Becoming Good American Schools

Becoming Good American Schools

The Struggle for Civic Virtue in Education Reform

Jeannie Oakes

Karen Hunter Quartz

Steve Ryan

Martin Lipton

Jossey-Bass Publishers • San Francisco

Jossey-Bass books and products are available through most bookstores. To contact Jossey-Bass directly, call (888) 378–2537, fax to (800) 605–2665, or visit our website at www.josseybass.com.

Substantial discounts on bulk quantities of Jossey-Bass books are available to corporations, professional associations, and other organizations. For details and discount information, contact the special sales department at Jossey-Bass.

 Manufactured in the United States of America on Lyons Falls Turin Book. This paper is acid-free and 100 percent totally chlorine-free.

Cornel West quotation on page 308 is from *The Good Citizen*, edited by David Batstone and Eduardo Mendieta. Reproduced by permission of Routledge, Inc. Copyright © 1999.

Library of Congress Cataloging-in-Publication Data
Becoming good American schools: the struggle for civic virtue in education reform / Jeannie Oakes . . . [et al.].—1st ed.
    p. cm.—(The Jossey-Bass education series)
Includes bibliographical references and index.
  ISBN 0-7879-4023-2 (alk. paper)
  1. School improvement programs—United States. 2. Educational change—United States. 3. Public schools—United States. I. Oakes, Jeannie. II. Series.
  LB2822.82.B44 2000
  371.2'00973—dc21

99-050416

FIRST EDITION
HB Printing 10 9 8 7 6 5 4 3 2 1

The Jossey-Bass Education Series

Contents

To Emily, Haley, Evelyn, Alden, Elliot, and Joshua

Introduction

On the eve of America's independence, John Adams wrote, "Public virtue is the only foundation of republics." He also asserted that real liberty depends on "a positive passion for the public good."[1] More than two centuries later, we write this book as testimony to this passion being the foundation for what is good in public education. At the brink of the twenty-first century, violence, alienation, racism, poverty, and countless other social ills remain woven into the fabric of American life and American schools. Despair is one option. Another choice, the choice we argue for in this book, is to reflect on Adams's words and passion and seek public virtue.

Virtue has become a suspect term in contemporary American discourse, often hijacked by the religious and political right and used in the most narrow, individualistic terms. In the current political rhetoric, inadequate "family values" and selfish private choices—ranging from allowing children to watch television unsupervised, to mothers of young children entering the workforce, to abortion, divorce, and single parenting—signal the demise of virtue. In the 1990s, virtue has become associated with character education and the work of former U.S. Secretary of Education William Bennett, who asks us to kindle our outrage and preach one another and our children into moral behaviors. Although we have no quarrel with the value of the individual traits that Bennett seeks to cultivate in young people—truth, honesty, and courage—our deep concerns about virtue and education arise on entirely different terrain.

In this book, we argue from our decade-long study of reforming schools that the starting point for social and educational betterment is the collective. As Aristotle taught long ago, a person learns to be truthful, honest, and courageous by living in a political setting that enables its citizens to develop these virtues. We believe, then, with Adams, that civic or public virtue must come first. A passion for the public good focuses our collective energy on making our country a fair and just place to live and learn.

Becoming a virtuous society requires far more than individuals embracing better values or making moral choices for their own lives, as if social conditions are neutral. It requires a democratic public life that, in the words of Cornel West, "keeps track of social misery, solicits and channels moral outrage to alleviate it, and projects a future in which the potentialities of ordinary people flourish and flower."[2] Rather than simply an aggregate of individual virtues such as honesty, loyalty, and courage, we use the term *civic virtue* to refer to an interconnected core of values, beliefs, and dispositions, deeply rooted in the American experience, that define how citizens must forge a common, public good. From this democratic perspective, Americans must come together in a public sphere, apart from the marketplace and outside their homes and churches, to deliberate and solve collective problems. This public sphere brings politics together with learning; a democratic civic life must support continuous learning for individuals as the foundation of democratic deliberation and problem solving. Moreover, the public space must bring *all* potential citizens, not just a privileged few, together in relationships of respect and mutual interest as they actively learn, deliberate, and identify what is hopeful and what is outrageous. How different this view is from those of moral conservatives who have little to say about channeling outrage to alter the public policies or structures that underlie misery. How different, too, from the conventional approach to education reform.

In the decade since we began studying school reform, we have been struck by the abundance of civic passion in our nation's public schools. Wherever we found schools engaging their students in rich and challenging intellectual work, we found educators and policy makers driven by their commitment to the public good. This passion was palpable in school communities where faculty, students, and families were struggling to create more socially just, caring, and democratic learning communities. We came away from such schools convinced that the quest for civic virtue is the key to good schools. We learned that genuine school improvement happens when policy makers and educators pursue their passion for the public good by ignoring, circumventing, subverting, challenging, and sometimes even changing those countervailing pressures in the educational system that would otherwise crush their efforts.[3]

But watching schools struggling to reform also forced us to recognize how easily, and how often, positive passion for the public good is thwarted, misguided, and overwhelmed. After all, John Adams noted that American society requires this passion, but he did not suggest that it was the only passion that would make claims on the new republic. And, of course, many others do. Passions for private interests and individual gain are deeply rooted in American culture, and they press the nation's social policies and practices both toward and away from the common, public good. Moreover, even though the idea of the common good can focus diverse citizens on their shared interests, different groups of people often envision our shared public life and obligations to one another in quite different ways.[4]

For example, contrast the democratic view of civic virtue, above, with the increasingly popular conception of public life as a marketplace. From this perspective, Americans come together to exchange goods and services to optimize each individual's consumption, rather than to deliberate and alleviate social misery. Instead of making public life equally accessible to all potential citizens, the marketplace provides differential access to different consumers, depending on the resources they bring. Rather than developing relations grounded in a broad range of shared interests, we limit our interactions to the exchange of goods and services. People participate as consumers seeking to receive finished products, rather than as participants in the creation of those products. Clearly, a market vision of civic life is grounded largely in the nation's competitive, hierarchical economic structure, rather than in its more egalitarian political ideals.

Complicating matters further is Americans' unyielding attachment to education reform as a technical and rational process realized in what we call, with due disrespect, the reform mill. We watched schools struggle as they were prodded and impeded by a succession of prescriptions, training sequences, and all manner of what the reform mill calls "technical assistance." Too often, this reform mill short-circuits lofty reform goals through its overly technical-rational approach.

Recent scholarship on school change has faulted reform for failing to recognize the limits of an exclusively rational and technical approach.[5] School reform, the literature argues, is a cultural problem that requires local educators to support reform and then adapt it to the local context. Though this literature offers sensible principles to guide the change process, it doesn't press local policy makers or educators to recognize or challenge the normative and political dimensions of their efforts. Most often the reform mill solicits educators' buy in, seeking to deflect or ignore local normative and political resistance. It argues the reform message exclusively as practices that lead to more practical and efficient distribution of decision-making power and schooling resources.

Exposing norms to public inquiry and treating them as problematic can provoke calls to redistribute power and resources. Instead, the reform mill seeks to maintain a change and policy environment that is uncontentious. Consequently, the mill sticks with policies and innovations that rarely venture beyond the most abstract and uncontestable platitudes ("All children can learn"; "All children deserve to reach their potential"; "Schools must reach out to parents"). Its technical focus squelches important nascent questions regarding what constitutes a good school. In the current education policy environment, then, the reform mill provides educators with no legitimate avenues for questioning the values and politics that drive much contemporary school reform, particularly those policies and practices that require the predominance of marketplace values and interactions (for example, meritocratic testing, expert-driven change initiatives, etc.).

We learned from our study that a perspective we call "betterment" is a promising alternative to so-called reform. Betterment requires that policy makers and educators quit asking how the gears and pulleys of reform can be greased, and start asking how each school's reform efforts reflect Adams's "positive passion for the public good." Our conversations with teachers, administrators, parents, and policy makers and our observations of classrooms and communities revealed passionate, meaningful reflection—as well as bureaucratic, empty compliance. The passionate minority kept their focus on guaranteeing that their school would be a good place for every child who attended, without favoring those students who seemed to compete most successfully for scarce attention and resources. In this minority are the local heroes of our book. Seeking civic virtue, they challenge themselves, our schools, and our culture to be better than they are. There is much we can learn from them.

Becoming Educative, Socially Just, Caring, and Participatory

In the chapters that follow, we describe and analyze the experiences of sixteen schools in five states (see the last section of this Introduction). These schools participated in a major national reform project in the 1990s: the Carnegie Corporation–sponsored *Turning Points*[6]–reform of middle-grades schooling. Educators in these schools worked enormously hard to implement practices that would make the schools more supportive of students' intellectual development, more inclusive of children from diverse backgrounds, more caring communities, and more genuinely participatory institutions. The goals of the reform were extraordinarily appealing, not only because they promised to make schools more "effective" but also because they embraced American ideals of civic virtue. Our cultural lore evokes historical moments and actors that endure (although not always with historical accuracy) as exemplars of a passion for the public good. Most of us learned when we were schoolchildren that Thomas Jefferson insisted on a democracy that required an educated citizenry; that Abraham Lincoln waged war to extend membership in the American community beyond free, white men; that Jane Addams's work with immigrants around the beginning of this century injected an ethic of care into American civic life, and that Martin Luther King, Jr., struggled to have ordinary people take control of their collective well-being. These historical figures, among others, have become icons that represent Americans' commitment to an educated citizenry and a socially just, participatory democracy. The reform-minded people we met in the sixteen schools were passionately committed to schools' central role in creating and sustaining the version of public virtue represented by Jefferson, Lincoln, Addams, and King.

However, as the educators we studied strove to serve the common, public good by making their schools more deeply educative, socially just, caring, and participatory, their efforts brought into sharp relief other values that conflict with these seemingly unambiguous "goods." At every turn, their commitment to the common good confronted the culture's equally strong (or stronger) commitment to the individual's right to determine what is in his or her best interest and to the preeminence of marketplace values. Their efforts to advance public purposes ran afoul of an equally powerful zeal to protect private interests. Ideological and structural constraints to reform were widely imposed by communities and reformers outside these schools. However, as with most complex, human enterprises, the ideas were also embraced by many within the schools themselves.

In the chapters that follow, we stress Americans' attachment to Jefferson's (and the founding fathers') call for public schools to educate a citizenry that can sustain democracy. But as schools infuse curriculum and teaching with deeper intellectual inquiry, they run headlong into entrenched beliefs about the incompatibility of young adolescents' social development with expectations that they meet high academic standards. Schools also battle the widespread conviction that individual differences among students mean that not all are best served by an academically rigorous curriculum. They confront individual teachers' unwillingness to relinquish the order and predictability of traditional teaching methods.

Asking schools to serve diverse groups of children equally well taps into our collective (if historically oversimplified) memory of Lincoln denouncing slavery as inimical to American life. However, the schools' efforts to change structures and practices that systematically disadvantage low-income children of color evoke deep cultural tensions about race and social class as well as competing visions of the public good. Because reformers seek to disrupt the uneven distribution of high-status knowledge and learning opportunities, their efforts threaten the interests of privileged students and their families, who see themselves as benefiting from and deserving of more stratified schools and society.

Pressing schools to become caring communities calls up images of Addams's settlement house as a place that provided immigrants with respect and dignity instead of pitying charity. However, efforts to infuse this ethic of care into schools confront deeply entrenched deficit views of disadvantaged students, their families, and their neighborhoods. Moreover, a more powerful ethic of care challenges norms about the appropriate social distance between schools and families—norms arguing that relationships and well-being are private rather than public matters, and therefore beyond the proper purview of schools.

Urging schools to create participatory processes in which local educators, parents, and the community steer the course of programs and policies taps into our national pride in an engaged public sphere. This pride is exemplified in a tradition that extends from town hall meetings to social movements that range from the radical abolitionists of the nineteenth century to the civil rights activists of the 1960s and linger vividly in our memory of Martin Luther King, Jr. This tradition seeks power for ordinary people to shape the institutions and laws that govern their lives. However, schools' efforts to become more participatory threatened the differential power that individuals accrue by virtue of their wealth, rank, or expertise. They also threatened to change the delicate balance between issues that are seen as proper for public deliberation and those that should remain in the private sphere.

These contradictions are not uniquely modern phenomena. The historical icons whom the culture uses to anchor its democratic sense making are themselves examples of contradiction as much as they are examples of principle. We hear much of Jefferson, Lincoln, Addams, and King's struggles and contributions to the public good, but less about the social conditions and much less about the social values that made their struggle necessary. Their work and biographies reveal the equivocal reception society has given to the civic virtue they have come to symbolize. Further, in our romanticized and sanitized public memory, we often forget that these men and women were not themselves immune to the cultural conflicts of the times. In the lifetimes of those figures and ever since, Americans have never quit arguing over the noble ideals these figures have come to embody.

In this book, we argue that these cultural contradictions are fundamental to school reform. Understanding these contradictions can help policy makers and education leaders frame their efforts as a mission of cultural change as well as an educational effort to improve students' mastery over a personally and socially productive curriculum.

The Public Good and School Reform in the Twenty-First Century

After more than a decade of intense attention and hard work, nearly everyone judges current school reforms to fall well short of their goals. In March 1997, Anthony Jackson, Carnegie program officer and chief architect of *Turning Points,* joined colleagues from other major foundations in commenting on the state of middle school reform with a special collection of articles in the *Phi Delta Kappan.* The journal's editor introduced the articles by proclaiming that the evidence "demonstrates beyond a doubt that fundamental changes in the structure and content of middle-level education can produce substantial improvement in students' achievement—even for students in low-income areas."[7] This promising conclusion was based on reports from a longitudinal "self-study" of reforming middle schools. The study found higher test scores and positive affective outcomes in schools that had "fully implemented" reforms.[8]

Nevertheless, the data also showed a darker side. The promising findings existed side by side with equally powerful evidence that few schools in the middle-grades reform projects had actually made the recommended changes. The authors reported that "even relatively 'mature' and highly motivated middle schools . . . have not realized the full extent of structural changes that would fulfill the recommendations of *Turning Points.*"[9] They note: "Our most fully implemented schools are only part way there."[10]

These foundation leaders, like their reform-minded colleagues in the states and schools, were appropriately impressed with the difficulty and halting pace of school reform. "School reform is not for the literal, the timid, or the undecided," they wrote.[11] While they were "heartened" by the triumphs of those middle schools that used the reforms to become "high-performing," they lamented that "there are simply not enough" such schools. Exhorting policy makers and educators to recommit to reform goals and redouble their efforts, the foundation officers offered a finger-wagging explanation for the reform's limited accomplishments: "If middle-level school reform fails, it will not be because it was misguided. It will be because the effort—and not just of the schools, districts, and states, but also of the foundations—was not sufficiently comprehensive, intense, or long-lasting to sustain the schools' focus on creating academically excellent centers of teaching and learning."[12]

We offer a different analysis, drawn from different perspectives and data. Over the five years of data collection, we filled twenty-five file drawers with field notes and interviews from our numerous site visits to sixteen schools in five states.[13] The states—California, Illinois, Massachusetts, Texas, and Vermont—differed in their education policy traditions, their reform experience, and their relationships with local schools. The schools served diverse groups of students in communities that varied widely: affluent and poor, urban and rural, white and racially mixed.[14] This diversity of states and schools revealed how educators working in many contexts shepherded school reform from a widely heralded national report, to state policies and structures, to local practice. Many stories could be told from these data, including the one that the foundation officers chose to tell and the one we tell here.

This is a story of finding, nearly everywhere, individuals and groups engaged in astonishing—even heroic—efforts. It is clear that many of these efforts sought to do more than simply raise achievement test scores, avoid sanctions, gain recognition, or make schools orderly (although many schools accomplished all of these things). These educators wanted their schools to be "good" schools, of a sort that reform policies and implementation strategies barely touch. They wanted to create educative, caring, socially just, and democratic learning communities for their students. They set about reform in ways that were idiosyncratic, opportunistic, contextually appropriate, and often truer to the spirit of reform than policy makers could have anticipated or articulated in their mandates, incentives, curriculum guides, testing programs, or technical assistance.

We use Jefferson, Lincoln, Addams, and King to ground our local reform stories in American cultural tradition. Although doing so risks taking these figures out of their historical contexts and invoking them to serve partisan, present-day interests that would be incomprehensible to them, we use them to make clear that the commitment to the public good we found in schools is part of our mainstream (albeit contested) heritage. The dreams and ideas Americans associate so closely with Jefferson, Lincoln, Adams, and

King have never been fully realized or accepted. Yet few Americans would call them failures. Most would agree that the ideals they represent ennoble the country and were and are well worth pursuing.

By framing our accounts of school reform as ongoing reenactments of centuries-long pursuits, we hope to distinguish traditions of civic virtue from a market conception of the common, public good that separates the ends and means of civic life. That is, many leading reforms speak of becoming educative, socially just, caring, and participatory primarily for what these strategies will do to raise standardized achievement test scores. Often, they sound like business management programs that pose worker training, cultural sensitivity, friendly work relations, and problem solving as strategies for improving productivity. By mimicking this discourse, reforming educators find it easier to galvanize support of the business community, policy makers, and other educators. But they also cast learning and relationships as instrumental and lose the opportunity to conceive of schools as places to struggle for good. Without a consciousness of the deep differences between the democratic and market conceptions of public life, educators have no language to talk about why particular actions to make schools better matter so much, and they have no vision of democratic school reform to fall back on in the face of relentless opposition. We believe that viewing reforming schools through the lens of civic virtue can challenge citizens to enter the deep and rich schooling context, to get closer to the actual look and feel of the struggle for the public good.

We also believe that these stories suggest important answers to pressing policy questions. That is, although we offer no list of policy recommendations, no protocols for instruction or school restructuring, we believe that there is much in these chapters to enrich dialogues and action about what kind of nation we want, what we want schools to accomplish, and what steps schools can take tomorrow morning to become better.

What can be learned from *Turning Points* and other reforms that share salient approaches and ideology with *Turning Points*? Did reform make schools better or point the way to making them better? Is reform possible—and if so, under what conditions and to what degree? We judge *Turning Points* reform to be a qualified success. In many instances, reforms such as those we studied create a climate, a space, for passionate and willing individuals to take risks. We have great admiration for these individuals—these reformers— and we hope that this book stands behind them. Given a modicum of opportunity and support, they accomplish wonderful things on behalf of many students. However, we also know that the educational reform we studied did little to interrupt or disrupt the course of the nation's history, flaws, and inequity, its hegemony and racism. Reform that fails to interrupt or disrupt is at least an oxymoron—more a nonevent than a case of failure or success. Asking to disrupt a nation is a tall order—one that, we have become convinced, schools will eagerly follow but should not be expected to lead.

Part One, "Situating the Struggle," consists of two chapters. Chapter One, "The Struggle to Become Good Schools," tells the stories of three middle schools whose ambitious programs reveal the cultural and political contradictions that dogged their experiences with reform. We revisit images of their reform dilemmas throughout the book. Chapter Two, "Cultural Contradictions," places school reform in the context of the broad, historical struggle for civic virtue. The chapter finds in these broader cultural struggles the roots of today's polarizing visions of what it means for schools to be educative, socially just, caring, and participatory.

Part Two of the book, "Four Cultural Struggles," looks closely at four ways in which schools press to become places of civic virtue. Chapter Three, "Becoming Educative," addresses contemporary teachers' efforts to act on Jefferson's conviction that democracies must furnish all citizens with the tools of literacy and the sensibilities to consider ideas, form values, and make decisions for both their own and the nation's good. Toward this end, *Turning Points* admonished middle-level educators to "promote a spirit of inquiry" and develop middle schoolers who engage the world with a "reflective intellectual" approach—to become more educative, in John Dewey's sense of the term.[15] The chapter considers the conflicts schools experienced as they defined and implemented their educative mission in terms of curriculum and teaching. Interdisciplinary curriculum, a reflective intellectual approach to academics, and inquiry-based learning clashed with a more conventional anti-intellectual view of middle schoolers—at least those who are not the most academically precocious—and with traditional definitions of curricular rigor and good pedagogy. Efforts to make schools educative were constrained and frustrated by powerful regularities[16] in the culture of schooling and by community politics, as well as by the lack of opportunity for teachers to delve into the theoretical underpinnings of the practices they were expected to enact.

Chapter Four, "Becoming Socially Just," examines how states and schools attempted to enact Lincoln's legacy by creating learning settings where previously excluded children could succeed. Many reforms of the late 1980s and 1990s targeted equity issues, such as increasing resources and quality in disadvantaged schools, curtailing practices in student assignment that obstruct access to knowledge (such as gifted programs, special education, tracking); and promoting instruction that eases inclusion (for instance, cooperative learning). Most made modest gains; all confronted enormous obstacles. Each school had its own approach to becoming more socially just, but they all proceeded with caution—often under hypersensitive monitoring by their suspicious communities. Since the most common response was to create alternatives to ability-grouped classrooms, this chapter takes a close look at the course of tracking reforms. Nearly everywhere, local opposition voiced the conviction that different students had needs that should be addressed separately, and that socially just approaches would inevitably water down the curriculum and disadvantage high-achieving students.

Chapter Five, "Becoming Caring," examines how middle schools, in the tradition of Jane Addams, attempted to promote civic virtue by caring for all members of their communities. When school practices are guided by an ethic of care, individuals and whole schools emphasize growth, empathy, response, and continuity. These constructs guide the actions of individuals in ways that can create schools that look quite different from those guided by the *ethic of service,* or the distribution of services based on assumed needs, that shapes most schools. The schools struggled with varying success to free themselves from entrenched beliefs about the presumed deficiencies of students, families, and communities, particularly those who are poor and nonwhite. Instead they sought to form relationships characterized by school and community holding high and respectful expectations for themselves and one another.

Chapter Six, "Becoming Participatory," explores how educators sought to make schools democratic "public spaces" in which free and enlightened citizens shape the direction of their futures and provide for the common good. Most schools attempted to move closer to this ideal—so vividly rekindled in the American imagination by King—by enhancing the democratic quality of work life for adults in schools and enhancing relationships among professional educators and community members. When reforms challenged traditional power relationships in order to move schools closer to participatory democracies, opposition to the reforms typically escalated.

The third and final part of the book, "Becoming Better," makes clear that reform is a very fragile human process, not a technical one. Chapter Seven, "Struggling to Scale Up," looks at how foundations and states used technical assistance to frame the meaning of *good school* so that reform could be replicated widely and economically. This support and pressure in each state reflected both the larger cultural struggles and the peculiar state policy climates and leadership styles of those leading the reforms. The help that project leaders offered was shaped by the technical rationality of state bureaucracies, the vagaries and unpredictability of electoral politics, and the prevailing culture of school reform. Some of the most powerful successes occurred when highly placed foundation or state officials stepped beyond their traditional, formal role to connect personally with local educators in their local schools.

Chapter Eight, "Struggling in the Reform Mill," argues that conventional policy implementation attitudes can derail the most well-intentioned and hard-working school communities. If the *ends* of reform are to create educative, socially just, caring, and participatory places for students, then the *means* of achieving those ends—including changing how teachers teach—should also be educative, socially just, caring, and participatory. But the means of reform continue to chase the ends and still reflect old conceptions of teachers being passive and isolated consumers of knowledge and skills. Reform continues to be impersonal, hierarchical, and often authoritarian. Schools and their supporting agencies need to abandon this ends-and-means duality of reform. This chapter provides some concrete examples of how the reformers we studied struggled to do just that.

Chapter Nine, "A Passion for the Public Good," concludes with our assessment of what educators and policy makers can learn from the stories of the schools and states we studied. We encourage you to note that we do not hold up our cases as models to be copied. Rather, they are illustrations of how a betterment process, fueled by passion for civic virtue, can survive the reform mill with persistence, hope, and a capacity to bend without breaking.

We conclude with an Appendix describing the methodology of our study.

Sixteen Reforming Schools in Five States

California

Cesar Chavez Middle School. Enormous dedication and hard work—what Principal Ken Lawson and his faculty called "the Chavez way"—made this school the hub of its urban "port of entry" neighborhood. Ninety percent of Chavez's students are Latino, about 20 percent having immigrated to the United States within the past year or two. Only 10 percent speak English as their first language; all are poor. Determined to do more than keep students from dropping out or joining one of the neighborhood's sixteen active gangs (which included older brothers, uncles, and fathers), the faculty created a caring, college-going culture for its 1,650 students.

George Washington Carver Middle School. Carver's twelve hundred sixth through eighth graders (about half African American and half Latino) are among this big city's poorest children. More of them receive government aid for dependent children than do students at any other middle school in the district. Principal Sharah Kensington leads a faculty of mostly African American veteran teachers who take understandable pride in Carver's statewide reputation as a model urban school.

Canyon Middle School. Principal Tara Stickley oversees Canyon's fifteen hundred sixth through eighth graders as they enroll in one of the school's three tracks—orange, blue, or green—that filter in and out of campus, eight weeks on and four weeks off. The complicated year-round schedule accommodates this once-small, white, and conservative farming community's rapidly swelling population of young people. The Canyon community is now home to families of commuters who drive forty miles each day to work in a nearby city; a quarter of its increasingly diverse student body is Latino, 8 percent are African American, and 7 percent are Asian and Pacific Islander.

Countryside Middle School. Wanda Simpson, principal and sole African American staff member at Countryside, was the only person in the school's main office who could speak Spanish to the school's growing population of Latino immigrants. Countryside's 880 sixth through eighth grade student body (75 percent white, 15 percent Latino, and 10 percent African American) comprised children of long-standing residents of this small rural town (including its most affluent families) as well as those of newcomers who lived in a three-square-block, subsidized housing project.

Illinois

Washington Irving Middle School. Irving's 650 seventh and eighth graders—18 percent white, 4 percent black, 69 percent Latino, and 9 percent Asian—arrive by bus from five overcrowded neighborhood schools in the city's center. Sixty-three percent are low-income, and 21 percent have limited English. Under the leadership of Principal Sandy Tolliver, the school opened with a full array of middle school practices in place: teaming, block scheduling, advisory, heterogeneous grouping, and interdisciplinary teaching.

Inland Middle School. Twice recognized as a National School of Excellence, Inland is the only middle school in a Midwestern school district clouded by racial animosity and divisiveness. Covering 78 square miles, Inland serves a rural white farming community and four nearby towns: one mostly African American; one middle-income and white; one middle-to-high-income white, with a few well-off African Americans, and one quite wealthy and white. When shrinking enrollments forced school closures, dilapidated and overcrowded Inland became the place where the area's nearly equal numbers of black and white youngsters came together for the first time, under the leadership of Ben McCall.

Massachusetts

Horace Mann Middle School. Racial tensions have haunted Mann's working-class neighborhood for decades. About one-third of Mann's five hundred students are locals; the rest arrive by bus, including two hundred special education students, many of whom qualify for a citywide "prevocational" program. Principal Len Jacobi created grade-level teams to divide the school into smaller, more manageable units and worked with former social worker Kate Pontello to establish a staggering number of health and social services to meet students' pressing physical, emotional, and social needs.

James Madison Middle School. Madison opened in 1923 to serve affluent and blue-collar "ethnic" families living near the coast of its industrial, northeastern town. Everything changed in the 1960s when the town's major industry died, forcing many families to leave. By 1990, immigrants from Asia, Central America, Haiti, and Russia joined the shrinking numbers of white and African American residents. Today, most Madison students come from poorer neighborhoods, public housing, and temporary homeless shelters near the school, many of which principal Fred Antouli visits regularly. Half are students of color, and a third have first languages other than English, mostly Spanish. Politically well-placed whites circumvent attendance boundaries, sending their children elsewhere.

Lucy Sprague Mitchell Middle School. Mitchell's 650 fifth through eighth graders, mostly white, come from poor and working-class families. The no-nonsense principal, Goldie Fields, leads a faculty grouped in two- or three-member teams sharing responsibility for academically heterogeneous groups of students. Nearly all "special needs" students are mainstreamed into teams, which stay together for two years (fifth and sixth, seventh and eighth grades). The continuity allows teams to develop close student-teacher relationships over time and design engaging curriculum within a familylike setting.

Middleton Middle School. Middleton's seven hundred students are half white and half students of color. One-third receive free or reduced lunches. Students attend one of three distinct kindergarten through eighth grade programs—the Traditional Program, the Magnet, and the School of the Future. Although the programs evolved in response to individual parents' preferences, Principal Wally Vincent embarked on an ambitious campaign to involve parents in building a tighter whole-school community.

Mountain View Middle School. The only middle school in its proud Revolutionary War town, Mountain View has six hundred sixth through eighth graders, nearly all of whom are white. The faculty sees the school as diverse, given a handful of African American and Native American students and an increasing number of students from poor families. In partnership with nearby Mandeville College, Principal Paul Jennings established nine voluntary teacher "inquiry teams" as a way of helping the mostly veteran faculty learn about and shape reform proposals ranging from alternative scheduling to community partnerships.

Texas

Harriet Tubman Middle School. Principal Rebecca Owens, a spirited African American grandmother, leads two schools in one. Most of the 750 students are neighborhood children enrolled in "regular," special education, at-risk, and compensatory education programs, while a small group of specially selected high-achieving students take an "honors" magnet program. About half are whites who ride buses from other parts of the city. More than 70 percent of Tubman's families fall below the poverty line; more than half live in subsidized housing. Tubman builds strong ties to its troubled neighborhood through VOICES, a grassroots, multiracial coalition of church congregations and businesses.

Townsend Middle School. Torn apart by internal bickering, Townsend had to struggle mightily to make any change that threatened the status quo. The mostly white, veteran staff resented newly hired African American principal Harold Nance's aggressive marketing of what they viewed as newest-fad reforms. The school's high test scores masked racial differences between middle-class, mostly white neighborhood students and bused-in African American and Latino students, who were becoming an increasingly large part of the school's twelve hundred sixth through eighth grade student body.

Tanglewood Middle School. Suburban Tanglewood serves more than nine hundred students from affluent (mostly white) families. More than 80 percent of Tanglewood households include at least one college graduate, and in the early 1990s its per-pupil wealth was among the state's very highest. The "tight-knit" community is proud of its award-winning schools and funds them accordingly. Principal Brad Jelton took advantage of his community's competitive spirit to help his already successful faculty embrace reform and keep the school on the cutting edge.

Vermont

Martin Van Buren Middle School. Van Buren's three hundred white, predominantly poor sixth through eighth grade students are all members of grade-level teams. All of the school's special education students and teachers are mainstreamed into the teams. Principal Bob Davenport transferred a great deal of decision making to teams, which act as schools-within-schools and control their separate budgets, scheduling, curriculum, and more. Together with the principal, team facilitators form a school governance team that shares information across teams and helps maintain a whole-school focus.

Verbena Middle School. Verbena serves three hundred sixth through eighth grade students in an affluent, suburban town. Built as an "open" school, classrooms have only three walls, and open onto common hallways that converge in the school's wall-less library. Principal Sarah Chatsworth used the school's twenty-year-old alternative program—a multiage, experiential learning community—as a model to reorganize all students and teachers into heterogeneously grouped teams, which developed integrated curricula, portfolio assessments, and advisory groups.

Acknowledgments

The study reported in this book was made possible by the generous support of the Carnegie Corporation of New York, and in particular the encouragement of Anthony Jackson. Jackson and the foundation provided us with access to project meetings, participants, and documents. He also ensured our complete autonomy from the foundation's ongoing advocacy work. That our preliminary findings sometimes caused consternation among participants makes this promise even more commendable.

Among the researchers who contributed to this study, Jennifer Gong and Gretchen Guiton were pivotal in the design, data collection, and analysis for several years; Diane Friedlaender, Irene Serna, and Ash Vasudeva played key roles at important junctures. Their contributions to the study are reflected in every chapter. Karen Seashore Louis and Gary Wehlege provided remarkably helpful methodological and substantive advice at several key points throughout the project. Three anonymous Jossey-Bass reviewers' thoughtful comments substantially improved the manuscript, as did our UCLA colleague John Rogers's insightful read. We also benefited from the considerable editorial assistance of Lesley Iura and Christie Hakim at Jossey-Bass; Tom Finnegan; and Susan Auerbach and Cathie Gum, our UCLA colleagues.

Most important, we could not have completed this work without the tremendous cooperation of the educators in the state projects and schools we studied. These committed middle-grades educators and policy makers rearranged their schedules and gave us access to their schools, their files, and themselves. They spoke openly and at length with us about their work and their hopes for middle-grades reform. We are enormously grateful to them; only our promise of confidentiality prevents us from thanking them by name.

The Authors

Jeannie Oakes is professor of education and associate dean in the Graduate School of Education and Information Studies at the University of California, Los Angeles. Formerly a senior social scientist at RAND, Oakes received her Ph.D. in education from UCLA in 1980 after a seven-year career as a public school English teacher.

Oakes's research examines inequalities in U.S. schools and follows the progress of equity-minded reform. *Keeping Track: How Schools Structure Inequality* (1985) and *Multiplying Inequalities* (1990) document the uneven distribution of resources, curriculum, and teachers nationwide, and how this situation affects poor and minority students. *Educational Matchmaking* (1992, with Molly Selvin, Lynn Karoly, and Gretchen Guiton) details the interplay of race, social class, ability, and tracking practices in case studies of three comprehensive high schools.

Beyond the Technicalities of School Reform: Lessons from Detracking Schools (with Amy Stuart Wells, 1996), *Creating New Educational Communities,* the Ninety-Fourth Yearbook of the National Society for the Study of Education (1995, with Karen Hunter Quartz), numerous journal articles, and this book follow the progress of educators who are attempting to eliminate schooling inequalities and build more democratic school communities.

In 1986, Oakes received a Distinguished Achievement Award from the Educational Press Association of America. The American Educational Research Association awarded her its Early Career Award in 1990 and the Palmer O. Johnson Award for the Outstanding Research Article in 1997. In 1996, the Southern Christian Leadership Conference presented her with the Ralph David Abernathy Award for public service, and in 1998 the National Association for Multicultural Education gave her their Multicultural Research Award.

At UCLA's Graduate School of Education and Information Studies, Oakes directs Center X, where research and practice intersect for urban school professionals. Center X links three major UCLA professional education programs: the preservice Teacher Education Program, the Professional Development programs for practicing educators, and School-University Partnerships. Oakes's research at the center investigates teacher development aimed at social justice for urban schools serving low-income students of color. *Teaching to Change the World* (with Martin Lipton, 1999) explores the educational foundations, values, and approaches to teaching that are at the core of this work.

Karen Hunter Quartz is assistant research scientist at the Center for Research in Educational Equity, Assessment, and Teaching Excellence (CREATE) at the University of California, San Diego. She received her M.A. in Philosophy of Science from the University of Western Ontario in 1987, and her Ph.D. in the philosophical foundations of educational policy and practice from UCLA in 1994.

Quartz was research associate in the UCLA Graduate School of Education and Information Studies. She also participated in research projects on school and social reform for UCLA's International Studies and Overseas Program, the Anderson Graduate School of Management, the Southwest Regional Laboratory, and the Education Working Group of LA 2000. Currently, she is coprincipal investigator (with Hugh Mehan and Mary Kay Stein) in a Spencer-funded study, Co-constructing San Diego's Institute for Learning. Quartz has taught courses in education and philosophy at UCLA, UCSD, and the University of Western Ontario. She is also active in her local school's site council.

Her research and writing focus on the culture of school reform, social policy, and implementation of planned change. In addition to several presentations and articles, Quartz coedited with Jeannie Oakes *Creating New Educational Communities* (1995).

Steve Ryan is assistant professor of secondary education in the School of Education at the University of Louisville. He received his A.B. degree in 1987 in social sciences (socialization and child development) at the University of California, Berkeley, and his Ph.D. in 1998 from UCLA in urban schooling (curriculum, teaching, leadership, and policy studies). While at UCLA, Ryan was a research associate in the Graduate School of Education and Information Studies, research consultant for the Common Destiny Alliance research project Finding Alternatives to Ability Grouping/ Tracking, and research associate and team leader for UCLA's Center X Teacher Education Program. He served as assistant editor of *Educational Evaluation and Policy Analysis* (1995–96). Ryan also worked as a middle school mathematics teacher for seven years in East Los Angeles. His research and writing focus on teacher collaboration; teacher learning; moral dimensions of teaching; and the impact of school, district, and state policy on teachers' work. He has coauthored articles on caring school communities, standards in teaching and teacher education, and Web-based research and assessment.

Martin Lipton is a research associate with Center X. He has taught English in public high schools for thirty-three years, while applying classroom perspectives to his research and writing. His work focuses on learning, curriculum, and teaching in all school settings, particularly for those students who have the poorest prospects for success in school. He coauthored *Making the Best of Schools* (1995) and *Teaching to Change the World* (1999), both with Jeannie Oakes; he has also contributed to numerous other books and articles.

Becoming Good American Schools

Part One

Situating
the Struggle

Chapter One

The Struggle to Become Good Schools

Sarah Chatsworth did not expect to become a martyr. Ben McCall did not set out to be a hero. Fred Antouli did not think his tendency to be a renegade would become his leadership "style."

But then these three school principals became entangled in school reform. Now, some ten years after they signed on to a major, national school reform, Chatsworth has been fired; McCall has attained national recognition and has a fine new job; and Antouli continues to battle conventions and bureaucracy on behalf of his students. We can learn much from their efforts to transform their schools.

Sarah Chatsworth, Ben McCall, and Fred Antouli are three of the sixteen principals we came to know in our five years of studying school reform. Like most of the other educators, policy makers, community members, and parents we met, these three found very compelling a vision of school reform that emphasized the public good and aimed at making schools more effective in the narrow sense of raising students' achievement scores. This vision led them and teachers at their schools to craft new structures and practices that would make their schools deeply educative, socially just, caring, and participatory. Their efforts proved enormously difficult, their successes only partial. Together, the experiences at these schools suggest preliminary answers to central, if rarely articulated, questions that lie at the core of America's efforts to reform its public schools.

Beginning here with Verbena, Inland, and James Madison middle schools, and continuing with the stories of other schools in the chapters that follow, we place a set of difficult questions at the center of our analysis of school reform:

- Why, and how, do schools struggle for civic virtue in our complex multicultural society?
- How do schools make sense of the contradictions inherent in their reforms?
- How does this sense-making process have an impact on implementation?

With these questions, we seek to understand what contemporary reform reveals about our culture's ongoing struggle for goodness in its public schools and in children's lives. We also ask: How might education policy making and policy implementation better come to terms with the cultural and political forces that shape and constrain school improvement? We believe that such analyses have been missing from school reform. We also believe that, although the lessons in these schools' stories may not smooth the reform path, they certainly point out many treacherous spots along the way.

In this chapter, Sarah Chatsworth's, Ben McCall's, and Fred Antouli's confrontations with these fundamental reform questions begin to illuminate the considerable achievements and painful setbacks that we saw in most of the sixteen schools we studied. We use the stories of their schools—Verbena, Inland, and Madison—to introduce the fundamental dilemmas in American school reform. In the rest of the book, we dig deeper into the dilemmas that reforming schools face, the strategies they use to negotiate these dilemmas, and the lessons they hold for the nation's broader education reform agenda.

The stories of these schools help bring to life the ambitious agenda and reform process that many American schools are tackling. The sixteen schools we studied were engaged in a particular reform—the Carnegie *Turning Points*[1] middle-grade reform—but the challenges they faced are not unique either to the *Turning Points* schools or to the middle grades. As detailed in the *Turning Points* report, the reform sought to create communitylike schools that fostered meaningful engagement with ideas, as well as with caring people, diverse environments, and democratic processes:

1. Creating small, respectful communities for learning
2. Teaching a core of academic knowledge
3. Ensuring success for all students
4. Empowering teachers and administrators
5. Preparing teachers for the middle grades
6. Fostering young adolescents' health and fitness
7. Reengaging families in the education of young adolescents
8. Connecting schools with communities

In *Turning Points*, these democratic goals constitute both the means and the ends of school reform. But this agenda brought forth fundamental contradictions in the American culture. Other contemporary reform movements that seek to alter the deep structures, daily practices, and school culture to make them better serve the public good—the Coalition of Essential Schools, Accelerated Schools, and James Comer's School Development Program, to name just three of many—also raise similar contradictions.

The schools we studied also illuminate the cultural and political contradictions that threaten such reform at every turn. *Turning Points* enticed many educators and local and state policy makers toward civic virtue—that is, in the direction of norms, policies, and practices that promote the public good through a citizenry educated to come together across differences and solve common problems in a democratic public sphere. But these would-be reformers were also blindsided by the contested meanings of the common, public good. Many Americans—typically the most advantaged and powerful—take the common good to mean an aggregate of self-interested individuals who are free to be guided by marketplace values such as competition and the accumulation of social and material resources. For them, school reform would bring quite different policies and practices—specifically, ones that allow individuals to exercise their preferences, maximize their private and unequal resources, and compete effectively. So, although the reforms sometimes met with initial concordance, the harmony soon dissipated amid suspicion that reform on behalf of some would diminish schooling benefits to others.

These contradictions make clear the limits of technical and rational approaches to framing and implementing school reform polices. In these schools, we see that reforms that were meant to advance civic virtue galvanized considerable interest, provided pressure, and offered some support. However, they barely touched (and often provoked resistance from) powerful cultural and political opponents. Because the prevailing reform rhetoric and strategies were largely silent about the cultural and political dimensions of the changes they sought, few educators had opportunities to engage in their own learning about the broader implications of the new practices they hoped to implement. No wonder their struggle was so frustrating.

Fortunately, these schools' experiences also provide important insights about how educators and communities that are committed to public virtue can create better American schools. We found remarkable changes in schools, and some equally remarkable student responses to them, that make clear the efficacy of relationships among educators, reform leaders, and communities committed to transforming their passion into practice. Americans would do well to recognize that fundamental school reform is an essentially human process where teachers, administrators, students, parents, and community members come together to think critically about what they value.

One reason that school reforms are so difficult to implement is that their very nature tugs between our dual alliances to individual freedom and the common, public good; they force reconsideration of our cultural heritage. Yet framing particular reforms as a struggle for the common good is only one part of the puzzle. Schools also need to provide opportunities for dialogue around this fundamental issue. When this happens, schools begin to chip away at mountains of tradition. They blend their means with good ends; they participate in a reform process that in itself is a good. Unfortunately, such opportunities are few within the dominant culture of school reform.

Three Schools Tackling an Ambitious Agenda

In 1989, Sarah Chatsworth, well credentialed with a doctorate degree, won the principalship of affluent, white Verbena Middle

School, largely because of her reputation in Vermont as a "futurist" and an expert on middle schools. Her hiring fit Verbena's proud tradition of staying at the forefront of progressive schooling. Built in 1967 as an "open" school, Verbena's classrooms have only three walls and open onto common hallways that converge in the school's unwalled library. Over the years, most of the school had gradually shifted toward a more structured approach. However, the school's twenty-year-old alternative program, a multiage, experiential learning community called the Logos Team, still set the standard for progressive middle-grades education in the state. Verbena's three hundred students are among the state's very highest achievers.

Ben McCall couldn't be more different from Chatsworth. A former English teacher, McCall did not see himself as a cutting-edge reformer; he stayed in middle schools simply because he loved the life. Where else could he be the funniest man in the world by sitting in the hotseat of a rented dunking machine to earn quarters at school fundraisers? Where else could he be the coolest person ever when he took off on his motorcycle trip across the Midwest each summer? He was principal of all-white Inland Junior High, serving three prosperous Illinois suburban towns when, at the end of the 1980s, shrinking enrollments and a fiscal crisis forced Inland to merge with West Junior High. West served the sprawling district's African American neighborhoods. That these African American families were largely middle-class did little to quell white fears. Some whites, even today, call the West neighborhoods "the ghetto" and warn visitors not to drive there. In the white neighborhoods, a volunteer group (whose members call it a neighborhood watch while others say it's a "vigilante group") patrols on the lookout for "troublemakers," and some educators worry about "crack babies" in the schools. McCall's task was to create a new school for seven hundred seventh and eighth graders in a dilapidated and overcrowded building, where black and white youngsters would come together for the first time.

Fred Antouli, a scrappy former coach, is the long-time principal at James Madison Middle School in Massachusetts. Originally built in the 1920s to serve both affluent white and blue-collar "ethnic" families, by the mid-eighties Madison served students from low-income neighborhoods, public housing, and temporary homeless shelters near the school; about half the students were of color and a third had first languages other than English. In spring 1987, Madison became the city's first junior high magnet school. However, its reputation as the site of a rape and a shooting kept most white families away. That same year, the school gave 590 suspensions to its 575 students, attendance hovered around 67 percent, and teachers averaged nine sick days. One teacher put it bluntly: "Nobody was coming to school. Teachers weren't coming. Kids weren't coming; and when kids got there, they were getting thrown out." Antouli's task was to bring a "burning building" under control.

Verbena, Inland, and Madison were among the first schools chosen to participate in each of their state's reform project, funded by the Carnegie Corporation of New York's Middle Grades Schools State Policy Initiative (MGSSPI). The initiative aimed at fundamentally transforming middle-grade schools consistent with the reforms outlined in Carnegie's *Turning Points* reform document.

Chatsworth set the reform ball rolling at Verbena in 1991. Using the Logos Team as a model, she and the highly skilled faculty reorganized all students and teachers into heterogeneously grouped, multiaged teams and developed integrated curricula, portfolio assessments, and advisory groups. They sought to combine high expectations with a nontraditional structure and child-centered teaching to create a rich educative environment.

Ben McCall launched Inland's reform by attacking the school's system of tracking students into separate classes—a system that depended on highly questionable judgments of students' abilities and resulted in considerable racial segregation. With five tracks in math, three in language arts, and two in reading, the school's structure was so rigid that students rarely mixed for untracked subjects such as foreign language, science, and social studies. Because McCall required that all teachers teach some low-level classes, most were eager to eliminate them. Politically, it also made sense since, in his words, "the bottom . . . has very little political clout, and you're cutting them loose, it's like . . . you set these kids free." Nevertheless, he moved carefully. One teacher recalled that as students moved out of the low-level into regular classes, McCall was "smart enough not to . . . let us know . . . who they were." At the end of the first grading period, teachers learned the identity of the former "basic" kids. There was surprise that most of the students were doing quite well. By the early 1990s, McCall and the Inland faculty were well under way with detracking, and they had reorganized the school into teams. Teachers began using cooperative learning, interdisciplinary curriculum, and portfolio assessment. They researched and taught one another about learning styles and multiple intelligences; many brought multicultural content into classrooms.

Fred Antouli targeted both physical and educational deterioration at seventy-year-old Madison. He hired eighty students to spend one summer painting the school, and he pressed the art teacher to frame the front door of the three-story brick building with "Welcome to Our School" in more than a dozen languages. She and her students painted the interior walls with dramatic murals; they created a huge, colorful world map on the pavement of the interior courtyard (Madison's only outdoor space). The faculty adopted teaming, block scheduling, and mixed-ability grouping; they mainstreamed 80 percent of the school's special education and bilingual students onto "regular" teams. Each team controlled its own schedule, met during common planning time, and in most cases engaged students in long-term interdisciplinary units, with some leading to extensive community service projects.

Struggling for Civic Virtue

High academic achievement and a safe, orderly campus were important reform objectives for all three principals and their staffs. At Verbena and Inland, Chatsworth, McCall, and their faculties understood the unspoken agreement that high achievement test scores were prerequisite to pushing ahead with reform and that it would be allowed to continue only as long as scores remained high. As in many affluent communities, Verbena parents demanded evidence of high test scores to help them feel confident that their children would gain entry to the best colleges and follow their family's path to high incomes and status. One Verbena school board member shared what he saw as the prevailing parental attitude: "I want mine in the top 5 percent . . . and if you give me a standardized test I can pump the scores. I know how to work the system. My parents did it for me, and I will have my kid in Stanford." For these parents, working the system meant ensuring their children's competitive edge within a familiar (traditional) structure of test-driven instruction.

Inland's affluent white families were not so different. Maintaining solid test scores was essential in reducing community and district suspicions that the school's nontraditional practices would lower performance and scores. McCall and his faculty also knew that Inland was being watched closely by its racially charged community to make sure that the new, student-centered way of doing things didn't breed unruliness, or worse. "We gotta get the test scores up; gotta get those test scores up" was McCall's refrain. One year, he promised students that he'd shave his head if scores went up.

For Antouli and his Madison Middle School faculty, safety was the most pressing community concern. Test scores had been so low for so long, there was little to lose with reform.

As important as high test scores and school safety were at these schools, all three schools' reform goals went much further.

Struggling to Educate

Each school had its core of tradition-minded faculty members who favored approaches that matched their images of middle schoolers as large elementary students who needed developmentally appropriate, fun, and engaging instruction in basic facts and simple skills. Each school had another group who saw their students as miniature high school and college scholars who needed highly structured instruction in the academic disciplines. Teachers who were firmly committed to one of these camps generally resisted not only the other camp but middle-grade reforms as well. However, each of the three schools also had faculty members who recognized middle schoolers' powerful capacity to respond to a learning environment guided by a vision of civic virtue. These teachers welcomed reform suggestions that young adolescents could become lifelong members of democratic communities of problem solvers. In some cases, college coursework and staff development workshops had primed these teachers to be receptive to the reforms. Often, their own years of experience convinced them that conventional transmission teaching (lively or dull) that sequenced bits and pieces of content did not work well with their students. Some of these teachers on their own had developed an educative approach to teaching and learning that was engaging and fun while also challenging students to delve deeply and reflectively into significant problems that crossed traditional disciplinary lines. This group of faculty took readily to *Turning Points* and to the prospect that the educative practices they valued might become part of the teaching and learning culture—the mainstream—at their school.

At Verbena, for example, Chatsworth and faculty worked to create and sustain classrooms where students learned together across ages, skill levels, and subjects. They integrated curricula around themes, often including students in the planning. For example, the theme of origins grew from students' own questions about themselves, the world, and the nature and relevance of history and science. Activities within the theme included questions concerning the creation of the universe, life on earth, civilization, and more. The teachers often found themselves teaching together and making relevant links between their particular subject specialties and other disciplines. The math department adopted Math in the Mind's Eye, a curriculum that asks students to approach mathematics as a way of looking at and functioning in the world, instead of as a paper-and-pencil school skill. Day-to-day instruction became rooted in active learning strategies, and some teachers encouraged students to share responsibility for their own and the class's curriculum and activities. Revealing her profound conversion to participatory engagement in learning, one teacher told us, "It's really important that . . . we are no longer [exclusively] the disseminators of knowledge."

Struggling for Social Justice

The three schools also strove to be places where difference was not seen as a problem or an abnormality to be managed. As at most of the sixteen schools we studied, many faculty were solidly committed to the principles of racial equality and fairness, and they struggled with discrimination, inequality, and injustice. Not surprisingly, these were also schools that showed concern for gender fairness, and they also questioned and challenged many of the commonly accepted "limits" schools place on special education students. They tried to change their curricula and structures to expand access, provide extra support when needed, and improve relations among diverse groups of adults and children.

For example, McCall and Inland's faculty attacked the racial issues at the school head-on. This is partly why they pushed so hard on detracking. Community hostility was acute, and the principal worried about riots. Together, he and his newly merged faculty established a program, From Neighbors to Friends, as a series of informal social gatherings, games, and trust-building activities to engender a close community of diversity. Moms—black and white— became a familiar part of the school landscape. Inland didn't hide its conception of a good school as a socially just place. As McCall put it, "That's one of the things I've learned: if you believe it, write it down and put it on the wall . . . in the johns." (Signs throughout the school now proclaim that "different is not deficient.") He wanted to rid the school of what he called an arrogant belief that some students' capabilities are limited: "All kids have great potential . . .. Who the hell are we to decide who gets access to what learning?" McCall and the Inland teachers believed that their struggle went beyond ensuring the civil rights of low-income and racial-minority students. As McCall explained, they also were fighting for the betterment of themselves as individuals and society in general: "The struggle is not about blacks; it's about us. It's about what we as humanity will do to each other and will tolerate. That's why I get passionate about this stuff, I get excited about this stuff. This is where it's at."

Struggling to Care

Verbena, Inland, and Madison also tried to build close connections among educators, children, parents, and the neighborhood. They attempted to make the school itself a community that students belong to and help sustain. They worked hard to provide for many of their students' social and health needs, and to make their schools safer and more welcoming.

Madison's compassionate adults, for instance, expended enormous energy providing social support to students and their families, much like the settlement house school of a century ago. They developed before- and after-school recreation programs and a full-scale subsidized breakfast and lunch program. Madison's nurse counseled students about "social problems that they don't tell you about right away"—including their parents' drug and alcohol problems, and their own neglect. She referred them for pregnancy testing and to mental health agencies. Madison faculty and the probation department often joined forces to work with those in legal trouble.

Fred Antouli also forged personal ties with his school's minority neighborhood. Home visits had fundamentally altered his view of students' lives, and he encouraged teachers to follow his example. Many did. According to Antouli: "It's not the best neighborhood, but it's not the worst either. It's what you make it. I go outside, I walk the streets. I walk the streets on Saturdays and Sundays and stuff like that. Just so they know who you are around the streets. I think people look at strangers, and they say, "What's he doing here?" But if they see someone they know. . . ."

On weekends, Antouli worked with the Community Minority Cultural Center, a twenty-five-year-old group of African Americans and Hispanics. Madison provided Saturday programs at the center, where some teachers volunteer and many Madison students participate. Antouli also initiated a free spaghetti dinner (with himself as cook) to entice reluctant parents into the building; after three years he was serving more than 750 meals at his annual spaghetti dinner. He was proudest of his efforts to create a welcoming, accepting, and responsive community that was increasingly indifferent to racial, ethnic, and language differences.

Struggling to Participate

The schools also worked to make decisions democratically. Chatsworth convened a "transformation" study group of twenty-five community members, teachers, and administrators, paying much attention to developing a process through which difficult school and social issues could be spoken about openly. Working with the Verbena teachers was pretty straightforward—at least at the beginning. Unlike schools where trying anything new is a battle, most of these teachers viewed the sweeping reform effort as part of their professional duty. As Chatsworth told us, "They may be busy, they may be frenetic, they may be tired, they may not want anymore on their plate right now, but they are not resistant to change." She engaged the transformation study group in reading and talking about the literature on corporate change as well as educational research. She used change ideas familiar in the business world, such as "working smarter, rather than harder." She hired a high-priced corporate consultant to help the community and the faculty understand how to "shift paradigms and embrace transformation."

McCall's relentless and inspirational energy and talk galvanized the Inland faculty, and many teachers eagerly discussed and debated the school's mission. Because everyone saw him as a regular guy whose rhetoric was from the heart, he could challenge and even make people nervous without alienating them. He set up regular Friday morning breakfasts where the teams of teachers took turns hosting one another and having fun. Most important, he used these breakfast sessions to engage the faculty in talking seriously, if informally, about their efforts to change. His theory? "You want to change the school? Change the norms. Change the group norm. Get people infected with the disease that you want them to have." He worked to win parents over—and succeeded with many—through tireless, face-to-face contact. He took every opportunity for dialogue about how they could, together, create a community that reflected a passion for all of Inland's students.

Antouli, in contrast to Chatsworth and McCall, realized that a deliberative process wasn't a good match with his impatient and abrasive style, although he knew that a participatory process was necessary. So he named well-liked home economics teacher Rose Athens (who'd grown up in the neighborhood and attended the school) to lead the reform process inside the building. After spending a year examining Madison's problems, seeking best practices, visiting model programs, and selecting a school theme, Athens and her team of teachers recommended housing students and teachers in small clusters and emphasizing communication arts. Meanwhile, Antouli accompanied a social worker on her rounds to students' homes to solicit parents' help with attendance and discipline. He says that parents "got sick of my face." Although his car was stolen five times and he was shocked by what he saw, the visits energized him.

Resistance from Inside and Out

So much in the culture of the schools and their districts worked against reform. The three schools had to respond to a glaring spotlight of local public attention, district office skepticism, and jealousy from other building administrators. Sometimes (as later chapters show), even those who were at the core of the reform—in the state projects, for example—could act in ways that slowed or obstructed the reform. Policies, technical support, and resources frequently carried unanticipated and unhelpful consequences. Nevertheless, the schools did not shrink from pressure to demonstrate that reform works.

In various ways, each school provided this proof. Verbena's already high test scores held steady. Inland's early years brought minor ups and downs in test scores, and considerable and painful political fallout; but happily, the building stayed calm. Finally, in the 1994–95 school year and again in 1996–97, Inland showed clear achievement gains in writing, math, reading, and science. For two years running, all of the eighth graders passed the admissions test for college prep mathematics at the senior high school. At Madison, both teacher and student attendance increased dramatically—among students to about 95 percent—and students' behavior showed amazing improvement. By 1994, test scores reached the state's average.

In the end, however, the very proof that was demanded by those outside the school wasn't enough. Despite all her efforts to craft a reform process that would include her vocal, upper-middle-class community, Sarah Chatsworth became the target of angry parents. Many, it turned out, considered the much-acclaimed Logos Team a hippie-era leftover, rather than a reasonable approach for their children. They formed the Group for Educational Accountability, and—in a most uncollaborative move—presented a widely signed petition to the board of education demanding that Verbena return to a basic curriculum and traditional teaching. Some parents demanded that specific books be read and others prescribed specific amounts of time for certain lessons. The innovative Math in the Mind's Eye curriculum became a lightning rod for a group of fathers—many with degrees in science and engineering—who blasted the program as failing to prepare their children for the rigors of university. One former student, now attending an elite college, wrote to the local paper blaming his middle school experience and Chatsworth for his only being an average math student in his college class. One school member summed up the attack:

"These people are out for blood. I mean, they're with the 'I pay your salary' . . . stuff." With all the uproar, teachers began to feel that Chatsworth might have pushed "too fast, too much, too soon," eroding their professionalism rather than enhancing it.

Ben McCall confronted extraordinary nervousness from the Inland district office. He was sure that the superintendent was wishing he would just go away. The superintendent, fresh from a district that had experienced dramatic white flight, badgered the principal about changing practices in ways that might make families uncomfortable. For example, he balked when Inland adopted a different grading scale than that of the elementary schools, and he complained that the faculty didn't have a traditional homework policy. When the school took a slight dip in its scores on the "study skills" subtest of the state exam, the superintendent threatened to undo many of the changes they'd made. Not surprisingly, the superintendent's nervousness either fed or did little to assuage community fears that racial diversity at the school had brought a decline in academic standards. It also encouraged a political environment in which other district administrators cast McCall as a self-aggrandizing showman.

Fred Antouli and his faculty were bitterly disappointed that Madison didn't shake its image locally as a burning building or battle ground. Even after receiving a stream of visitors from other schools and recognition from the governor, Antouli lamented, "People—from the superintendent to the school community—are ignorant of what has been happening here, and that is kind of sad." Few of Madison's graduates gained entrance to the city's academic high schools. Antouli also became embroiled in controversy over bilingual education. He had integrated language-minority students—along with their bilingual teachers—into the regular teams because he felt the social isolation of Spanish-speaking students kept them from learning English and exacerbated behavior, attendance, and achievement problems. With characteristic impatience, he mistakenly dismissed Latino community activists' concerns as "absurd." That dismissal led the activists to file an official complaint with the state department of education. The ensuing controversy jeopardized the entire reform and eroded the hard-won local neighborhood support for the school.

Serious resistance of another type came from inside the Madison building. As hard as the school struggled to be caring, many faculty couldn't let go of their harsh judgments about students' families and potential; one told us, "With teachers only being able to go so far, and with some of the backgrounds [students] have, they will just not go the distance." Some thought the Latino students' futures were especially hopeless, given families who preferred to remain embroiled in gang warfare and living on public assistance.

Compromise

In the face of this considerable resistance both from outside and within their schools, Chatsworth, McCall, and Antouli made compromises that stalled their reforms and left the schools "only part way there." Chatsworth conceded to parents' demands for more traditional curriculum and instruction by creating a traditional team that avoided such progressive practices as active learning, integrated curriculum, and a classroom community environment. This team also closed its classroom, placed its desks in rows, and relied more on textbooks. Parents unhappy with the child-centered reforms were free to choose this "scholarly" team for their child.

McCall asked Inland's teachers to give up some of the time they devoted to the From Neighbors to Friends activities and multicultural curricula to drill students on the skills on the standardized tests. He never did persuade the district office to allow him to blend all of the mostly white honors English classes into the regular ones.

Antouli backed off on his efforts to integrate Madison's bilingual and regular programs and allowed parents to place their children in separate bilingual classes if they wished. To his regret, much classroom instruction remained quite traditional, in large part because too few faculty gave up their low estimates of the students' abilities. His participatory governance process never went beyond the small inner circle of Madison teachers whom he trusted to run the school. He continued to fend off district concerns by brashly ignoring administrative directives, and by effectively discouraging his teachers from electing a union representative.

Ten Years Later

Sarah Chatsworth left Verbena Middle School. Her attempts to instill meaningful curriculum, child-centeredness, and community ended bitterly in the face of parents' unrelenting pressure to retain a traditional curriculum and a school climate stressing individual achievement, competition, and upper-class entitlement. Rather than cave in, she agreed to resign when the school board offered to buy out the remaining year of her contract. All parties agreed not to discuss the matter publicly. She now works as a private educational consultant. However, today at Verbena, one traditional team exists side by side with three more reform-minded ones.

Inland's Ben McCall became a nationally recognized leader. He is regularly invited to speak at national and regional meetings on school reform, and educators from around the country phone him seeking advice about detracking their schools. But acclaim from the outside made it harder and harder for him to negotiate local district politics, and his superintendent made life increasingly uncomfortable. In 1998, McCall left Inland (with considerable ambivalence) to become the assistant superintendent in a school system on the other side of the state. Unlike his superintendent in Inland, his new boss told us that he hopes McCall will do in the new district's schools exactly what he did at Inland, and more. Already, McCall has connected with experts in gifted education who have begun to help him develop a dramatically new type of inclusive gifted program for the district. The Inland staff misses him terribly, and he misses them. But he also says that if what they created together has value, they'll carry it on without him.

Fred Antouli remains principal of James Madison Middle School. He takes great pride in his continuing reputation as a renegade.

The Culture of the Status Quo and the Culture of Reform

Despite the ubiquitous clamor for better schools and quite impressive energy directed at achieving them, the unsettling stories of reform at Verbena, Inland, and Madison are not surprising. As later chapters make clear, they are also not unique. Why? Although the *Turning Points* approach to reform was in many ways a best-case example, it provided little support for the most difficult reform challenges the schools confronted. In typical reform fashion, state reformers targeted policy changes, technical assistance, and new resources at changes in the schools' organization and classroom practices. As is usually the case, little attention was paid to the profound cultural and political challenges that lay at the heart of the reform.

The conventional approach to school reform treats it as a largely technical process. Ideally, policy makers, acting in the public interest, set ambitious schooling goals and enact policies (including those that provide technical support and resources) to ensure a schooling infrastructure that supports the goals. They also make policies that compel, "incent," and build educators' capacity to change practices so that they can reach the goals, and they work to make the policy system coherent by bringing prior policies into alignment with the new ones.[2] At the local level, school district administrators are expected to implement reform policies by making structural and procedural changes—for example, by adding new course offerings, rearranging school schedules, providing new materials, changing assessment and accountability strategies, and by engaging teachers in professional development. This approach assumes that school improvement is primarily a technical problem that can be solved by such technical means as coherent policies that send a clear and consistent message; resources and technical assistance that help locals acquire new knowledge and skills; and monitoring mechanisms that provide information for fine-tuning, holding educators accountable, and evaluating the reform's effectiveness. Such reform-minded policy making does not begin to capture how reform actually works. Reform is far less logical and technically rational. It is much more idiosyncratic—dependent on the context of local relationships, histories, and opportunities.

Confronting Cultural Contradictions in Schools

Current reform efforts also proceed as if there were strong consensus on the *meaning* of school reform. Typically, there is not. In spite of political and policy rhetoric calling for school reform that ensures "high standards for all students" and "excellence and equity," these goals lack common understanding. When acted upon, they are often little more than facile catch phrases, riddled with the contradictions and controversies that lie at the heart of the American culture. They embody, for example, the enduring tension between fostering in young people both rugged and competitive individualism and egalitarian civic-mindedness. Throughout their history, American schools have been pressured to preserve the status quo while changing (and juggling multiple competing visions of) what makes a school good.

We view much of the reform struggle at Verbena, Inland, and Madison and the other schools we studied as a struggle among venerable, though conflicting, American cultural values. The pressures the schools faced have deep roots in American history and culture. Exemplifying this complex cultural legacy, these schools were struggling to enact the ideals of civic virtue, searching for an appropriate mix of emphasis on the community's needs and the individual's rights and interests. At the close of the twentieth century, as individual interests and freedom from government interference (for example, deregulation, privatization, glorification of market forces) dominate social policy, reforms like *Turning Points* press policy makers and educators to revisit and act upon countervailing American traditions stressing civic virtue. As they attempt to enact a vision of the common, public good, without compromising an equally compelling commitment to individual liberties and private interests, educators find themselves grappling with profound schooling questions:

- *Teaching and learning:* How can schools deepen the intellectual quality of classrooms, when most policy makers, educators, and parents hold onto conventional ideas of teaching as a process of transmitting knowledge and learning as receiving it? How can schools combat the widespread conviction that individual differences among students are such that many students are not suited for serious academic study?
- *Dominance and competition:* How can schools attempting to become more inclusive and socially just deal with educators and communities who are wedded to an Anglo-dominated school culture? How can schools balance their obligation to educate all children well with the demands of those who vigorously pursue competitive advantages for their own children through schooling?

- *Dignity—of students and others:* How can schools broaden their academic mission to provide greater care for disadvantaged students without reducing them to needy and helpless clients who require condescending charity or bureaucratic social services? How can educators avoid detached professionalism and instead link respectfully with families and neighborhoods to promote engaging and healthy activities in safe, community settings?
- *Genuine participation:* How can schools wanting to pursue a vision of participatory democracy go beyond the conventional, largely procedural approach to collaborative decision making and superficial parent involvement?
- *The larger context of reform:* What reform policies and implementation strategies might help schools address the cultural and political dilemmas that such reforms raise, as well as develop the technical capacity to make changes in practice?

Reform as a Struggle for Betterment

Those who were expected to support local efforts were as unprepared to address these questions as were the reform leaders in schools, and the help that some schools got in these arenas was serendipitous. Furthermore, changing business-as-usual in the policy-making arenas of school district and state leadership was as difficult as changing the practices and norms within schools and classrooms, if not more so. For the most part, reform never entered moral discourse, even though it embodied normative ideals.

A technical approach to policy implementation stresses supposed best methods, incentives, and centralization; it neglects attention to habits, beliefs, and the salience of local power. Yet at Verbena, Inland, and Madison as in the other schools we studied, it was cultural norms and politics—local beliefs and power—that shaped the schools' reform goals, processes, and outcomes and to a greater or lesser extent altered (modified, thwarted, adapted, finessed, etc.) the rational and technical strategies designed by policy makers and program designers.

Educators at Verbena, Inland, Madison, and most of the other schools we studied sought to forge educative, socially just, caring, and participatory communities. It is these attributes that we associate with commitment to the common, public good. At the same time, they strove to guarantee that individual children were free to pursue their own moral, educational, and competitive goals. In the American liberal tradition, these schools took it as axiomatic that to pursue self-interest is to support the general good, and that to pursue the civic virtues of learning, wellness, diversity, and justice for all is to establish a climate in which individuals can compete and excel. These schools also struggled with the nation's ambivalence over race. Solidly committed to principles of equality and fairness, these schools stood up to persistent racial discrimination and inequality. Of course, much of the schools' attention also came under the glaring spotlight of national foundation goals and state policy interests. As is nearly always the case in such a heightened political context, the reforming schools were expected to attain success within a few years.

Struggle aptly describes these schools—not only because of the contradictions commonly thought to be inherent in what they hoped to achieve (equity and excellence, civic virtue and individual freedoms) but also because the reform process itself posed intensely difficult technical, normative, and political problems. In the face of resistance coming from within and outside the schools, educators in most of them made compromises that, to the unsophisticated eye, rendered their accomplishments meager. But this is not an account of failed school reform. Our close observations of schools suggest that the interventions were often catalysts that converted unproductive struggle (or absence of struggle) into genuine consensus on small achievements that served children better. Sometimes, because the change was embedded within the school culture (even if only recently), teachers did not see themselves as having changed their beliefs or done anything new. Sometimes change did not last long. And sometimes nine steps forward were countered with only eight steps back. In nearly all cases, tackling the complex and often contradictory task of creating good American schools made them better for children and adults than they would have been otherwise. But things should have gone better still for these schools, and in the end we argue that the lessons learned from their experiences can inform more enlightened approaches to school reform.

We return to these lessons in Chapter Nine and argue that a promising alternative to focusing on the technical aspects of reform (finding and implementing best practices) is to allow schools to have open dialogue on the fundamental moral issues underlying the reforms, and to have educators jointly construct new meanings and practices that both shape and realize their goals. This way, educators might engage in reform so as to marry the means and ends. Cultural shifts in schools are far more likely if the reform process itself is more respectful of individual capacity to construct new versions of the common good through democratic (though not the typical majoritarian "let's take a vote") deliberation and reform work. Reinventing the wheel might be wasteful, but reinventing democracy within the ever-changing landscape of schools is a pretty good idea.

Chapter Two

| Cultural Contradictions

Reformers at Verbena, Inland, and Madison saw their reform diluted or turned back by powerful forces inside and outside the schools. These forces were not political abstractions, philosophies, or enemies of children. They were real people—parents, policy makers, community members, businesspeople, and educators—whose vision of good schools differed from the visions that Sarah Chatsworth, Ben McCall, and Fred Antouli worked so hard to achieve. That these reforms were opposed at every turn should surprise no one. If reform were to be welcomed and consistent with the existing culture, it would not be reform at all; it would simply be a slightly altered status quo. In other words, genuinely reform-minded schools attempt to be better than, or at least different from, what the culture actually expects or wants them to be. The wonder of reform is not how difficult it is, but why so many in schools continue to try in spite of the profound technical, normative, and political obstacles they encounter when their efforts threaten the cultural status quo.

Why did Chatsworth, McCall, and Antouli, along with many of the educators at their schools and others, tackle a reform agenda that brought them such struggles and even bitter defeats? That they were decent people and dedicated professionals cannot fully explain their theory, practices, or motives. What drove them to create schools that were more than simply well run or effective (however that might be defined)? What were they after, if not simply to make their schools well run or effective? What resource did they tap into that they were able to pass on to their colleagues and students?

Chatsworth, McCall, and Antouli, like many other educators and policy makers, found that fundamental school reform called forth altruistic and deeply American civic values. These values fueled their obstinate, single-minded, and often successful work to make their schools more educative, inclusive and socially just, caring, and participatory—as well as effective in a conventional sense.

The changes these schools sought to make pressed them in the direction of civic virtue and the common, public good. Such civic virtue is deeply rooted in American ideology and (as we explore further in this chapter) valorized in cherished accounts of such historical figures as Jefferson, Lincoln, Addams, and King. However, built into the American culture (and into the lives and ideas of these cultural icons) is also a deep ideological commitment to individual liberty—one that often pulls the culture away from focusing on the common good. Alongside viewing a "good society" as one that presses individuals to fulfill their responsibilities to the community and that seeks common good with policies and structures that engage and benefit *all* Americans, Americans also see "the good life" as one unfettered by constraints on individual liberty. We define our well-being in large part as free pursuit of our self-interest.

Schools must accommodate and help maintain these dual, and often contradictory, commitments. They must simultaneously foster individual development and promote the common good. Reforms like those attempted at the schools we followed did not ignore responsibility for individual development, but they pushed hard on the civic-virtue side of American allegiances. In the late 1980s and early 1990s, social policies generally were following a trend toward individual rights, self-interest, deregulation, privatization, and competition. The school reformers we studied, however, were bucking that trend; they were trying to enact practices that were pedagogically effective as well as guided by the collective side of democratic principles. Indeed, they were simultaneously following and constructing a theory and practice that made collective democratic ideology and effective pedagogy indivisible.

Not all of these educators were necessarily conscious of, or spoke explicitly about, what we have come to see as their attempt to counter America's late-twentieth-century trend away from civil society. In the remainder of this chapter, we explore how this cultural struggle explains, at least in part, why their reforms proved so difficult.

Reform for the Public Good

After a wave of reforms following *A Nation at Risk,* the 1983 report that largely ignored concerns with equity or civic virtue, educators in the late 1980s and early 1990s welcomed comprehensive reform movements that promised to make schools good places, as well as academically effective places. There were Ted Sizer's Coalition of Essential Schools, Hank Levin's Accelerated Schools, James Comer's School Development Program, Howard Gardner's Project Zero, and others. Practitioners found a compelling image of middle schools as places of civic virtue outlined in *Turning Points.* Many eagerly signed on to Carnegie's Middle Grades Schools State Policy Initiative (MGSSPI), which initially funded reform projects in twenty-seven states and continued supporting fifteen of these states for a decade. Each of the sixteen schools we studied participated in its state's Carnegie project. That project used *Turning Points* as the platform from which to forge new state policies and local, middle-grade practices. Since all these "restructuring" reforms have core ideas in common, and since they all have, to some degree, shared a similar fate, the experience of *Turning Points* schools sheds considerable light on the fortunes of many other school reforms. Their experience may also offer insights into other arenas of civic-minded public policy reform.

Like most of its reform counterparts, *Turning Points* advocated a fundamental restructuring of the organization of schools and a reconceptualization of the relationships among teachers, students, and subject matter. These structures and relationships require dramatically new forms of (and attitudes toward) participation on the part of teachers, school administrators, families, communities, social service agencies, health providers, and individuals and agencies who make and enact public school policy. Only if reform extends to changing relationships and changing who participates can educators provide rigorous, high-quality academic instruction, appropriate social support, and a sense of civic responsibility to *every* young American.

Like many other comprehensive reforms, *Turning Points* drew its inspiration, and to a large degree its substance, from a combination of late-twentieth-century cognitive, developmental, and sociocultural perspectives on learning. The reforms also treated as problematic the uneven distribution of educational resources and opportunities among students and communities. "How do children learn?" and "Who receives learning opportunities?" became critical questions underlying many of the reform programs. Matters of distribution, access, inclusion, and diversity, though often treated exclusively as political or ideological matters, are argued in *Turning Points* and the other reforms to be central to what, and how much, students learn in schools. What, how, and how much students learn are matters that can be separated only temporarily and artificially from their social and political contexts.

Given this broader view, it followed that the reforms would link good education to the public good. *Turning Points,* for example, argued that "the future of this nation as a stable, prosperous democracy requires that all members contribute to the common good of society and meet their obligations as citizens."[1] Thus, *Turning Points'* specific recommendations went far beyond a simplistic call for more and better learning. To be sure, the report called for schools that were more educative; however, blended inseparably into this more recognizable educative goal were three clearly social traditions that reformers are less accustomed to including on their agendas: for schools to become socially just, caring, and participatory.

Schools were to approach being educative first by casting off the widely held notion that young adolescence is a time of intellectual dormancy. They were to adopt far more challenging academic goals for *all* students to make sure that *all* of them were prepared for productive citizenship in a cognitively demanding future. Academic programs should aim for more than having individual students accumulate knowledge and skills, although that was a critically important goal. They should also prepare a citizenry. *Turning Points* argued that this could be accomplished best if schools shifted from departmentalized, impersonalized, content-driven classrooms to child-centered, interdisciplinary learning communities, rich with opportunities for students to learn collectively and experientially through deep engagement in thematic, problem-based curricula.

Schools were to become socially just by adopting structures and practices that would foster greater equality in students' academic work and participation in school life across divisions of race, social class, gender, and presumed ability. For example, schools should detrack, by assigning students to heterogeneous classes. They should provide additional supports and resources to those students facing economic hardship and social prejudice. In addition, greater social justice had curricular implications as well; schools must organize academic learning around themes that allow students to explore diversity and fairness in their classrooms and communities.

Schools were to become more caring by responding to students as whole persons who have academic, social, emotional, and physical needs, rather than seeing them, at the extreme, simply as recipients (or resisters) of instruction and knowledge. To do this, *Turning Points* asked schools to devise structures and schedules that make it possible for adults to know students well and to support them over time. Schools should also extend to students a safe and healthy school environment, and access to the additional health and social services they and their families might need. It is important that schools do these things with an ethic of respectful caring that moves them away from treating students, particularly underserved students, as needy or dependent clients whom they instruct and refer for social services.

Finally, moving away from norms of bureaucratic hierarchy and authority, schools were to become participatory by changing who makes decisions about school and classroom policies. Schools should join with families and communities, so that all participate in educating *all* the community's children. These reforms challenged schools to distribute power more evenly among administrators and teachers, among educators and students, and between the school and its community. By melding attention to access, care, and power with concern for learning, school reformers tapped into broad social, philosophical, and political traditions that include pursuit of universal opportunity and widespread distribution of social benefits. In schools, these traditions are expressed in educators' loving, caring, inspired, relentless hard work, and belief in their capacity to help all students learn, as well as their faith that all students can and must learn. Although not an exclusively American tradition, this legacy characterizes much of the nation's sense of civic virtue, goodness, and success. We came to believe that one reason that *Turning Points,* the Coalition of Essential Schools, Comer schools, and other similar reforms were widely embraced, despite their enormous countercultural challenge, was that they resonated so strongly with these deeply rooted traditions. Though not blind to the irony inherent in a tradition-based countercultural challenge, we are also heartened by it.

Cultural Lore, Civic Virtue, and Schooling

Our culture venerates civic virtue in its portrayals of deeply admired historical figures. We first encounter their romanticized ideas and biographies when we are young schoolchildren. American heroes such as our quadrumvirate of Jefferson, Lincoln, Addams, and King remain throughout our adult civic lives as illustrative (but sometimes faded) emblems of America's ideological foundations. These four oversimplified legacies are useful background for understanding Americans' democratic longings. Yet in their own historic times, these figures also faced manifestations, in their own contexts, of enormous ideological and personal contradictions.

Although the context of their times may differ from the contemporary social one, a close look at today's reforms and reformers reveals groups and individuals caught in comparable social and personal contradictions. Jefferson called for a universally educated citizenry for the very purpose of democratic decision making for the collective good, but he also remained fundamentally committed to individual rights and enormously suspicious of government's infringement on the individual's free pursuit of self-interest. Lincoln may have emancipated slaves, but he did so only haltingly; and he doubted the capacity of different races to live together on equal terms. Addams's work at Hull House clearly brought to American civic life an institutional model for an ethic of care, but her model was also characterized by a strong dose of *noblesse oblige*. King struggled mightily to teach that ordinary people could take control of their collective well-being, but his own charismatic leadership and Americans' need for individual heroes often masked the grassroots participation that created the extraordinary power behind the civil rights movement.

Of course, these "buts" diminish neither the power of the ideas nor the heroic contributions of the historic figures. Given the contexts of their times, Jefferson was more the democrat than the class-bound pragmatist; Lincoln was more liberator than racist; Addams the model citizen will always outshine Addams the aristocrat; and King clearly was a champion for the powerless, even if the story we tell about him obscures as much as it reveals. These contradictions are not revisionist debunking of great persons; they are evident in their writings and daily struggles as they negotiated their civic and reform missions. That they struggled with themselves as well as with the times makes their contributions to a citizenry that is educated, socially just, caring, and participatory all that more heroic. In what follows, we elaborate these ideas of American civic virtue—the cultural lore and the contradictions shaping them—that have spawned theories of educational betterment that, in turn, find their expression in current social and school reforms such as *Turning Points*.

Becoming Educative

In 1779, Jefferson set public education in motion, defining a vision for good American schools—an educational vision that is foundational for all else that follows. For him, public schools—perhaps more than any other institution—bore the responsibility for ensuring that Americans acquire the cultural knowledge and skills of deliberation that could make possible a public process of determining the common good. He thought that a liberal education was essential to creating public spaces in which free men—each with his own individual, self-interested perspective—could deliberate and forge agreements on how their individual interests might give way to the common good.[2] Through this exercise, civil society could be virtuous.[3] Despite dramatically changed times and schools, many education reforms in the 1980s and 1990s, including *Turning Points*, adopted an essentially Jeffersonian rationale, arguing that schools must, first and foremost, impart to all young Americans the academic knowledge and skills necessary for democratic citizenship and the public good.

Jefferson envisioned that schools would bestow on all citizens the tools of literacy and a basic familiarity with Greek, Roman, European, and American history. This education—conveyed in three years of free, publicly provided schooling—combined with inborn moral sensibility and powers of reason would allow citizens to read political ideas in newspapers, form their own political values, and make political decisions. Jefferson believed that a public so educated would protect the new republic and help it prosper. Armed with these skills and sensibilities, citizens would be well-prepared "guardians of their own liberty."[4] For Jefferson, unlike many of his contemporaries, public schooling held the key to ensuring the public good. So much faith did Jefferson place in education that he tried (without success) to persuade the Virginia legislature to build brick or stone grammar schools at intervals of one hundred acres throughout the state, and to offer public scholarships to poor children.

Educative Reform Today

Much has changed since Jefferson's time, yet much remains the same. Both the length and substance of the education we see as necessary to prepare citizens have multiplied many times. Three years of common schooling have become twelve; President Clinton suggests that it be raised to fourteen. Significantly, during the past century most Americans have come to believe that enlightened and productive citizenship requires far more than basic literacy and knowledge of Western history, and much more than the rote teaching and learning methods that characterized postrevolutionary schools.

Turning Points, for example, implored middle-grade educators to develop the young adolescent into "an intellectually reflective person" with "a disciplined mind." It argued that citizens need skills far beyond the rudiments of reading and computation:

> Our youth will be able to analyze problems and issues, examine the component parts, and reintegrate them either into a solution or into a new way of stating the problem or issue. In developing thinking skills, the youth will master self-expression and be able to "hear" others through diverse media. These skills of self-expression and hearing include persuasive and coherent writing, articulate verbal expression, and familiarity with symbols and basic vocabularies of the arts, mathematics, and the sciences. Moreover, the student will be able to appreciate and absorb the perspectives of cultures (and languages) different from his or her own.[5]

Augmenting Jefferson's basic education, which included historical and scientific facts along with reading, writing, and computational skills, *Turning Points* called for a curriculum comprising coordinated, meaningful, challenging educational experiences and a full academic program for all students that integrates English, fine arts, foreign languages, history, literature and grammar, mathematics, science, and social studies, so that students can delve deeply into complex ideas, grapple with ideas that may span several disciplines, and create solutions to problems that reflect understanding, not memorization.

Moreover, ideas about how children learn have changed substantially. Anticipating, and unquestionably shaping, much current school reform, John Dewey argued more than sixty years ago that democracy requires an education that engages students in active participation with intellectual and civic ideas that matter. Dewey's view converges with conclusions from contemporary cognitive and sociocultural research on learning and achievement: "Learning which develops intelligence and character does not come about when only the textbook and the teacher have a say; . . . every individual becomes educated only as he has an opportunity to contribute something from his own experience, no matter how meager or slender that background of experience may be at a given time; and finally . . . enlightenment comes from the give and take, from the exchange of experiences and ideas."[6]

The Dual Commitment to Civic Virtue and Freedom

Importantly, Jefferson drew no distinction between the common good and individual liberty, and he believed that education could serve both. Drawing on the sentiments he saw within the early colonies and what he wished for the nation to become, he argued that the new republic depended on a citizenry that was *both* virtuous and free. Virtue would inspire service to the public good and sustain it. Freedom would foster equality and independence. Only through the deliberation of educated citizens who were both virtuous and free, Jefferson argued, could the nation govern itself and safeguard the inalienable rights of all equally created men.[7] This view is apparent in the *Declaration of Independence*, where he wrote that our inherent and inalienable rights include "the preservation of life, liberty, and the pursuit of happiness."[8] Far from an individual's hedonistic plea for personal benefit, the pursuit of happiness has Aristotelian roots as a collective end that demands the altruistic exercise of virtue.

Much has changed to make problematic Jefferson's view that public education would necessarily foster his dual commitment to civic virtue and freedom. Since the nation's founding, public schools have been guided by their increasing role in the nation's social-selection processes. Inherent in this selection is the belief that schools should certify which students will best succeed in their pursuit of individual social, economic, and political benefits because they also make the greatest contributions and best decisions on behalf of a good society. If these students gain the greatest material, social, and educational benefits, such gains are fair and just because they have earned the benefits by dint of their greater merit. Further, their example will serve the public good by motivating others to aspire to similar gains. Today, this assumed causality—that competition and private motives in schooling produce social betterment—distracts from and often overshadows schools' role in cultivating both knowledge and a passion for the public good. For example, the principal use of norm-referenced standardized testing is now to distinguish among and rank individuals. Little theory and no evidence has emerged over the century to support the testers' claims that these tests contribute to a synergistic balance of private gain and public good.

Understandably, the large-scale reforms of the late 1980s and early 1990s did not entirely abandon the view that focusing on individual development leads to a virtuous citizenry. However, they did recommend abandoning many of the theories and practices that schools used to sort and select children "meritocratically" for future educational opportunities and the life chances that follow from them. These reforms stood on cognitive psychology and sociocultural perspectives of learning that largely discredit traditional transmission theories of teaching and learning. Fundamentally, the reforms challenged schools' (and the public's) understanding and theories of how children learn. For example, the conventional notion that teaching is the transmission of knowledge from an adult to a child does not support the recommended changes in school organization or practice. Likewise, the idea that differences in what and how much knowledge students learn are determined by their individual differences in intelligence and motivation is a popular but grossly inadequate theory for explaining why some children succeed in school and others do not.[9] Neither did these newer theories support the conventional schooling practices so familiar to those of us educated in twentieth-century American schools: impersonal student-teacher relationships, lack of cohesion across the curriculum, emphasis on content coverage rather than content depth, and individualistic learning activities in classrooms.

These end-of-the-twentieth century reforms were explicitly Jeffersonian in their mission, affirming in the strongest terms that the future of the democracy depends on a public education aimed specifically at preparing citizens to decide together and act on behalf of a collective good. However, they have also gone far beyond Jefferson's knowledge standard for a basic education by adding a thinking standard. Like Jefferson, most contemporary reforms, including *Turning Points,* insist that self-interest and the public good are fundamentally compatible goals, arguing that development of the intellect is a fundamentally social process. As such, they eschew the traditional individualistic and competitive model of teaching and learning that most people still associate with unconstrained learning opportunities and the freedom for each child to reach his or her full potential. As we explore further in Chapter Three, this cultural shift was, at least in part, what made schools' efforts to become more educative so difficult.

Becoming Socially Just

In Jefferson's day, one-fifth of the nation's population was neither free nor equal—a matter that the nation sidestepped for another century and schools avoided for nearly two. For Jefferson, the idea of the public good was largely compatible with civic participation limited to white and propertied men. Jefferson, for all his democratic faith in an educated citizenry, placed firm boundaries around citizenship that excluded women and people of African descent.[10] His educational plan for Virginia proposed that only those students who showed promise should be provided more than three years of public schooling. At the time, stratification according to wealth and background was generally acceptable, and stratification according to race and gender was both desirable and a matter of law.

It took three decades after ratification of the Constitution before every state permitted all white men (not just property owners) to vote. It wasn't until the 1860s that Lincoln acted to expand Jefferson's conception of who should participate in civic life; yet he still remained consistent with Jefferson's democratic sensibilities.[11] As pressure from the Abolitionists grew stronger, as the North's war needs for manpower heightened, as blacks sensed the possibility of impending emancipation, as southern white opposition to slavery and planter rule mounted, and as the political response of the southern slave states grew more resolute, Lincoln understood that the nation's collective well-being was fundamentally threatened by individuals' continued freedom to own slaves.

In the minds of most Americans, Abraham Lincoln stands as the Great Emancipator, identifying then ending the moral evil of slavery and leading a Civil War based on the conviction that "this government cannot endure permanently half slave and half free." Ask any schoolchild. Indeed, by freeing the slaves, Lincoln changed who could be an American citizen. Those formerly excluded now had a legal, as well as a moral, platform from which to demand full citizenship and schooling. However, for the nation to end slavery when it did was a commitment to civic virtue only in the narrowest sense; now it was *possible* to have a good society for all; there were fewer legal barriers to a good society. Left open was the question of how Americans, whether Americans, and which Americans would embrace such a pursuit. Lincoln affirmed the basic humanity of blacks and denounced slavery as an evil institution, but he also supported the private right to act on racist, segregationist beliefs. This tangled racial legacy left us with complicated questions that are still unresolved as we enter the twenty-first century: Who is fully American? What does American citizenship bring? What does a diverse citizenry mean for the national culture and for the transmission of that culture in schools?[12]

A Legacy of Racial Ambivalence

Lincoln's Emancipation Proclamation and the constitutional amendments that followed did much to settle a matter of law, but little to resolve the nation's ambivalence about race. Lincoln abhorred slavery and argued that the law must disallow it. He believed that blacks were entitled to the natural rights of life, liberty, and the pursuit of happiness as affirmed by the Declaration of Independence. But he never supported full social and political equality for blacks, and he also made clear his own doubts that black and white Americans could or should forge a common society: "I am not, nor ever have been, in favor of bringing about in any way the social and political equality of the white and black races . . . I am not, nor ever have been, in favor of making voters or jurors of Negroes, nor of qualifying them to hold office, nor to intermarry with white people, and I will say in addition to this that there is a physical difference between the black and white races which I believe will forever forbid the two races living together on terms of social and political equality."[13]

Black Americans were offered what even for the time was considered the barest minimum of de jure protections against only the most egregious personal violations.[14]

Lincoln's brave abolitionist words in his debates with Stephen Douglas and in the Emancipation Proclamation brought only partial resolution to a nation divided, half-slave and half-free. The granting of freedom—and Lincoln's equivocation about the capacities of black Americans—fell far short of resolving the national skepticism about black and white Americans living together and governing themselves as one people. As W.E.B. Du Bois predicted at the beginning of this century, and Cornel West now reminds us at the end, the problem of the twentieth century is the problem of the "color line." Du Bois's phrase color line conveys the structural nature of the national attitudes and division over race. Lincoln's legacy is every bit as much the partial and cautious nature of the terms under which blacks became members of the American civil state as it is his emancipation of southern slaves.[15]

The Struggle for Socially Just Schooling

As public education developed and spread across the young American nation, laws in the South barred slaves from schooling. In the North, blacks were not legally excluded, although they were typically not welcome. Historian Joel Spring relays the story of the

Boston School Committee granting the request of a group of black parents in 1806 to open a separate school for their children as part of the city's new, comprehensive public school system. These parents thought that separate schooling would spare their children the hostility of their white classmates. Before long, however, Boston's black community charged that the facilities and teaching in the city's black schools were inferior to those in white schools, and in 1833 an official report concluded that segregated schools benefited neither white nor black children. It took more than two decades of protest before Massachusetts passed legislation that prohibited schools from denying admission because of race or religion; however, an 1849 state supreme court ruling that segregated schools were equal and therefore legal remained on the books.[16]

Segregated schooling continued after the Civil War, and outside the South exclusionary policies also restricted and segregated Chinese, Japanese, Mexican American, and Native American youngsters as well. In 1884, a Chinese couple were turned away when they tried to enroll their child in a San Francisco public school; after the courts supported the child's right to schooling, San Francisco and other districts established separate schools for Chinese, Japanese, and Korean students. Many Southern California school systems created separate schools for Mexican children.

Just before the turn of the twentieth century, the U.S. Supreme Court handed the nation what most people took to be a fair compromise. The Court ruled in *Plessy* v. *Ferguson* (1896) that segregation was constitutional as long as separate facilities were equal. *Plessy's* separate-but-equal doctrine held until mid-century, even though people knew that most minority schools were inferior to most white schools—at least in terms of dollars spent, facilities, and resources to support learning. In 1946, a U.S. District Court ruled in *Mendez et al.* v. *Westminister School District* (of Orange County, California) that the segregation of Mexican Americans had no legal or educational justification; eight years later, the U.S. Supreme Court ruled in *Brown* v. *Board of Education* that state-sanctioned racially segregated schools are inherently unequal. Efforts to use the courts to desegregate schools have continued throughout the century, with some gains and many disappointments.[17]

Structures that separate Americans by race have proven more persistent than the early National Association for the Advancement of Colored People and other civil rights advocates imagined. *Brown v. Board of Education* in 1954 and the Civil Rights Act of 1964 finally removed legal barriers to blacks' civil and voting rights, but they fell far short of resolving the larger cultural dilemma those barriers symbolized. Most American children still attend segregated schools—today a reflection of racially segregated residential patterns, rather than law. In racially mixed schools, racially distinct, "ability-grouped" academic programs and extracurricular activities have increasingly become the norm.[18]

Inclusion, Racial Ambivalence, and School Reform

For most of the twentieth century, Americans have attempted to balance freedom and virtue around race by pursuing equal opportunity—specifically, equal *educational* opportunity. Yet, even as equal opportunity sets the conditions for individuals to act freely, it often presumes racial neutrality. In the educational sphere, it requires school structures and procedures to ensure that the system is fair across lines of race and, increasingly, social class, language, gender, and sexual orientation. We use such metaphors as being "color-blind" to indicate normative conditions of fairness, and creating a "level playing field" to describe these structural efforts to make schools nondiscriminatory.

The two decades between 1954 and the mid-1970s witnessed a flood of educational-opportunity policies from government and the courts, including school desegregation, compensatory programs, and special assistance for language-minority and disabled students. But increasingly, the struggle moved beyond racial neutrality to a proactive stance for equality and inclusion. Lyndon Johnson's presidency tried to use public power to overcome the exercise of private prejudices and gave civil rights struggles new life. The civil rights movement of the 1960s and 1970s yielded landmark court decisions and legislation on behalf of a wide range of excluded Americans, with the centerpiece of this legislation being the 1964 voting rights law.[19] The federal War on Poverty created programs such as Head Start and supplemental compensatory education to equalize opportunities for poor children. In 1971, the Pennsylvania courts ruled that the public schools must provide an appropriate and free education to handicapped children—a ruling that led in 1975 to federal Public Law 94–142, requiring that schools develop individual education plans for these students. In 1972, Congress passed Title IX of the Higher Education Act, which provided for sexual equality in all educational programs supported by federal funding. In 1974, the U.S. Supreme Court decided in *Lau* v. *Nichols* that schools must provide special language assistance to students whose first language is not English. In 1975, a California court decided in *Serrano* v. *Priest* that the state's school finance system was illegal since it provided less to schools attended by poor children. In 1976, a district court in Washington, D.C., ruled in *Hobson* v. *Hanson* that the ability-grouping practices in the public schools discriminated against black students. Although the *Hobson* v. *Hanson* decision was later overturned by an appeals court, it set in motion a series of cases—some successful—and led to Title VI of the Elementary and Secondary Education Act, challenging the legality of ability grouping in racially mixed schools. Similar cases were filed and won by plaintiffs in states across the nation.

Early in the 1980s, however, under the Reagan and Bush administrations the federal government raised the banner of "excellence" and cast advocacy for equity as a threat to the goal of excellence. From *A Nation at Risk* in 1983 to *Goals 2000* at decade's end, a well-articulated campaign by social and political conservatives argued that the quality of the nation's schools—and with it, the efficacy of the nation's economy and the security of its defense—depended on government's setting high standards and holding schools and students accountable for attaining them. Counterarguments that government also had a responsibility to guarantee that all children have the opportunity to learn up to the specified standards fell on ears that had become not only deaf but disdainful of expensive (and, in their minds, intrusive and ineffective) efforts to equalize schooling. Thus began a period, extending to the present, in which successive demands for schools to improve were answered by research and policies that called for low-achieving students to attend schools in which highly qualified teachers had command of up-to-date teaching practices, generous resources, and full inclusion with a demographic cross-section of all the community's children; however, such practices were at least

partly at odds with the conservative national politics and social policies that demanded improvement in the absence of such inclusion.
Schools found themselves smack in the middle of this bind.

Contemporary Reforms for Socially Just Schooling

By the end of the 1980s, most civil rights and children's advocates
worried that hard-won gains toward equity and inclusion were
eroding. They despaired at a federal government and a judicial system that had turned away from framing new legal remedies and
enforcing those already in place. They were discouraged about the
disposition of the education system—and the culture at large—to
resist or circumvent the presumed spirit of legislation and court
decisions.

In the absence of government activism regarding equity, some
private philanthropic entities stepped into the breach. Though not
fundamentally challenging society's race-neutral, equal-opportunity
approach, a number of foundations, including Carnegie, initiated
new agendas that pressed educators to focus quite directly on
improving schools enrolling low-income children and those of
color. Reformers argued that full access to social and political institutions such as schools couldn't be accomplished simply by opening doors. Rather, the conduct of these institutions must be
changed to promote the achievement and school success of students from the diverse array of American cultures. The nation had
too much to lose—in economic and social terms, as well as in a
moral sense—if schools failed to prepare all children for productive work and good citizenship.

Reform projects such as *Turning Points* sought, in part, to
change educational practices that hamper children whom schools
see as "different": racial and language minorities, girls, children
with disabilities, and those considered to be normal but of "low"
intellectual ability. *Turning Points* argued for socially just school
structures—including heterogeneous ability grouping—and
changed classroom practices to make more socially just structures
work. Heterogeneously grouped classrooms, for example, were to
be supported by cooperative, small-group learning strategies, flexible scheduling, and learning opportunities expanded beyond the
school day (extended day, Saturday, and summer programs;

greater home involvement). Furthermore, *Turning Points* made clear that for disadvantaged students to overcome educational obstacles imposed by poverty and racial discrimination, schools must offer educational, health, and social services in ways and to a degree that would help them participate alongside their advantaged peers. The unmistakable implication of this would be for disadvantaged students to receive more resources, relative to advantaged students, than they currently received.

Such recommendations for inclusive and socially just practices, if actually implemented in schools and supported by state and local communities, would require breaking down old hierarchies of educational advantage and redistributing power and resources across race and class lines. Calling attention to the growing social and economic gaps within the school and national populations, these reforms moved away from a presumption of neutral equality to call attention to how educational supports were distributed. But in the political climate of the times, such implications for redistribution could not be made explicit and still get government support or the support of the private foundations funding the reforms. As a result, the broadest social, political, and economic consequences of the reforms were kept at a sufficiently high level of abstraction so that all political segments could buy the reform. This does not mean that the most ideologically sophisticated participants of the reform missed the redistributional consequences. Those who were comfortable with redistribution committed all their energies and passions to effecting the changes, convinced that the reforms would benefit all students, rich and poor. Those who opposed redistribution and favored the structural and resource status quo were, in the mildest of terms, less enthusiastic.

These reforms unsettled, if only slightly, Lincoln's legacy of ambivalence that placed racial equality as an ideal residing in an unspecified future, rather than an urgent imperative that must be enacted immediately. Required to enact obvious and well-documented inequalities, American schools continue to take cover under individualistic and competitive norms of equality. Following an almost Calvinistic notion of merit, schools sort children and distribute resources not explicitly by race or wealth but by indicators (standardized tests, language proficiency) that effectively serve as proxies for race and wealth. Those children who compete most successfully to acquire the best education and educational opportunities are presumed to deserve these advantages by dint of their individual hard work and intelligence—or even the sacrifices their parents are willing to make on their behalf. Of course, this meritocratic version of schooling stands little chance of pulling together an American society polarized by race and wealth. Reforms like *Turning Points* advocated a clear, if only partial, shift from purely individualistic and competitive goals and promoted movement in the direction of social justice as the basis for allocating educational opportunities and resources. Attempting to make this shift, however, placed school reformers squarely in a struggle over the meaning of civic virtue and freedom in American culture.

Becoming Caring

A century after Jefferson, social reformer Jane Addams came to stand as a symbol for the deeply rooted view that American social institutions, including schools, should be caring as well as educative communities, particularly for those with alienating work lives and living in impoverished neighborhoods. In 1889, Addams established Hull House in the midst of Chicago's burgeoning immigrant neighborhoods. Addams and a group of well-to-do young women spent their days there caring for children, teaching, nursing the sick, and helping immigrant families grapple with horrendous problems in their new lives. The education they attempted to provide went beyond the pragmatic basic skills of reading and writing, to include what these young women saw as essential cultural tools of mainstream middle-class life and dignity, including the arts, handiwork, discussion, and political action. Hull House also promoted a public sphere characterized by participatory debates and dialogues across race and class. Addams's work at Hull House exemplifies Americans' desire for social institutions, including schools, to enable people to attend to one another's well-being.

Caring as Civic Virtue

As in other progressive, big-city settlement houses of the period, the Hull House workers viewed the "problem" of immigrants very differently than did many influential Americans at the helms of industries, newspapers, government, and so on. The prevailing view at the time was that the immigrants themselves were responsible for increasing urban crime, squalor, and unemployment and must therefore be reformed. Addams, however, believed that the greed and corruption of wealthy industrialists had created the conditions that fostered these social ills. She argued that the solution was not simply to "Americanize" (more accurately, to Anglicize) the immigrants, but for social institutions—including government—to rebuild communities torn apart by industrialization and attend to the social needs of immigrant families. Addams meant for Hull House "to provide a center for a higher civic and social life; to institute and maintain educational and philanthropic enterprises and to investigate and improve the conditions in the industrial districts of Chicago."[20] In addition to offering education and culture at Hull House, Addams and her colleagues fought for stronger labor laws and health and safety regulations, ran food programs, gave shelter to prostitutes and battered wives, operated a maternity hospital and a nursery, and more.

The settlement house movement developed an ethic of democratic community that merged social, educational, and political goals and activism. Addams argued eloquently in public lectures and in her writing that democracy must have a social as well as a political function. She wrote, for example, that

> Although America is pledged to the democratic ideal, the view of democracy has been partial, and . . . its best achievement thus far has been pushed along the line of franchise. Democracy has made little attempt to assert itself in social affairs. We have refused to move beyond the position of its eighteenth-century leaders, who believed that political equality alone would secure good to all men. We contentiously followed the gift of the ballot hard upon the gift of freedom to the [N]egro, but we are quite unmoved by the fact that he lives among us in practical social ostracism. We hasten to give the franchise to the immigrant from a sense of justice, from a tradition that he ought to have it, while we dub him with epithets deriding his past life or present occupation. . . .[21]

Addams helped the nation understand that immigrant Americans living in contained neighborhoods and ghettos could, or at least should, be brought into civic life. Her and her colleagues' helping the poor was first understood as charity but came to be considered as work on behalf of the common good or social work. These social reformers, by argument and by deed, wove new threads to connect to the commonwealth the lives of the poor and disenfranchised. They helped the public consider that freedom to act on one's own volition and in one's self-interest, unfettered by public constraints, was roughly commensurate with one's resources, education, and status.

In the belief that political equality was insufficient to provide for the general welfare, Addams pressed for virtuous social institutions that exhibited care for people in addition to ensuring them their rights. Distancing her efforts from charitable motives that focus heavily on the individual giver and recipient, she developed a view of civic virtue that required care to be both private and public. She wrote:

> If in a democratic country, nothing can be permanently achieved save through the masses of the people, it will be impossible to establish a higher political life than the people themselves crave; that it is difficult to see how the notion of a higher civic life can be fostered save through a common intercourse; that the blessings and cultivation which we associate with a life of refinement and cultivation be made universal and must be made universal if they are to be permanent; that the good we secure for ourselves is precarious and uncertain . . . until it is secured for all of us and incorporated into our common life.[22]

Schools as Caring Social Centers

From early in the nineteenth century, the goals of transmitting the knowledge and skills needed for participating in the economy and imparting the habits and dispositions for responsible citizenship have driven most schooling policies. These values resulted from and contributed to the dominant view that classrooms—especially those enrolling poor children—should be run like factories, with strictly enforced rules of conduct.

Although this dominant mode suggests few imperatives to care about students, caring has nevertheless been a recurring theme in schooling. Johann Pestalozzi, a Swiss educator with a strong American following throughout the nineteenth century, wrote about the virtues of "domestic education," arguing that students learn best in an environment where teachers help them develop self-respect and emotional security. "Maternal love," in Pestalozzi's view, ensured trust and obedience, elevated the moral character of the young, and improved the lot of poor children. Similar concerns drove nineteenth-century Boston schools to seek women teachers, reasoning that they would make classrooms more nurturing and homelike places. Friedrich Froebel, who developed the first kindergarten curriculum aimed at promoting children's development through self-expression and cooperative play, argued that the classroom should become a miniature society; he believed that the cooperation they learned at school would help them become cooperative members of adult society.

The educational theories of Pestalozzi, Froebel, and others figured prominently in Jane Addams's efforts. She argued that education for immigrants must go beyond the basics of English language instruction and civics, to provide for the social and moral well-being of all who were poor. This meant attending to social and aesthetic needs with lectures, discussions, concerts, and an art gallery; providing vocational training; and giving workers an understanding of the history and significance of the industrial life in which they and their families took part. In 1892, Addams raised this issue in relationship to schools' capacity to meet social needs: "We find that all educational matters are more democratic in their political than in their social aspects. The public schools in the poorest and most crowded wards of the city are inadequate to the number of children, and many of the teachers are ill prepared and overworked."[23]

The settlement house movement went beyond the specific social programs it fostered. The ethic of social service that guided these democratic communities merged political, social, and educational purposes in an organization that was modeled more after an extended family—a community—than a school. Over time, the settlement house reformers persuaded schools to consider the family/community model. Schools responded with school physicians, classes for handicapped children, school lunch programs, and school libraries in a movement they called "socialized education."

Dewey's friendship with Addams and his support of her work influenced his thinking that schools might themselves become social centers modeled after the community at Hull House.

What a contrast these ideas were to the dominant mode in early-twentieth-century schools. Educational historian Herbert Kleibard recounts that in 1913, a factory inspector, Helen M. Todd, surveyed five hundred child laborers to see if they would prefer to go back to school or to "remain in the squalor of the factories." Todd asked them whether, if their families were reasonably well off, they would choose to continue working or go to school. Kleibard notes, "Of the 500, 412 told her, sometimes in graphic terms, that they preferred factory labor to the monotony, humiliation, and even sheer cruelty that they experienced in school.[24] Even as the rigid, factory model persisted, reformers pressed for more humane alternatives. Within the first two decades of the century, many city schools followed Addams's and Dewey's lead, offering health and social services as well as extended community education programs after school and in the evenings.[25]

Care and Contemporary School Reform

By the late 1980s, a growing chorus of school reformers were decrying that American secondary school students too often drift through classes without developing stable relationships with teachers (and, often, other students). "Departmentalization," once prized as a reflection of teachers' specialized expertise, came to be seen as limiting teachers' ability to accommodate students' personal and social needs, as they single-handedly manage the large number of students they have for less than an hour of instruction and virtually no time for personal interactions. Although schools have expected individual students to get what they can from this structure, reformers claimed it embodies norms that favor only the most motivated and highly skilled students—frequently, only those students with school-savvy parents who guide their children through the formal and informal structures surrounding scheduling and course selection, grading, discipline, and so on.

Echoing Addams, reformers in the late 1980s sought to make schools more familylike. Just as the settlement houses built close communities around the common goal of children's intellectual,

physical, social, and moral well-being, the Coalition of Essential
Schools, the Comer School Development project, and *Turning
Points* in particular challenged schools to reinvent themselves as
socially just and caring communities. *Turning Points* called for students who "will understand the importance of developing and
maintaining close relationships . . . that require great effort
and even sacrifice, but without which life is filled with insecurity and
loneliness."[26] It also asked schools to make structural changes that
would "create stable, close, mutually respectful relationships with
adults and peers that are considered fundamental for intellectual
development and personal growth."[27] Large impersonal structures
were to be replaced by smaller schools-within-schools, teams, and
advisory groups.

Such reforms were meant to highlight the interdependence
among students, teachers, and parents. The responsibility for
teaching and learning was not meant to fall on a single individual,
but should be shared in a strong and positive school community
with fundamentally communitarian norms intended to promote
close and caring relationships, trust, respect, common purpose,
and mutual support. Many reforms also argued that these norms
must extend beyond the school into the community. Schools must
establish "partnerships and collaborations to ensure students'
access to health and social services, and to use community
resources to enrich the instructional program and opportunities
for constructive after-school activities."[28]

Advocates for such reforms have been bolstered by increasing
attention to the concept of care in the schooling literature. A compelling exploration of schools and classrooms as caring communities is found in the work of Nel Noddings, who wants an "ethic
of care" to shape the social, emotional, and academic conditions
(the culture) in classrooms. She believes that "schools should be
committed to a great moral purpose: to care for children so that
they, too, will be prepared to care."[29] Noddings proposes caring as
the centerpiece of school reform, defining it as a relation between
two human beings—one caring and the other cared-for—rather
than a set of behaviors or an individual trait. Such caring requires
commitment to foster empathy and responsibility for others and
for maintaining continuity in relationships. Recent thinking about
school leadership also supports this approach to reform, arguing

that when school leaders act on an ethic of care, they can influence the development of shared values that help schools build a foundation of moral commitment and trust.[30]

This ethic of care represents a considerable shift from the individualistic charity and service ethics that characterize how schools try to meet student and community needs. Typically, schools provide "needy" students with screening, information, or actual basic health and social services, often through the school nurse or health classes. Some schools encourage students themselves to do community service, to help the needy through activities such as holiday canned-food drives. However, attending to the needs of others who are in desperate straits is not quite the same as meeting needs as an unexceptional condition of living in one's own community. As educational historian John Rogers has noted, "While schools may have become sites for and conduits to an array of services, they have not necessarily become centers for community life."[31]

Some contemporary activists, Rogers among them, argue that schools must go through a critical and respectful process of understanding the circumstances that shape students' lives and the conditions in their communities.[32] They stress the relationships inherent in caring (relationships in which something is built and mutually held), as opposed to the transactional and service relationships inherent in meeting needs (relationships in which something goes from one to another). A relationship of care allows for an even or flat distribution of power or authority, whereas service nearly always requires a hierarchical distribution of power between provider and receiver.

Advocacy for caring, child-centered schools that attend to students' health and social needs has become a stronger, even if still minor, influence in schools.[33] Such advocacy draws from Addams's model for a caring community, which recasts freedom and civic virtue so they become less oppositional and more synergistic. To *freedom* society has typically assigned the values of individual volition, striving for oneself, and independence; and to *civic virtue* society assigns the values of collective decisions, striving for others' benefit, and community life. However, Addams and her colleagues saw the strengthening of community life for the less fortunate as the road to a fulfilling life for all citizens.

Becoming Participatory

The contribution of Martin Luther King, Jr., to American culture is usually encapsulated in his leadership of the civil rights gains made by blacks during the 1950s and 1960s. He is well remembered from film footage of violent white reactions to protesters' "direct actions" of sit-ins, marches, and boycotts. Our popular culture has focused on King's inspirational dream and his hope that "some day" racial minorities and the poor would achieve civic and economic justice. Like Addams, King was a heroic leader committed to public action, not for personal benefit but rather out of a virtuous concern for the common good.

King and the civil rights movement reasserted Jefferson's conception of citizen participation as the essential means for protecting individual rights and freedom. King and Jefferson might very well part company on the specifics of who should participate and what decisions they might make; for example, some of Jefferson's preferences might match those of today's social conservatives. Yet they both found coherence in the values of freedom and civic virtue. Jefferson posed the ideal of a democracy in which every citizen participates in public affairs—not just at the ballot box, but every day. In the intervening years, the nation accepted (more or less) that every citizen requires legal access to most fundamental rights. King struggled alongside ordinary citizens to make citizen participation a democratic reality, not simply a legal or theoretical possibility.

The Power of Collective Participation

Popular images of King and the civil rights movement obscure the actual participatory processes that characterized the struggle. King's vision and skillful, charismatic leadership, though surely remarkable, tell only part of the story. More significant was the power of the collective, grassroots struggle that was the core of the civil rights movement, the negotiations forced by such participation, and the considerable risk and courage it required of ordinary people.[34] Through its extraordinary collective action, the civil rights movement confronted the culture's uneven distribution of power. Its struggle for freedom was a struggle to participate, and it blurred all distinction between actions that would benefit individuals and actions to benefit all the people. In his "Letter from the Birmingham Jail," King wrote: "I am cognizant of the interrelatedness of all communities and states. . . . Injustice anywhere is a threat to justice everywhere. We are caught in an inescapable network of mutuality, tied in a single garment of destiny. Whatever affects one directly affects all indirectly."[35]

Rather than simply attesting to the power of courageous individuals, the civil rights movement and other social movements (such as the women's movement) illustrate the power of a determined community to sustain individuals as both the means and the ends of civic virtue. Moreover, these movements also demonstrate that participation stands the best chance of advancing civic virtue (and civic virtue stands a good chance of advancing participation) when diverse, heterogeneous groups of citizens struggle together to solve public problems.

Today, we imagine this public virtue to be conflated with what is popularly referred to as the "public sphere" or "public space." We see such a space, loosely, as an environment in which a free and enlightened public—a collection of people who may differ in their backgrounds, resources, and interests—work together, face-to-face to solve public problems, advance the common good, and shape the direction of the democracy. Indeed, in its ideal form, such an environment represents a public will or volition in which the norms for acting on behalf of the public good are so strong that no other action makes good common sense.

Participation Must Be Action as Well as Talk

King knew well that this participation meant including face-to-face relationships. Like Jefferson, he understood that such commitment could not rest on allegiance to a charismatic leader or be sustained by a desire for parochial benefits. Even so, King was no neutral shepherd, prepared to follow the meandering will of his flock. He was unequivocal in his identification of injustice, and he was nearly as firm in his views on how to accomplish the goals of the social justice movement. This certainty became a source of much conflict and trauma within the movement. King pressed for a process that accorded those who opposed his cause the same dignity and respect that he sought to gain for blacks and the poor. Nonviolence afforded dignity to the movement's opponents by presuming that their consciences, self-interest, and public spirit would allow them to make sense of the movement's aims in ways they previously could not, whereas violence presumes that one's enemy is incapable of a sensible or moral act. Accordingly, he believed that power inhered in the nonviolent means by which the powerless confronted and engaged their situation. Again in his "Letter from the Birmingham Jail," King outlined a process of democratic inquiry and action through which ordinary people become powerful enough to transform social and economic arrangements by collection of facts, negotiation, self-purification (preparation for nonviolence), and direct action.

Participation Is Both Means and Ends

King's approach resonates with the work of contemporary participatory democratic theorists, who argue that participating in local community projects—as distinct from the limited form of participation that voting represents—fosters community attention to their collective well-being, as well as care about their members. This civic virtue, according to political scientist Carol Pateman, encourages individuals to act as "public as well as private citizens."[36] Cornel West argues that the struggle for social justice requires faith in "the abilities and capacities of ordinary people to participate in decision making procedures of institutions that regulate their lives."[37] Not unlike King, West seeks a "prophetic pragmatism" that combines faith in democratic processes with a "critical temper." The process is one that, as we noted in the introduction, "keeps track of social misery, solicits and channels moral outrage to alleviate it, and projects a future in which the potentialities of ordinary people flourish and flower."[38] And in fact, some democratic activists begin with the premise that communal bonds and collaborative action give individuals the power to act in ways that can bring social justice to their communities.[39] In sum, America's democratic tradition allows for—but does not fully exploit—citizen participation in the public spheres of school and community. Participation is democracy, not simply a way of achieving it.

Ambivalence About Democratic Participation

Democratic participation; isn't the expression itself redundant? For how might one conceive of democracy in any way other than participatory? Who could object to citizens participating? As with the public goods of well-educated citizens, socially just institutions, and caring communities, Americans are ambivalent about their commitment to participatory democracy. The ambivalence often centers on power. If ordinary people, including poor people and people of color, become real participants, then institutions might actually change in ways that those who control the institutions may not want. Those in power also fear relinquishing control over change to the poor and disenfranchised, even when they agree with the change itself. So, as with the civil rights movement, they may modify stories of grassroots counterculture activity to appear as mainstream triumphs—rational and bureaucratic—rather than tangible, moral, and near-revolutionary victories.

Surely, King's status as an American cultural icon rests partly on his representing grassroots activists who fought for new versions of the common good, even in the face of terrible threats to personal safety. But a less countercultural image of King has been constructed post mortem—that of King as a good model for both blacks and whites, the leader who pursued a nonviolent dream under stable, Christian leadership. The sanctified image of Martin Luther King, Jr., and crowds singing "We Shall Overcome" obscures fundamental American dilemmas about power. Our individualistic thinking attributes the efficacy of the civil rights movement to a charismatic leader, a hero, rather than to the collective action of empowered ordinary people. From this perspective, we see grassroots participants as followers instead of everyday heroes who joined together in anger and power and with a vision of a virtuous society.

At the abstract level, Americans believe that the collective pursuit of the common good can peacefully coexist with individuals' free pursuit of their own self-interest. In the real world, we see how difficult it is for groups seeking to talk about and act toward the common good to withstand the press of individual self-interest. Most Americans in charge of institutions have considerable enthusiasm for participation, so long as it doesn't disrupt the greater power of those with privilege. Democratic participation evokes contrary responses because it is not neutral to the current distribution of power. We know, of course, that participatory politics can be quite reactionary—the "not in my backyard" restrictions of neighborhood groups, for example. But democratic participation is, at heart, advocacy for a more just society; it fosters relationships that strengthen those with less relative power. King and the civil rights activists recognized that conflict would be an inevitable and necessary part of such a process, even if it is fundamentally democratic. Resolving this conflict, many theorists argue, requires deliberation across differences in settings characterized by free exploration of ideas and egalitarian, honest, non-manipulative exchange.[40] Of course, as King knew well, such deliberations among people with vastly differing power in society rarely are entered into voluntarily.

Finally, many Americans simply avoid participation altogether. The important—even essential—representative nature of our government exerts a powerful tug toward a nonparticipatory citizenry. The rule of law, the rule of bureaucracy, and the "rule" of always having some business more pressing than civic participation all conspire to create the feeling that one's own vote or one's own action does not matter or may not be welcomed. Indeed, many observers today lament the decline of civic participation over the past twenty-five years. None of us needs to look too far for signs. In February 1999, for example, the *Los Angeles Times* reported that several small municipalities in Southern California had canceled their upcoming spring elections. From upscale Beverly Hills to the low-income City of Industry, no candidates emerged to challenge sitting mayors and city council members.[41] Scholars Harry Boyte and Nancy Kari at the University of Minnesota's Center for Democracy and Citizenship write that, in the 1990s, ordinary citizens have abandoned civic participation for what they call secondary roles in public life—those of "consumers, complaining clients, special-interest advocates, or volunteers who 'help out' but make few serious decisions."[42] As participation declines, Boyte and Kari argue, most people today see government less as a collective action of free citizens and more as a provider of services; they are willing to let experts make the decisions.

Schools as Participatory Democracies

Many wish fondly for schools to be sanctuaries from the harsh, real-life, rough edges of the larger society—places where children and their parents participate according to both the letter and the spirit of American public laws and public values. Many wish also for schools to be nurseries where children are raised with civic virtues that exceed those of their parents. Sometimes these wishes are partially realized, but rarely without confronting and struggling mightily against the fierce individualistic pressures that are manifest in the uneven power and privilege outside of schools.

Throughout the nineteenth century, small and often marginalized reform groups worked to make schools instruments of social justice, and therefore better places than the community at large. Particularly interesting are the efforts of African American women educators, often assisted by black churches and sometimes by liberal white groups such as the Quakers, to use the schools to improve the social, economic, and political circumstances of the African American community. These women used their classrooms and their leadership to teach reading and writing not only to their students but to adults from the community as well—a defiant act of social justice in the nineteenth century. For example, teacher Fannie Jackson Coppin organized tuition-free classes for freed slaves coming north and founded a school for their children. Believing that knowledge is power, Coppin intended her teaching to "uplift" the race. Other well-educated black women educators such as Anna Julia Cooper and Mary McLeod Bethune also went far beyond teaching their students technical skills or rudimentary literacy and attempted to teach in ways that would bring about social and political change. At the root of their efforts was the conviction that education was not about individual gain but about strengthening the community, a view captured eloquently in the motto of the National Association of Colored Women: "Lifting as We Climb."[43]

In the educational mainstream, first Horace Mann and later John Dewey envisioned schools as agencies of social reform for the further democratization of American society. Dewey stressed that classrooms are a part of life, not merely preparation for it, and to make society more democratic, students must participate in classrooms that are themselves democratic societies. Teachers must give students a chance to learn how their actions affect the success or failure of the group. In classrooms, students must develop their sense of civic-mindedness by sharing both the pleasant and unpleasant tasks that complex group projects require. Doing one's part as a member of a classroom group project prepares students to be both leaders and followers. In 1938, Dewey wrote: "The realization of that principle in the schoolroom [that schools are a part of democratic life], it seems to me, is an expression of the significance of democracy as the educational process without which individuals cannot come into the full possession of themselves nor make a contribution . . . to the social well-being of others. I said that democracy and education bear a reciprocal relation, for it is not merely that democracy is itself an educational principle, but that democracy cannot endure, much less develop without education. . . ."[44] When such classroom projects focus on issues of community interest, teachers and students can forge new, reciprocal relations with community members.

Later in the century, during the 1960s and 1970s, efforts to make schools participatory and socially just emerged in the movement for "community control"—most notably, perhaps, in the Ocean Hill–Brownsville neighborhoods in New York City. Black activists seeking community control of schools were more interested in changing institutions than they were in simply gaining greater access to them. They believed that collective action by ordinary people could create school conditions that would enhance the lives of neighborhood children and families. In Ocean Hill–Brownsville, parents and community activists won the right to hire and fire school staff and select curriculum materials. Teachers, feeling powerless and threatened, were caught between a school administrative bureaucracy that left them few professional prerogatives and citizens who seemed to be grabbing for the few remaining ones. They responded with a two-month strike that ended the Ocean Hill–Brownsville experiment.[45] This quite radical vision of the schools actually belonging to the central-city communities whose children attended them never reached the mainstream.

Most schools remain today locked into hierarchical and bureaucratic principles. Administrators have more responsibility and
power than teachers; teachers have more responsibility and power
than students. Parents have responsibility and power over their
children, but they have very little capacity to affect the school directly, especially if they are not among the community's elite.
Compartmentalizing administrators, teachers, students, and
parents into well-defined roles sustains these norms of authority.
Principals remain the official leaders of school activities, often enforcing centrally mandated changes in teaching practice and
school organization. Teachers normally have little official voice in
coordinating activities or enforcing changes, but once the classroom door is shut they exercise significant control over what gets
taught. Although granted some avenues for power, parents are normally considered outsiders, especially if they come bearing complaints. "Parent participation" nearly always means that parents
support the schools' work or that schools teach parents knowledge,
skills, and home routines that foster school success. Finally, students have virtually no official voice in their education, though
reactions to this prescribed passivity often surface in quite active
forms of resistance.

Today's Participatory Reforms

The comprehensive reforms of the late 1980s and 1990s sought to
change the prevailing structures and the norms that drive them,
arguing that democratic and participatory processes must be a key
component of fundamentally restructured schools. *Turning Points*
argued, for example: "Deeply ingrained in our society is the belief
that individuals can be trusted to make decisions for themselves
and for the common good. This belief is the bedrock of the democratic political system."[46] *Turning Points* also offered specific recommendations that would make schools reflect this fundamental
American value. Urging that decisions about students' experiences
are best made by those closest to the students, and recommending
that teams of teachers govern their own classroom budgets, space,
curriculum, teaching strategies, and scheduling, *Turning Points* also
called for committees composed of administrators, teachers, support staff, students, parents, and community representatives to

make schoolwide policies. It argued that closer relationships between schools and communities would build trust, respect, and common purpose. Partnerships with community agencies and businesses would bring greater coordination among youth-serving groups and garner additional resources for school programs.

Turning Points, of course, was less clear—and even silent—on many of the logical manifestations of these proposals. How does such participation disrupt local sensibilities? What does it cost? How long does it take for people to learn about each other and learn new skills for participation? What happens when parents, educators, and community members begin to fear that empowering others to participate will infringe on their own right to pursue what they see as best for themselves, their children, or their professional lives? Is change a rational, orderly evolution, working within and led by existing bureaucracies, or does it entail some of the chaos associated with a revolution?

Turning Points and the other reforms tended to keep discussions about the course of change at a sufficiently high level of abstraction to postpone answering these questions, as when the Carnegie report talked about change almost mystically: "This transformation is intended to create for every young person a community that engages those for whom life already holds high promise, and welcomes into the mainstream of society those who might otherwise be left behind."[47]

Tension Between Individual Liberty and the Common Good

The pull toward civic virtue and the public good embodied in contemporary school reform has deep American roots. So too, however, does the pull toward protecting individual liberty. In his 1996 book *Democracy's Discontent: America in Search of a Public Philosophy,* Michael Sandel reminds us that

> Central to republican theory is the idea that liberty requires
> self-government, which depends in turn on civic virtue. This
> idea figured prominently in the political outlook of the founding
> generation. "[P]ublic virtue is the only foundation of republics,"
> wrote John Adams on the eve of independence. "There must be

a positive passion for the public good, the public interest, honour, power and glory, established in the minds of the people, or there can be no republican government, nor any real liberty." Benjamin Franklin agreed: "Only a virtuous people are capable of freedom. As nations become corrupt and vicious, they have more need of masters."

The founders also learned from the republican tradition that they could not take civic virtue for granted. To the contrary, public spirit was a fragile thing, susceptible to erosion by such corrupting forces as luxury, wealth, and power. Anxiety over the loss of civic virtue was a persistent republican theme.[48]

The 1985 publication of *Habits of the Heart,* by Robert Bellah and colleagues, helped spark renewed interest in understanding the nation's culture and politics in terms of the tension and balance between individual and communitarian interests.[49] This framework opens useful windows for viewing how society conducts its schooling. Do humans naturally compete for the greatest individual gain? Does this natural tendency simply need a few organizing principles (say, free markets and competition) to be the engine that drives societal well-being? Or does public good derive from a commitment to social, rather than individual, practices and values (for example, cooperation, participation in public affairs) as the public engines of well-being? Does the individual's well-being necessarily result from—rather than produce—a good society? Also, if one or the other side is neither wholly correct nor wrong, what is the proper balance for this particular time in history or for a particular age of children, such as those in middle schools? Finally, *balance* may not be the proper term—suggesting as it does a zero-sum, as if favoring one side must come at the expense of the other side. Rather, the greatest good may come from seeking *harmony* among the contradictions of civic virtue and individual interests.[50]

Schools and Cultural Contradictions

What is the public school's role in maintaining the culture's balance? How does each generation persuade the next to be dutiful and wise citizens, and at the same time guard their individual freedom and choices? How does each generation convince the next that our collective national well-being requires autonomous individuals to compete dispassionately with one another? How do we teach that a diverse society must simultaneously uphold the ideal of political equality and preserve unequal social and economic structures? And how, amid a shifting professional view of best practice that gives primacy to sociocultural and often communitarian learning perspectives, can educators assuage fears and/or garner political clout to change the venerable and highly individualistic appearances of learning in schools?

Nurturing both freedom and virtue cannot be left to chance. Neither can it be entrusted to families or religious congregations—at least when these traditional social institutions emphasize small-group norms of loyalty and cooperation over those of individual development, autonomy, and choice. In a highly diverse society, if particularistic family and community affiliations are too strong, they can thwart the nation's ability to forge a meaning of the common good that all will share. Public schools are the one social institution in which members of diverse racial and other groups must by law come face-to-face to define and balance individual freedoms with the common good. Therefore, it is in schools where the national struggle to accommodate multiple, culturally shaped meanings of virtue and freedom takes place most surely.

Although the dichotomy between civic virtue and freedom oversimplifies today's public dialogue on culture and politics, it also reflects an enduring theme of today's seminal education issues of choice and vouchers, multicultural and bilingual education, the cultural canon and constructed or contextualized knowledge, heterogeneous and homogeneous grouping, accountability and standardized testing, and so on. Over time, educators such as Sarah Chatsworth, Ben McCall, and Fred Antouli believed that *their* students in *their* schools could thrive academically and socially only if their schools could balance or at least harmonize the norms of civic virtue and individual interest that characterize American culture. This reform challenge thrust these educators into a fundamental cultural contraction between the two goals of civic virtue and individualism, as they strove to make their schools educative, socially just, caring, and participatory. Of course, few argue for one or the other side of these (here polarized) values. All Americans today of whatever political and cultural stripe claim to ride the inside philosophical track to achieving both individual freedom and social good. And all point to the founding fathers, most particularly Thomas Jefferson, as their uniquely American progenitor. Today, in our era of intense individualism and marketplace values, reform-minded American schools strive to reemphasize and teach the young the rudiments of civic virtue, at the same time that they hone children's skills to freely pursue individual self-interest.

Tipping the Cultural Balance

Americans expect schools to be virtuous places, where citizens become educative, socially just, caring, and participatory in pursuit of the common, public good, and *Turning Points* asked schools to press toward these communitarian and civic values. Yet *Turning Points* could not expect Americans to abandon the culture's strong Jeffersonian interest in promoting and protecting liberty, including individuals' pursuits of their own good life. Indeed, most school reform recommendations are framed in terms of enabling young people to compete well and to gain better lives for themselves.

We have seen clearly that Americans prize individual initiative and other ineffable individual qualities such as character, talent, and intelligence as the principal contributors to a good society or a good school. This legacy of individualism remains strong by guarding against public or private constraints on individuals' pursuit of personal gain and advancement. Although this legacy does not preclude caring, social justice, and so on, it does not present civic virtue as the principal engine behind good schools. Rather, this tradition drives a competitive, merit-based approach to learning and achievement. It also fosters emphasis on learning as an individual activity, rather than as fundamentally social.

The success of *Turning Points* reform depended on policy makers and educators finding ways to redefine and then better balance civic virtue with freedom. Since making schools more educative, socially just, caring, and participatory embodies the traditional American tension between civic virtue and individual freedom, Turning Points reforms engendered palpable ambivalence in all of the states and schools. Some reformers found themselves embroiled in conflict, mired in their own local versions of larger cultural contradictions. Their struggle was to forge a virtuous compromise rather than seek a triumph of one set of values over the other. These are the stories of reform that played out at Verbena, Inland, and Madison middle schools, and in the other schools we studied. These are the stories we tell in the remaining chapters of this book.

To the degree that *Turning Points* propelled educators to press for greater emphasis on civic virtue and its compatible theories of learning and development as social processes, it was a truly reform-minded undertaking. However, once *Turning Points* entered the school, community, and state political environments through its dissemination, implementation, and incentives, pressures welled up to protect the individualistic tradition, diminishing the effects of the reform. The reformers found much of their hard work was lost to the children at their schools—much, but certainly not all.

Part Two

Four Cultural Struggles

Chapter Three

Becoming Educative

Jefferson's convictions have proven remarkably durable, reverberating in some version or another in nearly every contemporary proposal for school reform. Two centuries after he proposed that educated citizens hold the key to our national well-being, his views remain firmly embedded in the American psyche. Even though public schools have suffered withering attacks in the past two decades, most Americans remain firmly committed to the idea of public education.

Although Jefferson's commitment remains intact, his vision of the specific education that Americans need has changed as dramatically as the nation itself. Jefferson argued that citizens would be well prepared for democratic participation if they acquired the fundamental tools of literacy and a basic familiarity with Greek, Roman, European, and American history. His late-twentieth-century successors in the White House have demanded far more. Presidents Reagan, Bush, and Clinton, as well as lawmakers of both political parties, agreed that Americans now need higher-level cognitive abilities; specifically, they need knowledge of advanced mathematics, science, and technology to adapt to ever-changing global conditions and workplace demands and ensure security and prosperity in the twenty-first century.

An earlier version of the material in this chapter appeared in Oakes, J., Vasudeva, A., and Jones, M. "Becoming Educative: Reforming Curriculum and Teaching in the Middle Grades." *Research in Middle Level Education Quarterly,* 1996, *20*(1), 11–40. We acknowledge Vasudeva and Jones's considerable contribution to the analysis presented here.

Today, widespread support for school reform is predicated on a belief that American schools—especially in comparison with schools in other industrialized countries—are simply not up to the task. Popular reform rhetoric casts schools as academically flabby. Although some education scholars argue persuasively that the current crisis over American students' academic achievement has been largely manufactured by ultraconservative ideologues bent on dismantling public schools, these scholars also contend that much work needs to be done because schools could be so much better.[1]

The Press for High Achievement: A Brief, Recent History

In 1983, *A Nation at Risk* prompted policy makers throughout the United States to add more time to the school day, more days to the school year, and more math and science courses to high school graduation requirements, in the belief that more exposure to academic subjects would boost achievement. But by the end of the 1980s, most policy makers and educators had come to believe that simply adding more of the same was not enough. They believed in a rather abstract principle: that schools must fundamentally restructure the organizational arrangements that shape teaching and learning. Beyond that belief, there was little consensus. Educators, policy makers, and powerful national constituencies polarized around the questions of why schools were failing to educate students well and what the country should do about it. Generally, conservative observers believed that the country had strayed from traditional content, pedagogy, ways of distributing educational resources, and so on. Progressive observers contended that the country had not strayed at all, that these traditions were alive and well in schools, and it was the dogged adherence to some traditional perspectives that was at the heart of the nation's educational ills.

By the late 1980s, however, education analysts had also made clear to policy makers that the many elements of the overall educational enterprise (curriculum, teacher training, student assessments, standards, accountability, conceptions of learning, etc.), formed an interlinked system.[2] To alter any one of these elements significantly meant that other elements must also change. To take a persistent dilemma as an example, many schools trying to implement a reform curriculum continued to be judged by their performance on standardized tests that were based on the traditional (pre-reform) curriculum; therefore these schools felt pressure both to change and not to change their curriculum. Thus, by the mid-1990s, most states saw "systemic reform" as prerequisite to academically challenging teaching and learning. However, this systemic perspective did little to mitigate the divide between conservative and progressive ideologies as to the nature of good teaching and learning. Proposals to align and make coherent the many elements of schooling often provoked deepened hostility.[3]

School reforms such as the Coalition of Essential Schools, Accelerated Schools, Comer schools, Project Zero, and *Turning Points* were national movements aimed at influencing both schools and state departments of education. These were comprehensive reforms that hoped to address a broad sweep of schooling policies and practices; in other words, they tried to be more systemic than earlier reforms. Substantively, the projects argued for (and offered to schools) a set of reform practices—a vision of what a restructured school might look like. In addition to working school-by-school, many of these projects also attempted to help states align their curriculum, assessment, and school improvement policies with the schools' restructuring goals. The Coalition of Essential Schools, for example, worked with the Education Commission of the States to build a network of "relearning" states; Hank Levin worked with Illinois to make Accelerated Schools a statewide project; and Carnegie nested its *Turning Points* work with schools into a network of state projects, the Middle Grades Schools State Policy Initiative. Each state project began with a high-level task force that framed new middle-grades policies in the state and then used state-level staff to assist schools as they restructured to provide the rich and challenging teaching and learning that they believed all young Americans need.

Reform Requires New Theory as Well as New Practice

Recognizing that structural features of schooling and classroom practices both constrain and create learning opportunities, reformers advocated that schools take a hard look at these structures and practices and make each of them contribute to intellectually challenging teaching and learning. This would be a departure from the typical (nonsystemic) practice of targeting a single structure or practice to improve while ignoring other important and needed changes. These reformers criticized secondary schools' "egg-crate" organization of twenty to thirty students and the lockstep schedule of class periods, saying they forced rigid space and time constraints that work against developing fluid and flexible communities of learners. They assailed the large size of schools, saying it inhibited the rich, substantive conversations that are possible when teachers and learners know one another well. They attacked the strict separation of the disciplines into distinct courses as impeding the cross-disciplinary thinking needed to grapple with contemporary problems. They faulted the tracked structure of the curriculum (as in high-, average-, and low-ability classes) for artificially limiting most students' intellectual development. They criticized teacher-directed instruction and individualized learning activities as preventing students from actively engaging knowledge or developing learning relationships with peers.

From Transmission to Educative Practice

Some policy makers were asking educators to create different school structures and to change the way they taught. Some educators were asking for policies to allow practices that would appear very strange indeed to those sitting in statehouses and at home. The more fundamental the change, the more people would have to shift their concept of teaching and learning. It would not be easy.

Most traditional school structures and teaching methods are firmly grounded in conceptions of learning that are based on behavioral psychology and theories of individual difference. These conceptions, for the most part, frame learning as an individual matter. Students' minds are seen as empty vessels to be filled with knowledge and skills. Knowledge is thought to exist in the form of the conventional subject matters. In traditional views, individual variation in student potential, often coinciding with racial and social class differences, is taken to mean that learning needs and outcomes inevitably differ among races and social classes. Moreover, traditionalists believe that as youngsters transition from childhood to adolescence to young adulthood, their proclivities toward learning vary, with middle school often seen as a time of intellectual dormancy. Consistent with these theories, the teacher's job is to transmit subject matter knowledge and skills to students in ways that match their abilities and are developmentally appropriate.

In contrast, the new restructuring reforms were grounded in a competing set of theories, stemming from Dewey's conceptions of how humans think and learn, and the conditions Dewey called *educative* that nurture thinking and learning. However, unlike many of the early- and mid-century progressive reforms (and often excesses) offered in John Dewey's name, the late-twentieth-century reforms have been richly informed by recent cognitive and sociocultural perspectives on learning that are quite compatible with the entire body of Dewey's work.[4] These perspectives focus on learners' constructing their own meanings through interaction and experience. When learners construct knowledge, they make connections between their prior understandings and experiences and new ones in ways that can't be confined to traditional disciplinary boundaries. These theories also emphasize the commonalities across learners in their cognitive processes, rather than highlighting their differences. Moreover, they see differences among students as potentially enriching the learning context. The teacher's job, then, is to shape the environment, activities, and opportunities for rich and diverse interaction, and extend the help or scaffolding that learning requires. As a philosopher and social observer, Dewey anticipates later cognitive and sociocultural work. But going further, Dewey's thought also tightly links a civic or normative perspective to the cognitive and social; it also marries means and ends. These are connections that few others address, even now at the turn of the twenty-first century.

A Myopic Focus on Structure and Practice

Few reformers or educators in reform-minded schools paid much attention to the fundamental cornerstones of teaching and learning: cognitive and sociocultural learning theories, and civic virtue. Yet this is exactly what teachers and community members would require to make sense of the new practices. After all, restructured school organization and teaching hold promise not because they are simply the latest methods but because they are consistent with a coherent theory of learning and citizenship. Without attention to these conceptual shifts, traditional ideas continued to drive practice. Most educators and communities expected students to acquire the knowledge that teachers transmitted, and they expected schools to accommodate differences in abilities with levels and kinds of curriculum and instruction. Most continued to see early adolescence as a time of social development, but not intellectual development, and they continued to see students from disadvantaged communities—students of color, in particular—as less disposed to rigorous academics. The superficial attention paid to the foundational theories of learning and citizenship guaranteed that many of the changes in school would remain superficial.

Importantly, we do not see schools' avoidance of the theoretical as a basis for condemning the teachers' or communities' character or intelligence. This is not a culture that necessarily sees or trusts its public institutions as intellectual strongholds. Indeed, there is a decided preference for schools to be practical, commonsense places where experts already know what they are doing, rather than places to learn, solve problems, or inquire. An instantly understood and devastating accusation of schoolpeople—one most likely to be hurled within the school, by one educator at another—is, "Let's quit being so philosophical." In such instances, the meaning of the caution is clear to all: we do not have the time, the background, or the dispositions to deliberate deeply about reform before we act.

By remaining focused on implementing practices, however, and avoiding explicitly engaging the theories of teaching and learning that underlie them, everything in the reform implementation became negotiable. Moreover, discussions of best practice were rarely informed by theory. On the rare occasions when teachers had significant time to work with colleagues to do their own, necessary rethinking of their instruction, most teachers had few experiences, models, or consulting supports for the kind of theory-based inquiry that could be of much help. Thus, to the degree that local politics would allow extensive reform, these possibilities could not be exploited. Finally, the myopic focus on changed practice was particularly problematic since teachers and students were being asked to shift from individualistic approaches to learning and teaching, toward more collective ones. In other words, fights over best practice often became a proxy for fights between individual interests and the common good.

The accounts of teaching in the sections that follow provide some inspiring, even though small-scale, examples of educativity, where teachers' engagement with students embodied new theories as well as changed practice. The teachers enacted interdisciplinary curriculum, constructivist teaching, heterogeneous grouping, and cooperative learning, to help young adolescents become intellectually reflective and develop disciplined minds. These instances were far from typical, and some of these inspiring classrooms seemed only marginally related to the school's involvement with middle-grade reform. Far more often, teacher adoption of reform structures and practices did not lead to greater educativity. Rather, the reformed practices were enacted only superficially because they relied on transmission theories of teaching and learning that were ill-suited to new norms about the needs of young adolescents and the responsibilities of middle schools. In many cases, teachers simply rejected the reforms altogether. Their rejection was driven as much by deeply held normative and ideological concerns as by pedagogical or technical ones. In every school, overt or submerged social issues determined the broad course of the reform—issues such as race, social class, intellectual ability, merit, competition, and the role schools play in maintaining status and privilege.

Defining Educative Practice

Dewey's notion of educative practice set forth principles for intellectual growth in the academic disciplines. He argued that such growth required more than either "hard" traditional, transmission-style academic learning or "soft" high-interest activities that simply fostered student engagement because they were interesting. Dewey believed that learning experiences went far beyond the activities in themselves. Rather, in what can be viewed as a precursor to contemporary calls for higher-level thinking and problem solving, Dewey argued that an educative experience requires interaction, continuity, action, reflection, and the emergence of subject matter. By this, he meant that educative experiences must be social, connected to previous experiences, embedded in meaningful contexts, and related to students' developing understanding of content. However, experience without contemplating the meaning or purpose of that experience is just doing; educative practice requires doing, thinking about what you're doing, and considering why it matters.

Although most teachers drifted inexorably toward refashioning reforms to match traditional teaching and learning, we caught glimpses of Dewey's educative practice in some classrooms where teachers created nontraditional learning communities replete with intellectually rich activities. Of course, we cannot claim that such teaching emerged directly from the reform. What we do know, however, is that the reform opened up the space for these teachers to pursue their democratic visions. It offered a sense of common purpose in which they could place their own work. For examples, we turn first to Carver Middle School—in many people's minds, a most unlikely site for state-of-the-art teaching and learning.

Educative Practice at George Washington Carver

George Washington Carver Middle School is one of the few graffiti-free buildings in its neighborhood of public housing projects and run-down, single-family houses with brown lawns, iron window bars, and chain link fences. Carver's sixth through eighth graders (about half African American and half Latino) are among the city's poorest, and a greater percentage are on AFDC than in any other middle school in this large California city. For many Carver students, their federally subsidized lunch is the only regular meal of the day. Despite what was called rampant gang activity in the neighborhood and violent incidents in nearby schools, the campus defies the stereotype of an unruly urban school. The grounds are tidy; colorful student-painted murals of famous African Americans and Latinos line a well-scrubbed central courtyard. Students in brown and gold uniforms move about the campus in rambunctious, but orderly, middle school fashion. During class time, hallways are quiet. But as proud as they are of their safe haven, many Carver teachers don't settle for that.

Carver's reform relied heavily on structural changes. The shift to teacher teaming, block scheduling, and common planning time meant that, for a few years at least, teachers taught four classes and shared two common planning periods with team members; this enabled them to hold team and grade-level meetings, plan curriculum, meet with parents and students, and participate in a daily "student interest" program. We also saw classroom practice that approached Dewey's notion of educative practice.

Deepening Understanding and Building Skills

In Carver's seventh grade wing, Nancy Nelson built on students' prior knowledge to develop a sophisticated understanding of history as they celebrated Black History month. Nelson's limited-English-speaking seventh graders had just finished watching the video "From Montgomery to Memphis," about Martin Luther King, Jr., and the civil rights movement. Before the video, she wrote King's words on the board: "I want young men and young women who are not alive today but who will come into this world with new privileges and new opportunities—I want them to know and see that new privileges and opportunities did not come without somebody suffering and sacrificing for them."[5]

She also gave the students a sheet of paper with the quote written on it and asked them to take notes on that paper as they watched: "Keep a list of the privileges and opportunities you enjoy that the people in the film did not, and keep a list of the suffering and sacrifices that were endured to earn them for you." From this launching point, students brainstormed how they, as students who were not alive when King spoke, might respond to his words. Carefully questioning, probing, and listening, she led her students to arrive at two themes that they might write about: privileges versus sacrifice and past versus present conditions.

Nelson's lesson moved adroitly from the prewriting activity—talking about the film—to relaying her own experiences in the civil rights movement. She made herself a historical actor and then asked her students to do the same. To model the kind of narrative that she wanted her students to write, she built on her experience in the 1960s, when she was living in an all-white, middle-class Detroit neighborhood and the first African American family moved in. She told how her neighbors feared that the neighborhood would quickly become all black and how they mounted an aggressive campaign to ban the new family. As a young Anglo housewife, Nelson stood against her neighbors and became a support and a friend to the unwanted newcomers.

Using her own example, she asked her class of immigrant and black students, many of whom had had similar experiences when they moved to their neighborhood or this country, to write about how something in their own lives connected with what they were learning about the civil rights movement. Rather than using trivial, familiar matters such as popular music or current television programs to make her lessons relevant, she helped her students learn high-level school content about history, civil rights, courage, and more, by connecting these themes with their own experiences and with hers. Students who might otherwise find little value in their experiences, or possibly even feel shame from them, were able to see themselves as belonging to an American tradition—one of struggling to establish their own and others' rights to a dignified life, even when the law says they already have those rights.

In the initial brainstorming activity Nelson had provided much support and encouragement, or scaffolding, that she tailored both to individuals and to the whole class ("Getting started is the hardest part of writing"; "Try finishing the sentence, 'I have many . . .'"; "Don't worry about spelling"; "Just get out your ideas."). After students finished their first efforts and read their responses to one another, Nelson closed the lesson by asking them to complete short prompts: "I learned . . ."; "I am most proud of . . ."; The most difficult part for me was. . . ." With these questions, she assessed how her students were making sense of responses as they were thinking about them instead of waiting for the final essays to be turned in, or even for the first draft. She applied this information directly to addressing her students' individual needs for thinking about and writing the assignment. Completing first drafts, reading and commenting on each other's essays, and several rounds of revising and editing would begin the next day.

Interaction and Experience Make Abstract Concepts Accessible

We saw many examples of Dewey's idea that learning takes place through interaction, but perhaps none better than in Tom Katzir's mathematics classroom. Katzir engaged his students in an intense conversation about probability—using baseball statistics. During the fantasy baseball unit, Katzir's students worked in pairs to draft players into their teams; the pair then made a spinner in the form of a pie chart with wedges corresponding to each hitter's likely outcome for a given at bat (single, double, strike out, ground out, and so on). They calculated the size of each wedge based on the baseball cards that Katzir had given them when they first drafted their teams. (In this system, for example, slugger Mark McGwire would have a bigger home-run wedge on his spinner than the other players.) Then the students played a season of simulated games against other teams.

Throughout the multiweek unit, these math students wrote, discussed, and, of course, played the game. During one class, we watched the students deeply engaged in a discussion of batting order; they shared sophisticated probabilistic and statistical explanations about why batting order was an important consideration in terms of run production and ultimate team success. They also discussed what type of out is best, settling on a ground out, since it can move a base runner along.

During the lesson, even the most disaffected students began thinking statistically—the students who, according to Katzir, "have been defeated for years, and years, and years." For example, he predicted the response of one student who had a long history of math failure: "Eventually he's going to say, 'Yeah, it's going to land on strike-out more often because that's a bigger section than the triple section.'" When that actually happened—and only then—Katzir seized the opportunity to teach, largely by asking questions.

> I could tell them, but somehow discovering it and owning it, they say, "Yeah, you know, I found that out on my own." So now it becomes theirs, and they'll hold on to [it]. The things that you tell them—they get told fifty-million times, they get told rules for everything, and definitions, and this, that, and the other—that stuff just becomes filed with all the other things they're supposed to know. But something about finding it out on your own makes it that much more meaningful, and so it's [what] I'm trying to get to. So I always try to bite my tongue when I want to say to a student, "Oh, you know, it's just a ratio, you just have to divide that ratio, you know." They don't care why A over B equals C; they don't care

about why two fractions added together equal something. You
have to spark that little thing that says, "I wonder why that works."

In Katzir's lessons, students constructed knowledge through
their interaction. Repeating the teacher's words was not an option
here; students had to base their answers on their experience and
use the language of the discipline to communicate what they knew.
In short, they had to become, and then act like, mathematicians.
Moreover, he made sure he checked in with his students about
their learning. For example, during the class period in which the
baseball lesson took place, he asked about half of his students to
explain the thinking that lay behind their contributions to the discussion.

Connecting New Content with Prior Knowledge

Nelson and Katzir's colleague at Carver, social studies teacher
Bethany Houston, also used a pedagogy that delicately balanced
teacher direction and student activity. Whether through call and
response, open-ended questioning, reciprocal teaching, or paired
or group seatwork, students in Houston's classroom seemed always
to be actively engaged in learning. Their knowledge of social studies was emerging from her artfully pushing them to connect new
content with what they already knew.

For example, to begin their discovery of Japanese geography,
she asked her students to tell her everything they knew about
Japan. After listing their contributions on the board, she asked students to quickly scan the chapter on Japan in their geography texts
and predict what new ideas they would learn. After they identified
their prior knowledge as relevant to the upcoming lesson, they saw
themselves as even more likely to be competent participants in the
lesson. Only then did she begin activities that would engage them
with new, important concepts. "That's how you motivate a class—
by drawing questions from them and getting them interested, so
that they know the lesson is for them," she told us.

Focusing their attention on the map of Japan in their atlas,
Houston organized the students into four groups, one for each
island. She asked them to study the maps and then configure

themselves into a human map of the island. They moved their desks to create an open space and began moving into place, all the while checking the map and talking over how to form themselves into shapes of islands and neighboring countries. Throughout, Houston provided continuity by eliciting facts and concepts from students by questioning their prior knowledge of Japan, asking them to recall what they'd learned in earlier units, and referring them to their recent survey of text. She provided guiding questions ("Tell me something about the land") to keep them engaged in the topic. She constantly pushed their reflections deeper ("How can you tell?" "What do you think?"), giving them lots of time and opportunity to figure things out either by themselves or in consultation with classmates.

Nelson's, Katzir's, and Houston's classrooms were not typical of instruction at Carver. Their teaching, unlike that of many of their colleagues, was consistent with the *Turning Points* recommendations for constructivist teaching. However, what we saw in these three classrooms actually had its beginnings years earlier, in a period of far more intensive reform. In 1981, the existing Carver school was disbanded and then reopened with a hand-picked faculty. It was one of four inner-city schools that decided to reconstitute themselves to ensure that their low-income students would learn a challenging academic curriculum. Carver sought and won waivers from state and district regulations and secured enough additional resources to reconfigure as "schools within a school," reduce all teacher class loads, and allow time for teachers to develop close working relationships. They spent long hours over a number of years deliberating and planning how the school could live up to the late researcher and activist Ron Edmonds's assertion that inner-city schools can teach poor black children well. Carver's work brought considerable visibility and opportunities for professional growth. Katzir, for example, became a regional leader for California's innovative mathematics curriculum project. Thus he was on a statewide working group that designed units like the fantasy baseball unit we observed. Teachers from the region would visit Katzir's classroom for demonstrations of these units, and the state gave him considerable release time to coach math teachers at other schools.

By the early 1990s, however, budget cuts, a teachers' strike, and changed district policies had eliminated most of these supports (including the reduced teaching load and the extra, shared, planning period). The school's formerly African American neighborhood was rapidly transforming into a Latino immigrant community, and a race-motivated uprising (what most outsiders called a "riot") had destroyed much of the area's vulnerable infrastructure. Many teachers departed, and few qualified applicants replaced them.[6] In the face of all these changes, Nelson, Houston, Katzir, and a few others struggled to preserve the educativity of those earlier days.

Educative Practice at Lucy Sprague Mitchell Middle School

Across the continent, at Lucy Sprague Mitchell Middle School in Massachusetts, teachers Doris Davis and Roberta Simms offered examples of how students can have an active and purposeful role in directing their learning. In what follows, we illustrate how one of Davis's lessons that we observed engaged self-directed students, organizing new knowledge around existing knowledge domains.

Mitchell Middle School sits in a clearing between wooded acres and a working-class neighborhood, two blocks from a state highway. The extension of commuter rail service to the nearby city has brought into town both middle-class families wanting to "get away from crime" and "needy" immigrant families seeking more stable jobs and cheaper housing than are available in the city. Though Mitchell's 650 fifth through eighth graders come from poor and working-class families, most consider Mitchell the district's "country club" school—largely because its percentage of minority students is far lower than at the other two middle schools. And indeed, the fall's red and gold foliage provides a picturesque backdrop for softball, football, and soccer games on large grassy fields next to the two-story, 1950s brick building.

Most Mitchell students belong to small, familylike teams headed by two teachers who stay with them for two years. Because teams are responsible for their own schedules, no bells signal the start or end of class. Mitchell teachers spend little time badgering students to walk in single-file lines, not run, not chew gum, not push and shove, and so on.

Action and Reflection Help Students
Take Charge of Purposeful Learning

When we observed Doris Davis's and Roberta Simms's class five weeks into the school year, the rambunctious fifth grade children—mostly ten-year-olds—gave little outward appearance that they were ready to be initiated into the world of sophisticated science concepts. We were wrong.

While Simms leads a geography lesson on one side of their shared classroom, Davis puts on her white lab coat and introduces an investigation of the scientific method with a lesson on the senses. Consistent with Dewey's view that students' knowledge of subject matter emerges from experiences requiring organization of new knowledge around existing subject matter domains, Davis consistently aims activity toward deeper understanding of established disciplinary content—in this case, a quite traditional rendering of experimental scientific methodology.

With her students gathered on the floor in front of the blackboard, she begins by having them describe their existing understanding of the senses. After just a moment or two, she shifts to what it means to observe: "*What* can people observe?" Students begin calling out sense-rich objects (pizza, chair, flower, house, duck). At this point, Davis defines an *object* as "something that can be described using your five senses." Testing the definition, the students revisit *pizza, chair,* and so on. They appear intrigued, and judging from their darting glances we suspect some are continuing a private cataloging and sensing of objects around the room. Now Davis springs a perplexing riddle: What is a thing, but not an object? More discussion. A "nonobject" turns out to be "something that cannot be described by using your five senses." More examples: time, winter, and idea.

Significantly, students lead much of the activity, and the remainder of the lesson is generated by a student question. One asks if air is an object. Davis suggests the students propose an experiment to determine whether or not air is an object. Air could be cold, one says, and that proves it's an object. Another student inquires aloud, "Does air have atoms?" Other students propose going outside to test if they can observe air with their senses.

As students write in their notebooks, Davis explains what the steps of the scientific method are. They essentially walk through it, first stating the problem: Is air an object or nonobject? She wants her students to understand that a hypothesis is more than a wild guess. Prior to going outside, she asks, "From what you know, is air an object or nonobject?" and gives them a prompt: "I think air is a(n) _____, because _____."

Once outside, the young scientists begin watching and listening. The fall leaves rustle in the trees; a teacher comes out and claps her chalkboard erasers; all the while, the students record data. After ten minutes, they gather below one of the trees bordering the school to share their individual observations and reach a conclusion as a class. Students assert that the tree limbs moving in the breeze prove that air is an object. One girl notes that her cold face demonstrates that air is an object, because she feels the air on her face. A boy exclaims that chalk dust moves sideways, so air must make it move. Davis asks many questions about each observation, and students elaborate further. In the end, everyone is convinced: air is an object.

After the experiment outside, rather than switching students as they are scheduled to do, Davis suggests to her teaching partner that she keep her science students for the rest of the day. She wants to continue discussing the experiment with them and demonstrate another. Davis explains to us that this is not "Let's do a hands-on activity for the sake of keeping kids active." Rather, she is using the students' suggestion that they go outside as a way to give them a common experience on which to reflect and construct new knowledge together. At the same time, she demonstrates what an experiment is and, by extension, how scientists construct their own knowledge. She will be teaching these students science for two years, and they will return again and again to the ideas they first explored that day.

Structural and Cultural Supports for Educativity

Because Davis and Simms schedule their own time, they can be flexible when extending or shortening lessons; Davis does the same activity with the other half of the student team the following day. These structural supports—teaming, block scheduling, and sharing a room—are central to the *Turning Points* reform agenda, and Mitchell Middle School's adoption of them makes Davis's educative lesson possible. However, the supports don't ensure educativity; teaching like Davis's and Simm's is not found in every Mitchell classroom.

The two cultivated a professional collaboration, unlike most of their colleagues, and that relationship shapes their teaching. Over time, they developed shared values and goals, flexibility, trust, support, and respect. Their daily conversations are peppered with theories of learning and teaching, teacher expectations, student motivation, classroom relationships, and talk of their joint teaching. Rather than adopting the reform strategies wholesale, they have built a pedagogy by blending practices that help them enact the activity-filled, student-regulated teaching and learning they value. As Davis told us, "We really didn't want to throw out the old things that kind of worked, for the sake of all the new trends and the new philosophies. They have value and merit, but some of the old ideas did too." Their relationship makes it safe for them to experiment. As Simms explained, "She's very supportive of anything I try, and vice versa. . . . It's easier to jump in with two sometimes. I just know she's not going to criticize. . . . If we didn't have that relationship, it could be difficult to try something new, feeling like you might fail."[7]

Components of Educative Practice

In the popular reform rhetoric, adopting constructivist teaching and active learning strategies leads teachers to emphasize curricular depth over broad and superficial coverage. Thematic, interdisciplinary curricula press students to think across the traditional content areas and look for connections that enable them to see the relevance, complexity, and interconnectedness of what they are learning.[8] *Heterogeneous grouping* in classrooms makes rich and diverse learning resources available to all students. *Cooperative learning* activities make learning a social and interactive process. These changes are just some of the items on a long menu of changes in structures and practice middle-grade teachers were expected to adopt.

Implementing these reforms sometimes led to these educative outcomes; more often it did not. We next describe some additional instances where adopting new practices did help foster educativity. Then we explore why these outcomes were so difficult to achieve.

Curriculum Reform: From Isolated Subjects to Interdisciplinary Themes

The restructuring reforms pressed schools to reorganize into smaller teams (or, in the language of the Coalition of Essential Schools, into "houses") of teachers and students. All sixteen of the schools we studied formed small, cross-disciplinary teams of teachers and students. Typically, this meant that two to five teachers shared a group of students to whom they taught all their academic classes. In nearly all of the schools, principals strongly encouraged these teams to work across their disciplines. In some schools, they required the teams to develop a specified number of interdisciplinary units each year. The reforms argued that thematic units of study would foster students' intellectual development more than would lessons in isolated subjects. For example, *Turning Points* asserted that engagement in interdisciplinary lessons allows students "to inquire, associate, and synthesize across subjects," "connect new and old ideas" and "construct their own meaning of information." In short, these reforms in structure and practice were expected to create more educative classrooms, permitting lessons to embody continuity, interaction, action, and reflection, and to promote emergence of subject matter.

Many teams of teachers found innovative and uncontrived ways to engage their students in activities that blurred the disciplines and fostered serious academic inquiry among students and teachers. The best interdisciplinary units, such as the environmental one we sketch in the next paragraph, focused students on a concept, idea, or problem across disciplines and were co-taught by teachers in a variety of content areas. It was apparent that the high level of teacher interactions and their own critical thinking and inquiry powerfully enriched the quality of the lessons they developed with the students.

Inner-city Washington Irving Middle School in Illinois pursued what faculty called "problem-based learning." In a unit about waste disposal, Irving students studied landfills, incineration, recycling, and the rain forest such that they integrated knowledge and skills across subjects. In one set of activities, students conducted science experiments at a local garbage dump. They surveyed other Irving students and faculty about their views on relevant environmental issues and analyzed their numerical data. They published a magazine addressing the waste disposal problem from environmental and economic perspectives, devised a recycling program for the community, and sent an editorial to the local paper advocating their solution. Small groups of students wrote proposals for a school recycling plan, including a detailed budget; the school adopted the winning plan. These activities forged strong links between academic concepts and skills and real-world problems.

Instructional Reform: Constructivist Teaching to Deepen Understanding

American schools tend to expose students to lots of content, but only superficially—especially in comparison to other high-achieving nations. To remedy this problem, most reforms call for "depth" as distinct from "coverage" of a large amount of material. Teaching for depth engages students in active problem solving, calls upon a broad range of thinking skills (rather than simply retaining facts), and allows them to experience many levels of knowledge. Learning in depth allows students to learn large concepts and broad summaries, backed up with the reasons, history, small details, and personal experiences that support their developing critical-thinking capacities.[9]

Although probing deeply into a topic can take many forms, some features are consistent in deep lessons. The lesson or project lasts a long time—a week, month, or semester—instead of a few class periods. The best of deep lessons begin or tap into students' lifelong, self-generating interests, which might include their love of reading, music, sports, artistic pursuits, computer technology, and so on. In a way, classrooms model these individual learning passions. The lesson does not just allow students to select among many learning activities, pick one, do it, and be done. The lesson requires each student to participate in many activities, which might be writing; making models, clothing, or artifacts; reading; interviewing; individual study and individual subprojects; group activities such as skits or videos; a study of history; designing and performing experiments; and more.

At Vermont's small-town Van Buren Middle School, a team of sixth grade teachers let students choose topics and questions for study during a unit on the medieval period of history. But the team balanced the student-centered approach with considerable teacher engagement, always pushing students deeper into what the teachers believed needed to be learned. So, as students built castles, they also investigated what architecture revealed about medieval social structure and science; for example, they studied flying buttresses to learn the physics of how these buildings were supported. Predictably, a group of boys were interested in armor and warfare, so they studied how medieval people forged steel; they also sought to figure out how catapults were built. Students and teachers prepared a medieval feast for two hundred guests, and they served the meal wearing medieval costumes that depicted various stations in the social hierarchy of the period. These examples provide just the briefest glance at a unit that had many elements and many layers.

Grouping Reform: From Homogeneous to Heterogeneous

Research demonstrates that the commonplace practice of tracking (separating students into classes by ability and prior achievement) nearly always disadvantages those students whom schools judge to be less able; sobered by this realization, most of the restructuring reforms argued for heterogeneous classrooms. *Turning Points* was unequivocal in asserting that "tracking has proven to be one of the most divisive and damaging school practices in existence"; the report recommended abandoning tracking. In its place, teachers must learn to "effectively teach students of diverse ability and different rates of learning."[10]

The shift to heterogeneous classrooms was pursued enthusiastically at Mitchell and at many other schools. As the composition of their classes changed and they responded to the diversity of backgrounds among their students, many teachers turned to student-centered assignments. In Doris Davis's constructivist science lesson ("Is air an object?"), participation and learning did not depend on any particular ability level; much worthwhile learning could be mastered with a minimum facility in English.

Many also modified their grading systems so they could reward students for learning, no matter what the ranking among their peers. As teachers modified practice to address their diverse groups, most were pleased by the results. One of Davis's colleagues told us that students continuously "excel far beyond [their own] expectations." "It was just unbelievable," another reported, "They were heterogeneously grouped, and the strides they all made were ten times what I would have gotten in a traditional set up. So I'm an advocate."

These recommendations pressed educators, students, and parents to view student diversity as a potential resource that supports learning instead of an instructional problem teachers must overcome. Indeed, Dewey's theory of educativity, supported by recent sociocultural perspectives of learning, suggest that diversity in student backgrounds and abilities is an asset when students explore new ideas and develop new skills with their peers.[11] So when teachers like Davis treated learning as an active and social construction, they came to see that trying to fit classroom activities to students' current levels of achievement—as is the case in tracked classrooms—actually lowers expectations. Instead of scaffolding students as they stretch beyond their current capabilities, teachers in tracked classes often focus on what students can already do without much trouble.

Grouping Reform: From Individual Classwork to Cooperative Groups

Social interactions characterized the educative power of many classrooms we observed. Nearly all of the lessons described in this chapter included small-group activities. In fact, cooperative small-group learning was one of the most widely implemented reforms. At many schools, lessons typically began with teacher-led whole-group instruction, followed by group work in which students either helped each other on individual assignments or corrected homework.

Many teachers responded immediately to *Turning Points'* pronouncement that "learning often takes place best when students have opportunities to discuss, analyze, express opinions, and receive feedback from peers."[12] Some, like Carver Middle School's Katzir, created truly educative learning communities when students worked in groups. Throughout the fantasy baseball unit, student learning was facilitated by keeping the games moving along, turning students' questions back to them for team and group consideration, or posing more pointed questions about the various elements of strategy and contingency inherent in the minigames. Significantly, whatever guiding and probing questions Katzir was able to pose, his students always asked more of each other. He reveled in his students' ability to communicate their new understandings, but no more than in their increasingly sophisticated abilities to identify worthwhile problems and ask questions about them. Katzir's classroom was not just fun and interactive; it exuded a mathematically meaningful sensibility, where conjecture, inquiry, and deliberation were commonplace.

Educative Practice Bypassed by Reform

At every school, we found teachers who worked diligently with the educative practices we have outlined, to bring intellectual work into their classrooms. But sadly, many teachers who embraced the new structures and practices missed the educative intent. These were instances where the educative goals of *Turning Points* were undone not by its enemies but by its friends.

Pouring Old Wine into New Bottles

Overall, we were impressed with how incredibly difficult it was for teachers to use these reforms in structures and practice to engender academic rigor. As Andy Hargreaves has noted insightfully, new practices allow for "safe simulations." That is, instead of probing deep within the culture of schools and classrooms to construct activities and relationships that are more educative, and dismantle norms and practices that are less educative—either of which might seriously disrupt the cultural norms—the school institutes a safe substitute that poses no such threat. Students are allowed to "practice" cooperative learning (or other new modes of learning) in carefully controlled, adult-designed classroom groups that bear little resemblance to the conditions required for educativity.[13]

Subverting the reform's educative purpose may not have been the teachers' intent, but they followed a practical balancing of two important motives: the desire to gain the heralded benefits of the new practice for their students, and the need to avoid the unpleasant consequences of challenging traditional school norms. Teachers often had reasons to adopt reforms other than to make their classrooms educative. Some thought the practices would promote students' social development. Sometimes, they used new practices to "keep kids busy with hands-on stuff," so they would behave better or "like school more." Most extreme, some teachers maintained that academics just aren't that important in the middle grades. Reforms were usually introduced as techniques rather than as fundamentally different ideas. As a result, they did not confront the traditional logic that drives middle-grade schools. In the sections that follow, we make clear how commonplace norms presented far greater obstacles than did the technical challenges of changing structure and practice.

Missing the Point

When creating interdisciplinary units, most teams of teachers simply agreed upon topics that they would use to coordinate the lessons in their separate content areas. Unlike the interdisciplinary environment unit at Irving Middle School mentioned earlier, the following examples approached the curriculum quite conventionally. The only innovation was that teachers had to fit their personal, isolated instruction into an agreed-upon "topic." It is true that some degree of collaboration often took place and that this required some rethinking. But these conversations tended to be about selecting the topic or negotiating schedules, not about the content knowledge or pedagogy or teaching for the kind of conceptual synergy that took place at Washington Irving. The following sketches of lessons could be mistaken for capturing the reform's educative intent. Yet beneath the thin layer of collaboration and coordination, teachers spent little time together to explore how the lessons could extend students' knowledge across the discipline, how to make sure that students could act upon their new interdisciplinary knowledge, or how they might guarantee that students reflected on their experiences instead of simply letting them pass by.

One team at Inland middle school in Illinois used Africa as a theme. The English teacher introduced African literature; the science teacher created lessons on Africa's biomes; the geography teacher focused on the physical and social features of the continent; and the math teacher had students chart data from various African countries on graphs.

At affluent, suburban Tanglewood Middle School in Texas, the traditional social studies topic of "countries of the world" became one team's theme. The language arts teacher taught a lesson on essay writing using an imagined balloon trip around the world as the topic. In math, they collected data and created a huge graph about the countries the balloon crossed over. The social studies teacher structured one lesson around a novel about traveling around the world, focusing on how facts could be incorporated into fiction. Together, the teachers planned an exciting culminating event: a hot-air balloon would actually come to the school.

A team at urban Townsend Middle School, also in Texas, created a unit around elections, a topic that the social studies teacher would have covered anyway. The science teacher asked students to discuss environmental issues and public opinion. The math teacher devised word problems about the electoral college to have students practice the math concepts they were studying, and so on.

At Irving, one science teacher confessed confidentially that, even though most of her colleagues would be "horrified" to hear her say it, she disapproved of what she considered the intellectual flabbiness of many of the school's interdisciplinary lessons. "Interdisciplinary," she told us, "has come to mean a lot of projects thrown together to look good and to be a lot of fun. . . . There is nothing wrong with once in a while having a little entertainment in the school—but [does it work] as a unit that you have devoted every subject to?"

Embracing Reform for Its Contribution to Social Development

Just downstairs from Nancy Nelson and Bethany Houston at Carver Middle School, we found Bob Henry, a sixth grade math-science teacher and twenty-year veteran at the school who shared his view about teaching and learning in the middle grades. They are, he said, a "down time for kids' brains." He went on to argue that it's not that students aren't capable, but rather that they're experiencing a developmental plateau in mental capacity. This means middle school teachers really need to focus on socialization. Henry felt there is no reason to browbeat kids into trying to learn because it isn't that important. What is more important is trying to get them to learn how to work cooperatively with each other.

There were teachers at all of the schools who, like Henry, believed that young adolescents' affective and social needs outweigh their academic needs. Some argued that the goal of middle school is to provide a nurturing environment. A teacher at Mountain View Middle School in rural Massachusetts, for example, offered this: "The way I look at it . . . this is where you are making a life choice as to what kind of person you are going to be. And to me that is the most important part of the middle schools. It's dealing with the social well-being of these kids and helping them make choices."

Emphasis on social development is not necessarily a tale of bad practice so much as one of missed opportunities. We saw many promising lessons that were ripe for rigorous content knowledge, only to have the teacher stop short of treating students like scholars. In her unit on Mayan culture, for example, Jackie Julian, a seventh grade social studies teacher at Carver, had students work in groups to decorate plates with Mayan designs. "I really stress group work heavily," she told us. "Life is a group. They have to learn how to get along." Julian went on to tell us that the students made their Mayan designs from beans, cotton, corn husks, several kinds of peppers, and seeds of different colors—foods that Mayans grew or ate. She took pride in the fact that many students told her that, even though working in a group was hard, they were proudest that they had "all come together to produce one beautiful thing." "If I can teach them that, and good work habits," Julian told us, "the rest will come later in life." Not only did Julian fail to explore the intellectual potential of Mayan culture but even the social benefits were sharply confined to the students' familiar interactions around cooperative craft projects.

By thinking about her lessons as having to make a trade-off between academic challenge and social development, Julian missed the educative target for both domains. Far too few teachers appreciated the inseparability of the social and the intellectual, and implementing new structures and practices did little to help them learn.

Trivializing Student-Centeredness to Make Lessons Engaging

The next example, from Irving, captures a phenomenon we saw far too often in many schools: engaging students in trivial, superficial activities in the name of student-centeredness and active learning. Irving's eighth grade reading teachers wanted to extend students' learning after they read *Night* by Elie Wiesel. Because the book had stirred student interest about the Holocaust, the teachers decided to have them "act out" part of the book to better understand what the Holocaust was like. In class, teachers told students to stuff all of their belongings and anything else they could into their backpacks, put them on their backs, and run through the hallways of the school as if they were fleeing a captor. Students in the other classes had permission to shout insults and threats to those carrying their packs as they ran past the doorways. Afterward, the students wrote journal entries describing, in the team leader's words, "what it felt like to take everything that you had—everything out of your desk, everything out of your locker—and carry it with you and run."

Certainly, students find activities such as this one involving, perhaps emotionally memorable, and possibly upsetting. But we doubt that they lead students to reflect more critically on important ideas. In this instance, without a focus on oppression, danger, or anti-Semitism, it is difficult to see how students leave the class with a better understanding of complex events like the Holocaust. The teachers may have thought their activity would help students "learn to think, learn to express themselves," as one teacher put it, but this lesson not only trivialized profoundly serious moral issues; it lacked the intellectual power that, for Dewey, made active learning educative.

All significant learning is in some ways social; but not all that is social is significant learning. Much research, theory, and lived experience supports this view that the social and intellectual are not separate, not cause or effect, but aspects of the same phenomenon of constructing knowledge. At many schools, we saw disturbingly anti-intellectual activities masquerading in the name of getting students involved and constructivism, wherein adults abdicated their curricular authority or failed to insist on challenging content.[14]

Outright Resistance

Traditional, teacher-directed instruction remained firmly in place in the vast majority of classes. It persisted partly because of a catch-22 associated with systemic reform: the very comprehensiveness of the reform meant that schools must apply attention and resources to areas that many assumed were unrelated to curriculum and teaching. Further, in typical school-reform fashion, reform had to happen in a hurry, with little time to examine and question the existing norms. Addressing young adolescents' special physical, social, and emotional needs; producing a schoolwide change process (for example, developing a vision, using consensus decision making); and making structural changes (teaming, block scheduling, setting up advisor-advisee and community service programs) were intended to support teaching and learning. However, because they were not seen as integral to student academic learning, they often became ends in themselves—separated from such learning. In the press to establish programs that would accomplish these goals separately, the reforms dissipated time, energy, and resources. Because they were linked in the reform rhetoric, these seemingly "nonacademic" pursuits of the school often tainted constructivist pedagogy, thematic curriculum, group work, and other conditions for educativity.

In every school, interdisciplinary curriculum, constructivist teaching, heterogeneous grouping, and cooperative learning met intense ideological opposition from teachers and parents. Deeply held, conflicting, preexisting norms about the purpose of schooling and the nature of students fostered the formation of pro- and antireform camps, even before teachers could begin to explore the substantial changes on the horizon. Some conflict revolved around rather pedestrian concerns of whether classroom activities that foster engagement conflicted with efforts to keep order. Other conflicts were professional disagreements about what students needed to prepare adequately for the next grade, for high school, or for adult lives. Still others reflected much deeper philosophical disputes about how schools should treat their highest-achieving students. Perhaps most challenging were deep cultural and political differences about how schools should respond to students in disadvantaged neighborhoods. In the face of this polarization, it's not surprising that many schools followed a rather schizophrenic, approach-avoidance path to reform.

Objections to Reform: Undermining Order and Control

Many teachers, administrators, and parents expect an educative classroom to be quiet and orderly, with children seated and not talking to each other. For them, engagement might mean students' being attentive, tuned in, or listening carefully, but it does not mean speaking, gesturing, building, moving from place to place, and so on. For these teachers and others, such activity and relationships are the scourge of learning as they understand it—which is learning by transmission, not by construction of knowledge. Since educative reforms called for just such activities and increased interactions, resistance was instant among some of this group. For example, one Irving teacher characterized the effect and intent of the reform as "letting them run with the whip. We have a lot of teachers here who believe child-centered is letting the child be the leader. No, no, no, no! You have to be the leader and allow them to come up to your level."

Another teacher complained: "Some people equate [the middle school philosophy] with the view that they're supposed to be so buddy-buddy and pally-pally with the kids, that the kids don't know who the authority is. That's when you lose them." Perhaps one of the greatest ironies of middle-grade reform is that many of those who had always complained the loudest about the universally poor behavior of young adolescents (going back, at least, to Charles Dickens's Uncle Pumblechook) emerged as the severest critics of the reforms—claiming that the reforms suddenly caused good student behavior to decline.

Rule-bound schools with complex systems of reward and punishment were less likely to provide the deep and complex educative environments called for in the reforms. However, many teachers who had some considerable enthusiasm for the reforms still found it sensible to emphasize order and control, so convinced were they that strict discipline is a prerequisite to learning. Thus, what might appear to be a faculty unified behind reform could have several teachers, or a majority, believing that order and control are prerequisites—or even the main goal of reform. For example, many

Madison teachers used the reforms to control student behavior. They instituted block scheduling to improve their ability to supervise students, and increased conferencing opportunities to report misbehavior to parents. Pleased with the results, a few teachers branched out, using the new scheduling structure for thematic units. It was inevitable, though, that the norms in controlling behavior would inevitably spill over and affect most educative efforts.

One sixth grade team at Harriet Tubman, in Texas, considered its time well spent if children's personal habits were better organized. The team spent considerable time teaching routines they thought were second nature to successful students: how to open lockers, organize binders, be prepared with materials (each child was required to always keep twenty sheets of clean paper on hand), and so on. The inordinate amount of time spent on behavior at Madison and the Tubman team's preoccupation with routines must be viewed in terms of what economists call "opportunity costs." Time spent on these matters was not spent on discussing and formulating complex and engaging lessons. In contrast, other teachers at these schools and elsewhere reported that powerful engaging lessons were themselves most effective in supporting a productive and educative environment because they provided fewer opportunities and incentives for disruptive behavior.

However, as we detail below, these patterns also speak to the way educative practice is viewed differently in different socioeconomic contexts. As scholar Jean Anyon noted in the early 1980s, many teachers at low-income schools such as Madison and Tubman consider that lessons that teach students to behave well and to perform routine tasks correctly may be the most appropriate form of practice, while teachers in upper-income communities favor complex and open-ended learning activities.[15] That *Turning Points* sought to push beyond these differences may have been an additional source of teacher resistance. Some of this resistance is just crude racism, but some represents more complex beliefs about what "our kids" need to survive "here."

Objections to Reform: Coddling, Not Preparing

Many educators and others worried that reform would compromise academic achievement and student preparation for high school. Often, they were right to worry, even if they mistook their own application of the reform for its intent. One district administrator at Van Buren, for example, confided that community members thought the "touchy-feely stuff had become the overwhelming thing." Teachers at rural Countryside Middle and at Madison told us that the school was "coddling the kids too much."

Others believed that the reform emphasized knowledge and skills that were inferior to traditional curriculum. Some saw interdisciplinary curriculum and active learning merely as helpful add-ons, rather than replacements for traditional teaching. Many fifth and sixth grade teachers explained that they stuck with traditional curriculum and pedagogy because their students needed to master basic skills. Their eighth grade counterparts more often invoked preparation for high school as the reason. At schools facing intense pressure to have students score well on standardized achievement tests, many faculty faulted the reforms for neglecting the basic skills that are tested. Many Verbena math teachers, for example, along with influential parents, were convinced that the process-oriented teaching and integrated curricula meant "that you are going to lose the 'good' math knowledge." A Van Buren teacher told us that "children do not get the same amount of knowledge in [interdisciplinary] units as they would . . . being departmentalized." Another complained that the middle school philosophy had "lost all focus on content." An eighth-grade teacher at Van Buren told us: "We have to consider the reality. There is a high school experience coming next year that is radically different, and the kids need to have some skills to cope with that."

Such teachers need a much deeper understanding of why hands-on learning activities are preferred from an educative standpoint. Rigorous academic work doesn't mean lecture and skill-oriented drills; rather, it means, as Fred Newmann and his University of Wisconsin research team have demonstrated in their work, the construction of knowledge, disciplined inquiry, substantive conversation, and connection to the real world of students.[16] Surely, the intellectually engaging lessons we observed in Nancy Nelson, Tom Katzir, and Doris Davis's classrooms show how constructivist lessons teach basic skills—writing, mathematical reasoning, scientific inquiry—at the same time they engage students in important critical, higher-order thinking skills. But few teachers experienced a reform context that deeply engaged the underlying ideas of constructivist pedagogy.

Objections to Reform: "The Top Kids Get Screwed"

Despite considerable agreement with heterogeneity in theory, and cooperative learning's widespread popularity, these practices also engendered enormous opposition. The call for heterogeneous classes struck a deep chord within many teachers. Abundant research evidence could not be denied because so many teachers had their own confirming experiences. Most knew that the students judged to be able were more likely to get teachers' best efforts. Many dreaded an assignment to teach a "low" class—at the same time that they recognized that the newest or least-qualified teachers would often be stuck with those assignments. Most had had some experience with students' exceeding expectations when more was expected of them. Nevertheless, a teacher at Lucy Sprague Mitchell, a school that was for the most part heterogeneously grouped, put the common argument against change very succinctly: "The top kids get screwed."

Heterogeneous classes were strongly resisted at most schools; as we describe in greater detail in Chapter Four, no school succeeded in eliminating the practice of tracking students into classes by ability. Heterogeneous grouping triggered discomfort, in part because it reflected a view of educativity that didn't match with middle-class aspirations. Teachers and parents who advocated retaining homogeneous grouping also argued that grouping by perceived ability served individual students' needs and therefore, collectively, served the common good. Teachers tended to believe that many of their students who had been or would be identified as less able could never be ready for the rigorous intellectual activity envisioned by the reforms. Teachers often based their low estimates of what students could accomplish on their previous academic performance, or even family background—and they often settled for uninspiring exercises aimed at "getting them ready" for more serious academics in high school. The lethargic responses that teachers receive from students only reinforced their beliefs that most students just can't do high-level academic work. These responses and expectations were not lost on parents of students judged to be capable; this reinforced their self-interested and often politically powerful efforts to keep their children in higher-level classes.

Cooperative learning met with similar, though less vitriolic, resistance. It is not surprising that teachers with a transmission perspective of learning would have trouble teaching diverse groups of children. Heterogeneous classes and cooperative learning would disrupt the predictable high rankings that high-status students experience. Some teachers worried about losing control if they turned over too much responsibility for lessons to student groups, confusing control over the lesson (which the teacher retains) with control over learning (which the teacher gives up). One teacher lamented that with cooperative learning it is difficult to know "who is in charge"—indicating that he was not in charge, and he didn't like that.

Social constructivists in the tradition of Dewey would argue that such interaction in groups not only helps less-capable students engage in higher-level curriculum but also assists high-status students in thinking deeply about important classroom ideas. Rather than slowing down high-status peers, the presence of students previously labeled less capable can stimulate everyone to question their own understanding and sometimes approach problems in novel ways. They may press high achievers to explore possibilities often forsaken in pursuit of finding the right answer or being the first one to finish the day's assignment. Under these conditions, heterogeneous classes could provide a context in which students and teachers pay explicit attention to the civic virtue of striving for the common good while they develop individual interests and skills. Seldom did we hear educators or parents deliberating about heterogeneous grouping and cooperative learning in light of such educative possibilities. We return to these issues in depth in Chapter Four.

Objections to Reform: Not at This School or with These Kids

In addition to norms about teaching and learning that either obstructed or distorted the reforms' educative impact, school faculties also responded differently to the reforms in light of what they thought their particular students needed.

At sites marked by student diversity, teachers were far more torn about changing curriculum and instruction than were the teachers at more homogeneous schools. We saw the most ambivalence at racially and socioeconomically mixed schools that included a sizable group of white, middle-class children. Educators at these schools saw reforms largely in terms of their likely impact on an already difficult environment. Some racially mixed schools were concerned about losing their strong academic reputations and high test scores—and with them their holding power with white, middle-class families—particularly since "some kids were doing just fine" with traditional practices. Townsend's African American principal, Harold Nance, described what he called a false everything-is-all-right attitude among his colleagues, stemming from the achievement of their more affluent students: "We have been resting on our laurels because we have all these good kids from . . . $200,000 homes in this school, who, in my opinion, no matter what we do with them, they pretty much come prepared for learning as it is. And you know, we can do more with them. . . . If we were so great, we certainly would have more than 54 percent of our population passing a minimum standard test."

Because Townsend's advantaged students seemed to be successful, teachers saw little need to question curriculum, pedagogy, or assessment as factors in the failure of minority and low-income students. Rather, many teachers blamed those students or their backgrounds for their academic difficulties, citing lack of individual effort or parent apathy.

For these reasons Townsend teachers weighed the benefits of reform strategies largely by their impact on students' behavior. As we described earlier at Madison, Townsend's proponents of block scheduling argued that it would improve discipline because students would be in the hallways less; detractors countered with claims that students would be unable to sit still for ninety minutes. Neither side argued that its view was more educative. Those who resisted learning new strategies developed for teaching gifted students argued that what they really needed was training in classroom management and discipline. Nance wanted all teachers to use gifted teaching methods, but many of Townsend's white teachers thought his goal of teaching everyone an honors curriculum was foolish because their students were black.

Townsend wasn't the only racially mixed school that felt compelled to keep a tight reign on unruly students (even if they were not threatening). At Inland, where race relations were strained from the time the white and black junior highs merged, concerns about discipline—often framed as "white student safety" or "black student aggression"—clouded reform. The district superintendent worried that moving toward constructivist and student-centered practices might raise school safety issues and heighten white parents' fears of black students at the middle school: "I'm concerned when I talk to parents [who've left the system] who say, 'My kid didn't get a good experience there . . . [because of] racial interaction,' [meaning] aggressive black students who they felt weren't being controlled."

Teachers at all-white, low-income Van Buren, like their counterparts at Madison and desegregated Horace Mann, were extraordinarily sensitive to their students' impoverished backgrounds. For some of them, too, the perception of students as disadvantaged deflected attention from academic engagement. One told us, "You have to heal the child before anything is going to be successful academically." Students' backgrounds provided a ready explanation for academic problems, and few if any teachers questioned how they, as educators, may have contributed inadvertently to this outcome. Of course, not all Van Buren teachers shared this view. One who didn't told us, "I feel that [support for students' emotional concerns] must be strongly linked with learning; [I'd like more push toward] excellence in learning." She elaborated: "I just want my kids to have the best possible preparation that they can. . . . I guess to work towards excellence, because I don't feel like we're pushed to do that. I feel like I could come up with almost anything as long as the kids were happy. To me, that doesn't really [satisfy] my goals for myself."

In contrast to these low-income schools with largely white staffs, the two all-minority, low-income schools led by teachers and administrators of color—Carver and Tubman—placed much more emphasis on their students' academic learning. Bethany Houston and teammate Hazel Smith at Carver, for example, treated their low-income African American and Latino students with respect for their intellectual development. They understood the daily difficulties many of their students faced, but they didn't write them off academically. They believed that accepting less than their students' academic best was an unacceptable compromise. Houston expressed their commitment clearly:

> When people ask where do you teach, and I say, "Carver," they ask, "Carver?" and say, "Oh the things I've heard," and "Oh, isn't that a high-crime and low-economic area?" I say, "Yes, but behind those big tall gates up here, a lot of learning takes place," and I just turn it around. . . . Of course, there are bad times; there are some things that we may not like; no situation's perfect—they were up all morning washing, or they had to watch the kids, or the parents didn't come home last night, but they got everybody ready and off to school. And these are some of the things that you find when you counsel these students, or in homeroom. You notice these things. You notice the looks in their eyes. But regardless of how many dope houses these children have to pass or what they have to do to get here, a lot of them really want to learn. And that's our job—to teach them.

Quite different from teachers at diverse and low-income Tubman and Carver, teachers at the two affluent white schools, Tanglewood and Verbena, were unabashedly motivated by professional pride in being on the cutting edge of reform. They were also under considerable parent pressure to bring their high-achieving students the best curriculum and teaching and to ensure students' academic competitiveness in high school and beyond.

Objections to Reform: This Community Demands . . .

When white and wealthy parents demanded rigorous traditional education, they, too, often blocked most reform practices. Their objections stemmed from a view of educativity quite different from that of the reform. These parents did not see how the alternative posed in *Turning Points* was "good" for individuals or the collective, and the normative case was never made. The case most often made was that the new strategies would result in comparably high test scores, and few parents found that argument compelling. At Verbena and well-funded, suburban Tanglewood, where 80 percent of the households include at least one college graduate, white parents were enormously skeptical about proposed changes in teaching, particularly in core subjects such as language arts and math. This community skepticism put Verbena and Tanglewood teachers in an odd position. Their own high levels of professionalism pushed them to stay at the cutting edge of middle school reform. But since their students already did well on traditional outcome measures, teachers had little chance of demonstrating dramatic gains from reform practices. At the same time, they were likely to trigger fears that they were compromising students' stellar records for the sake of innovation.

As we saw in Chapter One, Verbena struggled with its vocal parent constituency's opposition to the reform. Parents were largely unimpressed with the school's statewide reputation as a progressive school, and many said both privately and publicly that they were frustrated with what they saw as constant change. Claiming that traditional methods worked well in their affluent community, a substantial number of parents organized themselves into the "Group for Educational Accountability" and launched a back-to-basics movement. Most teachers saw these parents as being "out for blood," demanding that particular books be read and specific amounts of time be spent on particular lessons. The math faculty's interest in problem-based curriculum met with resistance from highly educated parents, particularly those with strong quantitative training, such as engineers. Some math teachers worried about losing their jobs amid the acrimony.

Like their counterparts at Verbena, many Tanglewood parents—accustomed to exerting a great deal of power in their everyday lives—kept a careful eye on whether the school seemed to give high priority to their own children's individual interests. One teacher told us, "Parents have a voice; they have a large voice." Another added, "Parents are listened to, and parents feel like they have a lot of power." Parents routinely negotiated such matters as their children's placements with particular teachers, the amount of homework assigned, and grades. Even highly academically oriented teachers weren't immune to criticism. Tanglewood teachers vividly recall that a handful of parents made a distinguished former colleague's life "a living hell" by pressuring the district to take action against her because she was "working their kids too hard." Because teachers had little deep knowledge of the reform's intellectual underpinnings—for example, about educativity or social and cognitive learning theory—they could not engage their well-educated parents in compelling discussions about the learning theories or research that gave rise to reform practices, although there is no guarantee it would matter if they could. It was at these schools where debates over best practice seemed, in part at least, to be a proxy for fights between individual interests and the common good. In white communities where parents were less pushy, schools more easily instituted various practices that were included on the reform menu but, as we noted earlier, often with little of the rigorous learning that educativity demands.

How Might Reformers Better Promote Educativity?

Typical of blue-ribbon education reform reports, *Turning Points* included a list of reform structures and practices. It emphasized the goodness of the practices themselves, rather than a well-grounded explication of why and how such practices, well employed, can enable deep and powerful student learning. Some branded such recommendations as a faddish, anti-intellectual education reform mantra and bristled at mention of cooperative learning, interdisciplinary curriculum, block scheduling, heterogeneous grouping, hands-on activity, constructivism, and authentic assessment. Indeed, this litany is often rattled off simply as the way to update or "improve" classrooms currently dominated by lectures, traditional texts, textbooks, fill-in-the-blank worksheets, and multiple-choice tests.

Beneath these surface recommendations, however, was a call for a profound shift in the conception, as well as the practice, of teaching and learning. Juxtaposing the notions of community and learners, *Turning Points* drew upon the work of cognitive psychologists as the foundation of their emphasis on integrating how and what children learn, to replace the norms of transmission, specialization, and separation that currently dominate. It asserted that academic learning for middle schoolers is social, and therefore best done in communities with people they know well instead of working alone or in haphazard groupings. Doing so, *Turning Points* also looked backward to Dewey's concept of educativity and anticipated sociocultural research that would further close the conceptual gap between learning and social interactions.

The reform rhetoric challenged schools to create conditions wherein students engage authentically in rigorous and meaningful academic work. Many educators embraced this agenda enthusiastically, working to embed these ideas in practice. But theirs was a struggle—to learn new teaching techniques, to grapple with firmly held beliefs about teaching and learning, and to battle community politics that worked against their educative goals. Unable to reconcile the competing demands of improved academic engagement with social demands for safe, orderly, and appropriate learning environments, few teachers succeeded in developing academically rigorous lessons with coherent objectives building on increasingly critical, independent, creative thought. In short, we found only sporadic indications that the middle school's traditional anti-intellectualism had been altered. Powerful normative and political forces worked to keep traditional transmission teaching and learning firmly in place in the great majority of classrooms. This disappointing outcome was not for lack of trying.

The tensions we saw between transmission teaching and educativity connect closely with Americans' efforts to juggle individual rights and freedoms with the common good. Transmission teaching in its crudest form sees in each individual learner (or, as in a lecture, multiple individuals) an empty vessel waiting to be filled with school knowledge. Transmission teaching begins with identifying individual students' current level of knowledge, so new lessons continue the filling-up process precisely where previous ones left off. That way, each individual can pursue his or her leaning, unconstrained by the differing needs of others. Constructivist teaching, on the other hand, emphasizes the social nature of learning—that is, knowledge is created in the context of interactions with diverse others. Here the emphasis is on creating learning opportunities that allow students to engage one another so as to bring new understandings. In this way, both educative schools and citizenship that is focused on the common good draw upon the skills, dispositions, and mastery of nuance that sustain social interactions and relationships. Thus, joint work (whether it is learning to multiply, building a bridge, or sitting on a committee) draws from the same mental and social processes. A wide range of opportunities allow students and members of a community to engage actively, socially, and flexibly; no one need get locked out or left behind in a setting in which they can reason, participate, adjust, find a different way, get help, and so on. Affording the widest range of opportunities for all to engage in such processes is at the collective heart of both social learning and citizenship.

Compounding the normative challenges about teaching and learning that cut across schools, reformers' insistence that this educative vision is appropriate for and needed by all children taps into deep cultural tensions about race, social class, and culture. Large-scale reform that asks schools to think differently about learning, child development, and the roles of schools and teachers remains situated within a fundamentally stratified society. Because new practices disrupt the conventional, uneven distribution of high-status knowledge and learning opportunities, they may threaten privileged students and their families, and these reforms thrust educators in racially mixed communities and schools into political uncertainty. On a daily basis, educators who want to reform the middle grades and become part of good American schools take a political stand through their actions and words, and they find that those stands often trigger vociferous political reactions.

Also clear from the schools' experience is that when educators attempt seemingly technical and neutral changes, they also challenge their own beliefs, including their taken-for-granted conceptions of teaching and learning. These changes touch upon deeply felt cultural norms and politics. The major challenge for school reform, then, is to provide a language that connects educators' daily work with its cultural and political implications and supports them as they confront these challenges.

Chapter Four

Becoming Socially Just

As schooling expanded at the end of the nineteenth century to include children of recently arrived southern and eastern European immigrants, reformers transformed the purpose, character, and organization of elementary and secondary schools. What was, in 1890, a haphazard assortment of mostly ungraded (separate classes and rooms for eight-year-olds, nine-year-olds, etc.) "common" primary schools and a handful of secondary schools serving a small and privileged segment of the nation's youth became, by the late 1920s, a bureaucratic mass institution, characterized by such organizational strategies as distinct school subjects, age grading, ability grouping, and curriculum differentiation and tracking. For the most part, secondary students from immigrant families took a vocational curriculum to prepare them for factory work, and students from advantaged families took a traditional academic curriculum.

These reformed turn-of-the-century elementary and secondary schools gave great significance to individual and group differences in intelligence. Schools were expected to serve democracy by providing lower-class, immigrant children, who were considered of lower intelligence and diminished moral capacity, with specific and direct training for responsible citizenship and work. Equity would be served by what one sociologist, in 1929, called "followership for the duller intellects."[1] Reforms that provided education advantages to everyone, even the dullards, would be an instrument of economic and social stability; and offering an academic education to the established middle class would preserve the traditions of the educated classes. In this way, separate education for different groups was seen as equal because each individual could receive and contribute the maximum usable benefits to himself or herself and to society. Of course, before *Brown* v. *Board of Education* in 1954, this separate-but-equal doctrine typically meant separate and unequally funded school buildings for black and white children, achieved by law and residential segregation.

Today's social and economic turmoil is disturbingly reminiscent of the conditions that shaped schooling nearly a century ago. Immigration brings fears about the demise of our national language and culture. Powerful stereotypes about the newcomers' abilities also stigmatize citizens of the same race or ethnicity whose families have been citizens for many generations. Economic insecurity and unsettling shifts in the nature and organization of work add urgency for schools to socialize and train newcomers, as well as other "underprepared" groups, to be efficient workers who will keep the economy going. Like a century ago, many doubt not only the possibility but even the desirability of a mainstream that includes both white children and children of color, both poor children and children from affluent families; these doubts still shape society and schools. More than four decades after *Brown*, school segregation remains, as do racially distinct, ability-grouped academic programs and extracurricular activities in racially mixed communities that can no longer legally segregate their schools.[2]

Within schools, these segregative arrangements continue to be bolstered by the argument that equal opportunity in a democracy requires schools to grant each student access to the kind of knowledge and skills that best suit his or her abilities and likely adult lives. To make the argument more palatable in a culture that, rhetorically at least, prefers to see itself as abiding by classless and color-blind policies, educators and policy makers have reified categorical differences among people. So, in contemporary schools we have gifted students, average students, "Title I" students, "learning disabled" students, and so on, in order to justify the different access and opportunities students receive. Assessment and evaluation technology permits schools to categorize, compare, rank, and assign value to students' abilities and achievements in relationship to one another (as well as to students in other schools, states, and countries—past and present). Schools then group students for instruction with others in the same category, and they tailor curriculum and teaching to what each group supposedly needs and what the culture expects. Lurking just beneath the surface of these highly rationalized practices, however, are the illusion of homogeneity, the social construction of classifications, the prevailing biases of race and social class, and self-fulfilling prophesies of opportunities and outcomes.

Today's Reform Mantra: "All Children Can Learn"

Many Americans, policy makers, and educators push relentlessly to move the country beyond this legacy of "including" all Americans—but within fixed categories where opportunities are allotted according to one's category or rank. Most of the restructuring reforms at the end of the 1980s argued that schools must not only educate all students but also do so in ways that would bring students who are members of marginalized groups into the educational and social mainstream. *Turning Points,* for example, posed problems of racial and social class exclusion in society and schools as one driving force behind school reform: "For many of these young people [poor children and children of color], the American dream ends with the recognition that they are not wanted and are of little value in this society. . . . What is left for these young men and women is a life on the edge of society."[3] Schooling bore at least part of the responsibility for these problems, and reform was expected to help ameliorate them.

Reformers and practitioners increasingly adopted an unabashedly optimistic view and conviction that schools can and must be places where *all* children, not just a few, can be "smart." Growing numbers of educators and researchers were subjecting to greater scrutiny beliefs and practices that had seemed rational and democratic for nearly a hundred years. Increasingly, for example, educational researchers were coming to understand intellectual capacity as developmental and multidimensional, and learning as an active process of constructing meaning, rather than a passive event of receiving information.[4] From a growing base of theory and empirical evidence, this new view argued that all children could be far smarter than conventional definitions and measures of intelligence seem to allow, regardless of gender, regardless of skin tone, and regardless of their scores on outmoded measures of intellectual ability.

This work pressed educators to shake the lingering suspicion that minority students aren't as intelligent as whites because they tend to score less well. It raised serious questions about how schools traditionally have responded to children who are judged, according to conventional criteria, to be bright, average, or dull. It also called attention to the racial and social class separations created by those categories. Increasingly, policy makers and educators could no longer find anything equal or fair about students' differential access to the curriculum content, learning experiences, and qualified teachers that accompany racial segregation between schools and ability segregation within them.

These evolving notions of equality (among some policy makers and educators), coupled with the belief that schools were not doing a good job, led them to investigate more than their school's curriculum or test scores. Reformers began to ask: Who receives what most would agree are the best educational opportunities? What is their color? What meaning do the answers have for membership in the American community? Encouraged, badgered, and inspired by the rhetoric and commitment of prominent reformers, many in schools and communities worked valiantly to make schools more equitable. Local educators sought to create socially just structures such as heterogeneous grouping, special education mainstreaming, and so on, and to adopt instructional practices that make learning accessible to diverse groups of students (for example, cooperative learning and multicultural curriculum).

Reformers confronted enormous obstacles; but many also achieved important gains in their schools' willingness and capacity to be socially just. As they did with their efforts to become educative, schools faced normative and political challenges that proved at least as difficult as the technical ones, and probably more so. Each of the schools in our study approached these reforms in its own way, accommodating them to a community that was always suspicious of greater social justice. None of our schools was in a community that demanded greater equity than the school was prepared to give. Nearly everywhere, local opposition was voiced in terms of the conviction that students had needs that should be addressed separately, and that socially just approaches would invariably water down the curriculum and disadvantage high-achieving students. As we noted in Chapter Three, heterogeneous grouping and cooperative learning were consistently criticized by opponents—both in and outside the schools—who were convinced that these reforms promoted social inclusion at the expense of academic rigor. The opposition was most virulent at racially mixed schools, where racial politics lurked just below the surface of arguments about ability and quality.

Diversity, Scarcity, and Equity Policies

By the early 1990s, the increasing diversity and poverty of young Americans, and the undeniable inadequacy of the schools they typically attended, had triggered considerable public concern and sent education policy making in two quite distinct directions. One was to turn away from so-called ordinary public schools. This turn took policy leaders to either special public schools (such as magnets, charters, and other "choice" schools) or to public funding for private schools (such as vouchers or direct public support) as the means to ensuring high-quality schooling. The other turn was to redirect state policy makers and education agency officials—often with pressure from the courts—toward equalizing resources among rich and poor public schools, and to eliminate school structures that obstruct access to knowledge (such as segregated gifted and special education programs, tracking, etc.).

In the early 1990s, many citizens of Texas, California, Illinois, and Massachusetts were making sense of their schools in terms of two phenomena: scarcity and diversity. Middle-class parents had strong images of what constituted high-quality school opportunities—images that typically included traditional teaching methods, school organizations, and classmates with ethnic and economic backgrounds similar to their own. All this, they believed, should constitute a fairly reliable pipeline to a better four-year university.[5] A majority of middle-class parents believe that high school graduation should lead to admission to one of their state's own top universities, or even one of the nation's highly regarded private universities. Countless reasons surfaced that escalated the public's (especially middle-class parents') fears that the best opportunities for a good education, a good college, and a good life were becoming ever scarcer—reasons as varied and complex as the political, economic, and social times themselves.[6]

Believing school quality to be a fundamental source of and solution to social concerns, state policy makers and local school officials made clear that the public wanted schools to "improve." Although people wanted schools to improve for all students, their first priority was for their own children to have good schools and good teachers. If necessary—and if they had the means—they might send their children to private schools, or they would move to new neighborhoods to find these schools; and if not one of these choices, they would do what they felt necessary to position their children to receive the best opportunities from their existing schools.

Given the structures, the norms, and the histories of typical schools in these states, it was perhaps inevitable that white middle-class parents would conflate their daughters' and sons' increasingly scarce opportunities with "problems" they associated with racial and language-minority students who were often poor. One of the most prized educational resources, in the minds of many influential white parents and school officials, was the large population of white middle-class students that seemed necessary to sustain their images of a good school. But, this was not to be—neither in the 1990s, nor in the new millennium.

About 12 percent of Texas students had first languages other than English, and about a fourth of that state's school-aged children lived below the poverty line. One of four California students had limited English, and only half of the state's students attended schools where one ethnic group was over 50 percent of the student population. Illinois students were about one-third nonwhite, and a third of the state's schools served at least some students with limited English. Nearly a fifth of school-aged children lived in poverty—from minorities in Chicago to low-income whites in rural areas. In Massachusetts, over half of the schools enrolled limited-English speakers. Between 11 and 15 percent of school-aged children were poor; many attended schools in industrial towns mired in economic recession since the early 1980s. In Vermont, where nearly all students are white, poverty among children hovered around 12 percent. Everywhere but in Vermont, urban centers had fought bitter battles over school desegregation, and most city schools had become mostly nonwhite. News photographs of adults shouting epithets at desegregating youngsters in Massachusetts still sear the memories of those who lived through the times—and of course, they affect the parents and children who still live in the communities. Texas and California suffer ongoing acrimony over immigration, affirmative action, and English-language policies. Increasingly, as these painful disputes played out in school, reformers found that they were not just struggling to change the status quo; they were frequently challenged to defend prior, supposedly secure reforms.

Equalization and the Competition for Social Justice

Although the federal government and many state governors in the 1980s and 1990s were nearly silent on issues of educational equity, this did not mean that all state and local equity advocates were ignored. At times supported by court decisions, their voices were heard in controversies over the equity of school funding. All five states we studied struggled to correct inequities in distributing school resources to children in high-wealth and low-wealth communities—a division that often paralleled white communities and communities of color. Battles over special education, tracking, bilingual instruction, and multicultural curriculum also appeared in some form in each of the state agencies and schools we studied.

Texas faced enormous pressure to equalize a funding system that supported disparities of as much as $10,000 per student in rich and poor school systems. The legislature tried repeatedly to frame a solution that would pass muster in court, but affluent communities were outraged by so-called Robin Hood proposals to redistribute the state's education dollars more equitably. As one highly placed official put it, "The pot is not expanding, and nobody wants to give up what they have."

California's battle for more equitable fiscal policies was fought during the 1970s. The equity "won" in California was followed by a dramatic drop in taxpayers' willingness to fund schools. In the decades before that, California's support for education had been at least as generous as that of most states, but by 1993–94 the state's average per-pupil spending of $4,921 was among the lowest in the nation and only slightly higher than that of Texas. Despite legislative remedies, not all California schools were equally impoverished.

In affluent communities, private community foundations raised significant sums to supplement meager public support.

In 1993, a Massachusetts education reform law called for increased state aid to guarantee all schools a basic level of support. However, the law did little to narrow huge disparities between high- and low-wealth local systems, and other measures have since restricted property taxes for schools severely.

Vermont's funding equity problems were linked to the relatively low level of education spending by the state compared to money from local property taxes and to large disparities in the local tax dollars raised by high-wealth and low-wealth communities. In 1993 Vermont was sued, and by 1998 the state was in the throes of acrimonious battles over revamping its school finance system.

By the mid-1990s, the state share of school funding in Illinois had shrunk to a third of what it had been. The highest-spending local system spent about six times the amount per student as the lowest-spending system. Only in 1998 did the state legislature pass measures guaranteeing a minimum per-pupil expenditure for every child in the state.

At the very least, this brief reference to fiscal equalization through the eighties and nineties reveals a legal or public-policy sense that such gross differences in school resources are wrong. However, they also reflect the limitations of legal and political pressures to affect the pursuit of the common, public good within schools, a pursuit that eludes both high-wealth and low-wealth schools. In response to pressure (keeping in mind that the biggest equalization moves were court-ordered, not initiated by legislatures and not embraced by the powerful locals), equalization was justified as a protection of individual rights of students rather than a moral or civic benefit to all those who lived in the state. Whatever public benefit would occur in the future was thought to result from the state's increased economic competitiveness in a global economy. The school reforms that began roughly in the same time frame as these funding adjustments were viewed with similar individualistic attention. Little policy concern was given to how communities might be better places for *all* to live in the present if the struggle for good and equitable school resources could slow or stop the continuing separation of racial and economic groups. In the absence of such discussions, attempts to equalize resources—although absolutely justified—brought inclusion in the best schooling opportunities under the umbrella of meritocratic arguments. After all, many argued, now that the playing field (funding) is level, and now that opportunities are "equal," *they* (racial and ethnic minorities and the poor) have nothing further to complain about. If they are not fully participating members of the community and if they do not measure up within competitive school environments, then *our* relative advantages are all the more justified. Clearly, funding equalization was and is a necessary condition for socially just schooling opportunities, but within the existing politics and values of schools, communities, and states, equalization is not a sufficient condition.

Detracking as Proxy for Social Justice

State education policy makers in the five states had also made efforts to press schools toward socially just student-assignment policies as they complied with the federal Individuals with Disabilities Education Act (IDEA), requiring increased mainstreaming of special education students. The states also tried to integrate programs for gifted, regular, and bilingual students. Texas passed legislation in the early 1990s eliminating remedial high school classes to ensure that all students participate in rigorous academic work. The Texas Education Agency adopted new guidelines that permitted compensatory education funds to be used to support such heterogeneity. These policies raised the ire of what Jane McIvoie, the state's middle-grade project director, called the "significant and politically potent force" of the state's association for gifted and talented students.

In the late 1980s, California's department of education issued statewide curriculum frameworks and reports on elementary, middle, and senior high school restructuring that prodded schools to move away from tracking and ability grouping. Between-class ability grouping (classes for students who are high ability, honors, regular, basic, etc.) and tracking didn't seem to be much of a problem to Californians because most schools in the state do not admit (or perhaps recognize) how extensive these practices are. The new California policies (such as the frameworks that recommended, among other curriculum reforms, much less tracking within schools) generated enormous opposition from the state's powerful lobby for gifted students—opposition specifically directed toward mixed-ability classrooms as well as the cooperative learning strategies that many teachers found helpful in heterogeneous classes.

Facing this political heat, California's superintendent of public instruction, Bill Honig, issued a letter "clarifying" that the state's recommendations for heterogeneous grouping never meant to imply that the department didn't support some types of ability grouping. Honig's letter forced state agency staff who were strong advocates for heterogeneity to adjust how they talked, so that "flexible grouping" was emphasized as well as heterogeneity. In California, as in other states, the beliefs and politics around heterogeneous grouping had strong racial overtones. One member of the state department of education staff, Curtis Jeffries, told us, "Parents [of high-achieving students] perceive that the educational program is being diluted to serve all of those 'other' students. . . . They don't really ever say 'ethnic minority students,' but that's the hidden charged issue. They don't bring it out unless I probe . . . but I hear that."

Massachusetts moved aggressively to mainstream special education students into regular classes. In 1990, the state board and the commissioner approved and distributed about fifteen thousand copies of a department report critical of ability grouping and advising all districts to move away from the practice. Subsequent department reports discouraged grade retention and many of the prevailing discipline schemes, and focused on concerns that ability grouping exacerbated attendance problems. The agency held statewide and regional conferences, sponsored visits to schools that used heterogeneous grouping, supported study groups for educators at individual schools, and matched schools just beginning the transition to heterogeneous grouping with those further along. State project director Foster Davies worked with staff in the office of categorical funding to bring greater consistency among the state's policies on special education mainstreaming, federal regulations governing compensatory and bilingual education programs (best known as "Chapter 1" programs, given their legislative authorization under Title I and Chapter 1 of the Elementary and

Secondary Education Act), and their reform stance on heterogeneous grouping. They emphasized the importance of mainstreaming Chapter 1 and special education students into heterogeneously grouped regular education classrooms, and they funded districts to pilot this strategy. The agency funded professional development for teachers on integration and heterogeneous grouping, and staff awarded an "exemplary" teacher a fellowship to work for one year with schools trying to do a better job of teaching mathematics in heterogeneous classrooms.

Some equity concerns (especially in mostly white Vermont) centered on the superior opportunities afforded to wealthier students compared to low-income students. Vermont also focused on integrating special education students into mainstream middle school classrooms. These two concerns drove major state policy initiatives that pressed for heterogeneous grouping practices. The state board of education adopted a common core curriculum to enact its vision of "high skills for every student—no exceptions, no excuses" and new legislation encouraging inclusion of special education students in regular classes. A second policy initiative was challenge grants for schools taking the "risk" to "reinvent" themselves as places where grouping structures and teaching strategies create a challenging curriculum for all students. Both these initiatives faced a community context similar to that in the other states: many powerful parents would defend homogeneous ability grouping in order to retain advantages for their children. Of course, resistance to these reforms was not just about equity and race.

Unlike these other states, Illinois encouraged heterogeneous grouping without having an official state policy or any official state monitoring of grouping practices. Instead, state education agency staff developed and supported networks of schools that consolidated its separate projects related to Accelerated Schools, Turning Points, and Coalition of Essential Schools. Borrowing the appealing slogan of Henry Levin's Accelerated Schools movement ("don't remediate, accelerate"), the staff made it clear that traditional tracking practices would not advance the state's goal to bring high levels of achievement to all students.

None of the five states, however, pressed beyond structural or procedural reforms to confront how the culture of middle-grade schools, including the curriculum and relationships among teachers and students, might also work toward a socially just American society. Still, as we see in the sections that follow, some individual schools did head off in that radical direction.

Local Struggles for Social Justice

Nearly all of the schools attempted to change how students were grouped for instruction, both between and within classrooms, in the explicit attempt to make their schools more socially just. Given their concerns about the uneven access to school success that grouping brought, even all-white schools tackled grouping as an equity issue. Several moved solidly away from ability grouping in academic subjects by eliminating or decreasing the number of tracks, although none grouped heterogeneously across all classes and subjects. Many focused on including special education students in regular classrooms. California's Cesar Chavez Middle School, where only 10 percent of the student body speak English as their primary language (with the majority representing eight other languages, predominantly Spanish), aggressively recruited language-qualified teachers. Fifty-two percent of teachers are bilingual in English and Spanish, and all faculty members either possess or are seeking bilingual certification. Chavez makes clear its values for diversity as an instructional asset by integrating students of various English-language proficiencies. Other schools adopted multicultural projects, hoping to battle norms of exclusivity as well as racial tensions in classrooms by making the course content inclusive of the full range of American cultures.

Heterogeneous grouping requires major shifts in teaching, new materials, and different forms of assessment. Using such techniques as Socratic seminars, experiential curriculum (including project-based science and interactive math), and cooperative small-group learning, teachers promoted educative instructional conversations and supported engagement with high-level content in their classes. They crafted multidimensional assignments to challenge students of varying abilities. Many teachers adopted approaches they thought were appropriate for gifted students in their heterogeneous classes to permit a wide range of students access to higher levels of achievement. Some developed new forms of assessment, such as portfolios, to provide useful information about all students in a diverse classroom and to give students responses to their work that would encourage them to work hard.

In nearly every school, however, the perception among teachers and parents that students have fundamentally different and fixed capacities to learn shaped their attitudes toward heterogeneous classrooms, making these reforms extraordinarily difficult. One Horace Mann Middle School teacher spoke for many when he told us that such slogans as "everyone can learn" are meaningless because "there are, of course, some kids who can learn, some won't learn, and some can't. . . . They've reached their capability; they've reached their potential. They just cannot go any further in terms of academics."

Grouping and its consequences have meaning and exchange value beyond school. After all, homogeneous grouping, accompanied by public labels and status differences, signals which students should gain access to the university and the status and life chances that higher education can bring. Thus, tracking became part and parcel of the struggle among individuals and groups for comparative advantage in distributing school resources, opportunities, and credentials that have exchange value in the larger society. Therefore, it is not surprising that there were those with a clear personal stake in maintaining homogeneous grouping.

In racially mixed schools, grouping reform was doubly difficult. Educators invariably ran headlong into community values and the politics of race and social class, which combined with beliefs and ideologies about intelligence. In all of the racially mixed schools with significant numbers of middle-class or more affluent white families, these parents battled heterogeneous grouping. For example, in Texas, Townsend's concerted effort to bring gifted-and-talented curriculum and instruction to all students was met with significant parent protest against heterogeneous grouping, as we noted in Chapter Three. The outcry from this group led the district to require that all schools maintain honors-level and regular-level courses, but it allowed parents to override school recommendations and place their child in an honors class. When Townsend implemented this option, a handful of parents of high-achieving students complained to a district administrator that the academic rigor of honors classes was compromised, and Townsend teachers were subjected to an embarrassing review of their teaching by district personnel.

Parents and teachers also contested the cooperative learning strategies, fearing that the curriculum would become less challenging and that the pace of study would be slowed. A Townsend teacher summed up this argument by stating that cooperative learning "hurts some of the smarter kids because they're always having to remediate someone else in the group."

The stories that follow of Mountain View Middle in Massachusetts, Tanglewood in Texas, Countryside in California, and Inland in Illinois are examples that both inspire and give pause. Mountain View's efforts to integrate special education into regular classes and make all classes heterogeneous proceeded as smoothly as any such effort we saw at the sixteen schools. Although Mountain View's faculty prided themselves on the inclusive community they created, their reform fell somewhat short of its goal of completely heterogeneous classes, and skeptics both in and outside the school continued to raise questions about the soundness of the reform. At Tanglewood, powerful parents made extensive changes in grouping practices impossible. The highly competitive climate—driven, we suspect, by deep concern that children would not reach the educational or economic heights their parents enjoyed—abruptly halted the school's detracking. Racially mixed Countryside and Inland faced intense resistance motivated by racial fears as well as by academic anxieties. Countryside's faculty altered their grouping practices in part because tracking made scheduling teams of teachers and students so difficult. They countered early resistance by arguing the educational benefits of the new structures. However, after great acrimony and frustration the faculty realized that it was community anxieties about race, far more than about educational improvement, that drove the reform debate. Inland, by contrast, took racial concerns into account from the beginning. At Inland, structural changes were augmented with a more socially just curriculum and by building respectful relationships across racial lines. Inland's faculty addressed their community's racial volatility as being inseparable from its educational concerns, and their efforts were more successful than Countryside's. Even so, Inland's hard-won changes remained quite vulnerable.

As educators in these four schools worked for socially just practices, they made worthwhile changes that left their students better off than before. However, the efforts were grossly overmatched.

These good people simply did not have the social supports, the technical knowledge, the intellectual rigor or tradition, or firm de jure mandates to act out their impulses for justice, or even to keep them consistently in front of their own countervailing impulses toward exclusiveness. Social justice did not seem natural to many who wanted, above all, to make their lives technically smoother, or to many who had power and privilege.

Mountain View Middle School: As Good as It May Get

Mountain View is the only middle school in its intensely proud Revolutionary War town. Nearly all of the six hundred sixth through eighth graders are white, but Mountain View's faculty sees the school as diverse, given the handful of African American and Native American students and the increasing number of (in the words of one teacher) "kids from no-money backgrounds." Like many schools in Massachusetts, Mountain View's reforms were buffeted by financial crises. Hit hard by a loss of manufacturing jobs in the 1980s, the rural town's blue-collar economy spiraled downward, even as statewide fiscal troubles brought less state support for schools. Mountain View's building, a 1920s, three-story, Federal-style brick structure, showed signs of neglect. Some windows did not open, and the roof leaked. Colorful banners and student-made impressionistic stained glass window art did little to mask the dilapidation. District downsizing threatened to close Mountain View altogether and redistribute its students to other schools. Cuts in teaching positions had sent the most recently hired teachers to other school systems, and many of the thirty-five remaining faculty members were just two or three years from retirement. One veteran of twenty years called himself "one of the young ones."

Mountain View's efforts to become socially just focused on breaking down ability-grouping patterns in academic subjects and making regular, heterogeneous classes appropriate both for the eighty-five students identified as needing compensatory or special education and for so-called regular students. In addition, enough of the school's students qualified for federal, compensatory, Chapter 1 monies that two faculty members were designated "chapter teachers." Although race wasn't a factor in student designation, income certainly was. Several teachers told us that the students with the lowest incomes were also those that had learning difficulties. This mostly white school had its own version of "those kids."

Mountain View's efforts to become socially just, though not perfect, proceeded more smoothly than those at any of the other schools we studied. We came to believe that the process was certainly eased by the student body's relative homogeneity. But there were other significant differences between Mountain View and most other reforming schools. Principal Paul Jennings set up voluntary "inquiry teams" in which teachers could study reform alternatives, pilot new practices, and make recommendations to the rest of the faculty. We return to Mountain View's reform process in more detail in Chapter Eight. Here, we describe the significant changes the school made, under the guidance of what it called the heterogeneous-grouping and integration inquiry teams, in light of the school's response to students judged as either "slow" or "special."

Heterogeneous Grouping in All Courses—Almost

Mountain View's academic teachers and students were organized into two teams at each of the three grade levels; students rotated through four academic classes, an elective class, a study hall, and a skills class that offered extra academic help. Jennings violated his promise to have his faculty make all reform decisions when he announced at the end of the first *Turning Points* project year that, in the fall, all Mountain View classes would be heterogeneously grouped. He explained that grouping at the school was an "odd phenomenon where most people were practicing one way, but knew better." Some teachers were furious, but most were not. According to Jennings, "At least the majority of the staff were feeling like, 'Just tell us you want us to do it. Just tell us, will you please? There's going to be divisiveness. There's going to be arguments. There's going to be reluctance. Just tell us, will you? And we'll adjust.'"

The school's inquiry approach to reform, however, survived this autocratic move. The heterogeneous-grouping inquiry team read research, visited other schools, and piloted new strategies so the faculty could make informed decisions about how to make this reform fit the Mountain View context.

Math was the holdout. Like their colleagues at many schools, many Mountain View math teachers argued for homogeneous math classes, arguing that math was so sequential and students came with such uneven skills. Some felt that the school's inadequate math materials (too few calculators, inadequate manipulatives) prevented their teaching math in mixed-ability classrooms. Still others said that offering algebra to the most advanced eighth graders made math tracking necessary. Algebra, they argued, was the only way that Mountain View addressed the needs of its most capable students. Eliminating the school's most salient merit-based program would be pushing equity too far.

But the department's maverick, sixth grade teacher Tamela Carter, countered that mathematics, like other academic subjects, could be heterogeneously grouped. As a former teacher of remedial "chapter math" (the school's federally funded compensatory program), Carter attributed "low" students' misbehavior to the shame and defeat they felt when they were assigned to low-ability math classes. "They could not get it into their heads," she told us, "that this didn't mean they were inferior. So, in class they did absolutely nothing; they were behavior problems; or they were passive-aggressive in the sense they sat quietly but somehow never had pencil, paper, or a book." Carter also worried that "when you have a room of children who hate school and hate math altogether, there are no models for them. Even though you try to convince them, 'Hey you can do this,' they don't have any evidence of it."

As a result of her dogged effort, she and her colleagues detracked sixth grade math and adopted an "in-class" model, wherein the chapter teacher co-teaches and provides her charges with additional help: "If they don't take their assignment notebook out to write the assignment down, she'll remind them, 'Take your assignment notebook out now.' If we're on page 160, she'll check it. She is not identified [as being assigned] to them. She looks like she's helping everybody. I mean, they may personally know because their parent chose to tell them—she's contacted every parent—but no one really knows that she's theirs. Technically she is, but I answer their questions also. She keeps them in focus."

Carter argued in meetings, brought in a teacher from a nearby school that had detracked its entire math program, and tried to convince her colleagues that heterogeneous grouping would be the crowning glory of their already fine math program. She suggested that they organize extra study periods for students who needed additional math help and offer special after-school math clubs to challenge the most able math students. Even though her pushing brought what she called a "strong, strong conflict," her colleagues became less resistant as they incorporated new curriculum and methods, including using hands-on instruction. When our study ended, only two sections of seventh grade pre-algebra and eighth grade algebra pulled kids away from Mountain View's otherwise heterogeneously grouped academic classes.

Integrating Special Education Students into the Mainstream

In addition to mixing their regular students in academic classes, Mountain View's faculty integrated a sizable portion of their identified special education students into these classes as well, assigning a specialist to co-teach. Within three years, the academic integration program was expanded to all three grade levels and involved approximately half of the school's special education students. All special education students were integrated into homerooms, physical education, and exploratory classes. A few students with troubling behavior problems entered mainstream classes one class at a time; when these students were successful, the school added more students to the regular classes.

Most teachers seemed happy with the arrangement. Science teacher Gerald Darwin told us: "We have four, five, six special-needs kids in my first class, and I think three in my second-period class . . . all real nice kids, all willing to learn, and hopefully doing a good job. They seem to be a little confused from time to time, but look for help, and we try to give it to them. I think our special-needs kids are being served very well." Thomas Albans had eight or nine special education students integrated into the eighth grade English class he co-taught with special educator Mary Andrews. "They are in a group," Albans said, "in a heterogeneous group. I'm not sure the kids in the room could tell you who is special education. We have never divided them."

Andrews told us that, as a result of all this, teachers have become more open to special education students as regular kids. "Maybe I'm looking at things through rose-colored glasses," she told us; "most of our kids are really quite normal, anyway. And I think [teachers] are seeing that more and more." Interestingly, the inclusion also altered students' views of teachers. Albans made clear that his students don't necessarily look to him as the *real* teacher: "Frequently, it's more a combination. All the regular education kids are quite comfortable asking either one of us for help. So that's kind of nice. They rely on Mary just as much, which is neat."

Integrating these students into regular homerooms also brought unexpected bonuses. Students who'd previously been excluded from field trips, for example, were now considered a regular part of homeroom groups that planned and participated in outings. Special educator Shannon Levering told us, "We've taken kids with Down's syndrome, and we've taken our autistic boy. Some of the kids with a learning disability should have been included anyway, there's no reason for them not to be. But some of the lower kids have gone, like on a whale watch and mountain climbing. If they hadn't had a homeroom connection, that would not have happened. That was an important little first step."

But, Levering continued, field trips were not all the students gained:

> And then other little things . . . report cards. Kids, often, in these
> kinds of programs, would just get written comments but didn't
> get a regular report card. So, we decided that they should. . . .
> That doesn't sound like a big deal, but one mother came to me
> at open house the first year and said, "My son was so happy because
> he got a report card. He had never gotten one before in his life.
> Everybody else in his homeroom got one, and he got one, too,
> and he came home really, really excited by this." It was like,
> "Yeah, I'm part of this. They're including me in the school."

Heterogeneity and More

Mountain View's detracking seemed to invite new teaching practices. Co-teaching began to provide flexibility and additional support for heterogeneous classes. Teachers used cooperative learning strategies and student-centered curriculum to accommodate their classroom diversity. Science teacher Gerald Darwin told us: "One of the things that I see that works really well for me is the heterogeneous groupings. . . . The curriculum is designed to really take advantage of students who have high abilities and students who struggle a little bit more. There's a lot of room for abstraction.

There's also enough concrete activities, hands-on activities, so that students, no matter which level they're on, they can get a lot out of the curriculum."

Teachers also experimented with forms of assessment better suited to heterogeneous classrooms. Beverly Joyce, Mountain View's *Turning Points* coordinator, described their long-term goal as "getting teachers so that they take every kid in that classroom from where they are, and grade them on progress. That's revolutionary; and that's going to take a long time; and that cannot be done by commanding it to be done. It has to be done very slowly, but it has to be done."

Reflecting on grouping changes at Mountain View, Paul Jennings was enormously pleased with his teachers' response to heterogeneity, even though he'd initiated it with a directive, rather than through deliberation as he would have preferred: "That was one of the few times that I broke from my typical style and didn't regret it. At the end of the year, I had these old coots, these old language arts teachers marching up to me saying, 'I love it. I love it. I'm so glad we're doing it. I didn't think I'd ever say this, but boy I love it.'"

His assistant principal, Sam Lewis, shared his optimism: "Most [teachers] were glad that they did it. Now I think that people wouldn't want to go back to tracking." For the most part, our experience at the school confirmed this happy outcome.

Nevertheless, we also saw warning signs that made us wonder if the school's grouping reform was vulnerable. Many teachers retained serious misgivings, particularly in light of the community's demographic shifts. As the enrollment becomes increasingly poorer and from immigrant families, we predict there will be pressures to reestablish honors programs in order to mollify and keep affluent families. If Mountain View follows the pattern of other schools, they may increasingly see affluent families as bringing the school badly needed status and resources, especially if economic decline and changing demography continue.

Many teachers who went along with the changes clearly had only a marginal commitment to the academic or social justice foundations of the new structures or practices. One language arts teacher told us, "When I had a high group, I was able to do some things that I can't do now . . . that I feel I can't do. I can't teach introduction to Shakespeare and *Romeo and Juliet.* . . . What I would like is to have one high group." A second language arts teacher reported: "I really feel as if the kids who really are very bright are not quite getting a fair deal. Socially, this is a much better way of doing things. You don't have all of your problems in one class. It is like a see-saw. There are things that I like, and things that I don't."

Other teachers worried that cooperative learning strategies in heterogeneous groups had capable students helping their less successful classmates and not engaging in any additional learning on their own. Math teacher Ernest Rawlings told us, "What I am knocking is, if you're a capable student, you're spending some of that time teaching other kids, you're not getting the most out of your education while you're here in our school, in my particular class. There are more challenging things that I feel I should be exposing you to, furthering your education as opposed to asking you to become a teaching assistant, shall we say, in math. That's a drawback." In reality, teachers in some classes did have students "share the burden of teaching," as a result of the teachers' having little experience with or enthusiasm for learning how to set up cooperative groups in ways that avoid this problem.

At the same time, many affluent parents were turning to private schooling—most often when their children reached senior high school, but increasingly at the middle level as well. One parent of a Mountain View middle schooler as well as an older child in a private high school explained that a combination of heterogeneity and changing demographics may be driving families out of the public schools—in other words, inclusion of students of color, or who speak different languages, or who are poor:

> In many cases . . . it's the brighter students [who are going to private school]. The parents would like to see them more challenged. And I think there's a perception that maybe we're teaching a little more to the middle range and not offering quite as much for brighter students. I think that's something that people are starting to sense more. The population changed so that we have a lot more subsidized housing in town in recent years and so forth. We're having to deal an awful lot with things that have just been unknown in Mountain View, with students who don't speak English and so forth. That's all of a sudden becoming a reality for us. Elementary

school classes all have one or two kids who are Russian or Spanish
or whatever, so English as a second language is becoming something to deal with. There are just a lot of kids who are coming
not as ably prepared as kids in Mountain View always were.

In part, we worried about the Mountain View reform's vulnerability because of what we observed at Tanglewood. In contrast to
the Mountain View community, all-white and upper-middle-class
Tanglewood monitored the schools' grouping practices closely.
Parents were extraordinarily invested in having students identified
as gifted or honors, and giving them separate classes. Efforts to
move away from these practices brought enormous resistance.

Tanglewood Middle School: Fear of Falling

In 1990, sociologist Barbara Ehrenreich wrote a compelling analysis of social and economic anxieties plaguing the current generation of upper-middle-class Americans, anxieties she called *Fear of
Falling*.[7] Doctors, lawyers, college professors, business executives,
and other privileged Americans, Ehrenreich argues, have become
politically conservative because they fear that their own children
may not, as adults, attain their parents' affluence. They see education as the only hope for not sliding down economically, but they
worry, too, about spiraling college costs. They also fear that their
children might not have all that it takes to succeed in the years of
education that lucrative professional careers require. If Ehrenreich's analysis is correct, then the community of Tanglewood,
Texas, surely is a model case.

In the affluent Tanglewood community, being exceptional is
the norm: for students, their families, teachers, the school, and even
the school district. Indeed, the statistics are impressive: 99 percent
of Tanglewood's students pass all of their classes; average standardized test scores are consistently in the top 10 percent nationwide;
teachers average more than twelve years of experience; and nearly
all of the district's schools, including Tanglewood Middle, have
earned state and national recognition as exemplary schools. Most
in the community believe that even the district's average and below-
average students are exceptional. As Tanglewood teacher Natalie
Parker put it, "I think if you took our school population into, say,

the New York City schools, our entire school population would be at the very top."

A Culture of Competition

Not surprisingly, Tanglewood parents and teachers express considerable pride, but they also worry about accelerating competitiveness. Parents, thinking ahead to university admissions requirements, feel intense pressure around grades. As one teacher said, it is "not success but A's that are important." Since the state calculates grade point averages in terms of percentages, some press for as high an A as possible. Teachers said some parents complain about a grade of 95, and students told us they were yelled at and "got grounded" for getting B's. For years, the Tanglewood honor roll only included students with straight A's. It was a big, if symbolic, step when a second honor roll was added—the AB honor roll—for students who had earned nothing less than a B. At a school like Tanglewood, where so many students are successful, one might not think tracking would be an issue. Indeed, 92 percent of Tanglewood's eighth graders scored above the 90 percent cutoff on the reading test for honors classes. But in fact, tracking was a huge issue in Tanglewood, and it began in the elementary grades. A Tanglewood counselor told us that parents pushed hard for advanced class placements: "Even when some advanced students need to be in the regular track, the parents get them [advanced] because they want that as a badge; [for] some who are in honors [it's] the same way. And [the parents] just want that to say, 'Well my child's in advanced. . . .' And you can tell the parent that, but usually, . . . out here the parents usually get what they want. And so, we do that on a trial basis, but usually they stay."

The Struggle Around Tracking

When Tanglewood was chosen to be one of the first "mentor" middle schools in the Texas *Turning Points* project, Principal Brad Jelton began planning how the school would convert from its traditional tracked structure to heterogeneous, interdisciplinary teams. Social studies classes were already heterogeneously grouped, and science levels were being phased out, but language arts and math classes had several levels. In language arts, the problem of placing so many high-scoring students was solved by adding another, more difficult test. Top-track students had to score 90 on both to qualify.

Jelton began his "detracking" effort with mathematics. With classes organized into twenty-one levels, from low-level sixth grade math through advanced high school algebra 2, students were assigned by their scores on an end-of-fifth-grade placement test. The highest-scoring students (or those whose parents lobbied for a high-track placement) went right into algebra 1, bypassing middle school math altogether. Jelton and the math faculty used the occasion of adopting new, problem-based math textbooks to reduce their series of twenty-one math levels to two tracks in math in grades six and seven, and three in grade eight. The faculty's rationale was not aimed exclusively at social justice; many teachers simply believed that the previous tracking system was a poor way for students to learn math. One teacher said, "With so many tracks, kids would get to the high school and either stop math at their sophomore year, or have tremendous gaps in what they were doing. They missed the basic skills, and that prevented them from being successful in the upper-level math classes."

Jelton's plan for reform, generally, was to have "lots of parent involvement" to win support. "We'll start at the grassroots," he told us, "getting the parents talking. We can make it more or less their recommendation." That's what happened in math. Evening meetings on campus had allowed parents to listen and ask questions. Jelton told us that he and some teachers showed the parents evidence that because students accelerated their math classes, many of them had too many credits and left campus at noon. Also, because they finished high school math so long before graduating, they had trouble in their college mathematics courses. Presentations at the evening meetings included testimony from students who had experienced those problems. Convinced by the arguments, parents approved Jelton's reduction of math levels and tracks. A waiver process allowed parents to override the 90th percentile cutoff on the test score so students with lower scores could get into the top track on a trial basis. Students scoring in the 80th–90th percentile could waive into the class and remain as long as they kept up a grade average of 80 for each six-week grading period.

Jelton envisioned a similar scheme for language arts. If that didn't work, he had a plan for using test score data to persuade parents that heterogeneous language arts classes would be better. Jelton's vision for language arts was harder to implement. A year later, that department still had three levels at each grade. Jelton was hoping to reduce that to two, but, in his words, language arts was "a horse of a different color." Unlike their math colleagues, the language arts teachers weren't convinced about heterogeneous grouping. "The jury's still out," Jelton told us; "it's kind of the old school versus the new school. My gut feeling is we will not do anything this year. It's too late to really start talking about it for next year, but it will be coming down the following year. I would imagine in the language arts, if we did anything, we'd probably start at sixth grade level and then phase it in. There is quite a bit of support on the faculty here to do that. Let's try this [at] sixth grade and see."

In fact, there was little support among the language arts faculty. The department took pride in its highly differentiated curriculum, reflecting their very individualized view of learning. The honors, advanced, and regular levels read different literature, completed different projects, and set different expectations. One of the language arts teachers told us that with "a child that is so many grade levels ahead, as most honor students are . . . they don't need to be sitting in basal readers, and they don't need to be sitting in heterogeneous groups." Language arts teacher Natalie Parker told us that the idea of heterogeneous classes "scared" her, because "label-conscious middle school students could not be expected to sit in the same class and read different books than their classmates." Nevertheless, with heterogeneity strongly supported by the school board, district, and site administration, the language arts teachers were resigned to learning how to do a good job in a system they disapproved of.

"The Parents Had a Fit"

In the end, however, the plan for graduated grouping in language arts was stopped short by fierce parental opposition. One parent told us: "A lot of people pride themselves on 'my child is in honors. My child is in this.' I would think that [heterogeneous grouping] would not be well received." She was right. One board member reported that he'd received four hundred phone calls. Teacher Bob Mandrake reported: "The parents heard that heterogeneous grouping was happening, and they had a fit. It's all parental pressure. Last night [at the board meeting], the superintendent asked the crowd, 'You wanted three groups. And that's what you have, right?' So I think that they listened to the parents, they kept three groups."

The district and Principal Jelton pulled back. The following year, the tracking system remained as it was. Jelton, who later left Tanglewood, told us, "I'm not sure that this school will ever do that. I'm not sure that's what's best for this school, because of the population that we serve here." Four years after his initial optimism, nothing had changed. Teacher Hilary Richards put it bluntly:

> We have a lot of kids in the honors, and a lot of the kids in advanced. Are you going to go tell those parents? Are those parents going to buy into the idea that we're going to get out of tracking? I mean, they like going to the local grocery store and saying that their kids are in honors, and that their kids are gifted, and that their kids are . . . you know. I mean, that's what they talk about at Little League. To come and say, "Well, we're going to go strictly heterogeneous now . . ."—that's not going to wash in this district. It's just not, and it hasn't. And I haven't heard anybody talk about it.

In a community so gripped by the competition for individual status and privilege, a reform aimed at making schools socially just went too far against the cultural grain.

As difficult as the Tanglewood experience was, it did not approach the cultural complexity of those at the racially mixed schools. At those schools, reformers grappled with the added layer of racial prejudice and fear. Tracking cuts to the heart of our culture's ambivalence about social justice. African American, Latino, immigrant, and low-income students remain overrepresented in low-ability, remedial, and special education classes and programs; they are less likely to participate in college-preparatory and gifted programs. The belief in whites' genetic superiority has largely fallen from favor, and grouping explicitly by race and social class has become a schooling taboo. However, the persistent stratifying effects of schools' grouping practices continue to make deep, unquestioned sense to many in schools and society. The burden of defending such practices has shifted from racial superiority to competitively based notions of merit.[8] As we see in the next story, that of Countryside Middle School, treating the reform as color-blind may obscure these issues, but it does not make them go away.

Countryside: Color-Blind Reform

Once a small, nearly all-white farming community, by the early 1990s the city of Countryside was a rapidly growing bedroom community to two West Coast metropolitan areas. Population growth also diversified Countryside Middle School's traditionally white and middle-class student body; as Mavis Pearson, the school's longtime nurse and social services coordinator, explained: "We're becoming more and more a two-tiered type of school." In addition to serving some of the wealthiest families in town, "there's a group of very poor people. . . . [The] housing authority is packing them into three square blocks four blocks down [from the school]." Countryside's 880 sixth through eighth graders had also become one-quarter Latino and African American.

Wanda Simpson, Countryside's sole African American staff member, was also the only person in the main office who spoke Spanish: "[Latino] parents get me on the first ring," she told us. A former police officer with a strong yet gentle demeanor, Simpson has won state-level accolades as Countryside's principal. However, she replaced a popular "good old boy" principal, which polarized the gender-conscious school faculty. In the staff lunchroom a group of nurturing women, many of whom teach humanities, sit on one side of the room across from the "loyal opposition," mainly veteran males involved in the school's sports program.

The community's changing demographics were reflected in divisions among the students. As teacher Helen Lindquist explained, the school developed distinct student subcultures, often around race: "The blacks, the Hispanics, the whites, and then, even in those groups, you see the kids we call stoners—the ones with the baggy pants and the skaters and all of that. You see the real preppy kids, the kids in band and orchestra, together. There is prejudice against other groups. . . . It's still coming from home. I don't know where it's going to stop. These kids are learning it at home, so when they have their own kids, they are going to have it too. I don't think the cycle is ever going to break."

Lindquist believed that the school's tracking structure exacerbated the school's racial problems; "I think [prejudice] is actually going to get worse because we are getting so much separation between classes." In addition to the concentration of the school's Latino and black students in the lower-level classes, the growing group of Spanish-speaking students were increasingly separated from classes with their English-speaking peers.

Reform for a "Warm, Nurturing Environment"

Seeking connections with other middle schools, and intent on being a reforming principal, Simpson signed Countryside on to a California middle-grades reform network. She then brought together sixteen somewhat reluctant faculty members to be the "school reform committee" to lead the conversion from a traditional junior high arrangement to interdisciplinary teams. Teaming, they reasoned, would allow faculty to realize its fundamental reform goals. Those goals, in the words of one committee member, were to "base course content and instructional methods on students' developmental needs" and to "provide a warm, nurturing environment where every student feels connected to the school and can grow academically and socially." Nobody mentioned that the school might want to become racially just.

Race was rarely discussed at Countryside, perhaps because of the strong feelings that many thought were better left unspoken. For example, teacher Lindquist confided that although she never spoke about such matters to her colleagues, she was unhappy with the demands minority kids placed on the school. "I tend to resent these individual programs," she told us. "When they start having the Black Day and the Mexican Day and the Oriental Day. When was there ever a White Day? You can't say that to the kids, but after a while you start to think, "Why don't some of these ordinary kids get special attention?" In the Countryside community, Lindquist was not alone in her views.

When the reform committee realized that the tracking system would interfere with the scheduling and the composition of the

teams they wanted to create, they decided to make all classes heterogeneous. One teacher recalled, "Somebody came up with [the
idea], 'Well, why don't we offer advanced [English] to all of them?
Let's just put them all in next year.'" Because they saw this as primarily a technical (scheduling) matter, they were surprised when
it erupted in controversy a few months later.

Access for All Versus the "Gatekeepers"

When Wanda Simpson proudly announced at the parent orientation meeting that all incoming sixth graders would take the
advanced English curriculum, nobody spoke. Simpson told us: "I
remember standing up very naïvely saying, 'All students will be
offered the most advanced-level curriculum.' I mean, it was right
out of *Caught in the Middle,* that little speech. What we can offer?
They're all going to be in advanced English. I was thinking I'd get
this rip-roaring applause, but people looked at me and said,
'What?!' . . . And boy, it was as if I said, 'Tomorrow there's no sunshine.'"

Afterward, about fifty people remained in the cafeteria, where
a self-appointed spokesperson told Simpson, "Well, we want you to
know right here and now, we disagree with this because our students are gifted and talented. And they can't be in regular classes."

Across town, that same evening, the school board was preparing to consider the revised curriculum Countryside had submitted
for the proposed detracked English class. Simpson recalled: "Some
people went from my meeting straight to the board meeting. Beat
me there, you know . . . By the time I got in there, there was a battle roaring." Despite the controversy, the board approved the plan,
but she was shocked by what had happened. There followed a
spate of newspaper articles and letters to the editor. Some were
supportive, but the angry parents and students held the media's
attention. Amid the heat, the board asked Simpson to hold public
hearings to explain how Countryside planned to implement all the
state's middle-grades reform recommendations, including heterogeneous grouping.

In the thick of the controversy, the schools' middle school network provided moral and professional support. Simpson called
Heather Perkins at project headquarters in the state department

of education, who reassured her that schools all over the state were embroiled in similar controversies. She encouraged Simpson to call other schools for help. Perkins also sent relevant literature on the merits of detracking for the reform committee to use as they prepared. Simpson explained: "They had to read, go back and read things so that when parents questioned them, they could give them good information. You're an English teacher and I say, 'Well, now that you're untracked, how are you going to meet the needs of all kids?' You had better be able to answer that. And people ask."

The reform committee spent the day of the hearing rehearsing with "coaches" from other partnership middle schools who put people "in the hot seat and tried questions on them." Their strategy was to sell and implement heterogeneous grouping by arguing for student-centered middle schools. They hoped that, embedded in a larger reform context, parents would find detracking more palatable. Simpson worried, however, that all of the state's recommendations were at risk: "My biggest fear was this [middle-grades] program was going to die on the issue of detracking."

At the hearing, the committee members faced parents in the packed school library for nearly three hours. Simpson said they stressed why teaming was so essential: "We talked about a nurturing, warm, student-centered environment where the kids were going to be known. They were going to have their lockers in the same hall, and the kids were going to be accepted and they were going to do additional things. Teachers were going to have a common prep time, so if parents needed to contact them, they could contact one teacher and meet with all five of them together."

But many parents didn't see any connection between teaming—which they liked—and detracking—which they didn't. "What I heard them saying," Simpson explained, "was 'Put them on a team, but make it a GATE [gifted and talented education] team, or make it an advanced English team. Track within the teams. If you have to have some low kids, put low kids on the team, but just make sure they're treated differently as they move through the team.'" In short, the meeting was, in Simpson's word, "horrible": "People were angry. More angry people came to the meeting to question us than people [who] came to support. People who support the whole idea of the middle school movement stayed home because they didn't question." One assistant superintendent who came to lend district support told us that he "just about got skewered alive." Later, several still-angry parents complained to us that they had been ignored, that the committee did all the talking. One recalled, "No dissenting voices were heard."

Not long after the hearing, a core group of about twenty parents (who, in Simpson's view, "religiously" opposed the change) organized themselves as the "Gatekeepers," taking their name from the school's gifted-and-talented, or GATE, program. They affiliated with the state's powerful association for gifted education, which supplied them with advocacy material and support. At the peak of the controversy, the Gatekeepers claimed to have three hundred members. Their regular newsletters were meant to "keep folks abreast of changes that were being considered in schools." Simpson recalled: "These people were getting ready to lynch me. My phone was ringing off the hook. . . . They were out there networking. I couldn't even go places in town [without people noting] "There she is!" I couldn't even go to the grocery store."

Nevertheless, when students returned to school in the fall, one pilot team began implementing heterogeneity, grouping its students only in math.

Mixed Reviews from Teachers

Many Countryside teachers were enthusiastic. For example, one told us: "When you take those advanced kids and separate them from the regular kids, I don't think you help them. I think you punish them. In class, if I get everybody talking and they're all from different backgrounds, I have thirty teachers in my class."

But not all agreed. One explained that during instruction she "needed to slow down a little bit . . . and sit by and talk" to some students a little more. Another, revealing her conventional view that each individual needs instruction tailored to his or her supposed ability, confessed, "I feel bad because I have to take things down a level, where the majority of the students can understand it, and I know I am not challenging the upper students."

Content coverage was a major sticking point. Unfortunately, the faculty had done little inquiry into the nature of the curriculum and teaching for heterogeneous groups. Many teachers still used transmission, cover-by-telling strategies. Some felt set up to fail; they knew only a few students could quickly master the material that way. Another argued that cooperative learning slowed down the pace too much: "It's great when they can discover things, but if you have to take three days to discover something you can tell them in twenty minutes . . . well, we've got so much to cover." Some parents told us that teachers apologized for being unable to challenge high achievers. Others said that teachers warned them that advanced students would have to be responsible for their own learning and ask for more work.

Although detracking and teaming spread with enthusiasm throughout the seventh grade English faculty, resistant teachers retreated to "the sanctuary of the eighth grade." Then Simpson and the rest of the English faculty tried again to remove the GATE label from eighth grade English. Controversy erupted once more and was as fierce as the first round had been. The Gatekeepers forced a compromise: GATE English would go, but it would be replaced with honors English, a designation that allowed more students to enroll in the high track.

Changing grouping practices in math beyond the seventh grade proved even more difficult than English, partly because the most resistant math teachers had retreated to the eighth grade, and they soon formed strong alliances with resistant parents. Simpson explained: "I fought for a couple years, but I knew there was no way I [could] break the math department. And I'd have to wait until they were ready. Because we're talking about anarchy. You know, they'd be up in arms. But as math people retired, and I hired people, I hired people who I felt were going to look realistically at teaching all kids."

A handful of teachers left Countryside for the high school and other districts in response to the detracking uproar. Simpson saw this as healthy: "There has to be a way for people to exit the school who truly do not believe in the program." But some teachers believed that those who disagreed with her views were punished. "Instead of embracing those [with opinions contrary to the administration] and trying to work out something that meets all the needs," one told us, "It was more a matter of 'We're going to get rid of you.'"

Finally, after three years, seventh grade math went from four to three math levels. But the eighth grade never budged from its five-track structure. Two new math teachers did break ranks, however, by teaming up and combining their eighth grade remedial, general, and advanced classes to form heterogeneous groups. Nevertheless, Countryside continued to move slowly in the direction of untracked teams, and by the mid-1990s all but the eighth graders were heterogeneously grouped. After five years of reform, there were only five or six teachers left who, Simpson said, "still [wouldn't] budge." She had won the battle for structural change, but she and her reform-minded faculty were worn out by the constant battle to keep reforms (which seemed always to hang by a thread) from crashing down.

Success, Disappointment, and Caution

From a structural perspective, Countryside's efforts to detrack its school could be judged a success. After all, most classes ended up heterogeneously grouped. Yet, Simpson had learned a hard lesson. In the end, she realized she had confronted racism in the guise of concern over educational quality—a realization that brought deep personal disappointment: "Being a person of color, there was just something that bothered me. It was a whole issue of a different type of racism than I'd ever fought. So then I woke up, and I could deal with that. 'OK, you [white people] just don't want to be with them, because you don't think they're good enough.'"

Reflecting on the move to detrack English, Simpson admitted her naïveté at expecting the community to easily embrace a reform explicitly aimed at the common good: "If I look back at it now, I would never, ever make such a radical change. You know why? Because I thought everybody would just think like I did, that it would just make such sense. It was so democratic and fair. And when I look back at it now, I think, 'How could I have been so stupid? How could I have thought that there were people out there who would not want the good for everybody?' I mean, I was very idealistic."

She regretted that the battles they'd fought had deflected attention from making the school inclusive. "All that fighting and energy that we wasted," she said, ". . . we could have been building something for the school."

In contrast to Countryside, Inland Middle School in Illinois did build something for the school: a climate of racial justice that included heterogeneous grouping. As we described in Chapter One, Inland's story is generally a happier one than we found at many schools, although it too was fraught with racial politics and had a less-than-perfect ending. But by tackling the racial issues directly, the Inland faculty created for their students a place of considerable racial harmony in a community otherwise torn by hostility and fear.

Inland: Building a Socially Just Culture

Led by principal Ben McCall, Inland's faculty turned to middle school reform when the school became the focal point for their community's contentious racial politics. For years, blacks and whites lived in highly segregated neighborhoods with palpable racial animosity. Many whites expected violence if they ventured into the "ghetto" (one told us "they'd slit your throat"), and many African Americans feared harassment from the vigilante groups that patrolled the white communities looking out for "troublemakers."

In the mid-1980s, Inland's district, suffering a financial crisis and with diminishing student attendance, was forced to target one of its two middle schools for closure: either Inland, in the white neighborhood, or Lynwood, in the black. Described by one parent as "a horrible, horrible issue," the debate over which school to close grew more politically intense when it became clear that, while Lynwood had the bigger, better, and newer building, the white community "outvotes Lynwood easily . . . in terms of political power."

The school board came up with an incredibly controversial compromise by deciding to close the newer Lynwood Middle School *temporarily* for two or three years until some needed renovations to its air conditioning system and basic structure could be made. Meanwhile, African American Lynwood students would attend the more distant Inland, with its inferior physical structures. Although this decision angered Lynwood advocates, they were consoled by assurances that once renovations were completed, their middle school would be reopened as the district's sole middle school. McCall, then Inland's principal, was assigned to the now-merged school. The faculty was a mixture of Lynwood and Inland staff, some of whom were asked to teach at Inland and some of whom volunteered.

When the schools merged, McCall knew that many Inland students harbored their parents' racist attitudes:

> Parents will call me who are used to [their children] going to primarily white schools and say, "My daughter's in third-hour science with Mrs. Johnson and she's the only white kid in there." And I'll say, "You know, that's not true." And she'll say, "It's true. Don't call me a liar. Not only is the whole class black, but even the teacher's black. . . ." And I'll say, "You know ma'am, that's just not true. . . ." And I'll go down to Mrs. Johnson's third-hour class, and it'll be twenty-eight kids, and fifteen will be black, and thirteen will be white. That's the insidious nature of racism.

From the first year of the merger, McCall and the Inland faculty worked on changing both the program and attitudes. McCall explained that if all students were to receive a sound education, the faculty would first have to get along, talk to each other, understand one another's background, care what happens to each other, and work together with students. Consequently, during that first trying year, administrators and counselors made it their primary mission to create a communitylike culture out of the historically antagonistic faculties and student bodies.

Although their first attention was to students, Inland's faculty also worked to allay the fears of parents and community leaders. One teacher recalled:

> There were just tons of meetings. They were meeting with this PTO (parent teacher organization); they were meeting with another PTO; they were meeting with the band, they met with every possible group; and they just had talk sessions. They were very open: "This is what we know now. . . . What are your fears? Tell us what you want. . . ." They made sure that every single faction would be dealt with, so everybody felt that they were involved with this. . . . People were hearing, educationally, what was going into this school. We were talking about education. . . . I think that . . .

just kind of soothed their fears that we were gonna be some
armed camp.

School opened with a communitywide barbecue. Later, virtually everyone agreed that the potentially disastrous merger actually
launched a wonderful set of relationships within the school and
among parent and community groups—a sense of community that
in Ben McCall's colorful assessment "saved our butts." It also propelled their structural and curricular reforms.

The Illinois middle school association sent experts on multicultural education free of charge and offered staff courses on
"dealing with diversity." District money supported other sessions
on multicultural education and cultural issues in general, and Inland faculty "used our own best resources . . . ourselves" to develop
regular professional development about teaching and learning in
diverse settings. Then they went to work.

An Assault on Tracking

Inland teachers tackled tracking immediately, because they wanted
to educate their newly merged student body without disadvantag-
ing anyone. One Inland teacher explained: "It's not fair to put a
stigma on kids. They mature at different rates, and maybe their
readiness in reading or even math might not be here today, but
who says it's not going to be there tomorrow? And if you don't give
a kid a chance to grow and to compete against the best, or to even
work with kids who are brighter, they'll never know. They'll always
be at that lower level. And I think that's probably the reason . . . we
want the kids to grow up to do the best that they can do."

Strategically, it made sense to begin with the basic classes since,
as McCall told us, "The bottom—the low—has very little political
clout. . . . You set these kids free, and parents are not going to crab
about it." Significantly, because all teachers taught at least one low-
level class, most were eager to eliminate the difficult lower track.
Many shared (and nearly all respected) the principal's deep commitment to both equity and learning, and they knew that he believed
heterogeneous grouping would promote both. When he and the
Inland counselors eliminated the lowest classes, they didn't tell

teachers which students in their newly heterogeneous classes were formerly in the low track. When teachers found out after the first grading period who had previously been labeled low, they were pleasantly surprised to find that many of these children were doing fine in regular classes.

With the low track gone, McCall and the faculty moved to reduce the number of math levels from five to three, and eventually to two. A scheduling problem allowed them to quickly eliminate honors reading, but they moved more slowly to merge the regular and honors English classes. They ordered the same new English textbooks for both levels so teachers could prepare for heterogeneous groups; a committee conducted further research on detracking and drafted a statement to explain its intentions to the central office.

Seeking Socially Just Pedagogy

Many Inland teachers adopted new teaching methods. For example, along with eliminating honors reading classes, teachers decided to make both reading and English classes literature-based and to use a whole-language approach. Many English teachers found that this allowed slower students to succeed while the students with more skills also made good progress. As one teacher explained, traditionally oriented students (meaning: capable white students) can "learn a separate skill and then at a later time they can stick that where it belongs—low kids can't do that." Teachers challenged advanced students with supplementary enrichment activities included with their new textbook. Math teachers returned to a more fact-based curriculum for their honors and regular classes. Although this initially sounded less challenging, they also selected a text for some classes because it introduced algebraic concepts and included a diverse array of rigorous thinking activities for heterogeneous groups. At the time of our last visit, the math department had hired several new math teachers in part for their experience with manipulatives.

The science and social studies classes had always been untracked, and many teachers had used and were receptive to a project-based curriculum. One history teacher explained her unit on the Revolutionary War, during which students compiled biographies of black and white women and men who had an impact on the American Revolution. Because of their flexibility, Inland's science and social studies teachers joined English teachers from time to time to offer interdisciplinary, project-based lessons. Across departments, several teachers adopted learning-style or multiple-intelligences approaches to accommodate what they saw as students' preferences for the right or left brain, visual learning, and so forth. One teacher, who proudly described himself as an enthusiastic but traditional teacher (a "blackboard, piece-of-chalk-and-a-hearty-Hi-Ho-Silver kind of teacher") said that he made cautious changes, such as having students participate more by writing on the chalkboard and role playing. Several math teachers explained that cooperative learning works well in heterogeneous groups because "the higher kids get the benefit of seeing it a bit differently, because sometimes the lower kids do see things in a way that you really wouldn't think about."

Inland's teachers also tried new assessments. One based about half her grades on cooperative projects and homework. Another combined students' portfolios of their best work with some very traditional methods such as whole-group call-and-response and quizzes to check for understanding. Most teachers believed that portfolio assessments, when done correctly, gave more accurate measures than traditional testing.

In sum, Inland's faculty—motivated to make social justice work—found an abundance of appropriate materials and techniques. Further, after a few years they could bring in other like-minded teachers with important skills. Of course, enriching curriculum and learning new skills took place over several years—with some disruption and much trial and error. There was no way that all these reforms could have been put in place before combining the schools.

Including Knowledge of Everyone

Inland teachers worked singly and in teams to develop multicultural curricula. For example, one English teacher taught an "American values" unit to her classes that "deals with [the] ethnicity and background and families" in the big city near Inland. She wanted the unit to challenge students' stereotypes and prejudices by having them place their own experiences in local historical context and explore through the eyes of parents and grandparents their own history as immigrants and settlers. For African American History Month, three African American and two white teachers organized schoolwide activities. Various teams offered interdisciplinary units around multicultural themes, such as Africa, black Olympians, and black entertainers. Teachers began using literature that was more directly related to the African American experience, such as *Roll of Thunder, Hear My Cry; To Kill a Mockingbird;* and *Maniac McGee,* a book written in black dialect. Along with these readings, a new textbook was chosen partly because of its cultural pluralism.

A small but influential number of Inland faculty adopted a sophisticated view of multicultural education that went beyond students' simply learning *about* each other. Science teacher Trice Morris, for example, believed that teaching her students to be good citizens in a multicultural and democratic society was consistent with their learning science: "How can we teach them to become better people, have a better sense of the environment, have a better sense that Asians and African Americans—all people—have the right to feel good about who they are and what they are and what they brought to this culture?"

Thus, although Morris believed in instilling individual efficacy—the belief that "I can do whatever I decide that I want to do, and it doesn't matter what color I am"—she also wanted her students to learn the importance of contributing positively to society and making a difference.

But other teachers were clearly ambivalent about Inland's emphasis on African American history and whether the school inadvertently marginalized black students from the putative mainstream. One argued vehemently: "I don't think we do half of what we should do. . . . Every now and then, we do a little theme. But how are African Americans really a part of the full culture? I would like to get to a point where, when we study American history, we study everybody's culture. When you do African American History . . . you feel that you're stepping outside of the real curriculum." Another agreed: "We see a need now that it just can't be African American History Month. African American history is every day of the year." One must believe that this sort of multicultural controversy can only enrich the communitarian culture of the school and benefit children.

Many Inland teachers were teaching racially mixed classes for the first time. Like their students, they had to learn to interact without falling back on class-based and race-based stereotypes. Some white teachers spoke openly about their considerable discomfort, and they sought the advice of black colleagues. For example, one voiced her concern that discussions on slavery in her classroom provoked her African American students' hostility—which she didn't know how to handle.

Struggles with Prejudice Inside the School

Clearly, Inland made giant strides toward social justice, and most of Inland's faculty took pride in being fairly free of racial prejudice. However, old stereotypes were not easily extinguished. A number of white teachers struggled with the differences they found in their African American students. One saw black girls as brazenly defiant. Another confessed that he found black students "just vulgar and rude." Tending to define the "smart kids" by their conformity to traditional classroom expectations, some teachers fell back on stereotypical explanations for why their African American students acted "less smart" than white students: lack of individual effort and motivation, or social and cultural backgrounds (such as broken homes) that allegedly disadvantage blacks at school. One theorized that black boys suffered from what she called an "endangered species" problem that diminished their desire to work hard to earn a place in society. She explained:

> My own personal theory is [that] black male babies are a very precious commodity to the black community, and as they grow up and as there are more and more black males incarcerated, and more and more black males out of work, and so forth, and single mothers raising black males, I think they are very much, um . . . catered to, overindulged, spoiled, don't want to do anything to make them not love you to the nth degree. Give, give, give. "Maybe not my time, but I'll give you all these things. I don't have the time for you because I'm trying to make a living. . . ." You know the status is there because you are very precious—because black males are a very endangered species.

Other white teachers worried about "reverse discrimination" toward white Americans. As one told us: "There's a big to-do made of African American Month, and you know . . . you also have the point where, OK, where's the White American Month? And they're doing all women this month, so where are the men? I don't think that it should just be one or two groups chosen, like African Americans and women. I think that if they're going to do something like that, then they should do it for every single group."

Cooperative learning and strategies to address differences in students' learning styles also fell prey to stereotypes about high- and low-achieving students. For example, cooperative learning was less often used in honors classes than in heterogeneous ones. Teachers of honors classes sometimes claimed that a traditional format allows them to move faster and cover a greater amount of material, and they assumed that cooperative learning is a technique that primarily benefits slower students. A few suggested that cooperative learning burdens high-track students, since they sacrifice their opportunity to move faster in order to help their less-gifted classmates. Some teachers found it less relevant to accommodate different learning styles to present materials in honors courses than in other classes. Generally, many pedagogies touted as beneficial for multicultural education and for heterogeneous groups were found suitable primarily for low-ability students, thus feeding into the ever-present suspicion that multicultural emphasis and heterogeneity inevitably lower standards.

In contrast, one teacher told us: "Excellence is excellence. If you expect or if you accept less than my best, then you're telling me that I am less. I just have a hard time with that—a real hard time with that." For this teacher, not confronting a child about poor behavior and performance only cemented existing stereotypes. Others suggested that students' learning styles were rooted in their race's cultural traits, with black students more rambunctious and white students more studious. Learning-style theory may have inadvertently reified some teachers' conceptions of ability and behavior along racial lines.

White teachers rarely implicated their own conceptions of intelligence and ability as problematic for their curriculum, pedagogy, or assessment in racially mixed classrooms. On the other hand, some African American teachers were highly critical of white colleagues who they judged to be underchallenging African American students. Referring to some white teachers, one told us that expecting little of a child, regardless of his or her skin color, was "a cop-out" and a "dodge" and did nothing but allow the child to fail. African American teachers were also more likely than their white colleagues to engage students in dialogue about racism, and about racist practices at Inland.

Backlash from the Outside

Not only did Ben McCall and the faculty have to confront their own racism as they worked to make the school socially just but they also had to contend with considerable nervousness and some outright hostility from elsewhere in the school system and the community. For example, when McCall broached the idea of detracking honors English, "the high school teachers [at a districtwide curriculum committee] freaked out." They notified their high school colleagues and parents, who then inundated the superintendent's office with angry telephone calls. As McCall tells it, "The whole world was under fire. It became apparent very quickly that I had two choices: go to the wall with it and get beat, or back off." He backed off—at least for a while—and sought another approach.

Inland's faculty and administration decided that their next step must be to restore broad community and district faith in their "academic excellence" by raising their standardized test scores. They worked to raise scores without sacrificing the spirit and content of their reform goals. Moreover, they also worried that the public's expressed concern about scores might not really be the primary source of opposition to their reforms. Raising test scores could be a seemingly rational response to white residents' irrational fears about mixing black children, who they sometimes perceive as dangerous and dumb, with their own children. As one Inland teacher remarked:

> Quite frankly, I think the reason we have honors is parental pressure. It's a racial issue. An honors group is a white group. There are very few black kids who qualify to be in it. However, those black children that I have are my best students. I think it's really "white Inland" not wanting to do away with honors because then they'd have to mix with [the African American community].

I think it's strictly a racial issue. If that pressure were not out there
in the community, either via parents' telephone calls to Ben, or
the school board, or whatever, we wouldn't have tracking in
English.

An unspoken threat of white flight hovered over Inland like an
ominous cloud and was frequently used as leverage that accompanied requests for special treatment. This threat gained its real
power as it passed through a central office that was always very nervous about Inland's reforms. As the superintendent put it: "How
are we going to train the parents to understand what we're even
talking about? Because, what's going to be perceived is 'You're just
trying to give me a bunch of mumbo-jumbo so you can take care
of those black kids, and take away my rights as a parent.' We're
going to upset people and spend a lot of money . . . and what'll
happen is the white people will leave the system."

In fact, Inland's standardized scores rose quite dramatically
during their reforms, and faculty felt that their efforts deserved the
credit. However, no one was certain how long Inland's rising test
scores would convince the white community (and with it district
officials) to support the school's socially just reforms.

During all this time, administrators and teachers at Inland and
Lynwood community members were also anxiously awaiting the
renovations and the promised reopening of Lynwood Junior High.
Two years became three, and three became four, then five, then
six. Ten years after the compromise, Lynwood remains closed.

Lessons from Detracking Schools

Countryside's efforts to become socially just focused almost entirely
on changing the school's grouping practices in order to bring
teachers and students together in communities where all students
could have access to the highest-quality teaching and learning.
Inland's reforms (although including grouping) took a broader,
normative tack, seeking to change the culture of instruction, curriculum, and relationships among adults and children so as to
reflect and respect the racial differences that ruptured the Inland
community outside of school. Neither school had an easy time of

it, even though a committed, skillful, and much-admired principal led each.

Every appearance indicates that Inland's ambitious undertaking—aimed at changing the hearts and minds of community members as well as the school structure—fared considerably better than Countryside's more modest efforts. Furthermore, though Countryside's tumultuous reform was characterized by tension and uncertainty, Inland's equally contentious activity brought considerable solidarity to the school community. We are left with considerable uncertainty about why these schools' struggle for social justice played out so differently, but we were struck by a fundamental distinction between the two schools that we believe mattered a lot. At root, Countryside's reform process seemed to be the means to an end (structuring teams that then create a warm, student-centered climate); on the other hand, Inland's reform process appeared to be an end in itself (people behaving as inclusive and egalitarian in the process of reform). We return to these distinctions in our final chapters.

| Becoming Caring

At the turn of the twentieth century, reformers were grasping for responses to the poverty, disease, crime, and labor unrest they associated with concentrations of immigrants living in cities. Periodicals of the day lamented that these "nonwhite" Italian, Polish, and other southern and eastern European immigrants would not assimilate, would not assume their appropriate place in civic and economic life if they were left to their own devices.[1] The reformers turned to schools and other community agencies to do the job. Many reformers saw the new immigrants as culturally deficient, and to the degree that the immigrants' inborn limitations allowed, reformers sought to correct those deficiencies.

Except for the rare progressive schools of the day, urban schools in the early twentieth century looked a lot like the modern factories of the time, for which schools were preparing nearly all of their students. For the most part, schools relied on drill and repetition, valued memorization, and bestowed external rewards (grades, preferred seating) for high performance. Urban school teachers were charged with the responsibility to train students for industrial life and to give immigrants rudimentary cultural knowledge for their assimilation into the industrial culture. Teachers' work, like the work their students would soon be doing, was dominated by the prevailing model of scientific efficiency and the division of labor.

Social service agencies such as orphanages and other community relief agencies shared a widespread view of the urban poor that cast them simultaneously as pathetic and needing charity on the one hand, and dangerous on the other—a threat to the health, safety, economy, and morals of established citizens. Caring, in these institutions, was more about safeguarding the emerging middle class from the indigence of the lower classes than responding with compassion to an urban class created to support industrial growth. One turn-of-the-century reformer declared that "society must, as a measure of self-protection, take upon itself the responsibility of caring for the child."[2]

In contrast, Jane Addams at Hull House found strength in immigrant cultures. Rather than pitying her immigrant neighbors or treating them with a detached professionalism (in the name of scientific efficiency), she worked within the community, visiting her neighbors' homes and workplaces. Her personal interaction with her neighbors reveals her belief that social equality is a foundation for community life and individual expression. Dozens of classes and clubs met at Hull House, helping maintain the immigrants' expression of their cultures and easing them into knowledge of American ways and language.

The lesson we draw from Addams's work is to see caring as contributing to civic virtue when it includes, but is greater than, the community's aggregate of individual acts of support and compassion. She drew together disparate individuals and groups to form a community with community-minded norms. Hull House was a kind of home: a central gathering place, a community center, and a forum for political action. The norms and ethics of Hull House were to offer services to immigrants in ways that fit their strengths, perspectives, and capacities to serve others.

Contemporary Schools as Community Centers

Today's social and schooling problems resemble those Addams faced. Two million American children lived in poverty at the beginning of the twentieth century; more than fourteen million children live in poverty at century's end. The public's perception is that communities are in trouble, children are out of control, and schools are failing to endow students with the right values. Within this rhetoric of decay, education has been thrust into prominence as a response to multiple worries about children and the culture. Schools have been timidly nudged forward as places that might house comprehensive responses to social ills that go beyond traditional schoolhouse concerns.

Some of these comprehensive plans evoke images of Hull House. For example, James Comer's School Development Program has won considerable acclaim for its community-based approach, which establishes strong interpersonal relationships as the foundation for whole-school improvement and student development. Following such examples, in 1999 the Clinton administration expanded the Twenty-First Century Community Learning Center Initiative (with $600 million attached) to support school programs designed to keep students off the streets and strengthen community life. Although schools have always attracted teachers and other decent individuals who would expand their relationships beyond imparting technical and cultural knowledge, these reforms seek to formalize broadened roles for schools.

These programs aim to offer youths, parents, and community members engaging and healthy activities in a safe, community setting. Even though the concept is appealing, such policies as the Twenty-First Century initiative seem caught in an ambivalent view of local communities. Proponents argue that the program gets us "back to basics, back to active community involvement in raising and educating all of our children."[3] Community school advocates reason that such schools can be a safe after-school and summer haven for children, where learning takes place "in a building removed from the violence, drugs, and lack of supervision of children that permeate some communities in America."[4] This rationale betrays both the need for and the limitation of many current conceptions of community centers, employing a rhetoric that blames the communities whose involvement it seeks for the conditions that place children at risk. The distinctive feature of Hull House was not that it was a "haven" in a deficient community, but that it was a caring center where community members could strengthen community life.

Care: A Stance and a Practice

Turning Points sought to connect schools with their communities, reengage parents, and create small communities of learners within schools to make them caring places through a variety of services: coordination of health and social services, interdisciplinary teacher teams, and advisory programs. Although aimed at strengthening relationships, such practices do not connect students, families, neighborhoods, and schools unless they are guided by an ethic that supports development of caring communities, whether they be neighborhood, whole-school, or classroom learning communities.

Caring school practices are distinguishable from less caring practices on the basis of the norms that guide their enactment. A community meeting can allow people to speak and hear one another's perspectives, or it can be a time for the principal to report on routine matters or announce a policy change. Shared planning periods can give teachers a chance to plan lessons that challenge students to think critically, or the time can be coopted to fulfill administrative requirements. Advisory programs can foster supportive teacher-student relationships, or they can subject students to packaged self-esteem, antidrug, or other low-content activities that do little to foster relationships. Differentiating each of these examples is an ethical orientation related to one's perception of a good and proper way to treat others. Following educational philosopher Nel Noddings, we call this an ethic of care, to distinguish it from the usual instrumental and service orientations that prevail in schools.

In each of the paired examples above, not only is the first of the two practices to be preferred; *why* one prefers it, and the reasons given, matter considerably. Should people participate because it is a good way to get them to buy a program? Yes, but an ethic of care would have everyone participate to find dignity and understand the conditions that affect them. Is shared planning time an efficient way to produce challenging lessons? It may be, but an ethic of care stipulates that rigorous intellectual exchanges among trusting colleagues enables them to examine their own practices. Will student disruptions diminish if kids have a few individual moments with teachers each day? Possibly, but an ethic of care finds advisory programs warranted when they help teacher and student know one another more fully. When school practices are guided by an ethic of care, individuals and whole schools emphasize growth, empathy, response, and continuity.[5] These constructs guide the actions of individuals such that schools are created that look quite different from those guided by the *ethic of service* that shapes most ordinary school settings. An ethic of service can be thought of as a set of external principles that prescribe how things ought to be done; an ethic of care stresses adherence to these caring constructs.

Fostering Growth

Schools that emphasized *growth* took a broad view of students' needs and the school's role in their development. They avoided what Noddings calls a "shallow response to social change" by focusing on their students' cognitive, emotional, physical, and social development.[6] Focusing simultaneously on students' academic and nonacademic (cognitive, emotional, etc.) development requires educators to redefine their professional roles to include the broader social and economic contexts of their work and renegotiate their relationships with community members, parents, colleagues, and students.

Empathy

Schools and school leaders did not assume they knew what an individual or community needed, or (on first contact) even that they fully understood what they were saying; instead, they adopted an *empathic* stance. Such a stance requires listening continuously for others' meanings. It requires attending carefully to what others reveal about their experiences and how their perceptions are mediated by those experiences. It allows for the possibility that sometimes different meanings cannot be understood but must simply be respected. Caring schools, according to Chicago educational reformer William Ayers, see their mission as understanding the circumstances that shape students' lives and the conditions in their communities, rather than fixing a student's or community's problems.[7] Learning from others—including community members and students—is valued in caring schools; more correctly, such learning is what it means to care. It enhances, not replaces, teachers' skills and knowledge.

Responding

Caring schools *responded* to student and community needs by acting on the knowledge they acquired by listening to individual and community concerns. Response is the active part of a relationship.

For all of one's careful listening, respectful attitudes, and knowledge of another individual, it can hardly be said that two people have a relationship unless they communicate and take action that enhances one another's lives. If we are to speak of an individual's or family's relationship to the community or to the school, or the school's relationship to them, similarly active responses are essential.

These qualities of relationships do not produce a linear result (that is, growth leading to empathy, which leads to response). Rather, as norms, they are mutually reinforcing. If one is willing to attend to others so as to go beyond narrow professional definitions, there is a greater likelihood of an empathic response. Similarly, developing a high degree of empathy makes it likely that one finds it unsatisfactory to respond within a narrowly construed professional role. Caring requires more than acting on the knowledge of individual and community needs. Responding to others' needs requires educators *to act among* rather than *to do for.* This means that empathic responses must free individuals from common judgments and their labels, such as *incapable, unmotivated, too busy,* and so on. Under the weight of such judgments individual teachers, parents, or students stop *being* the community and drift toward becoming a less valued unit within the community. The distinction here, subtle though it might be, is analogous to a family whose strongest identification is that of being *the family* rather than individuals belonging to an aggregate of related brothers, cousins, aunts, parents, and so on.

Providing Continuity

In addition, caring schools increased the *continuity* among school, community, students, and teachers, through community service learning, interdisciplinary teacher teaming, and student advisory programs and other less formal activities.[8] Continuity requires educators to recognize the strengths of individuals and communities and investigate how to take advantage of those strengths, adopting a developmental rather than a deficit view. Although continuity extends spatially, across the school and community, it is also, as W.E.B. Du Bois notes below, temporal, reaching back in time to acknowledge the history of students' "class and group" and into the future, imagining a time of "perfect social equality."

A Sympathetic Touch

This complex version of care asks schools to exercise caution about creating hierarchies of need, and it treats students' physical, emotional, social, and cognitive needs as coequal and interdependent. It is not unlike Addams's plea to improve conditions for Chicago's immigrant families and children through public institutions, individual action, and commitment to democratic community. Addams's settlement houses were neither skill-training centers nor mental health counseling centers. They responded to the comprehensive, practical needs of competent people searching for help and resources. Similarly, the challenge to care in schools demands more than simply nurturing or empathizing with students' circumstances; it requires appropriate, sensitive, comprehensive responses.

As such, caring is more than a child-centered approach to education. It is a moral stance as well, akin to Du Bois's notion of sympathetic touch. In his 1935 article, "Does the Negro Need Separate Schools?" he argued: "The proper education of any people includes *sympathetic touch* between teacher and pupil; knowledge on the part of the teacher, not simply of the individual taught, but of his surroundings and background, and the history of his class and group; such contact between pupils, and between teacher and pupil, on the basis of perfect social equality, as will increase this sympathy and knowledge."[9]

Du Bois captures here the dual face of caring schools: empathic understanding and sensitive response. To borrow his language, sympathy without touch provides a convenient excuse to lower expectations, whereas touch without sympathy carries the threat of paternalism (or, in some cases, maternalism). Caring educators must come to know those for whom they care and respond in a way that is consistent with this knowledge, but they must also embrace those for whom they care as growing persons with a future. Acknowledging the future of those for whom we care is as important a dimension of justice as acknowledging the past.[10]

Care: Easier to Say Than Do

As we spent time in schools, we heard everywhere and saw everywhere talk, signs, and activities that paid homage to building a sense of community and caring for individuals. Sometimes on campuses where people spoke of and professed care in abundance, the care turned elusive; the more we looked, the less we saw. Other schools gave us a first impression that was chilly, with care nowhere to be seen; but soon we began to feel a deep warmth emanating from classes and play yards. Care, we discovered, was less a reform practice than a normative catalyst—an agent that could make reform powerful, though it would accomplish much less on its own. At George Washington Carver, Bethany Houston's teammate Hazel Smith explained: "I usually try to bond with the students first—make some kind of connection with them. When students feel that someone cares about them, they're more likely to listen. . . . I might get a different reaction than someone else who says the same things but who hasn't bonded with the student."

Every school has some teachers like Smith who bond and feel and act with care. Indeed, unusual is the teacher who has no moments whatsoever without his or her caring, empathic connections. But students and schools cannot thrive if care is confined to private, occasional moments: a teacher, a principal who stops because she notices a child in tears; a coach available after school; a friend who will listen at lunch. Most adults can remember people in school who cared about them, but few can recall many caring classes, a caring year, or a caring school. On the other hand, reform that has caring at its core seeks to establish an environment where students, parents, teachers, and other adults feel welcome, safe, and respected—all day, every day.

Transforming professional roles, renegotiating relationships, and changing values is a lot to ask for. Although some schools seemed well ahead of the others in these matters, we could never attribute a very large degree of their progress to the reform. Most of their care seemed to come from elsewhere. Many schools made scant headway transforming professional roles. Advisor-advisee programs, for example, did little to attend to students' social and personal concerns. Many teachers resisted advisory activities, preferring to maintain their professional distance and focus exclusively (even if ineffectively) on students' academic needs. These teachers felt such programs were hardly their "real" job and deemed them add-ons or burdens. "I'm no social worker," one teacher protested. It was an attitude that prevented many schools from addressing community or student needs.

Despite righteous intentions, several schools subscribed to a version of care that reinforced a view of students—especially those from poor and nonwhite families—as deficient physically, emotionally, and socially. Caring for students in these schools was tied to an understanding of sympathy that emphasized pity or compassion— quite unlike what Du Bois seems to be calling for: a mutual liking or understanding arising from sameness of feeling.

Caring and the Reform Mill

In Chapter Eight, "Struggling in the Reform Mill," we discuss how reformers renegotiate reforms to accommodate those who resist. In the face of inevitable resistance, reformers wear down and lose focus in their efforts to help school communities develop new norms and values. These negotiations and modifications of programs and initiatives prop up the status quo practices and traditional norms. So, for example, to appease faculty who objected to taking on an advisory role or activities oriented toward counseling or relationships, some schools implemented prepackaged, sometimes scripted advisor-advisee programs that could be taught outside of academic, social, or historical contexts. At the other extreme, faculty for whom an ethic and practice of care was a dramatic departure from their past practice (and a traumatic venture to contemplate) were sometimes demeaned as delinquent outcasts and told to "lead, follow, or get out of the way." Clearly, teachers would require the same kind of caring conditions for themselves that reformers hoped teachers would create for students. Most schools could not create those conditions.

For Every Need, a Program

Nothing was less controversial than the reform goal that schools should focus on meeting students' needs. How could anyone object to such a goal? Our schools developed programs and brokered services aimed at meeting academic, physical, emotional, and social needs. Many teachers at low-income schools sympathized with students' often-chaotic lives; they made sure that students felt supported and that they enjoyed coming to school. One Irving administrator explained, "If they don't get a feeling of warmth and comfort when they come to school, then it is difficult to learn if there's things that they're concerned with or worried about." At Carver, Mitchell, and Van Buren, teachers talked openly about the importance of student nutrition. Teachers at Tubman and Van Buren brought couches into their rooms to give students a comfortable place to read, or a place for tired or ill students to lie down. Tubman's superintendent reasoned that engaging parents and the community at the school contributed to the education of the whole child.

Schools addressed students' self-concept and nurtured their social development, often identifying and referring students for help. Teachers at all schools participated on committees to create or implement individual and group programs for students at risk academically and socially. Popular, too, were peer mediation and conflict-resolution classes to help students peacefully resolve conflicts with their peers and teachers.

Most schools tried to offer students a place to belong. They formed clubs, recognized student achievement (honor roles, award assemblies, reading student names over the PA system) to enhance students' self-esteem. At Tubman, African American students who were engaged in a variety of community service activities founded the Essence Club. Countryside and Madison launched teen centers. Chavez conducted college readiness assemblies, aware that the high school to which their students were going would make few such efforts.

Schools had a heightened interest in cooperating with local agencies or community members to help address student needs. Doing so brought two additional and related benefits: it strengthened the link between schools and local service agencies and reinforced the idea that schools could act as hubs of a system aimed at promoting healthy student development. Early on, Van Buren hired a home-school coordinator to be an interagency facilitator, help families contact agencies, and alert agencies to students who had broad family needs. Schools referred students to drug and alcohol abuse programs, support groups, and mental health and family planning agencies. Schools often collaborated with police and juvenile justice agencies on programs addressing students' self-esteem, mediation and leadership skills, and crime prevention and gang membership. Mann, Madison, Van Buren, and Irving paired students with successful adult mentors in their communities.

Programs Were Not Enough

The examples in the preceding section highlight some schools' activities and practices that had the potential to connect schools and communities. But these programs were only effective in establishing a caring environment if they were enriched by commitment to growth, empathy, response, and continuity. All too often, these norms were absent. One such school was Horace Mann. Its decent and loving faculty offered a flurry of services designed to fill what they saw as deficiencies in students' lives. In this culture of service, it was hard for many Mann faculty to find students' strengths.

Serving the Deficient: Horace Mann Middle School

Horace Mann's century-old, brick building is a landmark in its white, working-class neighborhood. Modest, well-kept homes; family businesses; and small, mostly Catholic, churches line the surrounding streets of this Massachusetts city. Many residents are children and grandchildren of European immigrants who settled here early in the century and still live in the houses where they were born, with as many as three generations of family members—all Mann graduates. In recent years, the community has added Vietnamese immigrants—many without legal status or eligibility for medical or social services—and some African Americans have joined the long-established neighbors and occupied nearby public housing. Many of Mann's veteran teachers, themselves members of the community, know the school's local students well. Lenora Jones, Mann's assistant principal for ten years, an African American and relative newcomer to the school, explained that teachers "have taught here long enough to know fathers and mothers and cousins. You spend twenty-five years in one neighborhood, then you see the blood lines coming through."

But only about one-third of Mann's five hundred students are locals; the rest arrive by bus. Ten buses transport so-called regular students, mostly African Americans who live in some of the city's most ravaged neighborhoods, as part of the city's school desegregation plan. Another seventeen vans bring two hundred mostly African American special education students. Some of these students have severe learning disabilities that qualify them for Mann's citywide prevocational program, which is housed in the school basement along with other special education and vocational classes.

Historically, Mann has experienced high racial tensions, and they still haunt the neighborhood. During one of our visits, a white shot an African American sitting in his car outside the nearby housing projects. State police occupied corridors for two or three years during the late seventies as Mann desegregated under a court order. One veteran teacher recalled that during those years, "Neighbors were up in the streets taunting the buses as these kids got off. It was terrible. It was a nightmare." Principal Len Jacobi, who has lived all his life in the neighborhood (an important source of his credibility and trustworthiness), was then an elementary school principal. His staunch support of desegregation pitted him against lifelong colleagues and earned him many enemies, some of whom hurled rocks through his living room window and made threatening telephone calls. Upon his arrival in the mid-eighties, Jacobi reorganized his "out of control" junior high into grade-level teams to divide the school into smaller, manageable units.

"School Is a Refuge"

With the help of Kate Pontello, a former social worker, Jacobi counted on the power of a child-centered perspective to bridge Mann's deep racial divide and carry the school to happier times. They first set up a student support team to address students' social and health needs. Jacobi, Pontello, and a core of enthusiastic teachers fought to achieve a kinder version of the school, one that brought adults and children together. They believed that educators must be willing to take on broad professional roles in order to help their students overcome the difficulties they faced daily. Pontello articulated the school's vision: "Until we really perceive our school as a community and as a family, we are not going to be able to reach all of our kids. . . . Yes, we are being asked to do it all. There is no doubt about it . . . and if that's not something that you believe in, then you don't really belong in an urban setting. You just have to buy into that old African saying that it takes the whole village to raise the child . . . that makes so much sense."

Just as committed to their quite different position, however, were several veteran teachers who dubbed Jacobi "Mr. Elementary" and complained: "Teachers see themselves as educators. They don't see themselves as becoming a buddy or an advisor or a counselor. They're not nuns and priests."

Undeterred by these teachers' it's-not-my-job attitude, Jacobi and Pontello established a staggering array of health and social services at Mann, which now form the core of faculty efforts to serve all the school's students. Most see the school's bused-in African American children as the neediest, and faculty try to make up for homes they judge to be dysfunctional and neighborhoods that are certainly poor and perceived to be dangerous. Social worker Charles Murphy told us: "School's a refuge. They'd rather be here than be home. . . . Why would they want to be home if they're going to get whacked in the head and lied to, promises broken? At least here they have a little more stability."

Murphy's concern for children was genuine enough, but his capacity for an empathic stance was constrained by his view that this community was devoid of resources, and perhaps moral standing. He could not see through the eyes of the people he was helping, could not imagine a loving family, a hardworking parent, or good clean fun. He was not alone. Nurse Fran Pietro, when asked to describe the students at Horace Mann, replied: "Their emotional health needs are really different. Some of our children are bused in from a neighborhood with a lot of violence . . . so they are coming to school with a lot of extra baggage." Teacher Barbara Vinney elaborated: "These kids need a lot. . . . You can't believe who [might be] coming in the next day. Their brother was shot the night before. Whose father was killed? Who has no clothes? Whose house burned down in the night?"

Surely, these problems were real and terrible. But for many teachers, the problems were all they could see.

Unloading Extra Baggage

Dealing with that "extra baggage" had become one of the school's main jobs, often outweighing academic instruction. In a recent year, faculty referred a third of the students for services. During our visits, intercom messages interrupted several times each hour to call students out of class for counseling groups, visits from mentors, and individual therapy. Teachers didn't seem to mind. One, Judi Soto, commented, "A child who is pulled out to see a therapist, I think that's just as important as his academic time." Principal Jacobi concurred: "I always say, 'If we do nothing else but remove the stigma of seeing a therapist when your family is in need, then we've been successful. . . .' Kids don't think anything of walking in here and sitting down and saying, 'You know, I really need to see a counselor.'"

This therapeutic school environment existed alongside an authoritarian code of discipline that also reveals much about Mann's approach to helping its students. Students are required to walk silently in single file through school halls. They sit in assigned cafeteria seats, and teachers use a rather military strategy to call students up row-by-row to eat, blowing whistles to signal when students can file out in order. Students carry with them at all times a package of "merits," coded by number, date of issue, student name, and homeroom. These are the currency by which faculty track and evaluate behavior. When infractions occur, adults confiscate merits. Clearly, these practices constrain students' liberty, and some students complain that Mann is "like a prison." Most faculty, however, agree that the payoff is well worth it. One argued, "You hate to hold things over kids' heads, but it's working, it's working."

Deficit Thinking Distorts the Enactment of Care

Despite Kate Pontello's deeply held belief that Mann needed to envision itself as a caring community, Mann's care generally amounted to distributing services, many of which interrupted students' academic growth and communicated a clear message that they needed to be "fixed." To be sure, Mann's students faced enormous challenges. Family, neighborhood, and societal circumstances placed many of them at risk; doing nothing would have been far worse. However, the school's approach rested on making up for students' inadequacies, relying on authoritarian standards of correct behavior and doing *for* rather than doing *with* or showing how. Mann's approach, as well intentioned as it was, echoes a

long-standing cultural view that assumes nonmainstream populations are damaged and need to be "repaired." In contrast, other
schools with similar student populations extended care that built
empowering relationships rather than providing services.

We next turn to some of these schools. Each was able in one or
more ways to establish programs and practices grounded in the caring norms described earlier, and to avoid the service approach that
permeated Horace Mann. As we saw in Chapter Three, many
George Washington Carver teachers balanced students' academic
and nonacademic needs, seeing high academic expectations as one
of several manifestations of their care. Educators at Harriet Tubman moved their school into the center of community life by forming close, respectful relationships with students and families that
capitalized on their strengths. Similarly, through empathic listening and responding, Middleton (a desegregated school) brought
white parents and parents of color together to respectfully construct a school vision that responded to the needs of all of the
school's diverse students. Pity and low expectations had no place
at any of these schools, and service proved unnecessary when students and parents acted on their own behalf.

Carver Middle School: A Sympathetic Touch

Bethany Houston's work at Carver over the years and her involvement in a local church have made her a mainstay in the Carver
community. She understands the daily difficulties her students face
but does not accept less than their best efforts. She views her job
as helping her students learn regardless of the difficult conditions
in their community. Both Houston and her teammate, Hazel
Smith, believe that getting students interested motivates them to
actively engage in their learning. But they also communicate firmly
their expectation that all their students are very capable and can
take responsibility for doing high-quality work. Smith explains
their no-excuses policy: "If Bethany gets something that's sub-
standard in her room, she knows what the capabilities are, and
same thing here. And if something is turned in that's sloppy, and
I know that they're capable of doing much better, then they don't
get away with that."

The duo's high expectations extend beyond cognitive tasks to include a kind of social contract. Smith credits her success to her ability to inspire students to produce good work and to show them that she is invested in them as people. That way, she hopes, "They won't want to do something that would be displeasing to me." Students have little choice but to rise to those expectations. Although students see Houston and Smith as strict, theirs is not a tough, callused stance reminiscent of the hard-liners at Horace Mann. The two, and many of their colleagues at Carver and other schools, reach out a welcoming hand—a sympathetic touch.

Houston and Smith's colleagues take expanded roles in students' lives. In one veteran's words, they are "an extra mommy, an extra daddy [to] give them values—to help them through these turbulent years." Unlike many at Mann, however, Carver teachers do not try to replace parents but see themselves as extended kin, an extra voice, another resource. Even though one reform leader insists that Carver is not the miracle school that some think, nearly everyone at the school seems deeply engaged in important child-centered activities. One thirty-year-veteran physical education teacher, who routinely takes students on weekend outings, coaches sports after school, and chaperones student trips, exemplifies this commitment: "I was one of those people who was raised without parents, so I have a real warm feeling for these kids. That's the reason I spend a lot of time with them, because most of the kids here are without a mother or father in their home. . . . So that's one of my commitments. I just think the only way I can do my job is by doing what I'm doing. So, I feel good about it. I feel good about the school, and I feel good about the response I get from kids."

Without relinquishing their concern for students' academic achievement, many at Carver gauge their success by the capacity to make students happy. One science teacher told us, "The way I judge how well the school is working is by what percentage of the kids I see smiling walking around the halls." Judging by the faces of Carver students in many classrooms we visited and in the school hallways, the school is a tremendous success.

Carver's vision of the good American school also emphasizes the importance of students' becoming good citizens, getting along well with others, and taking personal responsibility. Rather than implementing a system of rewards and sanctions to monitor student behavior, as the Mann teachers chose to do, many Carver teachers embed social supports for learning into daily classroom instruction, as we saw in the example of Nancy Nelson's teaching in Chapter Three. At the whole-school level, Carver has introduced Student Court, where student attorneys, judges, and juries adjudicate student and faculty grievances, such as the case of the apple missing from Nelson's desk. In a community where citizens have cause to question the fairness of the justice system, the court provides a forum for conflict resolution through a student-led judicial process. (Nelson's case resulted in respectful resolution of a childish prank and the return of the sentimental desk ornament to a loving teacher.)

Similarly, Harriet Tubman Middle School's faculty did not attempt to compartmentalize students' needs. Perhaps more than any other school, Tubman blurred the boundaries between school and the community, building relationships between neighborhood and school that demonstrated all four caring norms: growth, empathy, response, and continuity.

Tubman Middle School: Educating the Whole Child

Harriet Tubman Middle School occupies a treeless lot across from public housing with burned-out apartments. Despite the neighborhood's federally sponsored Weed and Seed program, drug dealers take refuge in a boarded-up apartment building nearby. More than 70 percent of Tubman's families fall below the poverty line; more than half live in subsidized housing. Many of Tubman's sixth, seventh, and eighth graders bear the scars of this tough world. "I saw a shooting," "I saw someone stab my neighbor," "Drug deals go on all the time," they tell their teachers. Like their peers at Mann, Tubman students "have seen everything," one teacher told us. After twenty-five years of court-ordered busing and voluntary magnet schools to combat racial isolation, less than a third of the seventy-one thousand public school students in this Texas city are white. Tubman's neighborhood and student body has shifted from white to black, from middle-class to very-low-income.

Ironically, school desegregation has also shaped Tubman into two racially identifiable schools on the same campus. On the ground floor of the main building and in five "temporary" bungalows, neighborhood children enroll in regular, special education, at-risk, and compensatory education programs. Upstairs, a small group of specially selected high-achieving students, about half of them whites who ride buses from other parts of the city, take an honors magnet program. Principal Rebecca Owens, a spirited African American grandmother, leads both the mostly black and female "greater school" faculty as well as the smaller group of mostly white magnet teachers. Although most teachers live outside Tubman's gang-ridden neighborhood, few fear for their personal safety—at least during daylight hours. One told us, "I don't fear anything in this neighborhood because I know right around the corner is one of my kids just waiting to say, 'Hi.'" Inside Tubman's graffiti-free building, green plants adorn the foyer, and cheerful red-and-white gingham curtains line the windows of the nearby cafeteria, where each table sports a tablecloth and a red plastic carnation in a white vase. More curtains and homey touches bedeck the offices of Owens and her staff.

In 1987, Superintendent Tom Beckerman mandated that Tubman restructure as a middle school, arguing that "somebody, somewhere has got to convince people that you have got to look at the education of the whole child." Owens was beginning her second year as principal, and because she was well known in the community Beckerman thought she was the perfect person to do it. Tubman became one of Texas's first mentor middle schools.

For Owens and the Tubman faculty, educating the whole child in middle school meant providing a familylike setting, increasing achievement dramatically, and promoting social justice activism. It meant struggling to redefine how schools respond to the often self-fulfilling term *at-risk student*. Tubman could be a good school, they believed, only if it helped children, families, and the neighborhood rise above poverty and discrimination. It had to be a hopeful place. So, Owens made clear that although teachers should be quick to reach out to students, they should do so in ways that would teach them to help themselves.

Like Family

Tubman faculty maintain the kind of structured environment that raising a large family takes. Owens explained, "I don't mind telling anybody that we are very structured; if we were not, the kids would not learn and they'd run us off." When the bell rings, students bustle quickly, laughing and jostling before depositing themselves in their next classes; there's no trace anywhere of the standard middle school favorites, gum and candy. Unlike the strict, adult-imposed military discipline at Mann, teachers stand by their doors watching the flow of students and chatting with other teachers. Monitors, walkie-talkies in hand, stand in hallway intersections keeping a watchful eye, sometimes quietly pulling students aside for reminders about strictly enforced rules. A polite "Sir" or "Ma'am" ends many a student remark to an adult.

Teacher Althea Mooney explained that she takes time in class to teach students how to properly address one another and their elders. She makes clear that this is all part of making the school more like home: "That's how we treat it. You would not do this in your home, and you're not going to do it here, and you would not talk to your Momma like that, and I'm certainly not going to let you talk to me like that."

Although not all teachers use Mooney's no-nonsense approach, nearly all employ "discipline" to promote academic achievement and healthy development. For example, Sarah Brown's more relaxed style lets Tubman students know that teachers understand their students' complex lives and are willing to listen and respond, or change:

> When [students] act out in class, a lot of times I don't send them straight to the office. . . . I will ask them . . . [to] step outside for a few minutes, and then I'll join them and I'll say, "Now, what's the problem? Is something happening at home? Is something wrong? Did I say something?" I'm going to go down this list of things . . . and "If you can, if it's something I'm doing, let me know what it is, and I'll stop it. But if it is something that's bothering you that you brought to school, I can deal with that too, but let me know, so I know not to step on your toes about that."

Down the hall, in Charla Walton's class, students turn each day to a well-worn sheet of paper; much like the Pledge of Allegiance, they chant together in powerful unison a creed about self-respect that Walton got from an inspirational Chicago teacher, Marva Collins.

Within this orderly environment, teachers display considerable affection for their students, offering them a pat on the back or a warm hug. For science teacher Tom Scott, one of the fundamentals is "to make a kid smile once a day as a result of something a teacher did." To help ease the harshness of students' lives, several teachers regularly bring students meals and school supplies. This kindness often extends beyond the school day, as teachers accompany students to church. Some teachers encourage students to call them at home and, on occasion, to join their families for meals. One regularly takes students home with her after school to earn money baby-sitting and then spend the night.

Empathy and Response: Keeping Standards High

Though acutely interested in easing students' tough lives, most Tubman faculty feel strongly that their hardships must not become excuses. In teacher Darla Smith's words, "You can't take the attitude that the kid is never going to do better." So for both substantive and political reasons, Owens and the faculty insist on the kind of student achievement that shows up on the state's standardized tests. The Texas Education Agency published a humiliating list of "low-performing schools" each year, and Tubman was determined not to be on it.[11] The school joined the College Board's Equity 2000 project to increase minority college-going by detracking mathematics; it also participated in the New Standards Project's effort to develop standards-based testing. The school-based "Helping Hand" project provided a college-preparatory course that offered guidance, preparation for entrance exams, and advice about financing college.

Worried about "low expectations on the part of we who are educators" for special education students, Owens included these students in regular classes and gave special education teachers a common planning period to help make the plan work. Working with the school psychologist and a counselor, Owens started a pull-out program for eight to fifteen students having particularly severe problems. No one wanted to "help" by creating a group identified as second-class students for the remainder of their middle school years, so the program made sure that struggling students rejoined their team in less than a year. "They do a marvelous job of getting those kids that are at risk to stay in school and introduce them to a lot of things," said one admiring teacher.

Continuity: Blurring School-Community Boundaries

Owens and her staff assumed that to act on the care they felt for their students, they must connect with parents and the community. Tubman parents helped with fund raising and school improvement projects and volunteered to work in the office and in classrooms. This involvement was not simply a service that parents were offering to the school. One parent explained, "We also get to know the kids in our neighborhood by volunteering at school, and I see them in stores, and they come and talk to me." The boundaries between the school and the community were permeable, so school became a place for parents and other community members to connect with students as they might in any other part of the community.

VOICES, a local community organizing project, shared Tubman's commitment to work within the community rather than trying to fix it. In Chapter Six, we describe how VOICES helped Tubman become a more participatory place. But we also found the VOICES association with Tubman reminiscent of Jane Addams's relations with her Hull House neighbors; relationships and shared commitment to improving community conditions drove their shared work. Through VOICES, Tubman linked with the local churches that played a vital role in community life. Ministers sat in Tubman classrooms to check up on students, and they would read the names of high-achieving students during Sunday morning services. Together with Tubman staff, they monitored students' academic progress and provided students support, giving them a true sense of continuity between school and community life. As one of the VOICES organizers explained, "the church can give credibility to the school by emphasizing it so much. It is a permanent part of community life."

Relationships between families, VOICES, and Tubman faculty were not pursued to make something else happen at Tubman, as is the case in many schools where parents offer schools a service or lend legitimacy to the school's operations (that is, so the school can say it had community input). One Tubman parent explained that "the school should belong to the community, which is different than controlling the school." An administrator agreed: "School is not separate. . . . They're realizing that home, school, and community, it's all in one. It's all part of their lives." Relationships at Tubman were worthwhile as ends in themselves—a clear confirmation of an ethic of care. As VOICES organizer Felicia Landers put it, "What's important is human dignity, a sense of community, and a sense of power in your life."

Few schools are able to cultivate the kind of community that allows faculty to be empathic and responsive supporters of children, families, and parents. Tubman did. So did Middleton Middle School, although in a very different way.

Middleton: Continuity Between Home and School

Adjacent to a Massachusetts metropolitan center, Middleton's city of about one hundred thousand takes pride in its diversity and public schools. As a result of a carefully crafted and much heralded districtwide voluntary integration program in the late 1970s, all of the Middleton community has, for more than two decades, maintained a racially balanced enrollment—half white and half students of color—and a reputation for strong academic programs. White flight, most Middleton citizens eagerly report, just hasn't been an issue. State funding was generously supplemented by local property taxes, resulting in a very comfortable resource base.

Nestled within a lightly wooded old neighborhood, Middleton's imposing concrete building stands in stark contrast to the modest, traditional homes that surround it. Both architecturally interesting and functional, the school's exterior is cubelike, punctuated with rows of steel-framed windows. Inside, youthful exuberance offsets the gray unfinished walls. Brightly colored bulletin boards and hand-lettered signs announcing upcoming events add warmth to exposed cinder block, as do the seven hundred K–8 students who scurry along hallways carpeted in primary colors, into the school's comfortable and well-equipped classrooms. If the student body were not so diverse, a visitor would probably guess Middleton to be an affluent, suburban school, much like Tanglewood (described in Chapter Four). Principal Wally Vincent assured us that, although the school is technically urban, it's far from a "classic inner-city school." Nevertheless, Middleton has its share of the tensions that diverse city schools face.

A brand new school by Massachusetts standards, the Middleton building opened in 1977. Over the years, it capitalized on its innovative physical design to respond to community demands for "school choice" with three smaller school-within-a-school K–8 programs. Families could select the progressive Follow-Through school (featuring multigraded classrooms and interdisciplinary, project-oriented curriculum), the Traditional Program, or the School of the Future (which integrated computer technology into the all subject areas). The Middleton plan worked, and its K–8 student body represents the ethnic and socioeconomic diversity of all areas of the city. However, although not as starkly segregated as Tubman Middle School in Texas, Middleton's progressive Follow-Through students are predominantly white and affluent, and its Traditional Program enrolls most of the school's minority and low-income kids.

By the early 1990s, when Wally Vincent became principal, the school was moving toward restructuring once again. Although the middle school reform movement was the primary impetus, some, including Vincent, were also eager to strike a better racial balance in the school's programs. He hoped to merge the sixth, seventh, and eighth graders from the three separate programs into a single interdisciplinary team at each grade. But creating a common school community out of these three programs, each with its history and supporters, would not be easy. A major challenge was changing a school that most parents did not see as broken—a task complicated by the fragility of the school's racial equanimity and overall stability. Many faculty were convinced that the Follow-Through parents, who closely scrutinized every aspect of the school's program, would no longer keep their children at the school without "their own private school" within the magnet.

The parents surprised nearly everyone by readily agreeing to the plan. Then, after intense months of planning, the middle school opened the following fall, with racially balanced teams and parents as happy as parents of middle schoolers ever are. One might wonder why these parents were so accommodating.

Vincent's accessibility to parents, his interest in them, and his respect for all the members of the school community over his first few years at the school had conveyed care and built enormous trust, which seemed to make change possible. As one teacher explained, "He did a lot of reaching out to parents"; still another says, "When parents come in and have a complaint or have something to say, he's accessible and willing to listen." This style, though perhaps more subdued than what we found at Carver and Tubman, sent a message to the entire school community that Middleton belonged to them. The trust between community and school evolved in such a way as to make clear that care comes far less from programs than from the ethic that pervades how educators respond to everyday events.

Responding to Parents

At the same time that Vincent accepted his post, in the summer of 1991, a politically powerful group of parents became outraged by the possibility of serious environmental contamination at Middleton. The school, built on a landfill, was being monitored regularly to detect any possible danger to student and staff health and safety; then a test detected methane vapors. Parents were worried that Middleton's ventilation system could not adequately remove toxic fumes that they feared would seep into the school. Some faculty were sure that this was simply another in a long line of frivolous parent complaints. One told us derisively, "the parents were really making a stink" by pressing the district to close the school and find an alternative site. Many suspected that the parents wanted the school closed anyway.

Vincent tackled the crisis head on, with listening and talk. He wondered whether the problem was primarily the environmental issues, or other agendas. He knew that parents had raised problems for a very long time. But he set aside any skepticism and worked hard to get to know the parents and listen to their concerns: "I had parents calling me at home, I had parents calling me when I was on vacation. I would drive home. I would drive over here in a minute. I went to homes, I went to meetings in houses. I knew that was something that had to be done. I had to reestablish the fact that the principal was not going to hold them at arm's length, but answer their questions. And if I couldn't answer them, it was my job to find someone who could."

Vincent's open, empathic style took everyone aback. Some anger remained, but most were relieved. He told us: "Most people interpreted it as, 'Finally, an outsider with no axe to grind wants to build an open and safe environment.' I attended many meetings, where I was able to convince people I wouldn't hold their complaints down. I was able to establish sincerity, credibility, with long, long hours."

After further testing, the fumes proved to be organic compounds that presented no danger. The leaky air conditioning system was twenty years old, so Vincent had it replaced. He used the crisis to build strong, supportive relationships with parents that would weather some uncertain times to follow. Sometime later, he told us: "In a way, the environmental situation was to my advantage as a manager because I was able to very quickly, and under emergency situations, establish credibility. Because I still think it was more of a communications issue than it was an environmental issue."

Knowing and Respecting the Whole Community

Vincent responded to his new faculty similarly. In essence, he dealt with the school's adults in the same way he wanted adults to deal with students. "I think the children need to be known by everybody that works with them," he told us. "Every single child needs to think, 'I'm known here,' and, 'I'm comfortable. . . .' I think it's important that those teachers know those kids. It's important that the kids know the teachers and know each other." He made a similar argument about his faculty: "I think the staff has to get to know each other in contexts outside the teachers' room. Get them in the gym for a volleyball game. Get them on an overnight. Go on a retreat. . . . They have to get to know each other in another light."

For Vincent, the same held true for parents; he needed to know them, and they needed to be known. "I have to be accessible," he told us. "I make phone calls, and I talk to people. Was it time-consuming and tiring to allow myself access to everybody? Yes it was, but it needed to be done."

Rather than solving problems for them, as Len Jacobi and Kate Pontello at Mann tried to do, Vincent empowered parents, including those of color who had not previously been part of the powerful parent teacher organization. Gently, he formed a new parent council that he hoped would be both "a policy-making board for the school" and an advocacy group for the school: "It won't just be the principal slamming the phone down and being frustrated and angry, but it will be the school council calling up the school committee [the district's school board] and saying, 'Are we going to be given the opportunity to manage this building, or are we still going to have to deal with somebody who doesn't care?'"

This wasn't simply about politics. Rather, Vincent wanted to build a community of talent that the school could draw on. "We talk about the talent pool of teachers; there is a talent pool of parents, too." To make sure that the new council would not be dominated by powerful white parents, Vincent purposely asked leaders of the PTO not to run: "I asked them not to run. I sat down with each one of them individually and explained why. I wanted people to look at the school council differently than they do the PTO. Everybody readily agreed; they understood exactly what I wanted."

Vincent then "beat the bushes," in one teacher's words, recruiting prospective members from each of Middleton's other programs. The schoolwide election yielded a diverse council, with two parents from each program.

Over time, the new council developed a set of core values for the school and pressed ahead with middle-grade reform. Later, when the newspaper published an article exposing how most of the city's so-called desegregated schools maintained considerable racial isolation, Middleton wasn't among them. Vincent told us: "Our school wasn't mentioned because not only is the whole school balanced but all three programs are. . . . That was out of efforts of the school council, and myself. About a year ago, the council asked the student-assignment person to come to our meeting, which he did, and he worked closely with us. I stand up at every meeting I can and say that the best-balanced program in this city is my middle school—in terms of racial and economic balance."

Importantly, Middleton's relationships weren't all about hard work and seriousness. The school community also had fun. They held parent dances, auctions, and an international potluck dinner that drew about 250 people, who came in costume and brought a dish and some music from their homeland. They had a Cinco de Mayo night that was well attended by families from all backgrounds. Each year, Vincent and his wife hosted the Middleton faculty, staff, and their families at a huge Christmas party. Vincent's relentless pursuit not just of parent involvement but of knowing everyone well created a new set of norms at Middleton: that students and parents were to be listened to, that teachers and parents should be partners in solving problems, and that the school should be a reflection of the community—a shared undertaking in a caring place.

How Reform Made Caring Easier

Some of the specific reforms recommended by *Turning Points*—teaming, student advisory programs, "looping," and child-centeredness—helped schools become caring places, as we shall see below. But reforms were not enough; caring reforms in themselves do not make caring schools.

Routine and trivial activities at typical schools may become powerful foci for reform at others. Conversely, large-scale, heavily organized programs with the loftiest-sounding objectives may turn out to be entirely routine, doing little to change prior relationships or bring people closer. Many factors might go into the chemistry of how members of school communities interact, feel committed, distribute power, and so on. Schools with many people participating in many activities have opportunities to learn more about one another's needs; they can nurture closer relationships than schools with pro forma, one-way, or token interactions. Though not a prescription, a principal who is determined to beat the bushes is to be preferred over one who rationalizes low levels of participation.

Teaming: Creating Small Communities

The most important school structure implemented in our schools was teacher teaming. Although it was often described as a strategy to help teachers integrate their instruction, teaming fostered a climate of support for students and teachers alike. Teachers at more than half of our schools, serving the entire range of student populations, told us that teaming helped them get to know students better and changed how they thought about children. As one Tubman teacher put it, "They are more yours. You are looking out for their welfare because you can track them all day long, and you know that their other teachers are looking out for them also."

According to one teacher at suburban Canyon Middle School in California, teaming also allowed teachers "to really look at each child as an individual, talk about their needs, try to meet those needs." Teaming enabled teachers to share more than information; they found a way of sharing skills with one another. The mutual support that teammates could extend to one another not only meant there was less chance that students would fall through the cracks but also had an impact on students' classroom behavior (as we discuss in Chapter Eight).

Student Advisory Programs: Knowing All Students Well

Formal advisory programs complemented teaming practices at more than half of our schools. In general, advisory programs were designed to meet students' emotional and social needs by cultivating closer bonds between teachers and students, giving students opportunities to know a teacher in a nonacademic setting, and allowing students and teachers to discuss issues not ordinarily confronted in a classroom. Many schools rearranged the school day to incorporate a formal advisory time, much like a homeroom period although with a purposeful program of activities. The depth and quality of relationships in advisory programs is what mattered, however; the mere existence of a program did not ensure growth, empathy, response, or continuity.

Looping: Continuity over Time

Maintaining close teacher-student relationships was the foundation of reform at a number of the schools. At Verbena, teachers stayed with students for three years. At schools without formal advisory programs—Carver, Madison, and Mitchell—some teachers took on a similar role to meet students' needs for connecting. At Mitchell, teachers and students stayed together on teams for two years (grades five and six, and seven and eight), and the idea of an advisory program seemed redundant because teachers were able to build close teacher-student relationships over the longer time period. Doris Davis and Roberta Simms took great advantage of the two-year teaming structure. Davis explained: "Two years ago, the last group that left us—I hadn't cried when a group left in many years, and that year we did . . . both of us did. We absolutely loved that group, absolutely loved them, they were wonderful. But some of the things that we did with them, and were able to do with them, I hadn't been able to do in a long time."

As described in Chapter Three, Davis and Simms shared a classroom with fifty students and worked from the very beginning of each two-year cycle to provide a consistent, supportive environment that meant multiple opportunities for students to take charge of their learning and behavior. Although the duo never allocated time for "advisory," they were constantly adjusting and readjusting their teaching and their individual and collective interactions with students to address students' academic and nonacademic needs and maintain close contact with all of them. They regularly talked to their students about health issues, linked with the school counselor on a self-esteem unit, and always reminded students that what they were learning in class had value beyond the classroom walls. As Davis commented: "We always tell them, 'You're learning this for the rest of your life, not just to pass sixth grade. This is for always.'"

Child Centeredness: Centering Learning in Real Life

Turning Points' emphasis on child-centered pedagogy supported teachers' efforts to encourage discussion of teen issues and students' real-life experiences. These experiences could be incorporated as relevant elements of the curriculum. One Chavez teacher said, "I think it's great that you can integrate the education with their lives and not just say, 'This is my agenda and I'm going to teach you this.'" As one Tubman teacher put it: "You're not just trying to pour this information into these little heads, you know. You're trying to teach the child, not the [subject]." Teachers had students work in cooperative learning groups because they felt it was important for students to learn to work as team members in society.

Many interdisciplinary units took advantage of the community as a laboratory for student study, exploration, and service. In so doing, caring teachers saw and treated students as having lives outside the fifty or eighty minutes a day in their classrooms. Students participated in multiple community service learning activities, particularly in Massachusetts, where students at all of the schools we studied engaged in such activities as serving meals to families and working with the elderly, the homeless, and young children. Mountain View and Mann students also worked on environmental projects. Community service learning opportunities both acknowledged students' roles as community members and brought the school into the center of community life. As one Mountain View teacher remarked, "There's a definite need for children to be involved in their community and to give back to the community in some way."

Caring Beyond Reform: Beyond the School Day and School Yard

Some school communities extended their care far beyond what any reform would dare suggest: "You're mom, you're counselor, you're dad, you're grandma, you're everybody." This statement, from a teacher at Harriet Tubman, captures the extraordinary level of care we saw at several schools.

At Cesar Chavez, in California, for example, teachers and staff knew their Latino immigrant students outside of school; many relationships lasted well beyond the students' middle-grade years. Chavez teachers spent long hours before and after school—and on weekends in some cases—as tutors, companions, mentors, and big brothers or sisters; as many as twenty Chavez teachers roller-skated with students on weekends. One Chavez staff member "adopted" a pregnant sixth grade student and made sure she had proper prenatal care, emotional support, and admission to the teen mother school. She even took the girl to the delivery room. "Her way of saying thank you," this staff member told us, "was to name the baby after me. . . . That's how deep I am with these kids. I dance at their weddings, they name their children after me."

Teachers found support for such extraordinary caring from one another. Teaming afforded them collaborative support for professional growth, gave them ownership over their work, and allowed them to connect school with their out-of-school values and interests. But caring did not arise from a team's organization. Rather, teaming reinforced a family feeling; teacher teams often compared their relations to marriages. Mitchell's Roberta Simms explained, "We [Doris Davis and I] do agree on a lot of things. Nobody's perfect, but we agree on those kinds of basic goals, like in a marriage, where you have the same goals for the future, the same goals for life." Like a good marriage, good teams helped reduce teacher stress and burnout as their roles expanded. One Mountain View teacher said, "It was very enlightening to find out that, at times, we all had a similar problem. . . . In the past we were all isolated and felt that it was maybe something we were doing wrong."

With such relationships, teachers found renewed energy for teaching and greater willingness to experiment and take risks. One Middleton teacher remarked: "There's tremendous power when adults get together and plan together. . . . The ideas just fly. People are able to start each other and inspire each other and think of some things that they weren't able to think of before."

Such teaming relationships energized even some veteran teachers. A Canyon teacher told us about a meeting the previous evening with her teammate. "[We] spent three hours together, and I got so excited that I didn't sleep all night. My adrenaline was going—and I've been teaching for seventeen years." Eloquently expressing what so many told us, she continued: "Just having a peer to work with that you respect [helps] you know the education that you're going to be giving your students is going to be above anything that you can imagine."

Why Didn't Reform Help More?

Care is no small feat. Caring simultaneously for children and adults means that sometimes the needs of one group must be asserted over the needs of the other. Expanding professional roles to address students' broader needs, as we saw at Mann, often drove schools to place students' nonacademic needs ahead of their academic needs. Even when educators agreed that they should avoid creating hierarchies of needs, they could not evade demands for rising test scores or high school readiness. In addition, communities and schools do not always agree on which needs are most important or how to best address them.

Competing Needs

Lacking time and human and financial resources, schools relied on teachers who were willing to give more of themselves than could realistically be expected. For example, advisory programs frequently pitted teachers' needs against those of their students. Advisory programs often left teachers feeling ill-equipped to deal with students' personal problems, or feeling that they had to take on an extra class. Burdened by the heavy demands of reform, teachers at Townsend, Carver, Mountain View, and Inland resisted advisory programs or turned them into study halls that teachers would supervise (and try to catch up on some grading or other paperwork) rather than use as an opportunity to form closer relationships with students.

Teachers did not necessarily resist hard work as much as they disagreed with priorities. Many teachers, such as a number at Mountain View, bristled when advisory time was taken out of core teaching time. One veteran science teacher argued: "I'm not going to take time out, nobody is going to take time out of a core class to do that, nobody. I guard my core time jealously. . . . I want them to learn science when I have them."

Similarly, although teachers generally favored teaming, it was difficult for many schools to give teachers time for shared planning. Union contracts, scheduling issues, financial difficulties, and sometimes only tepid interest on the part of teachers and administrators all exacerbated the problem of finding time to meet during the school day. District budget cuts meant that teachers at Carver and Mountain View actually lost planning time. Even when teacher teams had shared planning time, many teachers objected to forced meetings. Some felt that time spent on individual work was more worthwhile than "giving away" their time to the team. One Tanglewood teacher thought that team planning limited her classroom creativity: "Sometimes you feel like you don't have time to sit back and say, 'Instead of just teaching this out of the book, how could I be more creative in teaching it?'" Some teams simply compensated by focusing their planning time on issues that reduced their work but did little to make their teaching practice responsive.

Competing Educational Values

Calls for high-stakes testing, national teaching standards, and teacher competency tests are aimed at increasing accountability and permitting the public some measure of quality control. Similarly, many calls for greater teacher collaboration seek strengthened professional communities as an accountability mechanism against incompetent teachers. *Turning Points* sought a different approach to improving teaching and learning, one partly predicated on strengthening interpersonal relationships. Nevertheless, teachers could not fully escape the impact of the prevailing educational environment: the tyranny of high-stakes testing, the push to recertify all middle-grade teachers, the demands of high school readiness. Thus, when many principals and teachers spoke about middle school reforms, they referred to them as markers of effective practice, rather than moral practices that emphasize growth, empathy, responsibility, and continuity.

Teachers' commitment to an ethic of care was also challenged at the classroom level. Although the addition of elementary credentialed staff at Chavez, Carver, and Van Buren brought "a more caring, kid-oriented perspective rather than a subject-oriented perspective," teachers often told us their actions were guided by state frameworks and district guidelines, not students' needs or interests. This conformity might please some reform advocates, but they should not be greatly heartened. To us, it echoed of hollow compliance, generating little of the energy and passion teachers exhibited when they were driven by an institutional and personal ethic of care.

Too often, shallow compliance with the reform agenda meant teachers spent countless hours on the routines of cooperative learning or thematic units while paying little attention to whether students learned to take an active and interested role in their learning and evaluation. Likewise, teachers often mistook students who were engaged with lessons and having fun to mean that students were learning something worthwhile. As Mitchell's superintendent, Ray Fierro, argued: "I think they [teachers] use a lot of activity in lieu of substantive, hard, rigorous learning. . . . Learning can be fun, . . . but if you want to look like Arnold Schwarzenegger, don't think you're not gonna sweat, and if you want to be like Albert Einstein, don't think you're not gonna sweat intellectually."

Competing Social Values

Caring schools often engendered resistance from parents and school boards that felt individual freedoms were threatened by expanded school roles. For example, conservative parents, school boards, and political forces—fearing promotion of sexual behavior—blocked new health and social service roles at Tubman and other schools. Of course, parents and others who could make best use of these expanded services did not necessarily defend their use, and sometimes schools had the difficult job of both selling the service to those who might benefit from it and fighting to be allowed to continue to provide the service. For example, although Tubman and Mann used eligible students' Medicaid and Chapter 1 funds to pay for on-site health services, parents at Tubman and other schools were often leery of public agencies and failed to follow through on referrals. They could not be counted on to be a vocal force for maintaining the services against active opposition.

In a political climate that emphasizes individual responsibility and limitation of public support to meet individual needs, few schools could feel secure that their programs would continue to be funded. The list of services cut from schools in our study is about as long as the list of surviving services. It includes a variety of health programs as well as nurses, counselors, attendance officers, home visitors, transportation, supervision, tutoring . . . and the list goes on. Yet caring schools would sometimes move with astonishing ease (though with substantial regret and anger) from a cut or diminished service to a new service or a new configuration of an old one.

Competing Goods

Schools differed in their acceptance of responsibility for students' broad needs and varied widely in how they acted upon these responsibilities. Some schools, like Mann, treated students' needs as deficiencies that prevented competent development; others, like Tubman, Carver, and Chavez, regarded similar needs as part of students' growth and ongoing development.

Recasting parental involvement was not easy. As we saw in Chapter Three, school leaders in white and wealthy communities had an especially difficult time wrestling with the tension between parental involvement and parental control—keeping parents involved enough to garner support for reform, but not so much that they would take over. In diverse schools, some veteran teachers described parental involvement in terms of what parents could and were willing to do to help schools and teachers achieve their goals. One Townsend teacher expressed her frustration: "[The parents] you call don't want to talk to you. They don't want to hear about it." Ironically, some poorer and less educated parents, believing that the school did not want to be bothered by them and therefore feeling they were deferring to the authority of school professionals, contributed to the view of some staff that parents did not care. In each of these examples, parental involvement was treated as individual currency—a vote at a PTO meeting, or a stern reprimand at home for classroom misbehavior—rather than a norm of a caring and inclusive school community.

Much tension was the inevitable result of renegotiating participation and power. Schools spent a good deal of their energies seeking equilibrium between their frontal pursuit of the common good and opposition from those whose conception of the common good is derived from individual students and families' cumulatively pursuing their own individual interests. At half of the schools, affluent parents and parents of higher-achieving students were more likely to participate. As schools broadened the scope of care to include all students, the parents of traditionally successful groups of students felt that their own children might lose some advantages. The strategies used by these traditionally influential parents and other reform opponents varied. A common tack was to exert political pressure by using low test scores to show that schools were not fulfilling their academic mission. Sometimes parents relied on anecdotal reports of their children being unchallenged or bored.

Teachers faced similar tensions in their classrooms, particularly in the diverse schools, where defining those needs was more complicated than in schools serving relatively homogeneous populations. Townsend and Inland—two schools with a history of serving affluent, predominantly white populations—fought to convince parents that all students could be served in a heterogeneously grouped classroom. As we saw in Chapter Four, Ben McCall was successful in leading his teachers in understanding the need to offer a high-quality curriculum to all Inland students, but Harold Nance encountered staunch resistance from Townsend's veteran faculty when he tried to force through similar reforms (as Chapter Six describes in detail). These teachers used high test scores (relative to other schools in their district) to argue that the reforms advocated by Nance were unnecessary.

Many of the tensions surrounding classroom reform centered on issues of power: who has it and how it should best be used to create a caring school. The very words *power* and *care* may seem antithetical, but changing the relationships between schools and communities, teachers and parents, teachers and administrators, teachers and their colleagues, and teachers and students challenged conventional notions of schooling and made fertile ground for confrontation. As principals and teacher leaders searched for the proper pace and direction of reform, they fought to balance the school's academic and social functions. At the same time, political pressure from the state, district, and community levels meant that the buck stopped at the principal's desk; caring leadership came face-to-face with the external press for cutting-edge reform and the public's demand for better test scores.

Strengthening Relationships and Developing Communities

These days, one cannot escape hearing that American society is in trouble. For many, a lost sense of community is to blame. Remarkably, but perhaps not surprisingly, this rhetoric of lost community is not unlike that heard near the turn of the century, when massive waves of "unassimilable" immigrants—the individuals Jane Addams and her colleagues cared for—came to this country. Now as then, families—particularly poor families—are also viewed as culpable for the moral decline of our nation. Usually, it does not take long for public schools to receive their share of blame. Lacking a state church, it is left to public schools in our country to socialize America's youth—who are so often referred to as "the future."

All the schools in our study labored to redefine the school in caring terms to address these concerns. They worked hard to break down artificial barriers between school and community; teachers reached out to students by creating nurturing learning environments and linking student learning to the world beyond the classroom. These changes required more than structural innovation. Teachers took risks to care—to develop open and trusting relationships among colleagues, school leaders, and the larger community.

America's faith in individual achievement contributes to a view that individual, caring teachers make and break schools—and, by extension, the future. Pop culture is filled with images of teacher as savior. The broad appeal of teachers—we need only mention Jaime Escalante of *Stand and Deliver* fame—is testimony to the popular view that good teachers can overcome the conditions in which they work. Although the teachers we studied—particularly those in high-poverty schools—did make a difference in the lives of their students and communities, it would be wrong to conclude that any of these teachers did it alone. Teaming, administrative and community support, and ongoing professional development fostered trust and experimentation rather than compliance and standardization.

We see in these schools that reformers must be ever mindful of potential dangers in creating schools as caring community centers. In some communities, such creations can breed the kind of moral superiority that turns even well-intentioned educators—like those at Mann—into enablers of lowered expectations. In others, parents may choose to take their children out of public schools that they view as overstepping their bounds in passing down the wrong values, sending them instead to private and religious schools or keeping them close by for home schooling.

To guard against these and other disappointing effects of reform, parents and policy makers must engage in a sustained public discourse—largely absent today—about the common good, individual freedoms, and the meaning of caring American institutions.

Chapter Six

| **Becoming Participatory**

Thomas Jefferson posed the ideal of a democracy in which every citizen participates in public affairs, not just at the ballot box but every day. Jefferson (and more recently Martin Luther King, Jr.) wanted ordinary citizens to engage actively in public affairs. Their participation must entail more than climbing onto a bandwagon or following a charismatic leader. Clearly, King's twentieth-century conception of grassroots activism for reformed social policy was far more inclusive than Jefferson's eighteenth-century view of citizens making dispassionate judgments about their leaders. But both sought a public sphere in which free and enlightened people—who may differ in their backgrounds, resources, and interest—work together to solve public problems, advance the common good, and shape the direction of the democracy.

As it is to the public goods of well-educated citizens, inclusive institutions, and caring communities, however, American's commitment to participatory democracy is ambivalent. King's popular legacy, constructed as much by social elites as by the people King sought to empower, obscures the pivotal connections he drew between power and participation. King sought to mitigate unrestrained marketplace participation, with its inevitable winners and losers, by way of the moral argument and force of collective action. Further, the target of this collective action was not confined to social conditions of the moment; it extended to future generations and distant communities. For King, participation was

We are indebted to Jennifer Gong for her significant contributions to earlier versions of this chapter.

both a vehicle for demonstrating collective will and a way of being—of living one's life—that combined personal dignity and high social purpose.

The call for participation that reemerged in the comprehensive school-restructuring reforms in the late 1980s is reflected more in superficial structures than in the core intentions of King and the civil rights movement. Some reform strategies tried to break from this trend, which cast participation as an instrument for getting people to buy into corporate or institutional ends without examining the full social consequences of their participation. *Turning Points*, the Coalition for Essential Schools, Accelerated Schools, the Comer schools, and others placed collective inquiry and action at the heart of a democratic reform process. *Turning Points* suggested, for example, that values of mutual support, equality, and appreciation could open genuine opportunities for traditionally disadvantaged parents to participate in the educational process. The cultural press to dampen or extinguish these goals of participation has been fierce—and largely successful. But we saw, shining through the dark and frustrating reform landscape, glimmers of democratic participation that let us know why these schools found the struggle worthwhile.

Most of us have sat in school and community meetings—school site councils, parent advisory groups, or committees with delegations of parents, teachers, and others—where participants were expected to share the power and responsibility for creating good schools. We listen to presentations and vote for or against them. Sometimes we leave these meetings feeling that we contributed something important, that we are wiser and more connected to a larger group; other times we leave none the wiser and alienated. In our study of middle schools, such meetings represented the bulk of the schools' efforts to be participatory and to empower those who were typically able to exercise little power. Does such participation signify reform? When we examine them closely, we find that these gatherings were always under the press to maintain the schools' existing practices and relationships, even when their goal was reform.

For example, do such structures actually break down traditional authority relationships and lead to more equal power sharing within schools? Do they allow diverse participants to rise above their self-interested perspectives and make decisions with an eye to the common good? Have these schools become places where citizens can participate every day in the way that Jefferson hoped they would? Are they settings where democracy can be lived as well as learned, to paraphrase Dewey's ideal? Or where ordinary citizens can gain access to and shape public institutions, as King sought?

Nearly all of the schools we studied embraced in principle the idea of teachers, parents, and community members being involved in instructional decisions and in school-based management and shared governance. Nearly all formed new policy-making bodies to institutionalize comparatively egalitarian decision-making structures and processes. To a degree, these councils, teacher committees, and parent associations did reflect a press for greater, and more democratic, participation. Indeed, we include in this chapter examples of participation that were driven by a democratic and inclusive passion for the public good and sustained by face-to-face relationships among parents, teachers, consultants, and others. In these instances, democratic participation became a way of life in the schools. Democratic relationships sometimes brought important shifts in educators' and parents' roles and the work they were able to accomplish for students.

On the other hand, much that we saw did not reflect civic virtue. Representation often became a proxy for the virtue that reformers sought. Schools occasionally created the participatory structures called for in reform—teams and site-based governance committees—but these structures rarely gave people the means to sustain substantial reform. The meeting, the vote, the training, and the shared responsibilities were clouded by bureaucratic, budgetary, and political constraints that failed to promote—and in some instances extinguished—the personal relationships that must form the core of participation. Rarely was power really thought about or distributed differently than it had been before. This is what we saw in most schools, though not all of them.

Participation and Civic Virtue as Reform

Like most other national, state, and local reform initiatives, *Turning Points* was unequivocal in its support for participatory school practices. These reforms argued that participation would result in more effective and more efficient decisions. Greater effectiveness would result from having those closest to classrooms and students make decisions about students. Greater efficiency would result by freeing schools from a stifling array of bureaucratic processes and regulations that mark typical top-down, district-office governance.

Reformers also argued that participation would make schools more democratic and more virtuous. Making parents and community members active participants in the work of the school would help create a shared vision—often called a mission—for the school, reduce the school's isolation from the community, and foster a climate of trust, respect, and common purpose. Participation could also lead parents and educators to become more powerful citizens generally. Partnerships with community agencies and businesses would promote youth service activities and health and social services. They would garner additional resources for school programs and further communitywide responsibility for all students.

Moreover, these benefits would have a salutary effect on students. Echoing Dewey's argument that democracy requires students to participate in schools and classrooms that are themselves democratic societies, *Turning Points* asserted "students who witness teachers making decisions and discussing important ideas can envision what it is like to participate in decision making. Increasingly, they can become part of decisions affecting their education. . . . The empowerment of school staff is a necessary and desirable step in creating a transformed middle grade school that produces responsible, ethical, and participating future citizens."[1]

We met many educators in the schools and state projects who themselves had an intense respect for participatory practices as a route to socially just institutions. However, they did not seem to come by these practices as a result of the culture of their schools. Instead, many appeared to develop their democratic and participatory practices in places other than their schools or education agencies. For example, several—among them, Nancy Nelson at Carver and Len Jacobi at Mann, whom we met in previous chapters—had powerful memories of exhilarating participation in movements for social betterment; many Latino, black, and white educators hearkened to the social-activist movements of the 1960s as the inspiration for their teaching. Others—including Carver's Bethany Houston and Tubman's Rebecca Owens—brought from their church experience a trust and sense of common purpose that they could apply to their schooling work.

This chapter explores what happened when educators implemented participatory structures in their schools. As the accounts here illustrate, schools established committees so teachers or teams of teachers could help make decisions that were previously the purview of administrators. Some councils and partnerships included parents, community agencies, and local businesses in shaping school policies and addressing the health and safety matters that jeopardized students. As we saw in the last chapter, Harriet Tubman Middle School joined forces with a community organizing group to address the academic and social problems. But simply creating participatory structures and processes did not make these schools empowering or socially just; in fact, the new structures and processes typically reflected, or even reinforced, preexisting organizational or social hierarchies.

Authentic democratic participation implies opportunities for self-reflective, critical inquiry, where participants engage in open and egalitarian deliberation about ideas and knowledge.[2] It suggests that schools and communities should develop relationships that build on the strengths of those with less power, advancing civic virtue by having diverse groups work together to solve public problems. The exercise of voice and deliberation can take many forms in different sociocultural contexts, but nowhere should they be undermined by experts or by those who would coerce them into participating in someone else's agenda.[3]

For the most part, we found little of this sort of participation in schools. Some principals tried to use their governance groups to legitimate what they wanted to do in the first place. Even those with strong commitments to reform were caught in an institutional bind and very cautious about relinquishing control. These principals worried that if they gave up some of their authority, they would end up with less power to accomplish important objectives. They continued to be held responsible by district offices for traditional outcomes and processes while being directed to include new decision makers who had no such accountability.

In some cases, educators with power treated the parents and community members whose participation they sought as "clients," dependent on the school for expertise or goodwill, rather than as equal partners. A few administrators simply ignored or overturned what their teachers or community partners wanted. Finally, sometimes resistance to giving up control came from those who also protested they had *too little* power. Since it was inevitable that power-sharing activities would sometimes be frustrating and acrimonious, participants often lost patience with the process and complained that the principal should make the decision.

Few schools could breach the entrenched habits that allowed nonteachers to discuss some topics (for example, homework or tardy policies) while reserving for teachers the more fundamental, "professional" matters (such as teaching practices or curriculum). Firm boundaries often preserved the individual rights of teachers and worked against collective efforts for socially just school practices, especially those that required public, outspoken support. A powerful ethic prevailed for supporting a colleague's autonomy even if it hindered one's own commitment to reform; the positive spin given to this support was to declare that everyone cares about the kids and has her own way of doing good work.

Despite these negative pressures, we also saw illuminating evidence of direct participation. In a number of schools, efforts to increase participation did allow groups to make concrete their vision for transformed practice and to develop agreements about how they would work collectively to achieve it. When this happened, and when participants actually worked together over time to implement their agreements, they developed new relationships built on familiarity and shared experiences in their joint work. Instead of jockeying for power and protecting self-interest, people carrying on joint work could generate the collective power needed to solve problems. Over time, such relationships also allowed participants to grapple openly with dilemmas of teaching and involving parents—dilemmas that usually remain behind closed doors if attended to at all. It was also in these relationships that educators could begin to consider how their practices intersected with questions of social justice.

However, these instances of direct participation had to exist alongside, or embedded within, larger organizational environments that followed familiar hierarchical reporting and accountability patterns in which a few individuals would represent and speak for a constituency. These representative groups often limited their deliberations to formulating policies, making plans, and writing grants or reports; they left it to others to enact the policies. Not surprisingly, there was often slippage or lack of fidelity between the work of the executive decision makers and those they counted on to carry out policy. Our observations suggest a pattern: when individuals' interests were represented by others, they were less likely to learn from and inform the participatory process and less likely to form new relationships. When individuals spoke for themselves, they were more likely to work with others and further a collective vision for their schools. In this way, the instances of direct participation we observed allowed both individual expression and collective work.

The stories of four schools reveal how participation thrust them into the cultural contradiction between individualistic and collective visions of the meaning and exercise of power. Educators at Townsend Middle School and Harriet Tubman in Texas, Martin Van Buren in Vermont, and James Madison in Massachusetts all worked enormously hard to develop highly visible strategies for increasing participation. Townsend charged a new schoolwide governance team with developing the school's reform policies. Van Buren turned most of its reform decisions over to small teams of teachers. Madison sought to increase parent participation. Tubman joined forces with a grassroots community group, organizing parents to take action that would improve the school and the neighborhood. Townsend's and Madison's efforts fell considerably short of the participatory ideals. In both of these schools, participation deteriorated into power struggles that distracted everyone from the reform agenda. Though not perfect, Van Buren's and Tubman's experiences provide hopeful examples. In these two schools, we saw participants working together to create power to solve important school problems.

Townsend Middle School: Seeking Schoolwide Consensus

In the mid-1980s, newly built Townsend Middle School drew its students from prosperous nearby suburbs. Test scores were among the best in the district, and the popular principal helped the school win a Successful School award from the Texas Education Agency.

All that changed by the early 1990s. Rapid growth in the city's population, migration of many white families into the suburbs, and changed attendance boundaries following construction of another school left Townsend, in the mind of one district administrator, more like an inner-city middle school. The faculty felt daunted by their new students' hardships. One noted that "[students] see people selling drugs all the time and stuff like that, shootings, killings, all the time. . . . Just being here every day is an [accomplishment] in itself."

To grapple with these changes, the district assigned Harold Nance—an inexperienced, young African American principal—to, as one teacher put it, "bring [the faculty] into the twenty-first century." Passionate about equity issues, Nance arrived at Townsend eager to persuade the teachers that middle school reforms would enable them to extend the school's prior success to its low-achieving and lower-income, minority students. He was sure that small, student-oriented learning teams, block scheduling, interdisciplinary curriculum, heterogeneous grouping, cooperative learning, and advisory programs would serve the school's changing student body.

The Townsend faculty wasn't convinced. Some younger teachers were eager to try reforms, but most of the veterans considered themselves already effective. Many thought that the only hope for preserving Townsend's success lay in stressing traditional content, rewarding students on academic merit, and providing a tough administrative response to discipline problems. Nance's proposals, they believed, threatened all of these practices and would compromise the middle-class students who had done well at Townsend in the past.

Shared Governance to Spur Reform

In line with new Texas state policy mandating site-based governance, Townsend's district decreed that each school create a site governance council. Townsend's twelve-member council (made up of teachers elected by each department, a librarian, an assistant principal, a counselor, two parents, and a manager of a local business) would meet every other Thursday from 7:30 to 8:00 A.M.

Nance decided to piggyback his own reform goals onto to this state and district initiative. He would use Townsend's new council, he decided, to forge a consensus among the school's divided faculty in support of middle-grade reform. His role would be "keeping the pot stirred" with powerful reform ideas and advising the group about "what the research says" in ways that would make clear that the reforms he advocated were what the school needed. So, before each meeting, Nance distributed background readings on reform, in addition to the list of agenda items submitted by team members and others in the school.

The group's work did not proceed as Nance had hoped. Teachers filled the meager thirty-minute meetings with requests that seemed far afield from reform. Faculty wanted the council to develop new policies about lockers, pep rallies, backpacks, and dress codes. They wanted tougher procedures for dealing with student absences, tardies, late homework, and graffiti. Some teachers asked the council to come up with a way to make sure that every teacher monitored the hallways during passing periods—a school policy that was ignored by some faculty members, much to the outrage of others. Some wanted the council to develop criteria for assigning at-risk students to classes that would not load up some teachers with more than their fair share.

Late starts often shortened the already-brief meetings, and the cofacilitators raced through the agenda, trying to devote at least some time to the readings Nance provided, as well as to all of the agenda items submitted by teachers. In addition, the council fought over what items should be discussed, in what order, and for what length of time—as well as over the substance of issues. Some team members complained that philosophical discussion of the principles underlying the reforms diverted attention from concrete concerns. Pro- and antireform forces staked out clear positions and argued heatedly.

Not surprisingly, most of the governance team's business went unfinished, and the group formed a raft of ad hoc subcommittees to follow up. In the end, a frustrated Nance made most of the decisions himself, sometimes overriding months of intense subcommittee work and compromises. For example, one group worked for more than a year, investigating the potential benefits and drawbacks of block scheduling—a reform that Nance strongly favored. Their report persuaded the larger governance team that block scheduling would require the faculty to give up too much else that they valued if they implemented the change. Determined to change their minds, Nance kept lobbying for the change—bringing in experts, arranging for visits to schools where teachers were happy teaching in blocks, and putting literature that favored block scheduling into their mailboxes. Eventually, he wore them down.

Instances such as this confirmed for many team members that their views mattered little. Some asked Nance to let them know ahead of time if he'd already made up his mind, so that they wouldn't waste their time. But he refused, arguing that doing so would hamper the group's open and free deliberation. With time and a growing sense that nothing important could come from these meetings, the disagreements (though no less sharp) ended up hidden behind silence as opponents simply let one another talk.

Disaffection with the governance team was not confined to members. The contentious debate spilled over into the rest of the faculty when council representatives reported back to their constituents. Some teachers joked derisively about "site-based indecision." Others complained that their interests were not represented in the meetings because members didn't talk with them or ask for feedback. One teacher told us: "There are a lot of bad feelings that the leadership team is sort of a clique. So it's not working. It's a joke. . . . We get less of a voice as a faculty." Others charged that they only heard slanted accounts of the meetings and that written minutes were not telling the whole story. Few trusted the team to decide important issues, and most preferred to deliberate controversial issues privately with like-minded colleagues. Rather than developing schoolwide consensus about what and how to reform, the team enlarged the breach among faculty. The controversy it fostered left the teachers who favored change feeling even more burdened when they tried to reform, and it made those who opposed change worry that payback for their resistance was just ahead.

Much Ado About Little

Not surprisingly, reform at Townsend proceeded slowly, buried in meetings about process, structures, and logistics. Four years after

Nance arrived, Townsend adopted a planning process based on the Accelerated Schools model, switched to block scheduling, and hired several new teachers interested in change. However, many teachers continued to charge that Nance wanted change just for change's sake. One argued that he was pushing change "just to be different, to be in vogue, to be modern or whatever . . . whether it works or not." Many veterans argued that the pressure to change encroached upon their professional judgments and that reform was being "shoved down their throats." More discouraging, even those teachers who were themselves interested in making changes in what and how they taught were very reluctant to engage less-reform-minded colleagues in such discussions. The painful price of such discussions seemed just too high, even if they might lead to important schoolwide changes in practice.

The deep philosophical differences at Townsend were clouded by racial politics. The school's minority student enrollment had increased dramatically, and a reform-minded African American principal had taken the leadership reins from a much-loved, traditional, white administrator. Both of these changes led many powerful, mostly white parents to worry that the reforms were being mounted on behalf of low-income children of color, and that any changes would necessarily disadvantage their own children. It is not clear whether any participatory governance strategy could have bridged these deep divides unless matters of race were made as salient to the reform goals as curriculum, schedules, and other more comfortable school-specific topics. Certainly, these racial issues profoundly complicated the reform conversation at Townsend.

Keeping the Private Hidden

What is clear, however, is that Nance and the Townsend faculty never found or created a participatory forum in which they could elevate their differences from private opinions and personal blame to institutional and societal problems that could be publicly probed and turned into an agenda of shared work. The group exhausted its time and energy by perseverating over who had the power to make decisions. Time was spent rehashing safe and familiar (even perennial) matters such as tardiness. Without shared intellectual and programmatic work, relationships stood little chance of developing, and without strengthened relationships there could be little trust and incentive for taking personal or institutional risks. Issues of race, educational opportunity, and fairness for the school's diverse and changing student body pressed heavily on Townsend's faculty and community; yet they never came close to serious, public deliberation and action about making the school socially just. One should not conclude that Townsend tried and failed at such deliberation and action. Rather, the organizing principles of social justice and civic virtue were visions that never rose above the horizon long enough to capture the collective imagination of the school community.

Unfortunately, Townsend's experience was not unique. Teachers at Carver, Canyon, and Tanglewood told strikingly similar stories of failed attempts to use shared decision making to spur reform. For a more hopeful account, we turn to Martin Van Buren Middle School in Vermont. At Van Buren, Principal Bob Davenport gave teams of teachers control over the policies that affect their teaching: scheduling, discipline, curriculum, budgets, student advising, and communication with parents. Schoolwide decisions developed from an iterative process in which teams would discuss issues, team leaders would work toward developing a consensus across teams, and the issue would go back to teams for further deliberation. Davenport emphasized the persuasive power of sharing good ideas over mandating (even if by a committee vote) best ideas into schoolwide policies. Importantly, he did not interpret this participation as diminishing his own power or hindering his capacity to lead the school.

Martin Van Buren Middle School: Sharing the Core Work of Teaching

Van Buren's new state-of-the-art building sits on a hill overlooking small, working-class Vintage City, as a symbol of its gentrification. Storefronts along Main Street sport new granite doorsteps, and polished granite signs have appeared everywhere to celebrate the city's bicentennial. A recent influx of young professionals—attracted by affordable housing and the proximity to a midsized city—promises to reverse the decades-long outflow of middle-class families to affluent surrounding suburbs. However, families here are still mostly poor: one-third of Van Buren's three hundred sixth through eighth graders live in the city's two housing projects, and more than twice that number qualify for free or reduced-cost school lunches.

The commitment of Rick Mills, who was then Vermont's commissioner of education, to curriculum, instruction, and assessment reform provided a broad policy framework within which Van Buren could freely pursue its reform agenda. The state's small size meant that the Department of Education staff could provide steady support. Principal Davenport was enrolled in a doctoral program in education and was studying school change. His strategy was to bring a background of school change theory to his mostly mid-career staff—theory he believed would guide them through the risks he and his faculty must take to transform their traditional junior high into a middle school. A receptive state policy climate, ready technical support, and a savvy and informed principal combined for a powerful synergy to allow reform to take its course.

A summer professional-development institute in 1990 sponsored by the state's education department sparked Van Buren faculty interest in middle-grade practices. But Davenport was convinced that genuine commitment to reform would only come through dialogue and experimentation: "I don't know how else it's going to happen, other than to just continue to communicate and continue the conversation." Vermont's long and proud town hall meeting tradition of public deliberation and decision making contributed to predisposing faculty and others to dialogue. Davenport was well received by the Van Buren staff, other Vintage City educators, and community members when he reasoned with them that they could best improve their school by talking and working together. The principal's first priority was to build in ample time for this dialogue and reflection. He saw his job as keeping these change activities linked to a vision of the kind of school and relationships that were consistent with middle-grade reform.

Teams Take Charge

As at most schools, Davenport and the Van Buren faculty formed teams of teachers at each grade level to create small, student-centered learning communities. However, the Van Buren teams were not only to work together; they were to govern their own practice.

The teams shared blocks of space and time for meeting, planning, and teaching that they could use to shape their own budgets and schedules, plan curriculum, and frame discipline policies as they saw fit. Each team agreed to pursue an interdisciplinary curriculum, alternative assessments, and community-based learning. These reforms did not come with recipes or mandates, and each team was to devise its own strategies for making the reform work. Davenport and outside consultants would be standing by, ready to help with guidance and resources.

Some teams' early interactions were heated, and a few teachers earned the reputation, as one fellow teacher fumed, of being "negative for no reason other than to be against something," but gradually the sharing of time, space, and students allowed most of them to form relationships that overcame their reluctance to make decisions together. Early on, the seventh grade team formed a tight bond that they then sustained over the five years we studied Van Buren's reform. Team leader Oliver Bradley credited the atmosphere of "safety, confidence, and mutual respect" for the group's ability to make reform decisions easily. Equally important was their agreement to respect one another's idiosyncrasies. Over time, other teams followed suit, and the Van Buren faculty developed a schoolwide ethic that respected differences while persistently seeking change. Although sometimes frustrated by the slowness of their deliberations, most teachers came to believe that pressuring colleagues to change would never bring true reform; as one explained: "Until you internalize it, it won't happen. You've got to be willing to commit." Another teacher agreed, saying "you're not backed into a corner, which is the nice part about working in this building."

The relationships that held together Van Buren's teams strengthened teaching and learning by making public many dilemmas that were typically private regarding teaching, student engagement, and learning. Though these dilemmas are apparent at all schools, they are generally broached in what novelist Richard Powers calls a "culture of complaint." By contrast, Van Buren slowly built up a culture of problem solving. Seventh grade team member Brad Glass commented that "prior to being on a team, no one could question what you did in the classroom because no one ever saw." Rather than resenting their practice becoming public, many teachers felt that the increased collegiality more than compensated for greater visibility. Glass, for example, said that with teaming "I've lost negative things like a sense of isolation, a sense of being in this on my own, a sense of 'Well, I'm in this hand-to-hand combat with these kids every day,' and the sense of frustration that 'I'm not reaching the kids.'"

Team meetings, formal and informal, allowed teachers to draw on one another's content and pedagogical expertise and be recognized for their professional knowledge, cleverness, and wisdom. Further, they could share in the recuperative powers of being with like-minded colleagues. Talking about their classrooms with trusted teammates brought greater accountability, as teachers articulated their beliefs and justified their actions to one another.

Innovative assignments and lessons emerged as a direct result of the autonomy given to teams and the relationships on those teams. Colleagues on the seventh grade team, English and reading teachers Barbara Sullivan and Donna Silver, worked with guidance counselor Sharon Keller to develop an interdisciplinary conflict-resolution unit that spun out of the novel *A Girl Who Owned a City*. Darryl Reynolds and Brad Glass's math and science curriculum became more inquiry-based; and Oliver Bradley, aided by a new state-of-the-art school library, was pushing student-centered inquiry in social studies. He worked with the English teachers to craft challenging writing projects that were also authentic, performance-based assessments—far too daunting an effort for one teacher to take on alone.

Significantly, the team developed a level of comfort, mutual respect, and tolerance that allowed them to collaborate, even when they disagreed. As Sullivan explained:

> Over the years we've found out some of the issues that we stonewall on, so we already know how people feel, and unless it's really important to the function, something that we need to hash out, [we don't worry about it]. . . . You know, it's sort of like a long-term relationship. You know those things that you can change, and you know those things that you probably can't. So you don't spend too much time on the ones you can't, as long as everything else is going well. . . . In our team there's just been an understanding that we would [get along]. It doesn't feel like we spend a lot of energy trying to get along because we just accept it. That's how we work

best. If we have a problem with someone else, well, get over it, you know? . . . It frees you up to do other things besides worry about getting along or not getting along.

Reynolds explained how this way of working pushed reform ahead: "Everybody kind of gives up a little bit, and bends a bit, and accommodates a bit. . . . You don't build up the tension, you don't leave the room saying, 'Geez, I'm not going to do this because I don't want to do this.' In some cases, you find yourself doing things, and maybe you were a little opposed at first, but boy, it seemed to work out pretty good. Hey, why not? I think we've had that kind of success where we're not so structured and regimented that we will do it only one way."

At least on a few occasions the teams allowed teachers to grapple directly with some of the largest reform issues. An experience of the seventh grade team illustrates the strengths and risks of team-based decisions when dealing with an equity-related reform such as tracking. It was a serious test of the principal's commitment to giving teacher teams power to reform.

After a few years of working together, Bradley and his teammates decided that they wanted to resume grouping their students by ability level. Doing so would clearly violate Davenport's deep commitment to heterogeneous ability grouping and require that he set aside all of the social justice arguments he'd made around the issue. Davenport struggled with his response. On the one hand, to rescind the authority given to the teams would make shallow his commitment to teacher empowerment and shared decision making. On the other hand, to stand aside while the team tracked its students would undermine his commitment to a socially just school. He argued with the teachers emphatically, presenting the best case he could without pulling rank on them. They were unmovable. In the end and with considerable uneasiness, Davenport decided that he would not stand in the team's way.

Soon the team had second thoughts. By midyear, they began to recognize in their own classes problems with ability grouping that indeed appeared in the literature (and in Davenport's arguments). They found that their low-ability classes "lacked spark." The teachers' hope that they would make greater progress by tar-

geting their instruction toward students' lower ability did not mate-
rialize. That Davenport had argued against—but not fought—their
original decision made it easy for them to change course. They re-
grouped their students heterogeneously and found other ways to
accommodate the diversity in students' skills that had originally
prompted their decision to track. For example, the language arts
teacher designed a way for all of her students to share the books
they read with one another. This allowed her to keep the lower-
skilled students motivated and engaged with a wide range of literature, even if their own skill and pace limited what they could read
on their own. At the same time, she encouraged higher levels of
reading among the skilled readers. Together, the teachers arranged
their schedule to instruct students who had difficulty keeping up
with the pace in the heterogeneous classes. In the end, Davenport's
absolute clarity about his vision for a socially just school, combined
with his sharing of decision-making responsibility with the seventh
grade team in the face of his fundamental disagreement, garnered
support for heterogeneous grouping and established authentic
participation as central to Van Buren's reform. Certainly, not all of
Davenport's risks with his convictions ended so well. But this outcome spoke loudly of the power of democratic participation to
help create virtuous schools.

School Governance from the Bottom Up

Like most of the principals we studied, Davenport formed a school
governance team at Van Buren. His knowledge of the school change
literature, though, made him wary of simply creating the form and
not the reality of democratic reform. Consequently, he designed
the governance team to build collective decisions that would support the teaching teams' control over their own work, rather than
as a body that would decide what the teams should do. Davenport
asked the five team facilitators, including Oliver Bradley, to join
him on the governance team. The group's specific purpose would
be to keep the teams moving in harmonious directions, or, in Davenport's words, to keep "everybody within a reasonable eye's distance of each other." He viewed his own role as making sure that
all faculty members had the chance to interact and share ideas.

Twice a month, the governance team gathered in the back room of a restaurant down the block from the school for a two-to-three-hour session. As members trickled in from school, they would chat casually, catching up socially. Sitting around one large, square table, Davenport often ordered platters of onion rings and fries to sustain them through the long meetings. The facilitators had the responsibility to generate discussion in their own teams so they could bring that thinking to the governance committee, and the governance committee's thinking back to the team. Often an issue required several iterations of discussion. One member described the process this way: "Usually a question will be brought up, we'll discuss what our [the governance team's] opinion is, take it back to the teams with certain things we're looking for. Each facilitator brings that information back to governance, and we try to make an informed decision. . . . Many times we don't make the decision right then and there. We revamp what we are saying, and say, 'OK. Taking into consideration everything that's been given to you, how does this sound?' Each facilitator takes it back again for more input. It's usually not an easy process. I don't think consensus ever is."

Van Buren's iterative process demanded vigorous discussion to ensure that decisions addressed rather than deflected concerns. Of course, not all views could be accommodated, and the fundamental rule of consensus meant making decisions based on what everyone could live with, rather than insisting on anyone's version of the ideal. The group focused on generating new ideas and was skeptical about conventional or stock solutions. Contentious discussion, with some team facilitators routinely locking horns, generally gave way to productive compromise.

Occasionally, the governance team relied on the principal as a kind of tiebreaker, or as someone who might take the responsibility for decisions that were sure to displease colleagues with whom they would have to continue to do their daily work. In these cases, Davenport could say to staff as a whole: "We're going to [do] X now. Too bad. Sorry. Conflicts. That's the way it's got to be." Although this was never the preferred solution, one teacher admitted that "sometimes the team has too much vested interest in [a decision] so you need to let an outsider make the decision." Even so, most Van Buren teachers felt well represented on the governance team. In sharp contrast to what happened at Townsend, at Van Buren extensive deliberation about substance, shuttle diplomacy among team facilitators, and consensus building meant that most teachers felt they actively participated in the school's decision making.

Reform Through Deliberation and Collective Action

Davenport's style of patient pressure could never be mistaken for laissez faire leadership. He did not simply stand by and watch. One teacher remarked how, although he "never forced anything," the principal was "always pressing forward." Bradley credited Davenport's emphasis on consensus building and trust as crucial ingredients in creating a nurturing school environment. The realization that everyone's view would be respected tempered some resistance to change. Even after Davenport turned Van Buren over to a new principal in 1995, the faculty's determination to be a school where everyone could talk and be heard continued. So, too, did a level of commitment and work not often attributed to public school teachers.

On our last visit to Van Buren, we saw that the faculty had also made strides to include community members and social service agencies into their participatory processes. Together with local health, recreation, and educational agencies, the school received a five-year, $1 million federal grant to support a collaborative effort to give Vintage City kids "a variety of developmentally appropriate academic supports and enhancements and employment readiness and career exploration activities." One teacher remarked that it was "an exciting time to be in education in Vintage City." Another eagerly looked toward the future: "We've had the seeds planted. Now let's go on. What more can we do? . . . We're always striving to be better, to try something, to see if this will work better or that will work better."

Van Buren teachers approached reform through day-in, day-out participation in democratic and substantive deliberations and joint activity. They met, talked, and made decisions together, but only a portion of these interactions occurred in formal decision-making meetings. Most conversations at the school that affected policy took place as the teachers worked together—talking about students, planning lessons, sharing good ways to teach. Power at

Van Buren was thought about as the "power to" do the work of the school, rather than the traditional conception of power as that which enables people to get their way because they have "power over" the rest. As a result, at Van Buren the policies and the theories and values on which policies were based were alive in practice. Change was opportunistic and filled the environment. Sooner or later, it found a way into most teachers' thinking and practices. "How do you make somebody believe something they don't believe?" asked Bob Davenport. "You just don't. I think if people have their door open a crack, belief systems can change, but you have to want it."

We turn now to two schools where community participation and parents took center stage in reform. Here we see Madison's efforts falling well short of the engagement reformers hoped for; Tubman's quite unusual approach, on the other hand, yielded astonishing results.

Madison Middle School: Engaging Needy Clients and Complaining Consumers

James Madison Middle School took seriously the *Turning Points* recommendations for engaging parents and community. As principal Fred Antouli's story in Chapter One details, he and many Madison teachers took extraordinary steps to connect with parents. They enlisted community groups to facilitate out-of-school activities and enrichment for students during the school day. Antouli himself took great pride in the increasing number of parents he cooked for at the school's annual spaghetti dinner. However, the school's enthusiasm for parent involvement did not mean including parents as fully participating members of the school community. At Madison, parents had their place.

Despite a state law mandating parent participation in school councils, Madison's faculty reached out only halfheartedly to include parents or community groups in dialogue about the school's goals. This may explain why, despite the faculty's hard work, when parents and community members tried to help shape policy and practice, they and the school found themselves in acrimonious conflict.

Coping with Parents' Deficiencies

Madison's compassionate adults expended enormous energy extending social support to students and their families. Antouli's home visits made him a recognizable neighborhood fixture, and the big spaghetti-dinner events communicated heartfelt concern for his students' families. The school's wide range of social services made that concern concrete. Moreover, Antouli and some teachers worked weekends at the Community Minority Cultural Center, the school invited Spanish-speaking officials and professionals to talk with students about careers, and a vivid display in the neighborhood's many languages adorned the front door; all of this signaled the school's efforts to be a visible and valued member of the diverse community. Despite these efforts, Madison educators complained repeatedly that parents were simply not interested or did not want to be bothered by the school. They were upset that although a few parents were willing to contribute to bake sales or monitor school dances, most didn't participate at all in school activities.

Teachers tried to be sensitive to differences in cultural values. They hired an Asian community liaison to contact parents whom they needed to come to the school. Some teachers attended black churches to get to know parents better. Generally, however, teachers judged their efforts to involve parents as unsuccessful. One attributed lack of parent support to the life difficulties these parents faced, noting that "the parents are just trying to survive"; others told us welfare dependency and gang activity kept many parents—especially Hispanics—from engaging with their children's schooling.

Yes, sometimes the Madison faculty's best intentions actually seemed to discourage parents from participating in the life of the school. Problems with students triggered most teacher contact with parents. Teams regularly made appointments for parents to come in and sit down with all of the teachers at once when students had problems in a number of different classes. Even though many teachers believed that "there isn't really too much we can do," most felt that "You have to try and reach, keep trying and keep failing, and keep trying." Some faulted their peers for forgetting how difficult it was for these parents.

The Madison faculty had a limited view of what families and neighborhood resources could contribute to the school, and this view severely diminished the effectiveness of the well-intentioned hours of hard work the faculty devoted to serving their students. Hoping to serve students and lend social stability, faculty brought to the school mental health services, social service agencies, and the police department. They sought tutoring services from local colleges and businesses to make up for the community's limited academic resources. These partnerships could have been vastly more helpful if parents had participated in identifying problems and were prepared to see these services as helpful.

Antouli actually took steps to limit parents' participation in either making school policy or working to accomplish the school's goals. He did not comply with the Massachusetts law that established school councils. He stacked the committee heavily with teachers who shared his view of reform and then appointed three token parents. The committee only met sporadically. He refused to allow parents to form a parent teacher organization, which he believed interfered with the smooth running of the school. His assistant principal agreed: "I think that they lose sight of what they should be doing."

The High Price of Nonparticipation

Antouli's exclusion of parents and community members (and often Madison teachers) from policy making did not further his reform agenda. During the summer of 1992, he decided to mainstream all of the school's Spanish bilingual students into the school's regular teams. He worried that the separate bilingual program had kept his Hispanic students in almost complete social isolation from the rest of the school. In effect, Madison was two distinct schools—one for Spanish speakers and one for English speakers. He also was unhappy that many Hispanic students spent a number of years in bilingual education, never achieving the skills necessary to leave or refusing to leave because they felt more comfortable there. In typical Antouli style, he rearranged the new schedule without consulting anyone—district administration, teachers, parents, or Latino community groups. Much to everyone's surprise, school opened in September with all bilingual students mainstreamed and bilingual teachers assigned to support limited-English-speaking students in regular classes. Regrettably, although Antouli had strong convictions for students to retain and benefit from their Spanish-language skills, he did not communicate this conviction as a foundational piece of his mainstreaming intentions. It was an oversight or an attitude that surely would have been mitigated if he had had teachers and parents involved in the decisions that they would be affected by or would be implementing.

The reaction was swift. Strong advocates on the faculty and in the community were furious about what they saw as elimination of bilingual education. Still unwilling to subject the matter to public or faculty deliberation, Antouli faced the bilingual advocates, in his words, "willing to do battle." He flatly rejected community opposition to mainstreaming: "The lawyers and everyone else want the students to be taught in Spanish, which I think is absolutely absurd." He also belittled the teachers who opposed his mainstreaming reform, noting that "it's easier for the entire faculty if the students are taught in the native language separately."

Had Antouli engaged the community and teachers, someone might have reminded or encouraged him to get a waiver from state law requiring that students receive academic instruction in their native language. The community political action committee (PAC) representing Spanish speakers secured a court order requiring the school to reopen its separate bilingual program. Reluctantly, Antouli offered one for students whose parents requested it. The following year, he once again opened the school with all students mainstreamed. This time, the PAC met with the superintendent, who directed the principal to offer separate classes with a certified bilingual teacher for all students whose parents wanted such a program, and to offer Spanish-speaking parents the option of English-only classes for their children. So few parents requested that option that by midyear Madison had reverted to a very traditional, separate bilingual program. But by the next year, there was enough support for a program to allow a choice between the two approaches.

It need not have happened this way. Much in the Madison context could have supported a politically, socially, and academically acceptable solution. After all, Antouli and most of his opponents on the bilingual issue agreed on the fundamental goals for Spanish-speaking students: challenging curriculum, language support, and social inclusion. Eventually, the district hired staff to identify and provide resources to help monolingual teachers better address Hispanic students' learning needs. Once convinced that Antouli also wanted to give Latino students primary-language support, the middle school project staff and the bilingual group in the Massachusetts Department of Education helped Madison use bilingual teachers as members of regular teams. Sadly, rather than generating a serious educational debate between those who viewed mainstreaming as a gateway to greater access for Latino immigrant students and those who saw bilingual education as an effective pedagogy, the conflict deteriorated into acrimonious attacks on the character and motives of the opponents.

Yet in many other ways, Madison's reform achieved notable success, and its story is not so much one of failure as of opportunities lost. The school's shift to teaming, interdisciplinary curriculum, project-based instruction, service learning, and its provision of a range of social and health services greatly improved the climate and raised student achievement. Even its bilingual-versus-mainstreaming battles settled on a structure that improved what one powerful faculty member publicly characterized as "almost like apartheid—separate and unequal, as a matter of fact." Finally, one lost opportunity may be the most telling for Madison's sixth, seventh, and eighth graders. Lacking exposure to adults who have mastered civic participation, they may still be waiting for their first opportunities to be apprentices in citizenship.

In striking contrast to Madison, Harriet Tubman Middle School joined forces with a community organizing group to marshal families' energy and resources. Rather than maintaining power over its parent and community participants, however, Tubman's faculty sought to generate power with them. Strikingly, it was never clear at Tubman which group actually was "in charge." The school seemed to view the joint project as its initiative. The community group seemed to view the school as its project. What was clear was that democratic participation thrived on this ambiguity.

Tubman Middle School: Organizing for Empowerment

In Chapter Five, "Becoming Caring," we described how Tubman connected with its impoverished African American parents and neighborhood in supportive and respectful ways. Principal Rebecca Owens informed parents with data about their school. Her goal was to engage 90 percent of them because she thought this high level of involvement would increase achievement at the same time the school became a center of communitywide empowerment.

When VOICES, a multiracial and multidenominational coalition of twenty religious congregations throughout the city (and the local arm of a national network of grassroots political organizations started in 1940 by Saul Alinsky), approached the school with a new reform strategy, Owens jumped at the opportunity to further her agenda.[4] "VOICES works to empower the powerless," she told us, "That's why I fell in love with them." A longtime community member and activist herself, she knew that churches played a vital role in Tubman's community life and could be a powerful force in the school.

VOICES had also selected Tubman carefully. One pastor who helped lead the group told us that "the school had to be in a place where VOICES had a constituency, . . . it had to be within the self-interest of our people to get involved in this particular school. . . . Beyond that, there had to be a principal who wanted this." Once Tubman passed the test, VOICES provided a full-time organizer, Felicia Landers, to connect the school and its community. Landers, a former radio and TV news reporter, had grown up in the neighborhood, attended Tubman as a child, and sent her daughter to the school. She herself was an example of how VOICES worked to find talent within neighborhoods and help them develop into powerful leaders and teachers of others.

Connecting Community and School Improvement

VOICES viewed school quality as inextricably tied to other issues such as economic development and believed its work must help community members recognize these connections. It must show residents how to participate in the political processes (schooling included) that have an impact on their lives. At the same time, VOICES believed that this work would also help schools improve. As Landers put it, "[Harriet Tubman] can never really be different until the people who are part of the community of the school have some power, have some leverage, and have some sense of belonging. . . .

A school cannot survive if the community and the people around it don't exist. We are here physically; we look like we exist, but we're not community. So our focus is to help build community. To find leaders and begin to build community."

Using community organizing strategies, VOICES rallied Tubman parents and community members around school issues and relationships that benefited both the community and the school. Landers explained VOICES' reform strategy as one of connecting people with their own interests:

> How do we get people from participation to real involvement where they feel like they are vested? We call that self-interest. . . . Universals that permeate the concerns of the people are things like human dignity and the sense of community, or needing to belong somewhere, needing a sense of power . . . not just in terms of your child's education, but in terms of your world. . . . This whole idea of organizing is different . . . in the sense that we're not looking for a program. There's not going to be a panacea. I don't even think there's going to be any one collection of things that's going to work in every place. . . . Organizing is the only thing I've seen that touches all of those and takes them into consideration as we're trying to bring people to a level of leadership.

Organizing Nontraditional Parent Participation

Landers also described how her organizing differed from a traditional parent-involvement strategy, describing her job as "agitating" people in the school and community. Rather than doing things for them, "I don't have to be there to make it happen," she told us; "it's not my job to do for them what they can do for themselves. I will not go in and do something that they can do. But I do spend a lot of time kind of agitating different people into some form of action."

Landers began working with parents with a series of *what-if* questions that tapped into their deepest hopes for their children: "What if Tubman had 75 percent of its students achieving? What if there was no gap [between black and white achievement]? What if the gap was very minimal? A 10–15 percent gap between the Anglo students and the minority students? What would that look like? How would we feel if that were so? What kind of parents would you need, to have that be a reality?"

Landers and members of the VOICES congregations led a door-to-door survey of every Tubman family to elicit parents' views. Then they held separate forums for small groups of parents and teachers to examine their concerns, along with a series of joint meetings to discuss the issues together. Building on these activities, VOICES organized Saturday "community visitation" days. This time, the faculty joined VOICES volunteers in walking the neighborhoods, visiting homes, and saying hello to parents of Tubman children. Many of the stops included serious and substantive conversations with families.

Landers said that such conversations helped parents get to know teachers by name, learn the ins and outs of school policies, understand how to read a report card, and gain a sense of such basic educational concepts as what performing at grade level means, as well as build parents' confidence generally. Such knowledge, she thought, would have revolutionary consequences. "One of the things you have to have," Landers told us,

> Is an involved parent. We also think that you have to have an informed constituency. Those parents, to be involved, must be informed. They cannot be ignorant or led around by the nose. They have to know some things. They also have to have some sense of power, which is your question around control. They must be parents who want to have some of that control, to be a part, and a stakeholder in—a caretaker, if you will—in the shaping of how things turn out for the kids. So then when the children achieve, and it's wonderful, they know how that happened.

VOICES and Principal Owens hoped all these experiences would prompt parents to express their hopes and concerns more efficaciously. One VOICES pastor said: "You cannot have a good dialogue with people when they're angry. So we want to create an atmosphere where parents will come to the school before they get angry and build relationships with teachers." Owens hoped that parent activists would demand a better education: "We are trying to empower them so they will demand change. It is threatening, but it makes the school a better place because parents will demand more of us."

Tubman became the hub of parent activity. One parent, for instance, volunteered at school for eight to ten hours every day and organized ten other parents who worked almost as much. These parents followed their own creative agenda rather than just responding to the faculty's requests. One established a regular job for herself, attending to sick students whenever the part-time nurse was off campus. The PTA, headed by a grandmother, rejected its traditional role of raising funds through candy sales. Instead, the group focused on activism for school safety. It lobbied successfully for a twenty-mile-per-hour traffic zone around the school, built a fence around the property, increased the security patrol, and spearheaded drug surveillance at school by calling police when anyone suspected drugs. The group established a school uniform policy to cut down on wearing of gang colors, reduce the temptation for students to steal in order to have the "right" clothes, and more easily identify people who don't belong on campus. When the school needed resources, the PTA put its newly acquired organizing skills to work. As one parent told us: "I'll knock on every business door to get them. Ninety percent of people in the community buy from these stores."

Connecting Teachers and Parents

Confirming Landers and Owens's view that informed parents would get more involved at school, parents' increasingly independent activities spurred connections with teachers. Large numbers of parents began attending formal school events. One evening meeting brought nine hundred parents, and a daylong series of parent conferences brought five hundred parents. Teachers typically worked individually with ten to fifteen parents a month. One math teacher donated two nights each week to math instruction for families.

VOICES, the PTA, and the faculty worked together with the specific purpose of changing the school and community culture. As one parent reported, "We want the PTA, the school, the church, and community leaders all to be saying the same things to our children: 'You can learn; you can achieve; you are somebody; you are a citizen; you are a responsible person; you are important.'"

PTA parents contacted others whose children had academic problems, to tell them: "You need to get involved because here's your child over here, failing. You say, 'I can't do anything with this child.' Let me show you how to help your child with his homework. Let's find out where this child is failing. Let's see if we can get some tutors to help."

One parent prided herself on knowing not only all the students' names but their class schedules as well. Local pastors regularly stopped by the school to verify students' grades for recognition in church. Many visited classrooms to say "Hi," to spend an hour or so sitting next to a troubled youngster, or to counsel those in difficulty. They also used their Sunday sermons to encourage parents and community members to become involved in the school.

Joint, Public Work

Over time, the collaboration among administrators, teachers, custodians, parents, community members, and pastors from VOICES extended deep into the inner workings of the school. Notably, the faculty came to see their community partners as resources when political issues threatened their work. In one illustrative case, they took a potentially demoralizing change in state testing and accountability policies as an occasion to build greater community power.

By 1992, the Tubman community's enormously hard work had moved the school from being the lowest scoring of the district's twenty middle schools on the state achievement test to being one of the highest—a feat that brought a great sense of accomplishment to the community and parents. That same year, the legislature replaced its traditional basic skills test with a new one, the Texas Assessment of Academic Skills (TAAS). The TAAS worried the Tubman community, both because the new test claimed to emphasize higher-order skills and because it came with a heavy accountability mechanism that would publicize low-scoring schools. Some at the school thought that the higher-order reasoning and problem solving might help students "think and learn the way the world is and the way the world is going to be in the next century," as one parent put it. But many felt betrayed by the state's elimination of a test on which their children had finally scored well. Some even worried aloud that the TAAS might not reflect "the way minority children think, or . . . the way that their homes are oriented."

Taking immediate action, Landers, Owens, counselors, and teachers organized workshops to have parents "look at how the testing has changed, look at what . . . thinking is, look at what reasoning is." Counselors provided copies of the TAAS test booklets, with items and answers, so that parents could begin to understand what the test measured and how they could "begin to do some of that at home . . . and reinforce what the child is learning at school." The strategy worked. Even though Tubman students did not score high enough to reach the state's top category of "recognized" schools, they did score in the "acceptable" range. To everyone's relief, Tubman escaped the dreaded designation as a low-performing school (the fate of many Texas schools with poor students). Tubman has slowly increased its TAAS scores in the years since.

How did the Tubman community manage to work together so effectively? In the words of Felicia Landers:

> It's a relationship, a public relationship, not a private relationship—not your best friend, your family—but a public relationship where we decide overtly, consciously, we're going to work together to do this. It's the fact that we know each other, that we have a sense of one another, and a sense of where the other is coming from. So that if I cross the line or if I'm really out of line, that person can come to me and say, I felt you were pushing too much. . . . Because I have a relationship with them, I can also go back and agitate them and say, "I'm an organizer and I'm not going to do this for you, so if you want this to happen. . . ." When you do things in a relationship, it's just not that hard. You'd have to maybe wrestle and fight in another setting, but when people have a relationship, they don't question one another's commitment. We know we're on the same team. It's just a matter of how we're going to get done what needs to be done.

Conditions of Participation

Reforms in the 1980s and 1990s have been unequivocal in their support for greater participation in schools. *Turning Points* also made clear the connections between participation and civic virtues that extend beyond the school. Recall from Chapter Two that the report argued: "Deeply ingrained in our society is the belief that individuals can be trusted to make decisions for themselves and for the common good. This belief is the bedrock of the democratic political system."[5] *Turning Points* also suggested that the important work of school reform must be done collectively, declaring that "a large and activist constituency . . . must be created if systematic improvement in the education of young adolescents is to occur. It will require well-planned, collaborative, and sustained efforts, beginning in individual communities and extending to the nation at large."[6]

When participatory reforms suggest that activist local constituencies could be the engines that power reform in the direction of civic virtue, they merge a school change agenda with one for broad social change. This merger proved to be one of the most countercultural elements of American school reform movements of the late twentieth century. Not only did funding agencies, powerful political interests, state departments of education, and school districts have too little capacity or will to create local activist constituencies but the effort also embodied difficult contradictions—Carnegie had clear substantive goals (vis-à-vis detracking, for example) that required ignoring or acting against participatory voices of many parents and community members who wanted tracking to continue. However, if these larger units and social powers lacked the capacity and will to open fertile ground for participation, some individual schools did turn the slimmest of opportunities into productive local action.

Each of the schools we studied used incredible amounts of staff resources to set up and maintain participatory policy making. Some schools devoted the greatest share of their energies to managing and controlling participation; other schools, such as Van Buren and Tubman, worked hard to put power into the hands of the participants. Some school leaders, notably Harold Nance and Fred Antouli, saw themselves as needing to exercise greater power to keep unpredictable—even unruly—participants in order, while others, such as Bob Davenport and Rebecca Owens, saw each successful move to distribute power as adding to the total empowerment of the whole school program.

Constraining Participation

Dilemmas with participation in schools mirror the participatory dilemmas of the larger society. We recognize these constraints in the business, professional, and social service worlds—not just schools. In our study, at Madison for example, we found much fear that empowering ordinary people—especially those who received services—would lead to steamrolling by an uninformed majority. We saw many examples, such as Countryside, of participants who thought their self-interest was threatened by appeals to the common good. Others, such as teachers at Tanglewood, worried that shared decision making would overpower legitimate professional expertise. Arguments about structure and rules, or process (whether an appropriate venue for discussion existed, who had access to it, what topics could be addressed, and what decisions could be made), such as those at Townsend, often replaced a debate of substantive issues. Very frequently, participation was misconstrued as gaining superficial teacher and parent input and acceptance of the latest administrative initiative. This thinking invariably led some to explain the failure of programs or whole reforms with a facile "lack of buy in" analysis. Others crammed discussions into impossibly brief meetings or controlled agendas that deflected attention from important issues. Some groups focused on overly abstract matters (for example, framing a mission statement) while others were overloaded with procedural or trivial chores.

When schools and parents held different values, it was especially difficult for them to join as equal partners. In many disadvantaged areas, participation meant helping overcome deficiencies that interfered with the schools' traditional agenda. Fred Antouli at Madison and Len Jacobi at Horace Mann, for example, construed participation as charity instead of collective action; as being kind and helpful, rather than part of a genuine redistribution of power and resources. When this occurs, those being "helped" by reform are consigned to continued powerlessness, often seen as "poor things." In other communities, small groups of parents were used to wielding power (and usually getting their way) outside the official participatory school structures. These powerful parents were not so interested in altering patterns that had proved effective for promoting or squelching policies in ways that fit their self-interest. So, for example, despite their attempts to engage parents as reform participants, one Tanglewood teacher accurately characterized the school's reversal of its detracking reform this way: "The parents heard that heterogeneous grouping was happening, and they had a fit."

Enabling Participation

Reform leaders fared better when they eschewed conventional notions of power as control. Certainly, having strong leaders mattered a great deal in schools such as Van Buren and Tubman, but both Davenport and Owens were more than simply strong. Each led his or her school with a vision of how working together might actually create more power for the school, rather than trying to figure out how to redistribute power differently. Neither replicated the conventional, hierarchical power relations that often arise with strong and charismatic principals. This may be why participation at these schools went beyond a struggle over who gets to make decisions to creating new, bridging interests among participants.

Participation also seemed to work best when the people who were making decisions worked together to implement the decision. Representing others and deciding what they should do did not usually turn out well. Schools such as Van Buren and Tubman gave participants the power to act on their decisions in the context of their core work. Rather than only making schoolwide governance decisions, teachers studied, decided, and acted on matters of teaching and learning; parents and community members studied, decided, and acted on civic projects both in and outside the school. They used the schools' participatory processes to help people find new ways to act together to solve problems, thus reinforcing democratic practice in schools.

Above all, relationships were responsible for the success of the structures and processes we saw at Van Buren and Tubman. Likewise, the schools were successful in their reforms because they had brought people together, not only to dream and give their stamp of approval but to engage them in work that mattered to all of them, work that was sustained over time. Their talk and work was about themselves—what they could and would do, rather than what others should do. Such work created strong and lasting bonds that permitted participants to take risks and trust one another's support. Over time, they developed the power to accomplish far more than they could have working alone or in casual partnerships. Where participatory goals were realized, we saw groups of individuals—educators, parents, and community members—working collectively on specific schooling projects. Their decisions were inextricably connected to (and often created) their power to carry them out.

Moreover, when educators viewed engaging others—whether they were more powerful or less powerful than themselves—as drawing upon resources and as an exercise in power creation rather than as getting buy in or eliminating constraints on the school's agenda, they came closer to collective, democratic participation. This was especially powerful when the agenda was one of social justice. Tubman's work illustrates this clearly. Rebecca Owens believed strongly that Tubman indeed was a powerful school; she also believed that the school's power had been created through the participation and collective work of ordinary, otherwise powerless people to take charge of their neighborhood and school. As community organizer Landers said of Owens, "Now she knows she has power." Not only did Owens know that she had power but she also knew it was generated through the collective political action of parents, community members, and school faculty; she knew as well that this power lay behind the gains the school had made. So when Owens was occasionally charged by her peers elsewhere in the school system with being too "political," she would smile and say, "Thank you."

Part Three

Becoming Better

| **Struggling to Scale Up**

Each of the schools we studied was part of a national network of state reform projects attempting to take the promising ideas outlined in *Turning Points* and replicate them in middle schools. These projects were staffed, for the most part, by people who were strongly predisposed to make schools educative, inclusive, caring, and participatory. Like many of the educators in the schools, many state leaders were deeply committed to schools as places of civic virtue.

The reformers faced formidable challenges. They had to use considerable political finesse to develop strategies consistent with *Turning Points'* vision of middle-grade reform and with their own state context (that is, their agency's history of working with schools, and current education policy priorities). Ever present was the accountability they felt to demonstrate to Carnegie that they had brought deep, cultural changes to project schools and to show state policy makers that the reform was a success statewide. Of course, all of their work was also conducted in environments characterized by ambivalence about schools as places of civic virtue.

The state project activities to advance reform generated great enthusiasm and leveraged some changes in policies and practices. Yet while the state policies and implementation strategies appeared largely technical and rational, few state staffers were prepared for the turmoil that arose when reforms upset traditional practices or redistributed resources and the power to make decisions. State project staffs were prepared—to the extent that their resources would allow—to show, train, and lead schools in changing school structures and teaching techniques. However, few had the frame of mind and none had the resources or political mandate to help educators pursue genuinely untraditional practices along with a new way of life in schools.

Although the technical approaches were generally inadequate to address cultural changes, there is much to learn from some important exceptions. Some state projects did help the schools move closer to the civic virtue called for in reform rhetoric, and on occasion staff battled explicitly with the cultures and politics in their states, their own agencies, and local schools. In nearly every case, these struggles called for project staff to step outside their official role of bringing technical innovation to schools.

The "Scaling Up" Challenge

For policy makers and philanthropic organizations, *scaling up* is the current shorthand for taking ideas and practices that have worked well in a handful of places and replicating them in large numbers of schools. Absent the ability to scale up effective schooling strategies, many fear that the flurry of innovative reform initiatives of the nineties will simply add another painful chapter to the dismal history of planned educational change.

Because the history of education reform is largely one of failed or aborted efforts to spread new practices, 1990s reformers have tried to approach scaling up differently. Theodore Sizer's Coalition of Essential Schools, for example, translated success at a small number of high schools (such as Deborah Meier's in East Harlem, New York City) into a set of broad principles that schools across the nation could use to frame new organizational structures and practices. Henry Levin produced a cadre of change agents and training protocols to replicate nationally an inquiry process that he and educators at San Francisco–area elementary schools used to create Accelerated Schools. Robert Slavin and Nancy Madden at Johns Hopkins University translated their thoroughly researched reading strategy, Success for All, into a carefully crafted set of materials and a training program that could be adopted by schools where the faculty made a clear schoolwide commitment to the approach. The New American Schools Development Corporation created "design teams" to provide technical support to schools deciding to adopt one of its eight "research-based" designs for effective schools. The list goes on and on.

Scaling up was exactly the challenge the Carnegie Corporation staff faced once its Task Force on the Education of Adolescents released *Turning Points*. As we said in Chapter One, the report argued that eight principles, or turning points, characterized the good middle school:

1. Creating small, respectful communities for learning
2. Teaching a core of academic knowledge
3. Ensuring success for all students
4. Empowering teachers and administrators
5. Preparing teachers for the middle grades
6. Fostering young adolescents' health and fitness
7. Reengaging families in the education of young adolescents
8. Connecting schools with communities

The challenge was to get middle schools nationwide to embrace these principles and adopt new practices that would bring them to life. *Turning Points* recommended specific practices that the task force drew from a handful of successful middle schools that seemed to embody the reforms. Blue pages scattered throughout the report highlighted schools where teachers worked productively in teams, adults maintained supportive advisory relationships with young adolescents, all students learned rigorous academic curricula, heterogeneous classrooms using cooperative learning strategies were the norm, students developed community service projects, and parents and teachers shared leadership through democratic governance structures. Like Sizer, Levin, Slavin, and other school reformers of the 1990s, Anthony Jackson (see Introduction) and the Carnegie staff sought to create the conditions to scale up these practices. Carnegie called its strategy the Middle Grades Schools State Policy Initiative (MGSSPI).

The high-profile Carnegie Task Force on the Education of Adolescents (including then-Governor Bill Clinton, heads of major philanthropies, and highly placed education leaders), together with its widespread dissemination, ensured *Turning Points* considerable publicity. The report set out clear national and state norms for good middle-grade practice. Carnegie also took an activist role in moving its reform from a highly visible report to state policies and then to local practice. The MGSSPI funded efforts in two dozen states to create new middle-grade schooling policies, a goal that was almost universally accomplished. Then, for nearly a decade, Carnegie committed additional money through MGSSPI state grants to support local implementation in fifteen states; this was a strategy meant to support local educators' work and help leverage broader changes in state policies. Over the course of nearly a decade, Carnegie spent a total of $22 million to scale up *Turning Points* reform.

At Carnegie's urging, the first step taken by most states was to convene a highly visible task force made up of those who could actually change state policy: governors, state school chiefs, heads of health and social service agencies, legislators, middle-grade educators, leaders of other school reforms, and those in charge of teacher licensing and state educational testing. Their job was to set the state's vision for middle-grade reform and to make recommendations for aligning policies with this vision, such as urging new state curriculum frameworks and designing incentives to attract teachers to the middle grades.

Carnegie expected that a small central project staff in each state would carry out the task force work by fostering collaboration among education, health, and social service agencies; establishing networks of reforming schools; providing professional development for middle-grade educators; and documenting their reforms. Carnegie also contracted with the staff of the Council of Chief State School Officers (CCSSO)—the organization to which each state superintendent or education commissioner belongs—to extend technical assistance to the state projects. The group organized meetings and conferences of the network of "Carnegie states," published an MGSSPI newsletter, and helped states document their efforts.

Carnegie's vision and its first three years of fiscal support, technical assistance, and networking among the state projects emboldened these participants and schools to take middle-grade reform seriously, and many began changing policy and practice. They began by helping policy makers and educators respond to the new technical challenges of middle-grade reform, including school structures such as teams and advisory and governance committees;

teaching techniques such as cooperative learning; and curriculum design such as integrated curricula. But little from Carnegie and the CCSSO staff helped states recognize or deal with the cultural contradictions that soon emerged.

However, it would not be long before Jackson would come to believe that implementing *Turning Points* required far more than structural changes and that reform cried out for new, radical strategies. He and his Carnegie colleagues realized that the early course of the states' reforms and the frustrations some states and schools were experiencing were not resistance to the structures and strategies themselves so much as a response to the ideas and values they represented. Jackson hoped the state project leaders and local educators would realize that the structures and strategies were simply techniques to help schools educate children well, care about them, and become democratic places. States and schools would have to address values, beliefs, and expectations; grapple with redistributing power and authority; and focus explicitly on schools serving low-income children of color. None of these imperatives matched what policy makers and reformers knew how to do, saw as their role, or necessarily agreed with.

In response to this growing appreciation of the reform's normative elements, Carnegie became far more prescriptive about state activities. Perhaps the most significant shift was when Carnegie asked the states to designate a small number of schools with concentrations of disadvantaged students as "systemic change schools" and to use them as demonstration and training sites. Jackson's "bottom line" for these schools was that they be viable, working examples showing how high-quality educational opportunities could affect the learning and life chances of poor, minority youth.

State Strategies: The Same, and Different

Some similarities among state projects resulted from Carnegie's funding requirements, and some were products of the constraints that all of the state projects faced. All the project leaders were keenly aware of their precarious role, given the limited resources, the enormity of the job, and past failed efforts at school reform generally. State staffs understood that their success partly depended on synchronizing the middle-grade reform with existing state priorities and programs. They also believed that scaling up hinged on whether they could move beyond their intensely political state landscapes to steer their work into schools and convince educators that the state really wanted to help and could provide that help. Finally, they saw two consequences of their projects' high visibility that demanded a sometimes skittish walk between the clout and the vulnerability that publicity brings.

As agents of the state, project leaders felt compelled to bring reform to all of the schools in the state, not just a few model schools that already had the capacity and inclination to change. They also felt they had to guard against the perception that they favored some schools with more state resources than others, even though some schools might clearly require more resources. So to accommodate Carnegie's press for intensive work with a few schools, most states targeted a small number as a starting point from which they would scale up reform throughout the state. Differences between Carnegie's and the states' conceptions of these change schools was slight, but enough to add some tension, some nervousness, on the part of project staff. When they concentrated on working with many schools, they felt they were neglecting the change schools; when concentrating on the change schools, they felt pressure to spread their resources.

Other commonalities across the projects stemmed from the widely shared conviction that although middle-grade reform was coming from the state, and Carnegie funding was to be directed to a limited number of schools, widespread implementation could be promoted by bottom-up initiatives. This view led most states to develop networks of schools that would support one another as they created local versions of *Turning Points*. Another strategy, driven in part by scarce resources and used by all of the larger states, was the cascade or trainer-of-trainers approach. Here, state project staff worked directly with the faculties of a small set of schools— often those farthest along in reform—and they in turn provided the same technical assistance to the faculties of other schools.

Despite these similarities, each state developed a distinctive approach to scaling up *Turning Points*. Each framed its project to fit the size of the state, its political environment, and the history of state and local education policy. Each state project also proceeded uniquely because of the distinctive talents and idiosyncrasies of its staff. Local educators generally saw the reform staff as allies whose passion for helping and for change significantly supported local educators to do the things that mattered most for themselves, their students, and their school communities.

In the remainder of this chapter we examine these scaling-up efforts.

Texas: Cheerleading, Commitment, and Accountability

MGSSPI came at a propitious time of political change in Texas. In 1990, voters swept Governor Ann Richards's liberal Democratic administration into office, and in 1991 Lionel "Skip" Meno, the newly appointed commissioner of education, campaigned to transform the state's education system. Texas schools were reeling from a decade of contentious education reform policies. Since the early 1980s, with Ross Perot leading the charge, members of the legislature, governor's staff, the state board of education (SBOE), and the Texas Education Agency (TEA) had forged prescriptive get-tough reforms, including curriculum standardization, basic skills testing, teacher competency testing, and merit pay. Many well-heeled residents deeply resented the years-long string of court and legislative battles that threatened to equalize huge funding imbalances between the state's wealthy and poor communities. Texas taxpayers provided fewer per-student dollars than the national average, and educators were peppered regularly with such questions as "Why can't you do this bad a job on less money?"

Meno's reform agenda focused on the national interest in setting high standards, establishing accountability with "indicators of the quality of learning in each school," and deregulating the schools. But he infused these initiatives with his own strong commitment to equity for the state's children of color, vowing to hold all schools accountable on new state achievement tests. According to a colleague, "his message has always been the same. . . . You cannot be an excellent school if you have minority children who aren't performing . . . even if you are an all-white district, and you only have fifty minority kids. . . . You can't be called excellent." Meno found middle-grade reform compatible with his own interest in moving the state agency away from compliance monitoring and toward helping schools improve. He liked *Turning Points'* commitment to equity and welcomed the additional political clout that Carnegie brought to eliminating senior high remedial courses and middle-grade tracked classes.

Katherine Merchant, a member of the SBOE and longtime middle-grade champion, chaired a twenty-four-member Texas Task Force on Middle School Education, made up of representatives of the governor's office, the legislature, and the state's departments of health and human services, as well as local educators and university faculty. Within a year, the SBOE endorsed the Texas task force's version of *Turning Points,* called *Spotlight on the Middle,* as state policy.

Middle-Grade Reform, Texas Style

Texas's middle-grade reform faced enormous challenges. How could the small pool of Carnegie funds leverage reform in more than fifteen hundred middle schools in this large and diversely populated state? Convinced that "reform needs to be modeled, not just talked about," as one staffer put it, state agency staff and Merchant quickly selected nineteen geographically and demographically diverse "mentor" schools from a pool of seventy-three applicants. Affluent Tanglewood and inner-city Harriet Tubman were among those chosen. Few of the mentor schools actually had middle-grade practices in place, but they agreed to lead a network of other schools that could learn from their efforts to reform. The goal was to include all of the state's middle schools in a reform network within three years. By fall 1992, six hundred schools, including Townsend, had signed on.

In 1992, Jane McIvoie took the helm of the state MGSSPI project, and the project swung into action with schools. A former middle-grades principal whose own graduate studies focused on those grades, McIvoie led agency staffers in the new Middle Grade Division much as a reform-minded principal might lead a faculty, confronting much inertia and spotty support with her passion, pragmatism, and hard work. McIvoie and her staff contacted schools and educators and quickly added new mentor schools and networks. By 1994, eight hundred Texas middle schools had become part of the MGSSPI reform network.

McIvoie and her staff spent most of their time on the road, visiting lead schools and lobbying districts to adopt the educative and inclusive middle-grade reforms. Matching her approach to the state's achievement goals, she regularly displayed achievement test data to show the state's sorry record with its most disadvantaged students: "I shove down the statistics about children in our state. . . . What good is it going to do for us to educate properly one segment of the population when we are losing 50 percent of the others? We are going to have a third of our students with high school diplomas, [and] the rest will have either a very mediocre education, miseducation, or they will have dropped out. What kind of economy and society are these children going to live in?"

One of McIvoie's primary goals was to avoid trivializing interdisciplinary curriculum and student-centered lessons by ensuring that teachers remain deeply committed to subject-matter content. She described her frustration when teachers superficially implemented an interdisciplinary unit on "walls" (the Wailing Wall, the Great Wall of China, etc.) that teachers found attractive initially because, in McIvoie's words, they thought "it's neat, it's interesting, it's current, it's relevant":

> What we're saying is, "You have to be more responsible than that. So, you take it to the thematic level. Yes, go ahead and do walls. That's great. But connect it up here [points to her head] with a theme, first of all, such as prejudice or . . . totalitarianism, and then develop concepts that you want every discipline to address in developing children and ensure that children understand when you're doing these units. Then decide, before you start, what skills you want to develop, what basic skills, what research skills, what products you want, so that we don't end up all building the Alamo and not know why, and have that be the 'biggie of the unit.'" It's just a more responsible approach. I'm very frightened . . . by what I see.

Controlling the Message

McIvoie searched for strategies that would take schools beyond superficial implementation of the reform. In particular, she wanted

to monitor—perhaps control—the network activities very closely
to avoid having corrupted versions of middle-grade reforms passed
along from one network school to another. She told us:

> I was very concerned about the network conferences that were
> going on—from my observations in the first year. . . . You can't
> just bring somebody in because they want to share something,
> and they think it's wonderful, when . . . you haven't looked at it
> for substance. There are many bad messages that we don't want to
> give. Academic teaming was one of them. We had presentations
> where the teams of teachers from our mentor schools were saying,
> "Oh, this is so wonderful. We meet one or two times a week. . . . "
> [That was] everything opposite of what we wanted to get out as
> the message. So we have really regrouped. We're not going to say,
> "Don't allow the teachers to present it. . . ." You get good ideas
> wherever you go. But what we decided is this: we're going to keep
> coming in behind with the message we want to get out.

The Texas project produced and widely distributed their
Source Book of Notable Programs, listing one hundred practitioner-
recommended programs and practices for middle-grade students.
McIvoie told us, "I feel like the state needs to be a leader in providing examples. . . . I don't think it's something that you can just
sit down and do, even if you are willing." The concern over superficial implementation also led McIvoie and her staff to beef up
their trainer-of-trainers approach. They organized state-led summer professional-development activities to prepare educators in
mentor schools to convey accurately the substance of reform and
to deliver that substance in a good professional-development format. As McIvoie explained: "We train a core in school, they train
the rest of the school, and they train the network, and that is how,
hopefully, it will evolve. . . . This is one of the reasons we want to
provide them the very, very best. They really are getting the cutting
edge stuff. . . . The mentors are kind of like the hub in a wheel."

State project staff also produced print and multimedia training materials so that the reform message would be repeated with
fidelity. Each mentor school and regional center was given a large
loose-leaf notebook of overhead transparencies and a script to use
when assisting other schools with reform. McIvoie also set up an
electronic network, published a newsletter, and developed videos

to be used in conjunction with the staff development provided by the mentor schools and the regional centers.

Backlash and Unlikely Bedfellows

Not surprisingly, the demand, from the commissioner and the middle-grade project staff, for high achievement and inclusion of low-income students of color in rigorous academic programs brought political backlash. The Texas Association for the Gifted and Talented—whose membership was predominantly white and middle- to upper-income parents and certified teachers of the gifted—became a significant and politically potent force in Texas. Angered by the possibility of losing separate programs for gifted youngsters, this powerful advocacy group organized against heterogeneous grouping.

In part to counter this pressure, McIvoie forged a new alliance between her office and the TEA's Gifted and Talented (GT) office. The partnership meant that professional development for middle-grade project schools would focus on curriculum and instructional strategies identified with gifted students. Together, McIvoie and her counterpart in GT, Gwen Jefferson, hoped to both improve the quality of instruction in middle schools and reassure anxious parents by infusing a gifted curriculum into heterogeneous classes. McIvoie knew how politically important this was: "We have really tried to present a united front. We're all about the same thing: we're all about kids. We both have the same philosophy and beliefs. . . . If we don't come together on this issue for kids, then everybody loses, because gifted is not going away. Those parents are not going anywhere."

The collaboration had a fiscal payoff as well. McIvoie and her staff persuaded the GT unit to support expansion of the networks with their federal Chapter 2 monies. Over time, most of the project's funding came through the GT office. This helped enormously because the Carnegie funds were spread so thinly across the state.

In 1994, when Carnegie pressed the states it was funding to target their efforts to a handful of low-income, mostly minority schools, Jefferson assumed responsibility for these targeted schools, while McIvoie continued her focus on the bigger state picture. Jefferson mounted intensive curriculum workshops led by a nationally recognized expert on gifted education. This innovative political strategy served the project's inclusive goals in ways that few would have anticipated. Teachers of some of the lowest-achieving, low-income African American and Latino students in the state had access—most for the first time—to the intensive, high-quality professional development usually reserved for the teachers of the state's most privileged children.

"There Is Nothing to Stop a Freight Train"

Fueling a demanding work schedule with her passion, McIvoie and her staff built momentum for change. Her colleague, Carl Kent, told us, "We really get things done by doing them, not sitting around theorizing. Just do it." McIvoie argued the reform's inevitability, confident that it "sells itself" and that people just "sign on." She also told us with a laugh: "I usually do not fail—do not believe in it, will not accept it, will not tolerate it. It's not even in the picture. . . . There is nothing to stop a freight train. You can get on board or you can get out of the way."

At Tubman and Tanglewood, mentor school principals Rebecca Owens and Brad Jelton both spoke of McIvoie with high regard. They appreciated having her ready-made materials to use when they presented elements of reform to other schools. Owens was extraordinarily pleased to receive intensive training in how gifted educators designed curriculum. Tanglewood was used to such treatment, but for Tubman it was a rare privilege.

Mostly, both principals were amazed at McIvoie as a person. Her boundless energy and commitment to middle-grade reform heartened them. Plus, she actually seemed to like middle-grade students. Owens spoke enthusiastically about McIvoie's visits, noting that McIvoie didn't stay in the front office but wandered into classrooms and chatted with teachers and students. She stepped beyond official technical assistance, and sometimes she went where a dispassionate person might not. She shook her head at her own brazenness as she told us about meeting with a superintendent of a small Texas district: "I went in and spent the whole day. We'd go through the whole thing and see if they had any problems, [and the superintendent said, 'We] can't afford to do this.' I said, 'What is your athletic budget?' It was a million dollars. I said, 'You cannot afford three more teachers for your junior high schools, but you have a million-dollar-a-year athletic budget?' When the superintendent tells me that [he] cannot afford to do that, I say, 'You cannot afford not to do this? Where are the priorities? I can't buy [these priorities].'"

Only later, when her state project colleagues were dumbfounded at her audacity, did McIvoie realize that the district she went nose-to-nose with was the subject of a popular book about the sovereignty of high school athletics in central Texas. It was that kind of intensity, more than all of the polished technical assistance she delivered, that caught the enthusiasm of the schools with which she worked. That spirit, coming from a state official, may have also buffered the schools from district-level pressures that would otherwise make their reform work more difficult.

Most striking in Texas, though, was the state project's internal conflict over civic virtue that underlay the middle-grade reforms. At the same time that the project team was working for deep understanding of interdisciplinary curriculum, it also pressured schools to increase their scores on the state's TAAS test (see Chapter Six), which emphasized basic knowledge and skills. At the same time McIvoie argued for making all students the recipients of the very best that schools had to offer, her partner-in-reform Jefferson remained accountable for ensuring that the state's identified gifted students had different and richer opportunities. This schism was mirrored by Tubman's maintenance of both a "high achieving," mostly white magnet program and a nearly all-black "greater school." So, while Commissioner Meno and some of the state's MGSSPI project staff shared *Turning Points'* commitment to making middle schools equitable communities, they found little in the state culture to buttress their stance.

California: Marketing What Matters

In 1987, California's own middle-grade report, *Caught in the Middle* (*CIM*), actually anticipated *Turning Points*. Like the latter, *CIM* stressed both social and intellectual goals for the middle grades, making it a priority that all students have equal access to rigorous academic curriculum. *CIM*'s first principle was that "every middle grade student should pursue a common, comprehensive, academically oriented core curriculum irrespective of primary language and ethnic background." It pressed schools to move toward this principle by grouping academic classes heterogeneously; informing students and parents how course taking affects high school and college chances; and making a "heroic effort" to have "underrepresented minority" students pursue ambitious academic goals. This challenging agenda spoke loudly to the gaps between California's white and Asian students, on the one hand, and its African American and Latino students on the other, at a time when Latino students were soon to be the state's majority.

Caught in the Middle was only one of many initiatives that thrust California into national prominence in the 1980s. After securing support for an omnibus school reform bill, State Superintendent of Public Instruction Bill Honig led the department of education through development of an innovative set of curriculum frameworks and student assessments. As one staffer put it, "[Honig] is a visionary. Thank God we have people like him. He pushes the agenda." However, the 1990s brought a flood of changes: decline in the state's economy, the Republican governor's shift further to the political right, dissatisfaction with public schools, and Honig's ouster in the midst of criminal charges peripherally related to his work as superintendent. Controversial issues such as school choice, educating undocumented immigrants, multicultural texts, affirmative action, bilingual education, and low test scores overwhelmed attention to middle-grade reform and empowered many who opposed the ideological tenets of *CIM*.

When the Carnegie MGSSPI project began, Honig named as director Derrick Tilson, a savvy African American on his way up in the agency. He gave Tilson and his handful of enthusiastic middle-grade "consultants"—Olivia Murphy, Heather Perkins, Steve Bradley, and Curtis Jeffries—a free hand to blend Carnegie's initiative with other state priorities. For Tilson and his team, most of whom were former middle-grade teachers themselves, "what's best for kids" was the standard against which they weighed alternatives. Murphy enthused: "There's a middle-grade philosophy at work in this office. . . . There's a middle-grade answer to things." Risk taking was an unwritten unit policy. As Tilson put it: "We've been willing to stick our necks out. . . . We've been willing to do some things and ask questions later when we thought we were right."

Selling "The Middle-Grade Answers to Things"

Despite the high profile of California's education policy making, implementation could not be heavy-handed. Since state law prohibits unfunded mandates, Tilson and the team spread the word about *CIM* and worked to make signing on attractive to schools. They blanketed the state with copies of the report and presented at California Middle School Association meetings. They offered seed money and promised to create supportive networks. In return, schools had to promise that they would implement *CIM* reforms, serve as a catalyst for other schools, and strive for "uncommon excellence." Tilson's team hoped their marketing and inducements would create momentum. It did.

Schools were enthusiastic. In the years following the release of *CIM*, middle-grade reform became *de rigueur* in the state. Phase One began in 1988, with ten regional networks of ten to fifteen schools each. Rural Countryside and inner-city George Washington Carver were members of these first networks. One foundation school in each network, chosen because it was farther along, received a small grant to assist the other schools. Ten Phase Two networks, an additional 100 schools, formed in fall 1990. These included both suburban Canyon and inner-city Cesar Chavez. In 1991, 450 more schools indicated that they'd like to become members of reforming networks, and 62 signed on to Phase Three in fall 1992.

This was the reform context that Carnegie's middle-grade initiative would augment. Since the team's press for reform lacked mandates, it relied on persuasion and marketing efforts. They used Carnegie funding to produce a slick, five-part videotape series with glossy guidebooks and training protocols for facilitators. The first video, hosted by the star of television's "The Waltons," Richard Thomas, whose own twin sons were about to enter middle school, gave an entertaining overview of *CIM* and examples from some of the network schools. Staff hoped "that those on the margins of the reform effort will be impacted by the commitment of those who are already working on the cutting edge." Tilson's staff sent videos to each network principal, to county offices of education, statewide organizations, and key school reformers; all were asked to use the tapes at workshops and meetings. They sent brochures to one thousand local school boards and advertised in the journal of the school board association.

Securing an "Uncommon Commitment"

California's middle-grade initiative coincided with its economic downturn, and funding problems plagued the project as the state budget faltered. Initially, the consultants gave some hands-on support to the regional networks, visiting schools and attending network meetings. Soon demand outstripped unit resources. "We're running out of people," consultant Murphy lamented. Funding cuts eliminated support for nearly all travel, so any on-site visits had to be finessed within the department, paid for out of local schools' funds, or "donated" by the consultants. Despite frustration, the state middle-grade unit doggedly and optimistically invented cost-cutting strategies.

By Phases Two and Three, the new schools had to bear all the costs of their participation. In characteristic fashion, Tilson put the best spin on the state's unfunded mandate prohibition and resource shortage. Consultant Bradley noted with some amusement: "Derrick Tilson never lets lack of money be a deterrent; you just do it anyway. Everybody knows that the term 'uncommon commitment' means no money from us (laughter) . . . but we expect you to do it anyway."

Complementing the unit's emphasis on educativity and inclusiveness, Tilson favored a participatory scaling-up process and stressed the agency's commitment to schools' choosing and shaping their own reforms. Appropriating state law as his unit's own policy decision, he told the Carnegie national network, "We decided not to mandate anything. We would become brokers and facilitators." The team adopted a kind of "customer is always right" approach, inviting schools to select from the menu of reforms in *CIM*. They saw self-motivation and choice for the schools as pivotal to taking ownership and implementing change. They hoped that peer pressure and a positive competition within the networks would keep the schools moving. Murphy spoke to this point, saying, "The power and the synergy that has occurred has been one of the most exciting things that I've ever seen happen."

But at the same time the middle-grade team was encouraging schools to adapt the various reforms (teaming, advisory programs, and so on) to their own context, they also wanted to make sure that the central ideas didn't get lost in adaptation. Murphy told us, "In workshops we'd hold up [*CIM*] and say, 'When you sign on with us, this is your Bible for the next three to five years.'"

Beyond the Official: Negotiating Within the System

Over time, state funding for middle-grade reform shrank, and new, competing state reform initiatives emerged that weren't necessarily compatible with the values underlying *Caught in the Middle*. For example, concern about falling mathematics test scores in the state brought new pressure to emphasize middle-grade math as a discrete domain and stress basic skills, rather than approaching mathematics as part of cross-disciplinary learning activities or a problem-based curriculum. These regressive initiatives challenged the premises about educativity in middle-grade reform. So, too, did new projects aimed at better preparing low-income children in the state for college. The inclusiveness of the middle-grade reform was threatened by increasing pressure, from advocates for separate gifted-and-talented programs in the state, to rescind *CIM's* commitment to heterogeneous grouping.

However, rather than simply move on to the new agency priorities, Tilson searched for ways to head off, mitigate, or coopt the contrary initiatives wherever he could. He sought ways to bring other state units under his supervision, and he assigned the middle-grade consultants to spend part of their time working with other parts of the department. That way, they could piggyback middle school work onto other state projects and leverage those projects' resources for the middle-grade agenda. In Tilson's words, "We're making a big push. In essence, what I'm trying to do—without killing off each consultant—is moving more and more, and taking in more and more."

Consultant Perkins worked with the model curriculum projects that bore the brunt of the concerns about subject matter. Jeffries worked with the Chapter 1 unit "making presentations about middle-grade reform, and how it . . . merges with emerging changes in Chapter 1" and with the GT unit. Murphy took on the Middle Grades Postsecondary Preparation Program, a project to increase minority enrollment in senior high college preparatory tracks. Tilson told us, "We have our fingers in just about everything."

Beyond the Official: Ensuring What Matters Through Relationships

Working as collaborators with other state projects, the consultants held firm to middle-grade principles. For example, Jeffries worked ceaselessly with the powerful Gifted Education Unit that was adamantly opposed to heterogeneous grouping. "Internally," he told us, "the lines have been drawn." But Tilson argued that "it ought to be working so well that every classroom, hopefully, becomes a gifted classroom, every teacher becomes a teacher of gifted kids." Jeffries was also resolute; "we're going to continue to struggle, to push—at least at our middle level . . . the fight goes on and on." Jeffries openly confronted the contradiction between the middle school reform's press for inclusiveness and the links between gifted education and race and class stratification. To smooth the political waters, the team allowed that "flexible grouping" might be appropriate but stood firmly opposed to ability groups and tracking.

The state project leaders moved beyond their official roles as experts or authorities. Their personal relationships with educators proved especially important when the team pressed schools to aim for civic virtue. Close relationships allowed staff members to ask hard questions and exert pressure to keep schools from sidestepping the cultural contradictions they faced. For example, Perkins stepped in when racially mixed Countryside's white community opposed heterogeneous grouping. Perkins coached Principal Wanda Simpson almost daily, sent supporting material for the faculty, and brought the state's political muscle to bear on the district office. Yet Simpson saw this personal help and involvement as the most important support that she received from the state during the school's nearly decade-long affiliation with the project.

On one occasion, Murphy pressed a group of educators to grapple openly with racism at their schools: "We've been listening to you tell us that unless these problems are confronted and dealt with, you're not going to be able to do math, you're not going to be able to do science, you're not going to be able to do any of the academic stuff because all your energies are going to dealing with the results of intolerance and racism." Even though she later worried that she might be going too far, Murphy explained her thinking:

> We figured, Why beat around the bush? Call it what it is, and deal with it, and put it on the table. And we did. We got mixed reactions. . . . Some people walked out of meetings, the conversation still going . . . heatedly in the corner, but we wanted that. See, to us, that said it worked. If they had just walked out and [it] had been "Ho hum," and everything was rosy, we'd know we hadn't done it. Because if you don't create the climate for people to [have heated discussions], then it just gets swept under the carpet all the time. So we did it. It's risk taking, but you'll never know how to combat anything unless you bring it out in the open. It will stay [covered] for years. . . .

The schools were happy for any practical help the state offered. But what mattered most were the times when the middle-grade staff went far beyond their official roles. For Tilson this meant working around the system and circumventing standard procedures to break with the neutrality and rule-bound norms of his and most state agencies. For Murphy, it was a passion that could not let her tolerate racism (even when speaking out went against her best professional judgment and that of others). Clearly, for the California staff, promoting the middle-grade agenda was more than just their current professional project. As one staffer put it, they "stuck their necks out" and "asked questions later," as they worked to "do what's best" for middle-grade students and to maintain their equity direction.

However, because of California's physical size, many in the schools never saw this side of the state project and were uncertain about school involvement with the state and its impact. Carver teacher Tom Katzir's words reflect the views of many in the schools we studied: "People tell me I'm in a partnership school. I know of the other partnership schools, and I also know how they network with one another. I know because I've been to other schools, and I know that there's a relationship, mainly an administrative one. I'm not exactly sure how that's supposed to impact the kids.

There's not a kid in this school that knows what partnership means."

Illinois: Seeking Systemic Change

Statewide and state-led school reform is never simple, given striking regional differences. In Illinois, political tensions arise as "downstate" politicians representing white and poor rural people confront two political urban power blocks with contrasting interests: one advocating for mostly poor and minority Chicago, and the second advocating for mostly white and affluent suburbs. A school-funding formula dependent largely on local taxes makes matters even more difficult. In 1990, when middle-grade reform began, only in Texas did the education spending gap exceed that in Illinois, where the state's wealthiest district spent $14,000 per child, compared to $2,250 in the poorest district.

In the mid-1980s, Illinois education policy anticipated the national move toward standards and accountability-based reform. The legislature adopted state curriculum objectives, identified student outcome goals, and adopted a new state testing system. A succession of state superintendents tried to move the Illinois State Board of Education (ISBE) from a regulatory to an "assistance" approach—to a "customer service emphasis," as Superintendent of Public Instruction Joe Spagnola put it.

The push for middle-grade reform in Illinois came from grassroots advocates: middle-grade teachers and administrators. For a decade, Sarah Baxter, head of the Association of Illinois Middle Schools (AIMS), had worked with university professors to raise funds for middle-grade reform and research, including a $450,000 three-year federal grant in 1989. So, when the state superintendent in 1989 announced his interest in middle grades, Baxter, her fellow AIMS leaders, and University of Illinois colleagues persuaded the ISBE to develop and support a Carnegie project. Because the ISBE had no experienced middle-grade staff, Patrice Sherwood, a hard-working and respected agency manager, took the lead. Baxter and her team persuaded Sherwood that Illinois state policy must explicitly acknowledge the uniqueness of the middle grades. With some maneuvering "through all the politics," as Baxter put it, Sherwood won support from the board and the governor. Once funded, the Illinois MGSSPI project, like those in other states, began with a high-profile task force. Its report, *Right in the Middle,* sought to weave middle-grade reform into the fabric of Illinois schooling policy and practice.

Coherent Policies and a Network of Reforming Schools

Like the project directors in other states, Sherwood had two priorities: align state policies to support middle-grade reforms, and provide direct support to reforming schools. The project staff, collaborating with AIMS, worked to align the state education infrastructure with their work. In 1993, after two years of hearings and reviews, the state teacher certification board announced new middle school teacher preparation requirements, and ISBE and AIMS held conferences for the state's teacher training institutions to help them retool their programs. In addition, by 1995, the project team had also gotten middle-grade reform onto the professional-development agendas of the state's regional superintendents, as well as the Chapter 1 and special education units in the ISBE. Finally, Sherwood and her staff worked to make the state's new high-stakes school accreditation process compatible with middle-grade reform, knowing that schools would balk at reforms that put them at risk. As AIMS leader Baxter put it, if you "flunk [the accreditation], you can be taken over."

As with her counterparts in other state projects, Sherwood adopted an approach to reform emphasizing choice and support rather than mandates. In contrast to the high-stakes accreditation, Sherwood approached the work with schools with a light hand: "You can't get sustained institutionalized change by forcing someone to change. Now I know that other people don't believe that. Other people believe that mandates do work. But I can give you a lot of examples where they don't." Sherwood wanted to provide the schools with high-quality information on middle-grade topics that could help them frame their own reform direction and provide them with hands-on assistance.

Sherwood led a process to select thirty lead schools that were willing to embrace *Right in the Middle*'s reforms; they included small-town Inland, urban Washington Irving, and others across the state. Sherwood then asked agency staffer and former middle-grade teacher Will Darlington to organize the thirty schools into a support network. She, Darlington, and AIMS colleagues gave the schools a list of trainers who could help them learn more about middle-grade reforms; they published a pamphlet listing what each of the schools might offer the others; and they organized semiannual teacher-to-teacher and principal-to-principal exchanges. The AIMS group provided summer professional-development institutes for the network schools. "Giving advice rather than regulating was probably one of the best things that we've done," Sherwood told us. "People see the innovation as unrestricted, so when they call in here, they figure they can get some free-thinkers on the phone."

The Need to Go Deeper

Sherwood recognized early on that removing policy barriers, forming networks, and providing professional development wouldn't be enough to fundamentally transform schools. Like her counterparts in Texas and California, she watched with considerable frustration as educators rushed to adopt new structures and strategies without considering their deeper implications:

> People jump on the practices. [They say], "*Turning Points* is having teams." Well, why are we having teams? What is the purpose of teams? "Well it's just having teams." Interdisciplinary curriculum? "OK, let's do interdisciplinary curriculum." But why are we doing it? What are the purposes of it? What is our belief system about why we have interdisciplinary [curriculum]?" They'll never have those discussions unless you've got somebody asking questions to prompt that dialogue. They haven't had an inquiry approach to making decisions. I think that we've said, "These are the good practices for middle grades." So everybody kind of jumps on the bandwagon and does them without really thinking about the process of change and how do we make that change happen? And then some people think that because they've changed the structure, they're there.

To counter these superficial responses, Sherwood asked Darlington to work full-time supporting the lead schools—meeting regularly to push teachers' thinking about what the middle-grade reforms really meant. She also wanted him to educate and lobby district administrators and school boards to support the reform.

Darlington held lead school meetings, not only to provide information, but also to develop a statewide network of middle-grade advocates that would lobby for supportive policies.

To the extent his time allowed, he played an active part in helping the educators connect:

> I don't know if it's the culture here or what, but administrators seem to be reluctant to call on other administrators for advice or help. I don't know if that's admitting that I can't handle my own school, or what. . . . We have the network set up, and they can call on it, but they don't do it. But if you're sitting there on their team and say, "That's really a good idea. I know this school that's doing that unit right now. Let's give them a call and see if we can get the material here." Wow. It really works.

Spread thin, however, Darlington could only visit each of the thirty schools once or twice a year. "I visited the schools but did not take a really active role other than to meet with teachers, encourage them to continue what they were doing, and ask some really difficult questions."

The Whole Is Greater Than the Sum

To provide more support, Sherwood and Darlington devised a plan to combine the Carnegie schools with other statewide networks of schools that had been working with Levin's Accelerated Schools Project and Sizer's Coalition of Essential Schools. Arguing that the three reforms shared a common philosophy, Sherwood pressed the schools to pursue an "eclectic approach." Blending the three projects also enabled Sherwood and the ISBE staff to merge multiple funding streams, and they encouraged schools to do the same. Sherwood believed that this synergy was essential to make the reforms systemic and to scale them up statewide. By 1995, Sherwood and Darlington had pulled the state's various networks under one big umbrella: an eighty-school network that shared the resources of the three initiatives.

In 1993, when Carnegie asked the state projects to focus on a small number of low-income, high-minority schools, Sherwood and Darlington invited four such schools to join the lead-school network and engage in professional development, integrate health and social services into their programs, participate in the MGSSPI-sponsored self-study,[1] and work closely with the state project staff. The press to work closely with these schools enabled Darlington to begin using the Accelerated School inquiry process to help them push deeper. Darlington argued, "While *Turning Points* had the right ideas, they never had a process for it. I thought it was such a nice match that I began using it, not naming the process in the schools, but taking them through an inquiry process and looking at problem solving, problem-based learning."

A school "coach," Darlington reasoned, could facilitate sub-stantive conversations to keep reforms from simply reconfiguring the status quo, and help educators and communities develop a common set of beliefs or guiding principles. "To continuously improve," she told us, "You have to have an inquiry approach to learning. You have to continually ask why, why, why? Why are we doing this? Do we know where we're going? Do we have a way to get there? Are we asking the right questions?"

Coaching and Deeper Relationships

The shift to a smaller number of schools allowed Darlington to work intensively with educators, who spoke highly of his impact. Although Darlington had visited Irving in the early years of the project to bring information on grants, state mandates, state law, and so forth, when he became a coach the relationship changed. He found that, over time, teachers grew more sophisticated about the kind of help they asked for:

> It has changed dramatically. It's no longer superficial. They're ask-ing for time—"How do we create more time?" They're asking for a lot more on integrated curriculum—how to integrate curriculum effectively. They're looking for performance-assessment tech-niques. So I see them at a different level than they were before. . . . Do I have a part in the teams when it comes to, for example, inte-grating curriculum? I do because I'm on the teams. I actually do play a role there. I make suggestions. I share with them any infor-mation, training, manuals, resources that we have at the ISBE. It just surprises me sometimes, but maybe it's because I'm not so close. I'll hear a team talking about something, and I'll make a small suggestion that they just never thought of. I guess because

they're so involved with the everyday operation and management of school . . . they just don't always think about things, and yet, they're simple.

As coach at Irving, Darlington worked with the school's governance team once a week. Irving's Sandy Tolliver found Darlington helpful because he assuaged the concerns of those who were skeptical about reform: "Staff are very comfortable with him. He has enough authority because we have another group [of faculty] that has to be reassured that this is real. They won't necessarily take to me standing up in front of them, telling them this is a good process, but since this is the state, it's OK."

At Inland, Ben McCall had enormous regard for what Darlington was able to accomplish with the faculty that he, as principal, could not:

This new program, where Will visits us once a month, is awesome. It's a chance for an expert in middle-level education to go in and watch a team meeting and provide feedback. Because of my position as building principal, I couldn't do that. I can't go into a team meeting and when the team meeting is over, say, "All right, you guys didn't say one nice thing about that kid." Will Darlington can. Will Darlington sits in on a team conference and then they ask, "How'd we do, Will?" And he says, "Well, we sat here for thirty minutes and you didn't say one nice thing to the kid." And the team says, "Wow, you're right." Will says, "Have you ever had a conference with your boss for thirty minutes where he didn't say one nice thing about you? I have. How'd it make you feel?" See, Will is able to do that. . . .

Sherwood and Darlington believed that schools could confront the deeper cultural issues of reform if they and the coach used the schools' own data to generate hard questions. So Darlington integrated into the inquiry process data from the middle-grade self-study that AIMS leaders and researchers at the University of Illinois had developed and administered as part of a statewide project. "[Using the self-study] has forced them to begin looking at hard data. Schools aren't used to doing that. . . . It has really opened their eyes." Darlington organized teachers into study teams that focused on the "ideal middle school." Sherwood considered this inquiry as fundamental: "That's the underpinning of everything that happens. It's just like in a good marriage, you can have a lot of differences, but if you don't have a common, shared sense of purpose and values, you're probably not going make it, because things get too rough."

Darlington thought it was important for him to help the schools make good use of the data: "I don't know if they could [do it on their own]. They do rationalize it—not just the self-study data, but also standardized test results. When the scores come back low, it's because, 'Well, you know, it was a bad week. We had fog that day; school was delayed.' All kinds of things. But we still address it."

To supplement the data from the self-study survey, Sherwood and Darlington also asked the four schools to appoint "reform biographers": a faculty or staff member trained to become a critical observer and question asker. The biographers were to document the reform process with observations and with evidence, such as minutes from meetings and publications. Darlington believed that this biography exercise would bring continuity to the reform and provide a history "so that mistakes are not repeated." The written biography would also be a report to the community and to the state's policy accreditation office that could help the state learn what schools had done, thereby justifying the program to policy makers.

Coaching and Inquiry About What?

Both Sherwood and Darlington believed that their coaching and inquiry approach had worked well; Darlington explained that although coaches were "expensive," schools with coaches went much "further ahead" than those without them, some of which "became complacent." Sherwood added:

> It's kind of an odd situation, I know. I think it's reversed from every place else. Nobody else wants the state to come in. But our schools are firm that they want a state person to continue as their coach. I think it has a lot to do with the relationships that have been built up. They can see the bigger picture because someone from the state sees what's going on in a lot of different schools. They see the connections to policy. I also think they see themselves as being able

to influence us, since they are able to share with us. So it's a feed-back loop, almost. It's really two-way communication.

The Illinois team's coaching, inquiry, and self-study demon-strated great potential for a process that, if developed over time, might have a profound effect on the schools. However, its limited scope, resources, and duration ensured that the work of the team would be primarily a time-limited intervention rather than pro-mote enduring change in school culture. Their talking and work-ing together didn't penetrate to the deeper normative struggles around educativity, inclusiveness, caring, and participation. For example, although Darlington helped the Irving staff develop a set of interdisciplinary lessons, this work didn't confront the superfi-ciality of the lessons (such as the one we described in Chapter Three, where students role-played Jews escaping during the Holo-caust). At Inland, Darlington's assistance didn't help McCall and the faculty grapple more effectively with community racism and the constraints it placed on the school's efforts to develop inclu-sive, heterogeneous classrooms.

Massachusetts: Reform as the *Right* Thing to Do

Education ranks high among the policy interests of the citizens of Massachusetts. But for most of the state's history, this interest has been a local one. As one staff member at the state board of edu-cation put it: "This state is very decentralized . . . that's because of the history of local control. We [at the state] tend to shy away from statewide mandates on curriculum or other activities. The history of our agency is that we've generally been a less-visible partici-pant—more an encourager or a technical assister, rather than a monitor."

This analysis was offered before the 1990s, though, when the traditional role of the state agency changed quite considerably. In concert with remarkable changes in the political and economic landscape of the state, the change in role profoundly affected the course of middle-grade reform. Local control was sharply ques-tioned by the state's new Republican governor, William Weld, and by a group of the state's business and higher education elites. The governor attempted what some called "a hostile takeover" of the state education agency by creating his own cabinet-level secretary of education, and mounting a successful effort to merge the state's boards of education for higher education and K–12 education into a single body.

The governor's new appointees to the board included only one educator and several political conservatives. A report by the Massachusetts Business Alliance for Education, "Every Child a Winner," set the agenda for the state's first major educational reform legislation, the Education Reform Act of 1993. It established a new statewide funding formula and required teachers to upgrade their professional skills. These initiatives proved to be just the beginning of increasingly centralized education policy making. By mid-decade, the state had left behind its minimalist curriculum requirements, which specified thirteen years of physical education, one year of U.S. history, and one year of health. In its place, Massachusetts had a plan for state curriculum frameworks (a "common core of learning") in seven disciplines and a statewide assessment test tied to the frameworks, with the tenth grade test serving as a high school competency exam.

In Massachusetts the *Turning Points* project directors, Foster Davies and Zoe Sherman, grappled with how to promote middle-grade reform in this increasingly centralized policy context, and at the same time respect local communities' habits and preferences for local control. Davies was a former community organizer who now directed work at the department of education in student development and welfare (and later, after an agency reorganization, curriculum and instruction as well); Sherman headed teacher preparation and licensure. Together, they sought a synergy that would simultaneously alter middle school practices and preparation of teachers who would staff those schools.

But in the spirit of local control, they decided not to begin by pressing for new statewide policies. Rather, they would call for proposals from partnerships of middle schools and colleges, outlining how they would reform together. They had a vision of middle schools' becoming clinical sites for middle-grade teacher preparation programs while the colleges became resources for middle-grade school reform. Three of the Massachusetts schools we studied—James Madison and Horace Mann, in low-income urban neighborhoods, and rural Mountain View—were members of these early school-college partnerships.

To support the partnerships, Davies and Sherman convened regional meetings and statewide institutes featuring well-known middle-grade experts, and they deployed a small cadre of state consultants to assist the school-college collaborations. Before long, and in response to the enormous popularity of the partnership approach, Davies, Sherman, and their colleagues developed a two-tiered, top-down, bottom-up coaching approach. They created regional networks of school-and-college partnerships that included a fourth of the state's middle schools in eight networks. Small-town Lucy Sprague Mitchell and more affluent suburban Middleton were both members of these later networks. With Carnegie's 1993 mandate that the projects focus on a small number of low-wealth, minority "systemic change schools," Davies and Sherman added schools serving low-income communities to the reform mix in 1994—three concentrating their efforts on infusing a health focus into their schools, and three focusing on curricular innovations.

Forging Alliances

As in Illinois, the Massachusetts middle-grade staff also wove their project together with Accelerated Schools and the Coalition of Essential Schools initiatives. They brought federally funded Chapter 1 and special education programs into the mix, highlighting their compatibility with *Turning Points'* focus on disadvantaged schools, inclusion, and heterogeneous grouping. Forging these alliances required a great deal of skill and patience. As Davies remarked: "I spent the year building ties between Chapter 1 and special education so that we now have a team. . . . I've gotten them to front money from each account to support schools in the training. When we had a week of summer training, we invited all the special education and Chapter 1 staff to attend. . . . Because of that, we have all these Chapter 1 and special education staff running around saying how great Accelerated Schools are."

Sherman's department also wrote a proposal for a statewide systemic science and math reform grant to the National Science Foundation with the *Turning Points* schools in mind. Sherman targeted the NSF grant to the partnerships and chose participating middle schools as key project sites, using NSF resources to "leverage that change." They built other alliances as needed; when project schools wanted to administer a survey to assess their own progress, Sherman turned for help to another state department of education division: "So this year we corralled someone from the planning office who was sympathetic to our point of view and recruited him to work with each school with the design of surveys."

Reform as Adult Learning

Massachusetts reformers placed great faith in learning as a reform strategy—learning from research, learning from others, and learning as public engagement. Such learning was the means by which partnerships and networks would create reform. As Davies put it, "We think it's important to link schools to what research says is good, sound educational practice. It's time that schools stop operating in a vacuum and really take some serious self-reflective time to look at what research talks about in terms of good schools."

Moreover, to promote reflecting on and using expert knowledge, Davies commissioned and distributed a series of advisory papers aimed at illuminating the research base of good practice. Because they represent the authoritative view of a higher level of government, these widely circulated papers gained considerable visibility. Thus they not only publicized research but also shaped the reform agenda by displaying the expectations of the state. Balancing these expectations, Davies also recognized the power of local knowledge and placed high priority on schools and colleges' learning from one another. For example, the state consistently engaged school and college faculty as presenters at staff-development activities. One state consultant explained, "It's acknowledging that each teacher has something that they've mastered and that they can share with other teachers." Encouraging teachers to share with and learn from one another was the backbone of the Massachusetts networks.

Impressively, the project staff fostered its own climate of learning and experimentation. Admitting that "we probably screwed up and this is what we've learned" can be disarmingly effective, Davies argued. "Schools are so used to having institutional defensiveness put on them." Publicly acknowledging risks and mistakes actually enhanced learning. Staff revised their strategies to reflect what they had learned from other reform efforts and hired a documenter for the project to act as a sort of critical friend and help them reflect.

Nurturing Caring Relationships

Most of the staff agreed that building coalitions and community depended on caring personal relationships both within and outside the state agency. As one member put it, "The movement will come from the quality of personal relationships between the people who represent different agencies and the kind of work they choose to share across agency lines . . . it's a process over time, and it takes time for people to learn to trust that they can work together."

Staff entered these relationships with much more than an instrumental eye to gaining support. They told us that the connection can't be "on just a glad handshake kind of level, but you have to talk about what people's needs are," and "getting to this point requires coming to know who they are and what they do." Valuing relationships in this way, project staff built a solid record of fulfilling personal and institutional commitments. Moreover, the values held by state project staff carried over to at least some of the school and college participants. As we describe in more detail in Chapter Eight, for example, relationships between project participants at Mountain View and its partner, Mandeville College, appear to have enhanced considerable interdependence and enabled partners to challenge conventional roles and beliefs.

An Explicit Focus on Social Justice

Davies's most ambitious vision and the source of his greatest frustration stemmed from explicitly focusing on school reform as social justice. Unlike most of the project leaders and staff in other states, he used his bully pulpit to set a tone for reform that paid particular attention to the values and ideas underlying reform, particularly inclusiveness. He argued persuasively that middle-grade reform is not only more likely to improve student outcomes; it is simply the right thing to do. Whereas other reform leaders excused schools that were slow to pursue inclusion (often resorting to the argument that one size doesn't fit all), Davies and the project team pressed for a shared moral high ground for reform. They appealed to state policy, legislation, research, and (most often) a democratic vision for schooling to shape resources and assistance.

Davies walked a fine line as a state leader, maintaining an in-your-face commitment to social justice with a disarming conge-niality that won his group considerable respect. He noted, "People joke that we are a kind of renegade unit in the department." The team won support for its ambitious agenda. In 1991 (the state com-missioner of education later told us), "the very fact that we are tack-ling the toughest schools first—urban middle schools that have a whole host of other issues that people have to address—and trying to use those as the laboratory for addressing restructuring issues strikes me as a brave thing to do . . . that strikes me as impressive."

The equity goals envisioned by Davies and his staff were risky in a state where high-performing, mostly white and wealthy suburban schools stand in sharp contrast to racially torn, low-achieving city schools. They used Carnegie's prestigious name and its mod-est resources as levers to tilt more of the state's resources toward low-income children. As Davies told us (and everyone else), "The issues of social justice are in the forefront for me and our unit." He aggressively recruited urban schools to keep the rapidly ex-panding project networks from being dominated by suburban interests.

He struggled on other fronts to include all students and com-munities in the best schooling opportunities. An ardent supporter of the state commissioner's efforts to eliminate the general track in senior high schools, Davies pressed to include "equity indica-tors" in the state's new system of standards and accountability. These included measures of whether middle schools equitably pro-vided the conditions and opportunities for learning. Among these standards, he argued, was the requirement that students be offered courses in algebra in the eighth grade. Davies lent his own and his agency's support for many projects around grouping issues; for example, when Madison parents complained that the school's intention to mainstream bilingual students in regular teams would put the school out of compliance with regulations governing bilin-gual education, he responded by "taking a stroll down" to that divi-sion in the state agency. He persuaded them to grant Madison some additional time and political latitude so that the school could experiment with inclusive approaches to bilingual education.

A striking feature of the environment of risk taking in Massachusetts was that people had the courage to engage in public learning. Making things public, talking aloud about difficult issues of race and equity, and marshaling support through public appeal to the higher moral ground set a firm foundation for changes in practice. Staff believed that such public talk and learning about civic virtue allowed people to see the fundamental interests they shared with others.

Pressing Toward a Better Class of Problems

If middle-grade reform were to go deeper than other change efforts, Davies argued, schools and colleges must see their joint work as "embedded in their mission—that it's not another project that they're taking on; it's really a vehicle for systemic improvement and change." Just as urban schools must transform what Davies called "parochial" and "fatalistic" identities, colleges would have to challenge their individualistic cultures—blurring boundaries both within their own institutions and with schools. The most formidable problem, according to Davies, was that "the college culture really is very individualistic. There's nothing structural at the college level that requires people to work in teams and requires people to get on site, into schools. In fact, it's the opposite, that you have to do your individual research and get your papers published so you can continue your status within the university."

At the project outset, Davies and his staff focused on basic problems: helping schools and colleges get along and learn about the content of the middle-grade initiative. Despite the focus, he pressed harder on the core issues—sometimes being quite forceful about what really mattered. Over time, the level of discussion at schools and colleges went up a notch—to a better class of problems[2]—including conflicts over the meaning and practice of educativity, social justice, caring, and participation.

By 1996, however, Massachusetts had undergone a dramatic political shift. New conservative members of the state board—notably John Silber, president of Boston University, and James Peyser of the Pioneer Institute—were bent on reversing the state's progressive reforms. The curriculum frameworks that Davies helped develop were revised to look like the standards approved by the conservative Fordham Foundation. The board also adopted the Massachusetts Comprehensive Assessment of Skills (MCAS), which pressed schools in a direction diametrically opposed to the middle-grade emphasis on educativity. Equity issues dropped off the education policy agenda altogether. Believing that his efforts at middle-grade reform would also be undone, Davies left the agency.

Vermont: Dialogue, Consensus, and Community

Vermont's small, economically diverse, white population takes pride in its tradition of independence and local control. Town meetings often last well into the night as citizens grapple with local policies, taxation, and annual city budgets. Most residents are practiced in representing their point of view and working together. Education Commissioner Rick Mills, a Vermont newcomer, described the state's participatory culture: "Collaboration is expected. The place is very richly endowed with . . . people [who] have a lot of collaboration . . . skills. You rarely run into a person who can't stand up and give a speech . . . articulately. It's a tremendous advantage."

He learned quickly: "A political leader has to know how to listen. That's what you have to do as an educational [leader] too." As Mills and other policy makers listened, they also led through talk: "We deal with it partly . . . by talking endlessly about the goals of education, by painting word pictures . . . drawn from local experience." Talking and listening in Vermont take time, as policy making proceeds through a process of discussion, proposal making, and responses. For Mills, this meant that "every two weeks, I spend a whole day, early morning to late at night, in various communities."

One staffer in the Vermont Department of Education (VDE) warned that public support for middle-grade reform "could turn on a dime." In Mills's words, "Political campaigns are door-to-door, getting to the people. Transformation of the school is the same way. So, it's a matter of having a campaign for the children." Policy making is built "around involving everybody," and many in the VDE take pride in the tradition of broad-based involvement. Education policy emerges, Mills told us, from "maximum consensus—believing that we can hold our head high and say, 'We really did ask; we really did consider it; and we really did listen.'"

However, Vermont's local tradition has also meant that public support for education policies is marked by a potentially incompatible mixture of commitment to child welfare, rugged self-reliance, and ambivalence about government reforms. In fact, equity-minded reforms such as fiscal equalization ran into solid opposition from outspoken Vermonters who prized their individual interests. For example, author and Vermont resident John Irving's widely quoted vocal opposition to fiscal equity among the school systems framed equalization as "Marxism. It's leveling everything by decimating what works."[3]

A Reform Leader

Vermont garnered national attention in the early 1990s as a leader in adopting education reforms. In particular, the state's portfolio assessment project, studied by RAND, was closely monitored by national and state assessment groups. In Mills's judgment, "We have a national role that far outweighs our size." Rather than simply following national trends, however, Vermont has made reforms fit its own context. Mills believes that the state's stubborn insistence on being true to itself has enhanced its influence: "Our voice carries weight in these national discussions because we have thought this through locally." Local education professor Sean Christopher spoke for many others who are proud of this approach: "If it's possible to restructure American education . . . then it should happen here first."

Partly because of the insistence of local educators that Vermont deserved and needed a MGSSPI project, the VDE staff responded to Carnegie's first request for proposals. But without a middle-grade unit in the agency, staffers had little firsthand experience. In Vermonter fashion, they mounted a grassroots strategy. Staffer Walt Douglas recalled: "So we decided [that we] should get together the good old Mickey Rooney. You know, 'Let's get everybody together. Let's do a show. . . .' We just got everybody together, and it was . . . just layer on layer with enthusiasm."

Vermont's education reforms were driven by an ambitious and blunt vision: "High skills for every student—no exceptions, no excuses." Repeated regularly, the statement affirms excellence and equity at the same time that it anticipates common reactions by not allowing the usual escape clauses. In talks and reports to the state board, Mills measured all of the VDE's efforts against this vision. The MGSSPI was no exception.

The Vermont proposal, infused with notions of community and caring, easily won Carnegie support. Eight or nine VDE staffers from various divisions came together as an interdisciplinary MGSSPI team, while a cadre of middle-level principals, teachers, and professors who helped write the proposal became consultants. One, a widely admired education professor named Carrie Jacobs, took the lead. Douglas explained her enormous impact: "When she gets out her little laptop . . . and she's cranking stuff out, [or when she's] standing up there with a pen and drawing something that somebody else didn't see, . . . she had the people in the room . . . believing that the journey of trying to figure this out was worth it."

A statewide Middle Grades Task Force brought together teachers and principals, representatives from the Vermont Association of Middle Level Educators (VAMLE), staffers from state education and health and human services agencies, members of service learning groups, professors from institutions of higher education, and one elected official. The task force sought "to provide a clear and unified direction for middle-level education." Their report, *The Middle Matters*[4] (which placed the theme of "no exceptions, no excuses" in a context of caring and community for young adolescents), became state policy. It pledged to ensure that every young adolescent be intellectually reflective, competent, caring and ethical, productive, responsible, healthy, and committed to learning throughout life.

Interweaving Reforms

The specific *Turning Points* recommendations folded into the "much bigger educational reform initiative in the state," as Jacobs put it; "this project alone would have very little meaning in the state if it weren't for the other pieces." The team's strategy was to weave together a range of other state projects whose educative and inclusive goals resonated with *Turning Points*: projects aimed at developing a "common core of learning," curriculum frameworks, school delivery standards, and portfolio assessment. The state's NSF math and science reform grant also fit with the MGSSPI approach to school change, as did the state school restructuring initiative. Over time, the MGSSPI emphasis on interdisciplinary curriculum became a defining feature of the state's content-based curriculum frameworks and performance standards.

The multiple responsibilities of policy makers, education leaders, and teachers at trend-setting schools mirrored the interwoven substance of the reform. For example, Jacobs took the lead on both the state's middle-grade initiative and its common-core curriculum framework. Leaders constantly bumped into one another in their multiple responsibilities. As a result, their personal familiarity and knowledge of one another's business helped merge reforms that might otherwise have remained in separate offices.

Supporting Reform Locally

Over the course of the decade, three waves of schools participated as MGSSPI lead or demonstration schools. During the first wave, four lead schools, including affluent Verbena and low-income Van Buren, represented the state's range of demographic differences and grade configurations. Only schools that had been named by others as leaders in the middle-grade reform effort were chosen. But, true to Vermont's culture, these schools, rather than being stars that had already arrived, were simply making a solid commitment to get there. Jacobs explained: "The bottom line was climate. If there was . . . respect for and caring about each other among staff, there was probably a lot that you could do there, as opposed to a place where there was a lot of antagonism."

In the second phase, the project staff added seven new lead schools; the third phase focused intensely on four systemic-change schools that served disadvantaged students.

Finally, to scale up the MGSSPI , more than fifty schools participated in seven regional networks that would extend the reform throughout the state. With a lead school as the "hub in the wheel of a network," a VDE staff member explained, "people can see [the reforms]." Another argued that "the most valuable time for them [teachers] is communicating and speaking and spending time with other schools." Making the networks meaningful to participating schools was an ongoing challenge, and over time the MGSSPI team shifted away from region-based to issue-based networks that, according to one staffer, "build off of more natural relationships" of need and interest.

Eschewing Prescriptions and Pressure

Jacobs helped array a variety of groups that augmented the state middle-grade team's direct support. VAMLE built a grassroots people-to-people, school-to-school, resource system. The group organized conferences where local educators presented, sponsored visits to exemplary programs outside the state, maintained a Middle Grades by Mail resource library, and published a biannual newsletter and journal (in which educators write nearly all the articles). The Middle Grades Task Force's Young Adolescent Health Action Team, the Prevention and Wellness Group, and the Adolescent Health Task Force all offered services to help schools meet young adolescent health needs. Finally, in what education professor Christopher called an unusual "parity among those of us in higher education," faculty from five colleges came together as the Middle Grades Professional Development Collaborative—"just a group of people meeting every couple of weeks for two to three hours." This group developed preservice programs for middle-level educators; advocated for middle-level courses within the colleges; and offered professional development to experienced teachers, aimed at fostering student-responsive pedagogy. Although middle-grade certification was not mandated, by 1995 Vermont colleges offered five middle-level teacher-education programs.

The project's strategy for supporting schools developed over time, as Vermont's small size allowed college personnel to forge close relationships with local educators. What emerged was a highly individualized approach that emphasized local choice. Team members went to schools only when invited—a rule that, in the view of the state's Middle Grades Health Coordinator, Susan Sherman (no relation to Turning Points project director Zoe Sherman), encouraged schools' "willingness to work in a mutual way" and softened their wariness of the state.

The VDE middle-grade team built trust by posing questions to engage schools in learning about themselves—their goals, needs, and resources—and by evaluating reform options, rather than by giving answers. Because they got to know schools well, team members also understood each school's reform choices in the context of its history, traditions, and community dynamics. Acting as critical friends, they tried to help locals integrate middle-grade practices into the day-to-day life of school and support "what's happening, as opposed to making it a production in itself." Jacobs and VDE staff also tailored assistance to the needs and preferences of each network and school. For example, Van Buren teacher Delores Sullivan recounted how Jacobs helped resolve some personal conflicts that bubbled up on her team during one of the summer institutes: "She came and would sit in and listen. For some reason people finally felt they could be open enough to bring up things that were actually bothering them."

Exercising Caution with the Culture

Deference to local choices meant that the ability of the state project to press schools toward reforms that challenged cultural assumptions was minimal; as one state staffer told us, "we don't espouse anything when we're there." Instead of pressing for cultural shift, then, the cornerstone of Vermont's implementation strategy was to give teachers knowledge of middle-grade practices. State staff believed that flooding the educational environment with middle-grade professional and preservice learning opportunities would generate the reflection and discussion necessary to ensure buy in and fidelity to the vision. Jacobs and the rest of the Vermont team emphasized creating arenas for reflection in which educators could clarify goals, plan action, and understand results.

However, this cautious approach still allowed the team to help a school focus explicitly on issues related to civic virtue, if that was the direction the school wanted. For instance, in one network teachers wanted to work on inclusiveness by addressing the concerns of those in their schools who were resistant to heterogeneous grouping. In this case, the VDE staff member helped arrange a series of four all-day subject-area workshops on the topic, calling on nationally known teachers as speakers. But if such issues did not emerge on the initiative of a school or network, they were unlikely to be addressed. Despite the fundamentally democratic values that underlie the Vermont culture, if efforts to become educative or socially just went against the grain of the majority in a particular town, they would not likely develop into an initiative for change. Little in the Vermont culture welcomes pressure for antimajoritarian initiatives.

The Vermont project's emphasis on relationships along with its small size help explain the state's welcomed presence in the schools we studied. One Van Buren teacher explained: "It really opens your eyes to a lot of things you really didn't even know existed . . . never really gave much thought to. . . . It gives you a reason to go out and do more." Many found the informal meetings with the project staff to be most helpful. For instance, one teacher described how Jacobs attended her team meetings for support as team members worked through some interpersonal conflicts that were standing in the way of reform. In sum, much of what the state did was appreciated and useful.

However, the state's cautious presence proved insufficient to support the schools through the tough, significant implementation process they faced. Sometimes the schools felt they needed much more help from the project team. In other cases, at Verbena for example, some faculty saw the state's reticence to be more resolute as contributing to the difficulty of reform. One faculty member explained that the tradition of local control meant the state staff couldn't "get out and really push cutting-edge things" when the school faced intense local opposition. One school board member, frustrated with the state's laissez-faire approach, complained that the state project staff should have been more proactive in educating the community about Verbena's reform efforts: "Community members [should] know that Verbena is not alone, that we are not reinventing education in isolation. The state should do more spotlighting of schools that are delivering education in different ways and get us off this track of departmentalized, compartmentalized, standardized industrial-model schools. [The state] needs to publicize this."

Unfortunately, given the VDE's role as simply supporting local decisions, Jacobs and her team could do little more than sympathetically stand by as the Verbena community quashed the school's innovative efforts to become educative and then dismissed committed middle school reformer Sarah Chatsworth.

The Scaling-Up Dilemma

Looking carefully at the reform efforts in the 1990s, Harvard education policy analyst Richard Elmore concluded that "getting to scale" requires several key ingredients: (1) strong *external* norms that make clear what constitutes good practice; (2) close working relationships that "intensify and focus" these norms among teachers; (3) reformers who employ a sophisticated, yet practical, theory of how success at one school might be reproduced at another; and (4) structures and incentives that prompt teachers to engage in the hard work of learning new practices.[5]

Did these state projects scale up middle-grade reform? The state projects established an official vision of middle-grade schooling designed to give educators the political clout to try to make their schools better. Doing so, they provided strong *external* norms that made good practice clear. However, once the vision became part of the state policy systems, reformers focused on the structural and practical manifestations of the reform, often to the neglect of the principled reform ideas. Consequently, little in the states' strategies prepared schools to deal explicitly with the cultural and political contradictions that the reform ideas might bring to light. Moreover, the states' protective umbrella offered reforming schools little cover from the storms of local controversy brought on by these cultural contradictions. Project staff were not naïve about the new norms that their reforms embodied, or about the need for addressing them. However, so deep was the culture of their agencies and their own thinking that when they did seek to address these contradictions, as often as not they used technical means.

In a few schools, state project staff were able to establish close working relationships with educators, which, as Elmore put it, "intensified and focused" these norms among teachers. But because resources limit personal contacts, the good that came from face-to-face opportunities left out nearly all schools and teachers. Moreover, even if the state staff developed congenial working relationships, they still lived in different worlds and—with few exceptions, such as Will Darlington's connections with Irving and Inland—did not share local reform work over extended time. Their collaboration was by definition hierarchical, so the relationships couldn't really address the aims of those with less power. This, of course, is the same problem schools run into when they try to enfranchise less-powerful parents—they're doing *for* rather than *with.* Because the states realized they couldn't develop and sustain the kind of relationship that mattered most, they created networks of schools to flatten the hierarchies so that many schools could relate to one another. But few schools had the resources or inclination to develop relationships that would focus and intensify new norms. It appears that the top-down, bottom-up formulation must acknowledge the dual nature of this relationship: schools need to work collegially, as equals, with persons they perceive as having power greater than their own.

Did these state reformers employ a sophisticated, yet practical, theory of how the success of one school might be reproduced at another? Did they frame structures and incentives that prompted teachers to engage in the hard work of learning new practices? The experiences of the schools we studied led us to believe that they did not. As we elaborate in the remaining chapters, the schools we studied taught us that their theories of reform and scaling up bear little resemblance to a practical theory for becoming good schools. Rather, such a theory, we argue, must instill an ongoing process of the type we call betterment. Betterment is aimed at creating desirable outcomes for students, teachers, and schools. But in light of the lessons we learned, betterment must also be a "good" process. The hard work of becoming a good American school (making schools good) must itself be educative, socially just, caring, and participatory.

Chapter Eight

Struggling in the Reform Mill

If the administration wants to go with that program,
you've got to go with that program. Simple as that.
There's no point in kicking and making waves. . . .
You learn to deal with it. You don't get all bent out of
shape because you still want your job, so you have to go
along with the program. . . . You just wait for a certain
period of years, and then someone comes up with another
idea. . . . Change only lasts a short time. You have to
go with the flow. I try to do the best job that I can with
whatever I'm asked to do. It makes my day much easier.

SABRINA ARTHUR,
HORACE MANN MIDDLE SCHOOL TEACHER

We met very few teachers, administrators, or state project staff who were grumbling slackers. Rather, their steady hard work was often punctuated with bursts of upbeat, Herculean effort, and many educators were never less than Herculean. But their efforts rarely escaped the contradictions that pervade American culture—and American schools. Educators know that reform initiatives ask them to change conventional practices dramatically. They also know that the reform process expects them to go with the flow, get with the program, not make waves. But as initiatives make their way through the machinery of making policy and implementing plans into schools, the flow of the reform eventually arrives at the culture's lowest point, rarely a welcoming place for civic virtue. Thus teachers and principals attempt to go against conventional practices and norms while caught in a reform process guaranteed to preserve the status quo. We call this culture of school reform "the reform mill."

The reform mill grinds out reworked versions of the status quo that do little to address whatever initially motivated the reform. In place of making schools truly educative, the reform mill offers—but rarely delivers—higher standards and improved test scores. Behind the image of social justice, the mill tries to make schools meritocratic through competition, or it creates compensatory programs for those who can't compete. Instead of care, the mill services the needy. Behind the image of democratic participation, the mill gives a vote on a committee. Disappointed with the results of reform, policy makers, the public, and educators themselves judge the reform to be misguided, poorly implemented, or both; and so the next reform, waiting in the wings with new funding or new leadership, takes center stage.

Because most funding beyond schools' basic allocations is an incentive to reform, schools compete for a staggering array of new programs "to get as much as [they] can," in the words of Sandy Fraser, another Horace Mann teacher. The focus, or at least the priority, is often on doing or promising what is necessary to get the money, rather than developing a reform that may promise something different or take longer. Thoughtful proposals are discouraged by short application deadlines and a preference for using (or buying into) a plan that is being implemented elsewhere. As a counselor at affluent Tanglewood said, "Somewhere along the way the school district changed from wanting to be good just to be good, to being better than everybody." A teacher at Chavez noted that "there's a real strong desire to be on the cutting edge of things"; but another from Countryside pointed out "that cutting-edge is not particularly relevant, or particularly supported by data." Still another teacher said that "we're always changing, but we're not exactly sure why we're changing."

Professional judgments and self-judgments are often based on educators' willingness to embrace reform. The mill (or the culture of reform) sends them the message that they aren't professionals unless they pursue whatever reform package comes along. Many of the very best teachers and administrators we met—those most inclined toward and informed about reform—were being run ragged. Verbena's principal described her committed staff in these words: "They may be busy, they may be frenetic, they may be tired, they may not want anymore on their plate right now, but they are not resistant to change." At Tubman, teacher Sarah James agreed: "We just have so many things going on that you . . . almost get to the point where you just want to quit. The sad thing is that clearly outstanding people are the ones . . . who get real close to burnout. . . . The challenges that they take on are so involved that [they] require multiple hours of outside work."

Overwhelmed and frustrated by the absence of any real payoff for long hours, teacher Haley Marston agreed: "Most people were feeling that they can't do all these meetings. . . . It was turmoil. . . . All felt it was too fast, too much, too soon, everything in an extreme. . . . It's not the concept of change, but how much, how fast." Pat Lewis told us that it was not uncommon to see a teacher break down in tears because of the heavy load. In fact, many teachers did just that, wept, as we interviewed them about the demands of reform. "You are giving it all you've got," Lewis told us, "and you're still coming up short." Reform, as someone at Chavez put it vividly, "comes out of people's hides."

Why does this reform mill make sense to Americans, who are nearly unanimous in their view that it does not work well? Why do Americans insist on explaining the reform mill's failures through faulty parts (teachers, principals, low standards, monopolistic public education, bad parents, and so on)? We propose that the reform mill's purpose is to align the goals, ideals, and energies of reform-minded educators and citizens into an increasingly well-oiled, fail-safe system for educating youth—certainly a worthy (if narrow) reform purpose. We propose that the reform mill's failure is its inability and unwillingness to marshal social commitments to make schools places of civic virtue—places where adults and children experience educativity, care, social justice, and democratic participation.

In this chapter, we return to the early-twentieth-century origins of today's reform mill to better understand its logic. We then revisit our schools and state reform projects to suggest how the reform mill ground down the efforts of the most well-intentioned and hard-working school communities. We also find, however, impressive examples of reformers who struggled against the reform mill—who went against the flow. We hope that by exposing the workings of the reform mill and examining how educators battle against it, we can begin to formulate a humane and meaningful alternative conception—one of school reform as *betterment*.

At its core, a concept of reform as betterment goes back to Aristotle, who believed that we acquire virtue by engaging in practices driven by internal, not external, goods.[1] A practice in this sense is a shared activity that is undertaken because it's intrinsically valuable—because it is good in itself, collapsing the distinction between ends and means.[2] If we think of school reform as a practice or shared activity in this sense, then the goods internal or essential to reform include self-knowledge, analytic skill, critical stance, collaboration, active participation, and so on—goods that may be framed in terms of Americans' cultural struggles over educativity, social justice, care, and participation. In this sense, betterment makes little distinction between the process or means of getting an education and the product or ends of an education, both for students and teachers. In contrast, the reform mill is driven by external goods such as test scores (the ends) that may or may not be linked to educative, socially just, caring, and participatory means. As a result, even the most reform-minded teachers must struggle to hold on to the internal goods of betterment (self-knowledge, analytic skill, critical stance, etc.), their noble intentions mediated by an imposing set of structures, ideologies, and rituals set in motion nearly a century ago.[3]

Taylor Versus Dewey

In 1911, Frederick Taylor's immensely popular *Principles of Scientific Management* set the reform mill in motion by building on Max Weber's concept of the division of labor. Whereas Weber emphasized bureaucratic relationships among workers and the jobs they perform, Taylor accepted these relationships and focused specifically on the jobs themselves, dividing them into their smallest and most specialized components. Thus, Taylor further refined (made more "rational") Weber's hierarchical model by arguing that if an organization's goal is efficient production, the greatest good results when workers toward the bottom of organizational hierarchies perform ever more repetitions of increasingly simple tasks.

As Taylor explained, each worker might receive an instruction card, describing in detail "not only what is to be done, but how it is to be done and the exact time allowed for doing it."[4] Workers must "do what they are told promptly and without asking questions or making suggestions . . . it is absolutely necessary for every man in an organization to become one of a train of gear wheels."[5] Based on his belief that the desired ends should be divorced from execution or means, Taylor's new "planning departments" turned the quest for greater efficiency (a large part of what schools, today, call reform) into a science. Changing people's actions became as easy as distributing a new set of instruction cards. Taylor enthusiastically envisioned workers as automatons, exercising good habits and little intelligence. As Taylor put it: "All possible brainwork should be removed from the shop and centered in the planning or laying out department."[6] The rational thinkers, the planners, belonged higher up.

John Dewey, a contemporary of Taylor's, also looked to science as a model of progress, though his progressivism was driven foremost by democratic principles. Unlike Taylor, who advocated rule by an elite of scientific efficiency experts, Dewey believed that everyone was capable of careful, rational thought and should use this knowledge to inform democratic decision making.[7] Removing what Taylor called brainwork from the shop floor was antithetical to Dewey's core beliefs that improving the common good depended on the participation of all members of the organization. It would not be until the end of the century that American businesses would entertain (with rare fidelity, in practice) Dewey's conception that nonhierarchical relationships could work well for them, and efforts to improve *products* would also benefit from the active interest and participation of all. In 1908, Dewey explained it this way:

> The vice of the social leader, of the reformer, of the philanthropist and the specialist in every worthy cause of science, or art, or politics, is to seek ends which promote the social welfare in ways which fail to engage the active interest and cooperation of others. The

conception of conferring the good upon others, or at least attaining it for them, which is our inheritance from the aristocratic civilization of the past, is so deeply embodied in religious, political, and charitable institutions and in moral teachings, that it dies hard. Many a man, feeling himself justified by the social character of his ultimate aim (it may be economic, or educational, or political) is genuinely confused or exasperated by the increasing antagonism and resentment which he evokes, because he has not enlisted in his pursuit of the "common" end the freely cooperative activities of others. This cooperation must be the root principle of the morals of democracy.[8]

Better Schools Through Scientific Reform

Dewey's observations continue to be borne out. The "vice" of today's "social leader, of the reformer, of the philanthropist and the specialist" in school reform feeds off of Taylor's legacy and maintains school reform within the purview of the reform mill. More than twenty years ago, Paul Berman and Milbrey McLaughlin catalogued and documented the ineffectiveness of the methods of this "science" that splits rather than unites means and ends: reliance on outside consultants; packaged management approaches; one-shot, pre-implementation training; pay for training; and formal, summative evaluation.[9] Still prevalent today, these strategies and structures—along with others we detail below—define how we do reform.

Perhaps the most visible and politically salient products of this science are the *categorical program* and the *reform design*. Over the past thirty years, federal and state governments have constructed an elaborate network of categorical programs, aiming to fix specialized categories of citizens (poor, minority, learning disabled, etc.) by offering services that are delivered through an extensive array of prescriptions, rules, and bureaucratic regulations. An urban high school might have dozens of these programs to administer, miring local educators in complicated budgets and paperwork instead of engaging their students in serious learning.[10]

Categorical programs and other government reform initiatives have spawned hundreds of prefabricated and costly reform packages that inundate districts and schools every year with promises of higher test scores, improved self-esteem, and safer schools.

Michael Fullan noted that between 1979 and 1981 New York City schools piloted 871 such programs.[11] Despite more than two decades of research documenting the failure of external mandates (reforms to be faithfully implemented in schools), we seem unable to move beyond them. For example, the last reauthorization of federal Title I legislation mandated that schools that receive federal funds must adopt a "research proven" reform design. Although some of these designs allow room for local adaptation, others are quite prescriptive.

To help educators comply with regulations that accompany categorical programs and money, reform packages typically come in a friendly self-help format, complete with scripted training materials or consultant-provided training sessions. Although enterprising schools may in good faith adapt the prescriptions to fit their purposes, they are typically not encouraged to challenge or question packaged wisdom. Brainwork comes included in the package. Categorical programs and reform packages pass through schools as if on a conveyor. A teacher or principal who shouts "Stop! I want to consider this, make it better, inquire about its flaws" is as welcomed as a worker on the line bringing production to a halt. She had better have a good reason. She had better not do it too often. Many reform packages and programs try to make teachers student-centered and cognizant of learning as an interdisciplinary, socially constructed process, but they rarely add an approach that is teacher-(as learner)-centered; they avoid interdisciplinary content, and they attempt to transmit rather than have teachers construct new knowledge.

Practicing What We Teach

The very institutions charged with making changes, including the schools themselves, their communities, and their states, also have a great stake in making sure that change does not take place. When genuine reform seemed to take hold, it was often accomplished by skirting official reform channels. The most "successful" state project staff accomplished more through their personal relationships than by following the letter of their official, contractual role. They helped schools move away from reform as a commodity that could be provided by an outsider. These relationships among teachers, principals, and external supporters (including district, state, and university staff) were on occasion the foci of contextually relevant instantiations of principles that emerged from research and professional experience. In short, we saw evidence of co-constructed processes and programs that made schools better places for teachers and students even in the midst of community opposition and counterproductive legislative mandates.[12] But all this, as we shall see, was extraordinarily tough going, with the difficulty exacerbated at every turn by Taylor's legacy.

Becoming Educative Workplaces

It is a simple enough proposition: if teachers are not respected, not helped to respect others' differences, not encouraged to think critically, not permitted to speak their reservations, not allowed to work together solving real problems, and not given the time or resources to accomplish their jobs, then they are not likely to develop the norms or learn the skills required to fulfill even the most modest of reforms. Yet teachers rarely had such opportunities. Rather, the behaviorist learning theories and transmission modes of teaching that emerged with the reform mill were nearly ubiquitous conditions for teachers' learning.

Marginalized Learning Opportunities

"The all-day in-service is nice," Martha Sawyer, a Horace Mann teacher, said, "but you have one every three months. There's not a lot of give. Isolated days and isolated days and isolated days. I don't want to teach kids that way. Why would you teach teachers that way?" States or districts typically required teachers to fulfill a minimum number of hours of training per year. The California schools we studied, for example, ranged from six hours at Canyon to four days at Carver. Although everyone was "all for [teachers'] self-improvement," as one Mitchell teacher framed it, most teachers complained that training was sporadic and mostly unrelated to their daily worklives. Even schools energized by the reforms had to fight to hang on to their three or four in-service days a year. Van Buren's principal said he had been "hounding the superintendent for more time" and did end up with additional staff development, in spite of a school board member protesting that if teachers were truly committed to reform, they would be willing to pursue learning opportunities on their own time.

Packaged Brainwork

Teachers were expected to take expert knowledge and apply it on their own with little outside support. Over time, some state project leaders recognized this as a problem. Jane McIvoie, in Texas, told us, "The time for reflection has been missing. That's probably one of the biggest things we have discovered. My thinking was, if we just give them staff development and the knowledge, then it will happen. But once you have the staff development, you still need an inordinate amount of time to pull that together to apply it, to develop something. The demand on teachers, of what we, the gurus of the notion, are asking them to do—what sounds so good on paper—is unbelievable."

McIvoie asked staff from the state's regional education service centers to follow up with teacher teams after their "technical support" sessions. That way, she said, "in these team meetings, the teachers talk about concerns, and curricula, and so forth, and it is there that misperceptions can be clarified." The reform-mill culture, however, undermined McIvoie's determination to make available time and resources for constructing local knowledge and for the reflection that was required. Policy makers and administrators, both local and state, continued to emphasize strict accountability for planning time and were often preoccupied with the ends, or products, of these meetings at the expense of the means, or adult-learning processes.

Some experts actually limit teachers' and schools' capacity to construct new philosophical foundations for reform. Experts, or trainers, often reinforced the superficial, instrumental nature of day-to-day teaching routines. Instead of challenging current practices, especially those of the school or district administration (and maybe risk not being invited back), experts often presented reform ideas as nonthreatening ways to do better what teachers were already doing. Rarely did the experts, in their materials or presentations, help teachers anticipate the satisfactions to be found within the ongoing struggles that reform called for. Rather, they sent the message that if teachers carried out the new practices correctly and followed the plans, they would be gratified very soon indeed.

Many training sessions packaged not only the content but the presentation as well. Teachers found some workshops to be crowd-pleasing, fast-paced, laugh-filled events. Skilled presenters honed their shows, filling them with entertaining anecdotes, door prizes, handouts, even whole lessons (which many teachers received appreciatively). One could almost identify a school's reform history by listening for slogans that encapsulated their particular reform packages. One slogan urged teachers to shift from being a "sage on a stage to a guide on the side"—first uttered, no doubt, by a sage on a stage. Teachers in other schools were asked to go through a reform process of "forming, storming, norming, and performing." We heard slogans, principles, key points, and so on expressed identically from school to school and across the states. Not all were as euphonious as these, but they still indicated the broad reach of the reform mill's uniform messages.[13] Sadly, such shallow expertise rarely penetrated the school culture to cause deep reflection. Teachers were rarely invited to interrupt, to challenge, to ask for extra help, or to offer creative contributions of their own.

Teachers are a practical and resourceful group. Working with few materials and only simplistic training opportunities, most can salvage something useful—a handy hint here, a strategy there—from even the most ill-structured in-services. At Mitchell, for instance, one reform leader explained that teachers looked upon training as helpful for "updating their bag of tricks." However, a culture that invites such training is mostly debilitating. When Horace Mann teachers were about to implement a new inclusion model for integrating the school's special education students into mainstream teams, they begged for practical strategies such as a way to modify homework assignments so that both regular and special education students would complete them. When the school implemented inclusion without giving the teachers concrete assignments and plans, they felt ill-equipped to deal with their integrated classes. After not receiving the kind of professional learning they were used to—that which is delivered by an expert—they resorted to the only alternative available, namely, to struggle, teacher-by-teacher, on their own. Mann teachers had significant time during their regular team meetings that might have been used to read, study, and discuss ways to make their inclusive classrooms effective. Yet they did not recognize, nor were they encouraged to value and develop, their collective knowledge during that time.

Sometimes, packaged brainwork took the form of research findings that could be waved at teachers as evidence supporting a particular prescription. Because the research was presented uncritically (often prefaced with an unspecified "Research says . . . ") and rarely used to foster serious inquiry and learning, it undermined teachers' engagement and confidence in the reform. Superficial references to research tended to conflate all claims of authoritative knowledge. Thus, an article brought in from a practitioner or research journal might have no greater credibility (and be less likely to attract attention) than a secondhand telling of a feature on the nightly news. Careless bandying of research discredited the use of any scholarship; we often heard the familiar refrain, "You can prove anything with research."

In most cases, teachers had few opportunities to make the implications of research findings relevant to their own thinking and practice. Research is discounted when it does not offer direct practical applications, that is, if the teachers themselves have to interpret, modify, and construct new practices. One teacher told us: "Although the research is showing that it's better for the kids, a lot of times what happens [in a research study] is *not* what actually goes on inside of the room. A lot of things found in research are not actually practical. They do experiments, and they say: 'This would be wonderful; this would be good, this would be great.' Then, when they put it into a real, practical, everyday situation, it goes down the tubes."

Another teacher was similarly skeptical: "There are so many tenuous things out there, just so many things out there now that we don't have the answers to. Research says one thing, but statistics . . . I may be able to take the same statistics and make them say something else. That's the scary part."

In a culture of betterment, in contrast to the reform mill, staff developers would help teachers acquire competencies to seek out, interpret, evaluate, and engage in dialogue about the research that applies to their field. If such help had been available to the teachers who dealt with inclusion at Horace Mann Middle School, they would not have had to choose between packaged solutions or no help at all. They would have attained flexible, even generic, skills to make the daily and local adjustments that keep their practices aligned with the broad intentions of the reform.

Such an approach to staff development could also help educators engage their communities in similar dialogues instead of simply repeating the same "research says" justifications to often-hostile audiences. For example, when Countryside's staff tried to convince parents of the merits of detracking during a public hearing, they argued defensively that detracking was a state- and Carnegie-recommended reform, bolstered by research findings. As Principal Wanda Simpson told us, "I knew in my heart it was the right thing to do. It's just that I needed . . . who was [I]? I wasn't anybody. But I could get up and say [this researcher from this university] says, blah, blah, blah." She and the Countryside faculty used research to score points in an argument that they believed would be won or lost at a key meeting. They did not appear to see the research as useful for stimulating long-range school and public deliberations about the meaning of their tracking practices for educative and socially just schools in the racially diverse community. In the schools we studied, we did find examples of reflective and knowledgeable outsiders who played a crucial role in making schools better. However, this kind of help at schools was the exception.

No Time to Waste

Nearly all schools found themselves squeezing the school day to find time for teams of teachers to think and plan together. Ideally, teachers would use time carved out of the regular work schedule to reflect on students' learning and their own teaching. Such time could be used to refine their conceptions of good practice and integrate into their practice core ideas drawn from workshops and consultants. Teachers would meet to gather information, to learn, and to apply this knowledge directly to their work to make it educative and socially just. Unfortunately, the reform mill emphasized structure over substance. That is, the time is used well if spent in correctly designed teams with accountability for the resources and minutes spent. Teaming itself was the reform, not the quality of the teamwork or what teaming could accomplish.[14]

Many schools had to fight for paltry time allocations that came with strings attached. A Mountain View teacher reflected on a directive to her team to plan an integrated lesson during an afternoon training session: "That was a joke. We were never given any more time to do it. . . . It can't be an artificial thing . . . it has to come from us." Some schools had the luxury of daily meeting times, but very often "instructional leaders" in what Taylor would have called the planning departments dictated goals, structures, time allowances, and even the minutiae of the product the workers were to produce. Harriet Tubman's district, for example, required that teachers spend 60 percent of their team's meeting time on creating interdisciplinary units. During the remaining 40 percent, teachers were directed to make and review student profiles, noting each student's strengths and weaknesses and doing so every six weeks. Doing grades collectively and dealing with student discipline during team time—matters teachers considered especially relevant for them to have conversations about—were strictly forbidden. One district administrator would show up unannounced to check up on team activities. Accountability, if not outright distrust, saddled what could have been opportunities for teachers to develop their skills and knowledge by using their time flexibly. Townsend's principal, Harold Nance, designed his own accountability forms and required teams to report on the topics he specified for their discussion (such as curriculum and advisory programs). He checked team minutes to make sure teams used their time well.

Not surprisingly, faced with the task of swallowing expert knowledge while under the constant pressure of full-time teaching, many teachers viewed not just reform but their own learning and teaching as instrumental. Most saw themselves as being trained to achieve the desired result (implementation of a new structure or strategy—or more broadly, raised test scores) rather than engaging in a community of practitioners driven by the internal goods of increasing self-knowledge, analytic skill, or critical perspective.

Professional Development as Inquiry and Learning

We did see attempts to shift from Taylor's scientific management to Dewey's participatory and experience-based knowledge building. We saw evidence that structural changes could lead to greater educativity when combined with a disposition toward joint activities. As we discussed in Chapter Six, many schools developed participatory decision-making structures, often borrowing from the literature and practice of business organizations. Some formed groups (variously called inquiry groups, study or commitment teams, restructuring committees, quality circles, and transformation groups) that they charged with studying specific reforms. In many places, the reform-mill culture drove these structures and neglected attention to the norms that would enable teachers to value others' participation. The result was formal, instrumental groups producing few of the benefits of participation. Most teachers dismissed these activities as a waste of time. But elsewhere, we saw promising signs that such joint activities could shift the cultural tides around learning.

Inquiry and Learning at Mountain View

When the Massachusetts project staff invited Mountain View's principal, Paul Jennings, to form one of six school-university partnerships, he was wary that it might conflict with what he called his "very democratic, very grassroots" style. He approached Mandeville College, their partner institution, with a wait-and-see attitude. Over the next three years, contrary to predictions that his veteran teachers would surely resist change, Jennings helped Mountain View and Mandeville College faculties use a slow and deliberate process to attain a remarkable learning relationship. At the heart of this process were nine small, voluntary teacher groups, called inquiry teams, organized to explore the potential of teacher advisory programs, alternatives to retention, cooperative learning, effective discipline, heterogeneous grouping, integrating special education students into regular classes, alternative scheduling, school-community-family partnerships, and student assessment. As Jennings explained, "We looked at *Turning Points'* big ideas and realized that we had the makings for some really interesting work if we could set up these little campfires and gather people around each of the fires that they had a real motivation to study."

Each inquiry team devised its own strategies for learning about reform and developing recommendations for colleagues to consider. Staff-development resources were used to hire substitutes so teachers could visit other classrooms and other schools. They experimented with new teaching practices, attended conferences, and applied for grants. Mandeville College's role in the inquiry process was particularly touchy, as it brought to the surface long-standing norms regarding teacher learning. The teams were suspicious of experts coming in to tell them how to meet the needs of their students. One team member mentioned: "I see no use for experts. We're the experts. I don't know; we can do better. We know our kids. We know our community. What we need is to be given the time and the support to do it."

However, many Mountain View teachers were drawn to the value of research. After tentative conversations, the two faculties agreed that the college would provide reading materials and research to the inquiry teams. Stemming from this initial connection, and in a sharp departure from the university's tradition, Mandeville faculty incorporated this teacher-requested knowledge in courses they taught on the middle school campus. Mountain View faculty got the help they needed and in the process were able to earn college credit to meet the state requirement for certification as a middle school teacher.

Fifteen teachers met weekly for the introduction to middle-level education course. Their conversations were theoretical yet matched specifically to issues at their school. Going beyond this mix of theoretical and practical, the courses also affected the social climate of the school. One teacher noted, "[It] was particularly helpful to staff who were desperate to communicate with each other."

Although some teachers would have preferred direct training such as cooperative learning techniques within a given subject area, the partnership was generally held in high esteem. Jennings in particular was pleased that Mandeville didn't impose its own model of change and that his own staff didn't complain about outsider intrusion. Slowly, Mountain View and Mandeville forged a practice of collaboration around adult learning.

Becoming Socially Just Workplaces

Principals and teachers, department chairs and department members, advanced-placement teachers and regular teachers, white people and people of color, old-timers and newcomers, science teachers and art teachers, union members and nonunion, para-professionals and parent volunteers, and on and on—there is no end to how jobs and status can be divided up at school to justify who belongs and who should be listened to. Such is the traditional culture of the school. But there is also much in the American school culture that supports a pervasive (if quiet) press for social justice—that keeps nagging people in schools to learn from each other and with each other. The reform mill takes in this press for learning and for social justice, carefully reads the existing culture, and decides how much social justice the culture will bear. Typically, it is very little, and the role of social justice in reforms is kept small.

Sorting Adults

"Lead, follow, or get out of the way," said Larry Fowler, a Canyon Middle School teacher. This common and uncompromising stance reflected the sentiments of many enthusiastic reformers. Of course, at every school, one could find a range of enthusiasm for reform. Teachers would become passionately angry at their opponents while at the same time accepting the permanence of their adversaries' fixed opinions. Skilled peacemakers who got along with everyone were especially accommodating to their colleagues' intransigence. Because the reform mill had only limited strategies for adult learning and change—mandate, transmit, offer incentives—when these strategies failed to bring compliance or harmony, the solutions expanded to include two more: reject and ignore.

In one of many ironies of reform, those teachers most in need of new conceptions were often excluded from the best opportunities to change. This phenomenon is similar to criticizing uninvolved parents and making them feel unwelcome, or placing low-achieving students in unchallenging classes. Those who resisted reform were expected to get out of the way—to be uninvolved. Those enthusiastic about reform volunteered for staff development, sat on committees, traveled to conferences, and enjoyed elevated professional status. Gradually, they grew further apart from their more recalcitrant colleagues, and teachers' stance regarding reform—resister or enthusiast—became an indelible part of their identity. The resisters were not necessarily passive; some exerted energy against reform that rivaled that of the enthusiasts. Because they were ignored or barely tolerated in official reform dialogues, their primary work was behind the scenes.

Veteran teachers were expected to join or stand quietly aside, with early retirement held out as an option for those unhappy about reform. One teacher reported that her principal communicated that members of the "loyal opposition" had "outlived their usefulness." The message at Townsend, a teacher told us, was, "'If you're not willing to go along, then I'm not hearing you.' He [the principal] has presented this in meetings: 'You're just trying to hold things back. You're just being negative.'" Expressing a particularly callous rendition of this strategy, a Horace Mann reform enthusiast, frustrated with the principal's strategy of distributing enthusiastic and resistant teachers evenly across teams, commented: "That's not my job, to reignite the dead wood or get rid of it. That's the administrator's job."

Privileging Teachers of High-Status Academics

Because teaming was viewed almost exclusively as a reform suitable for academic or core subjects, teachers of electives and special education were excluded from or marginalized by new team structures. This segment of every school population, usually a large one, was often outside of the reform loop. As Townsend teacher Janice Farmer put it, "Elective teachers are the stepchildren in teaming."

In most schools, students attended elective classes during their teachers' team planning time. At Madison, even though elective teachers were assigned to teams they couldn't participate in meetings where the team discussed students' progress or planned curriculum and activities. This meant that interdisciplinary projects seldom involved exploratory or elective teachers. Not surprisingly, this group felt that academic teachers disregarded their credentials and abilities and devalued their subjects. Art teacher Kathy Frank complained: "I'm willing to do anything. I tell them, 'All you have to do is come to me and tell me what you want.' The problem is that most of the teachers do not consider that I have a curriculum. They don't seem to think that I teach anything in order. They don't take into account what kinds of supplies I have to beg, borrow, steal, or get-from-wherever to teach a class."

Another teacher reported that "we always feel isolated." Still another said, "We're somebody's coffee break." And another: "We are almost like baby-sitters in order for them to get their team time. Yet one more: "It is them and us . . . the core teachers look at us as frills." In keeping with this low status, elective teachers rarely enjoyed the same amount of planning time as the core teams, and only in a handful of schools did they meet regularly as a team.

In some schools, special education teachers were also left out of teaming reforms. Despite the fact that special education main-streaming is required by law, the teams' responses to integration ranged from thin, grudging compliance to the meaningful recon-ceptualization of special education that we begin to see at Mountain View (in Chapter Four). In most schools, asking regular teachers to share the work of special educators and work with disabled young-sters bumped up against a powerful reform-mill norm: Frederick Taylor's scientific management notion that work is most efficient and effective when it is divided up into discrete tasks and performed by specially trained workers. In this case, special education students need special education workers.

Divisions by Race and Gender

Because the reform mill treated change as an essentially technical problem, it was incapable of addressing racial and gender divisions and prejudice among adults. No technical, correct, expert-delivered package could ease adults' largely unspoken fears and animosities, or overcome their history of working separately and differently. As a result, the reform mill simply allowed educators and parents to ignore the racial and gender divisiveness among them. The exam-ples in this section (Horace Mann and Countryside Middle School) illuminate tensions that plagued many schools.

Most Horace Mann teachers were white, Italian Catholics who grew up in the neighborhood and attended parochial schools. The bitterness they felt toward school desegregation surfaced in the form of deep racial divisions in the faculty, even decades later. These divi-sions intersected with reform, creating and sustaining factions that prevented dialogue and learning. The African American and white teachers sat in their own groups during staff meetings, and the African Americans avoided the faculty room. Moreover, they formed racially separate social organizations within the school. The small group of African American teachers met at 7:15 every morning for a prayer meeting in science teacher Maya Lester's classroom. The white teachers contributed to the Sunshine Club to boost morale and support teachers; the black teachers circulated an envelope among themselves to collect money for people they wanted to reach out to. The Sunshine Club had to debate long and hard whether to send flowers to a colleague—an African American woman whose husband had died—who had not contributed to the fund.

Lenora Jones, the school's newly appointed vice principal, herself an African American, made it her goal to convince the black teachers to join the Sunshine Club. She felt she was making considerable progress toward better race relations when two or three black teachers showed up for the going-away party of a white teacher. It was symbolic of the tension that existed, however, when Jones decided not to participate in the black prayer meetings because it would be too divisive. As she explained the choice, she had to keep herself "real neutral."

Some whites were puzzled about the split, unaware of their own role in creating it. "Our minority teachers," one told us, "have been in this building forever. I can honestly say they're excellent teachers . . . but they're very insular in their relationships." Some African American teachers claimed that white teachers undermined their work with students. One told us, "They don't give you that support, and it's like the kids are . . . in a home with two parents. They play you against each other, and you can't put up a united front."

Other white teachers were openly resentful when it came to issues of race. Some claimed that minority teachers found racial issues where there were none. Others claimed that faculty of color were taking jobs through affirmative action, that qualified white teachers were being denied. One told us, speaking of a Mann colleague: "You know how good he is. I mean, he's wonderful. He runs that second floor. If there was ever a person that should be an administrator, he should be one. But he unfortunately is in his early forties and white. That's why he's not. And that's really sad." White teachers also were bitter about a white teacher who was replaced (according to them) for racial reasons. One faculty member recounted:

> I'll never forget the year we lost one of the most dynamic teachers we ever had in this building. We lost her because she was white, and because her department didn't have enough minorities. It wasn't that this building wasn't balanced, it was because that department wasn't balanced. And we got this little Hispanic snit [laughs with disgust] who had never worked with middle school kids before. He came right out of a junior college. I don't even think the man had his green card, and he was here in our building. The resentment towards him was unbelievable. It wasn't because of his color, it was just because of what created the problem. There was a lot of bitterness.

Gender issues played out in similarly painful ways. At Countryside, for example, Principal Wanda Simpson led a faculty that was "divided right down the middle" along gender lines. Calling themselves "a very fragmented faculty" and "polarized," teachers blamed the gender divisiveness for "wounds" and "suffering," as well as for blatant forms of exclusion. In some instances, the teachers acted out their gender separation much like middle school students. A new teacher, Andrea Battlinger, described her astonishment when she first went into the faculty lunch room: "[All the men] sit in the corner. They don't want any women eating at their table."

Countryside's gender split permeated the school's reform work. One teacher put it succinctly: "Women versus men." The men—led by a vocal coaching staff—opposed the reforms, arguing that discipline should be stronger, that teaming was a bad idea, that instruction should be teacher-directed, and that students should be homogeneously grouped. In contrast, most of the women—led by the principal and an activist English department—advocated strongly for the merits of teaming, cooperative learning, and heterogeneous grouping. The men viewed the women as overly nurturing and berated them for taking what one of them called "the counseling approach." Another chalked up the differing stances toward reform: "I think women are taught to be more nurturing and men are not . . . so I think teams work well with females. I don't think it necessarily would work well with the guys as much."

The racial and gender divisions that so powerfully distorted Mann's and Countryside's efforts to become good schools fall far outside of what the reform mill treats as matters to be considered in education reform.[15]

Reframing Implementation as Respectful Dialogue

Socially just workplaces require that schools reexamine what is often seen as the central challenge of reform: securing enough faculty buy in to smooth implementation. The thought is that if faculty can all agree on a set of specific goals and adopt a particular program or plan for structural change, then reform implementation can proceed smoothly. Because the reform mill sees neither commitment nor implementation as requiring ongoing inquiry and dialogue, it works in concert with (or at least doesn't confront) a culture built on either extinguishing or deprecating differences. But if the process of reform can include a respectful dialogue across divergent experiences, knowledge, and perspectives on schooling, then the reform process can become an inclusive and socially just one.

For example, the Massachusetts project walked a very fine line between local control and mandates with its social justice agenda. It attempted to respect local autonomy and diversity of views by framing equity concerns as compelling ideas about which educators could deliberate and decide how best to act. Generally, the Massachusetts schools were pleased with the state staff's democratic yet principled approach in dealing with them. One Madison teacher declared that the relationship between the state and the school continued to improve with time, even in the face of the state's considerable pushing on the school regarding the equity agenda: "We're evolving a relationship with the state as someone who's here to help, and not someone who's going to come down hard if you're not doing things just the way they want. And since we've become relatively close, we share our experiences, and they have sort of pushed."

The state's democratic approach was also reflected in the reciprocal nature of Mountain View Middle School's relationship with Mandeville College, where the diverse experiences of the two faculties were blended to make a strong teacher-education program.

In addition to supporting the inquiry teams' work, the Mandeville courses also provided a way for Mountain View faculty to become an integral part of the college's internship program to prepare new teachers. One course offered at the school was designed for faculty members interested in acting as supervising teachers for the university's student interns. Building on Mountain View's local knowledge and practical expertise, Mandeville hired two of the middle school's teachers as clinical supervisors—a bold move that challenged the university's traditional supervision role. Mandeville staff lauded the new strategy, saying that it gave the college's teacher-education students more immediate feedback and attention from experienced teachers. One of Mountain View's teachers told us that he really appreciated feedback on his teaching from the college faculty and the opportunity to learn from the interns.

Some schools worked explicitly to make racial inclusion central to the adult culture, as well as to students. Inland's faculty faced an enormous challenge when a less-than-friendly merger brought the historically antagonistic faculties of the district's African American and white junior high schools together. During that first trying year, Principal McCall turned his energy toward creating a communitylike culture among the school's diverse groups of adults—knowing that an inclusive culture for students would depend on it. Rick Marsten, one of Inland's counselors, developed a variation of the school's From Neighbors to Friends program for adults. Through numerous, informal social gatherings, name games, and trust-building activities, the two faculties were "married," and—as Marsten jokingly described it—"We've been quarreling ever since." Indeed, Inland's racially diverse faculty and staff had developed strong bonds of trust, dedication, and camaraderie. Time and again, we heard about friendship and affection that supported their strong desire to support one another professionally.

Inland's newly diverse faculty had to learn to reject the class and race stereotypes rampant in their local communities. McCall knew this meant people would have to change their thinking as well as practices. He also knew that changed thinking had to come from honest talk about differences. So he encouraged African American teachers to talk openly about how African American families value education highly and how they define it differently than members of the white community do. One teacher explained that "the African American community sees education as very important, but they define education as an awareness of the multicultural aspect of America, an awareness of the black experience, an awareness of social justice."

When describing the changes he'd witnessed, McCall was clear about his own changes: "I don't think anybody in the building, including me, hasn't changed at least 90 degrees from where they were when we started this. Racism is so insidious, I don't think anybody knows they've got it. I really believed that black parents were less caring for their children than white parents. I mean, I really believed that. But if you had said, 'Is that true?' I would have said, 'Hell, no!'"

Becoming Caring Workplaces

Acting on their caring sentiments, some faculties organized students and teachers into teams from which they could offer advisory programs (to build close relationships between adults and children) and align schedules (to work and plan together). Other schools focused first, and sometimes only, on the structures of these reform-recommended programs (teaming and advisory); they illustrated, as we discussed in Chapter Five, that new structures and programs do not guarantee the kind of social spirit Dewey or Addams might have envisioned.

Few teachers at any of the schools were overtly hostile or unfriendly to one another, and most welcomed any opportunity—including teaming—to chat and share notes about students. But unless they were bound together by a moral commitment to growth, empathy, and shared responsibility, teachers were as likely to replicate the prevailing school culture as to change it. Unless they applied their collaboration to educative, caring, socially just, and participatory activities, they continued to closely guard their classroom autonomy, be suspicious of the capacity of teaming to divide and balkanize their faculty, and distrust collaboration with those outside the school. Although adults often belonged to caring groups and had one-to-one caring relationships, such relationships were rarely expressed as integral to the moral ecology of their schools. They had caring friends, but only at a few schools did they teach at a caring place.

Contrived Collaboration

"You can't just demand a relationship," said Mountain View teacher Patrick Jackson. Forced into teaming, one Countryside team defiantly called themselves the "unteam." Most of its members saw themselves as the loyal opposition and preferred to be left alone in their classrooms. Exacerbating the situation, Countryside teachers were expected to hold team meetings during their only preparation period. Viewing their time as sacred, the team rarely met. Many teachers at Mountain View also resisted devoting their single preparation period to joint curriculum planning: "In the real world, we need that time to pull ourselves together," commented one teacher. Even in schools with an extra planning period, most teachers complained that they didn't have enough time to really collaborate. Or, as at Horace Mann, teachers were hesitant to make the emotional investment in teaming: "Everybody just wants to be above the board. Just skim the surface. Nobody wants to get into feelings or anything. The trust factor isn't there. There's no real feeling of teamsmanship." Clearly, the reform mill can lead teachers to meetings, but it cannot make them drink collaboration.[16]

Principals spearheading reforms often exerted considerable control over how teams were formed; at many schools, they set up teams with little advance notice or preparation. Some principals began by asking teachers to name those colleagues they couldn't work with; others described the process as "matchmaking" or "getting the chemistry right." Most often, however, principals created teams strategically, distributing strong teachers among the teams to share the wealth. Reconfiguring teams was also common practice. Several principals mixed teams to maintain or increase the momentum for change schoolwide. Madison's Antouli moved one or two of the teachers on each team every year or so. He believed that this switching helped make teaming a stable part of the school structure and kept teams from becoming too dependent on certain individuals or groups. When he moved the leader of an outstanding team to help another team in trouble, the result was just as most teachers suspected: members of the original team felt a deep loss. Other principals shuffled teachers if team members had repeated disagreements. Whatever the impetus, shifting team membership brought tension and reminded faculties that they served on their teams at the pleasure of the principal. Teachers nearly always preferred stable teams, estimating that it takes two years or more to get comfortable with one another, and that teaming can't influence instruction before this happens.

Competition and Comparisons Erode Care

Despite the widespread popularity and reform potential of teaming, in almost all schools teachers and others lamented the loss of schoolwide cohesiveness that teaming also brought on. As Hannah Dawson, a Van Buren paraprofessional, put it, "People forget we're one school. Everybody's so busy doing their own thing that they forget we're a whole." Teachers repeatedly told us that their team had replaced the school as the center of their worklives. Teachers in previously departmentalized schools often missed their department meetings, in which they could be secure as subject-matter specialists and relatively equal to other specialists in other departments.

Interestingly, this whole-school feeling of the past did not cause teachers to have a proprietary interest in what other teachers were doing. But when teams were working with parallel curricula, they sometimes felt that others were unduly concerned, or unconcerned entirely, with their affairs. As one teacher told us, "Many times we come up with ideas and want to do things. We take off and do it. The other team says, 'Well, why do you think you can do that? We didn't know anything about it, da, da, da.' So we have gotten to the point now where every time we come up with an idea to do something, we send that idea over to them. Why they're feeling left out, I don't know."

At some schools, the emergence of a star team fueled competition. At Van Buren, a seventh grade team jelled much more quickly than others did. During an intensive, state-sponsored summer institute held before teaming actually began at Van Buren, this group of teachers quickly developed a team identity, received some positive local press, and came to be seen as a model of what a cooperative, working team might look like. Needless to say, other teachers resented the comparison. It took two years of effort for schoolwide relations to mend. At Countryside, teachers were quick to acknowledge that their school's star team made extra efforts, but they also believed that the principal had set up some teams to succeed by putting the school's better students with the teachers most active in reform.

Just as sensitive and caring teachers struggle in their classrooms to acknowledge individual students' achievements without eroding class cohesiveness or making other students believe that they are not as good, so, too, principals tread a fine line between highlighting one exemplary team and implicating other faculty members' weaknesses. For example, one principal praised individual and team accomplishments in a weekly bulletin to encourage "healthy competition." To the degree that the bulletins simply communicated good ideas across teams and let teams be widely appreciated by their colleagues, the bulletins could support care at the school. The conventions of the reform mill, however, easily make such information instrumental—designed to motivate by creating informal comparisons and rankings among the best and worst teams. In such cases, care suffers.

At Tanglewood, teachers reported that the "whole school" previously felt united in its goals for children and against intrusions from highly competitive and efficacious parents. But as members of teams, teachers were drawn into the competitive spirit when some teachers or teams got more recognition, or when parents understood the consequences for their child's assignment to a particular team.

Similarly, competition soared at Verbena, where parent choice was especially important because students stayed in the same multigrade team, with the same teachers, for three years. Teachers presented their curriculum to parents at an open house, and parents were invited to visit and observe all teams. These meetings and visitations were staggered and continued over a period of several weeks each spring. Teachers generally found this practice threatening; some told us that they felt their jobs were on the line. One veteran said:

> I don't care anymore about the whole school. I care about my
> team and what's going on in my classroom, but there isn't enough

energy left to care about the whole school. Unfortunately, it's gotten to a point where parents come around and check out the teams and which ones they want. I wish we were more solid here and people knew . . . I mean we're professionals. . . . There needs to be solidarity. Our teams should be more alike. It's divisive. We were a very thoughtful and close faculty, but it's changed. You hear things like, "Don't tell the other team, because they might want to do it."

Fragile Alliances

Forging alliances with those outside the school and with people steeped in their own traditions and bureaucracies proved incredibly slow going. As within schools, a quickly designed structure for collaboration often took precedence over slower-to-accomplish changes in beliefs and relationships. Alliances with outsiders are even more likely than are within-school teams to be contrived, at least initially; they face even tougher obstacles in becoming genuine, self-sustaining relationships.

The struggle to forge alliances was most pronounced in Massachusetts, where school-university partnerships and interagency collaboration were a mainstay of the state's reforms. Unfortunately, the state, universities, and school districts could not constitute a stable and long-lasting environment in which many strong relationships might develop. Shifting political winds toppled many of the alliances that were just taking hold.

A common complaint—so common as to seem almost inevitable—was that universities, as one Madison teacher put it, "had no realization of what actually goes on." Lack of credibility in the eyes of teachers, combined with conflicting schedules and inadequate resources, never allowed Madison's university partnership to get off the ground. At Horace Mann, implementing a good, seemingly straightforward idea was pushed ahead of developing the understanding and trust that teachers would have required to accept the relationship. When asked by their partner college to mentor student interns, some teachers were reluctant to open their classroom doors. Would the teachers themselves be closely observed by strangers, and how would they be judged? Would the teachers know enough to mentor novices? Even so, over time—what seemed to teachers like a very long time—Horace Mann's relationship with its college partner matured. Even Mountain View's relationship blossomed gradually. But it took a long while before one university faculty member concluded, "[We're] a part of the team, we're a part of the school . . . it's just a really good relationship."

Of all the alliances, those with universities were actually the least problematic, though still problem-filled. After all, schools and universities did begin with some of the same assumptions, they had similar public missions and political pressures, and to a degree they spoke the same professional language. Relationships with other organizations, such as health providers, police agencies, businesses, churches, and so on, proved more fragile and often less satisfying. Madison faculty invested much time, energy, and hope in a state initiative that brought together eleven agencies; but the program was cut by the governor after an election. Reform leader Rose Athens told us, "It was awful, just awful. We've never been able . . . to get those people back on board."

When Relationships, Not the Reform Mill, Guide Betterment

As we saw in Chapter Six, Van Buren Middle established teams as schools within schools and gave them responsibility for scheduling, curriculum planning, grouping students, discipline, and parent communication. The seventh grade team clicked right away, but the other grade-level teams did not.[17] Saddled by personality conflicts and philosophical differences, the sixth and eighth grade teams enjoyed infrequent successes as some respite from the more persistent difficulties; but overall, things were made worse by inevitable comparisons to the seventh grade team. After several years of frustration, teachers from the sixth and eighth grade teams approached Principal Bob Davenport and asked that the teams be allowed to split up into smaller groups. Davenport, who was himself unhappy with the larger groups, happily agreed.

Betty Carlson and Mike Crawford became a two-member eighth grade team. Crawford joined the Van Buren faculty in 1993, after completing a teacher education program guided by student-centered curriculum and instruction consistent with middle-grade reform. As the language arts teacher on the five-member eighth grade team, Crawford had been frustrated that his veteran teammates were wary of the student-directed curriculum he envisioned. Carlson (the team's science teacher and a former college chemistry instructor) had complained for years about the rift between what she called the team's "skills" teachers (language arts and mathematics) and the "concept" teachers (science and social studies).

On paper, the two were hardly a match. Carlson had taught for more than twenty years, while Crawford was a relative novice. Carlson's teaching identity was as a subject-area expert; Crawford focused on process. As Crawford explained, even their biorhythms were different: "I'm just definitely a high-energy person; I'm strung out. I'm going all the time. I'm doing thirty different things at once, and her natural rhythms are just very much different." Still, the two were a team, and at Van Buren, this meant they shared the core work of teaching.

Sharing their work meant that they could not drift into the typical pattern of idealistic novice working with seasoned veteran. Carlson did not dismiss Crawford as a radical rookie, and Crawford never treated Carlson like an outmoded old-timer. Instead, the two worked at understanding one another's very different strengths. As Carlson noted: "Nobody is a totally perfect match for any kid. . . . We kind of fill in some of the holes. I am very, very weak in interpersonal relationships. It's not an intelligence that I have any strength in. And Mike has enormous strength in that. I have a great deal of intelligence in things like organization . . . so I do a lot of the clerical work, and it has nothing to do with me being female— it has to do with the way I work."

Similarly, Crawford told us: "My strengths are interpersonal. I feel the strongest thing about me is I know all the kids by September. I know what's going to set them off. I know what's going to make them productive. . . . I am a real disaster when it comes to anything like attendance, or notices home, or any of this school-wide organizational stuff."

Crawford pointed out that even though he carries the "generative flag" for the team, Carlson's strengths were invaluable to him, the students, and the team. Though they both acknowledged her role in keeping things organized, he also noted that her subject-matter knowledge was essential: "On a structural or curricular level, when we are putting things together . . . she is an incredible wealth of knowledge and process around sciences. I mean, she really understands things from that paradigm. I don't really have that way of thinking."

Guided by Davenport's conviction that the most important element of reform is "keeping the conversation going," and by their own curiosity and flexibility, Carlson and Crawford continually talked about practice. Before school, they opened the sliding partition between their classrooms and talked during their team's union meeting (when student leaders set the agenda for the day and answered classmates' questions). They talked during their daily planning time, which was theoretically divided into individual and shared planning time, but almost always ended with the partition open and the two sitting across from one another at a student desk. They even talked when they should have been working on report cards. During one ninety-minute planning period that took place the week report cards were sent home, Carlson and Crawford planned an interdisciplinary unit on Vintage City history. Together, the two critiqued the previous year's unit, improved the launch of the unit, and loosely scheduled four weeks of instructional time that began with students choosing a topic to study and engaged students with primary source material. As the teammates planned the day-to-day schedule, Crawford's desire to lead the lesson with information and activity, perhaps beyond their limited time, complemented (and was further strengthened by) Carlson's prowess as a practical manager.

Carlson and Crawford's relationship was a model for their students acting as a community of learners. The teachers shared students and planning time. They were competent in their work—including their teaming and interdisciplinary curriculum. They focused on one another's strengths, listened to one another's ideas, and helped make them better. They were the chief creators of this community and were among its greatest beneficiaries.

Becoming Participatory Workplaces

Over this century, the legacy of Taylorism has been partly responsible for the teaching profession being described (with good cause) as feminized, infantilized, subjugated, oppressed, and more. However, the structures and culture that rely on "power over" to shape teachers' worklives are met with teachers' own powerful resistance.

One form that teacher agency takes to counter their lowly status and often degrading working conditions is to step into their classrooms, close the doors, and whenever possible do as they please. This private work, this isolation, has not served democracy well, but it may also keep much that is good in public education alive. For many teachers, it mutes some of the dehumanizing effects of Taylorism enough to keep them teaching—keep them working with children.

Making the Private Public

In a manner of speaking, the reform mill invites teachers out from behind these closed doors. Appropriating communitarian, participatory, and democratic rhetoric, it offers a more fulfilling work-life, the promise of effective teaching, and perhaps greater status. Some teachers never respond to the call, but many cautiously step forward. For some, stepping into the public sphere allows them to experience an exhilarating, barely imagined dream of teaching. Other teachers experience what feels like a dirty trick; they are soon reminded of why they kept that low profile, and they disappear beneath the reform horizon.

Teachers' sovereignty in their classrooms gives them power to craft their content and methods of teaching. Increasingly, though, structures such as curriculum frameworks, required texts, and mandatory tests limit the scope of this power. Still, few norms are as dominant, as jealously guarded, as this autonomy. Attempts to make more of a collective, open enterprise must first counter this strong tradition, and second such attempts must deliver on what they promise: in Dewey's words, "a mode of associated living, of conjoint community experience."[18] The promise of participation is that the school become a public sphere in which free and enlightened people work together to solve public problems, advance the common good, and shape the direction of the democracy.

At several schools, teachers made sense of their strong norms of isolation and autonomy as meaning that all teachers have their own style, and that it would be inappropriate for colleagues to try to influence one other. Said one, "There is no such thing as a perfect teacher . . . I've never given advice to a teacher about teaching." Perhaps in some measure due to years of divide-and-conquer management approaches (often to counter teacher union challenges), teachers are quick to respond to any perceived attempt to create unequal status among their ranks. Thus, these nonjudgmental expressions of individuality and autonomy are also at the heart of teacher solidarity. One teacher reported that he and his colleagues did not "tread on each other's areas" or discuss each other's curriculum.

At one school, team meetings were kept at a business level dominated by administrative and scheduling tasks, rather than attending to curriculum or philosophy about which teachers might have to disagree. At another, a teacher reported: "I don't think that middle school means that each teacher on the team should teach the same way or should criticize any teacher who is not teaching the same way. We have that going on here. So, we don't have to all share a philosophy, but I think we should have to respect the fact that we may have different styles, but at least all the styles work."

Tubman's scheme to exchange lesson plans and observe colleagues' teaching fell flat because most worried that it would create an uncomfortable environment where some teachers would tell other teachers how to teach. Townsend principal Harold Nance replaced a team leader who pressed her colleagues to explain their reasons for their decisions and who offered help to some. A Tanglewood team leader told us that her colleagues would respond to discussions on teaching with a reaction like this: "Where do you get off telling me that I'm not doing my job?" She believed teachers responded to such discussions "as if they were evaluations" and that most teachers wanted teaching evaluations best left to administrators.

Reframing Participation

Breaking down the norms of teacher sovereignty would be very difficult even if teachers were to step out of their classrooms into a genuinely changed environment that respected participation and included time to learn new ways of teaching and relate to colleagues. Although such broad changes in norms or the environment rarely took place, we did notice enough new instances of participation to indicate that changes were possible and worthwhile.

Teachers find it risky to make public their private practices and thoughts. In a competitive environment, they are reluctant to share those practices and skills that they feel distinguish them from others. Thus, to participate freely, teachers must feel that others will anticipate and respect their vulnerability and that sharing will bring greater satisfaction than hoarding does. But whatever the concerns or fears, empathy must form the core of the participatory spirit. A Mountain View teacher explained how colleagues could tread lightly around these concerns without valorizing autonomy ("everyone has his own style") or disrespecting others' slowness to change or accept reform: "Working with a team, I had to deal with problems that I don't have in my classroom. You see, you're dealing with other people's problems, and you can't say to the other teammate, 'Well, don't you know how to teach?' You have to change your attitude. You have to all come to a conclusion—you're all in this together. You have to cooperate."

At Inland, a pair of teachers could request a substitute so as to make time to work together. Teachers believed these days helped them improve their teaching without calling attention to supposedly correct methods. One teacher explained: "Peer coaching is just a term that we use [for] two colleagues working together towards a common goal. I'm going to help you, you're going to help me. It's 'peer' because there isn't an administrator helping someone become better in what they're doing, so you learn [not] to say, 'Well, no that's not a good idea.' You say, 'Well, have you thought about trying such and such a thing?'"

A Chavez teacher told us that "people used to fear—I'm not going to share my ideas because I want to get credit for them." Another teacher commented, "Now I don't need to keep that to myself . . . we're working toward the same goal." Members of one of Canyon's few teaching teams explained it as coming to "look at things as a whole" and being "comfortable" sharing the work of teaching; one summed it up this way: "There's some harmony in that."

Moving Targets and Competing Reforms

Peter Armbruster, a Middleton teacher, was clearly frustrated: "There is just so much to do in so many different directions and no time to do it. It just seems like it's all fragmented. I don't think you should tackle a program until you really plan it through."

Reform is not an orderly process. Never was. Never will be. The reform mill responds to a proliferation of reform ideas not by engaging adults in the ways the mill expects those same adults to engage students—rather by imposing technical (rational, orderly, scientific, efficient) mandates and constraints on schools. Paying scant attention to the worklives of those who must accomplish these reforms, the reform mill—in thousands of small and large ways—demands that educators justify their work and worklives by making their activities seem orderly and rational. The mill demands quick results. Most pernicious of all, it asks for new reforms before schools are even aware that the old reforms are no longer desirable. Sabrina Arthur described her dilemma in terms of survival, a concern that overshadowed her strong desire for betterment: "You have to be able to change with the situations that come up within the school system. Every year, you're going to see change. You learn to deal with it. You don't get all bent out of shape because you still want your job, so you have to go along with the program."

Conflicting Local Demands

Everywhere, schools and teachers tried to accommodate conflicting views about how best to promote academic learning, but rarely was there a legitimate forum either for expressing their frustration or for working out how to make wise accommodations. As a matter of fact, to point out the discrepancies was to identify oneself (or one's school or agency) as uncooperative, not willing to be a team player, or simply a complainer. Those in positions of greater authority (such as the coordinator of a district curriculum project we describe later in this section) simply rationalized that the conflicting reforms did not really conflict at all.

To match her instruction more closely to the state achievement test, a Tanglewood teacher stopped teaching her successful interdisciplinary units even though she knew with certainty that her students would do well on the test: "I noticed that I became much more structured and actually tougher on the kids and much less fun to be with." District bureaucrats supported Van Buren teachers' efforts to work with the integrated curriculum of the state middle school project but also expected the school to implement the district's own curriculum scope and sequence. Because these guidelines clashed in some fundamental ways, the faculty puzzled about what to do; in the process they worked less collegially, not more. Teacher Sally Barberini proceeded cautiously with her interdisciplinary planning. Although it was her impression that fidelity to the district curriculum guidelines was not actively monitored, she still reported that the document "cast a shadow" that constrained faculty creativity in interdisciplinary studies. Her colleague, however, told us that the district curriculum director was "rigid" and that district policies basically meant, "This is the way it's done."

Many Mountain View teachers were frustrated by the district superintendent's demand that top priority be given to her pet project: developing a new K–12 subject-matter curriculum. The attention and resources they gave to this project kept them from their school's inquiry-based reforms. Making matters worse, the district project allowed no provision for teachers to explore the interdisciplinary potential of the curriculum under development. The coordinator of the district curriculum project concurred that integrating curriculum was important, but she disagreed with the middle school teachers' view that paying attention to curriculum integration could help the task force determine what is important in individual disciplines. She told us: "What you have to do is really frame your own discipline before you can really look at how it relates to somebody else. For example, maybe you need to really understand what concepts you are teaching in math before you can really talk about how you might pull writing in for them to learn how to explain what it is they are doing."

The teachers knew well, however, that curriculum integration was relevant and could stimulate rich and helpful conversations about *their own* disciplines. And they knew that their conflict with the district's initiative was a product of larger district politics. Specifically, high school teachers had used their clout and credibility as guardians of high academic standards to garner support in the community and therefore with the superintendent.

Inland's superintendent Tom Hanson was deeply skeptical about the commitment, on the part of McCall and his faculty, to heterogeneous grouping and multicultural curriculum; Hanson characterized Inland's goals as "touchy-feely." He believed that raising test scores would be the best way to reduce the community's concerns about the racially mixed school. He pressured McCall to focus on "academic excellence" and raising scores. McCall became increasingly defensive about the school's reform. English teacher Beth Fleming recalled: "They were riding Ben. We could feel it when we came back to school this year that the stress was there. We need to get these scores up. It was not like Ben. We spent so much of this year worrying about tests, standardized tests. You know . . . it's unfortunate. It's unfortunate because that's not what we're about, and that's not what we should be about." In response, Inland faculty spent more time teaching material that would be on the test (emphasizing study skills, for instance) and leaving less time for the school's From Neighbors to Friends program.

In at least two school systems, the entire middle-grade reform effort was jeopardized by macro administrative concerns having little to do with educativity. Prior to our final visit to Mountain View, for example, the superintendent proposed shutting down the aging middle school and redistributing its students to the elementary and high schools. Similarly, at Countryside, the district expected enrollment shifts that would warrant the sixth, seventh, and eighth grade middle school becoming a seventh and eighth grade junior high. The superintendent was clear that the shift "won't be based on educational preference," but rather on administrative needs. When Countryside applied for and won statewide recognition as a distinguished school, principal Wanda Simpson predicted that the award represented their "last big push." Although both Mountain View and Countryside have held on as middle schools, the specter of their reforms being dismantled for reasons so unrelated to schooling goals bred cynicism and dampened enthusiasm for reform.[19]

Conflicting State Politics and Priorities

Changing political tides in all of the states (in most places, a shift to the political right) pressed schools to show early and dramatic results on conventional measures. When such results weren't obvious, policy makers (many of whom were dubious, at best, about reforms that pressed schools toward the collective public good, rather than stressing competition and individualistic ends) rapidly shifted their attention to reforms concerning standards, deregulation, choice, and accountability.

California's project began in an environment of progressive curriculum and assessment reforms and with emphasis on equity for the state's increasing diversity among schoolchildren. These reforms were quite compatible with, and in some cases predated, *Turning Points*. The decade of the 1990s, however, witnessed almost complete retraction of those policies. The first blow was when the increasingly conservative state school board tossed out the California Learning Assessment System, a performance-based testing program. The conservatives complained that the test focused too much on how children feel, rather than what they know. For example, because students were encouraged on one subtest to support their views with personal experiences, the test was accused of being an intrusion into the privacy of the family. The state's curriculum frameworks stressing constructivist pedagogy and child-centered classrooms were replaced by subject-matter standards emphasizing phonics and basic math skills. Ballot propositions 187, 209, and 227 made clear the state's growing cautiousness and resentment regarding immigrants, affirmative-action policies, and bilingual education. By the end of the decade, the legislature passed new policies that would end "social promotion" and rank all of the state's schools by their scores on the SAT 9 (Stanford Achievement Test). Middle-grade reform is clearly out of step. The middle-grade staff remains part of the California Department of Education, but its role and influence in the agency have diminished considerably.

As noted in Chapter Seven, Massachusetts experienced a shift in education policy as dramatic and political as that in California. The state's 1993 Education Reform Act called for developing state curriculum frameworks and an assessment system, a task that the state department of education undertook using a grassroots strategy that engaged thousands of educators (including many from the networks of reforming middle-grade schools) and the public in a deliberative process that led to the *Massachusetts Common Core of Learning*. However, when Boston University's conservative president, John Silber, became the chair of the state board of education, the *Common Core* was rewritten, eliminating sections about inquiry- and project-based learning, interdisciplinary and multicultural curriculum, and authentic assessment in favor of narrowly specifying subject content with a strong Eurocentric emphasis. The board commissioned a high-stakes test based on the standards for grades four, eight, and ten, later to include other grades. All schools are ranked based on students' scores. The board also disbanded the state's networks of reforming schools.

Test-based accountability arrived sooner in Texas, and early in the Texas project. State project staff tried to help school administrators and teachers juggle the middle school project's emphasis on child-centeredness and interdisciplinary curriculum with the state's test-based accountability system. The new "Essential Elements" specified what students should learn in each of the disciplines, and they would be tested yearly on the Texas Assessment of Academic Skills. In 1994, the juggling act became far more difficult. Persuaded by promises of tighter educational accountability in exchange for more local control, Texans swept George W. Bush into the governor's office. The new administration overhauled the education code to eliminate most state mandates and to judge and publicly report school quality according to students' TAAS scores. Bush's education commissioner, Mike Moses, narrowed the state agency's role to basic fiscal and administrative tasks, reduced its staff by one-quarter, and transferred projects that offered assistance (including the middle-grade project) to regional centers. Not long thereafter, Jane McIvoie left the agency to become an administrator in one of the state's urban school districts. In 1997, working with the SBOE, Moses completely rewrote the state's curriculum standards and raised the scores students needed to pass on the TAAS. The new standards have been highly praised by conservatives, including the Fordham Foundation, for their focus on traditional content. Many districts have shifted from supporting comprehensive school reform to adopting specific programs that promise to increase test scores.

In Illinois, as in Texas, standards and test-based accountability existed side-by-side with middle-grade reform throughout the decade. But Illinois, too, experienced changes that proved wrenching to the state project. In 1995, a new state superintendent, Joe Spagnola, reorganized the agency. The middle-grade project was a casualty, although not right away. Spagnola created a new Division of Educational Innovation and Reform and moved the middle-grade project out of Patrice Sherwood's domain into the new division. The staff designated to pick up the project's work were doubtful that the agency could maintain the work that Darlington had nurtured, or whether, as a state agency, it should do this kind of work at all. Darlington negotiated hard to stay for a while with the schools he'd been mentoring. Today he works in the Accountablity and Quality Assurance Division of the state department of education.

Vermont's policy environment has probably remained the most supportive of middle-grade reform, but it too has shifted toward a standards and test-based accountability system that has complicated the middle schools' reform efforts. What began as a statewide attempt to develop an integrated, multidisciplinary curriculum framework was transformed by a conventional subject-by-subject standard-setting process. The innovative portfolio project gave way to conventional testing, and in 1998 scores on the state tests were published. The Vermont Department of Education identifies schools most in need of assistance by dint of their low scores. Although Carrie Jacobs has moved on to other things, the middle-grade project continues in the agency, and the university-based Professional Development Collaborative still works with project schools.

Reframing Reform as Betterment

In this chapter, we argue that school reform must be a struggle on behalf of adults as well as children, and that all who step inside schools must find the means to become better at what they do each day. Schools have a special social mission that calls us to further define this quest for becoming better as a collective construction of the common good. But much in the American character exhibits a decided preference for the individualistic and externally valued ends of reform. Counterbalancing these values with the instrumental and technocratic arguments, the reform mill, and Taylorism at its core, holds little promise. Rather, the experiences of the schools we studied argue that schools must interweave the means and ends of their work with the threads of a nonneutral, democratic struggle drawn from our culture and history. This interweaving leads to the constructs of educativity, care, social justice, and participation as our way of understanding how schools become good places for students, teachers, and society.

The Reform Mill and Betterment

We conclude this chapter with the stories of two California middle schools, Canyon and Cesar Chavez. Both joined state-supported middle school partnership networks; both sought major new funding under California's school-restructuring initiative; both schools' bids for these five-year grants failed. Yet that is where the similarities end. Canyon took the reform mill's bait: the promise of all that is good and true in schooling without needing to disrupt conventional practices and conventional thinking. The school became mired in its efforts to satisfy the mill's pressure to jump onto the latest school-restructuring bandwagon. Chavez, eschewing the same pressure, adapted the opportunities of the state's reform initiatives to develop and enact its own clear sense of betterment.

Reform-Mill Stagnation: Canyon Middle School

Canyon Middle School sits amid a sprawling suburb about forty miles from the city. Formerly a small, mostly white farming town, the Canyon community became racially and economically diverse in the 1980s and is growing increasingly so. In the early 1990s, one-fourth of Canyon's students were Latino, 8 percent African American, and 7 percent Asian and Pacific Islander. And about a third of all students' families qualified for Aid to Families with Dependent Children (AFDC). When Canyon's district moved to year-round education in 1989 to accommodate increasing enrollments, Canyon's fifteen hundred sixth, seventh, and eighth graders were divided among three tracks—orange, blue, or green—rotating in and out of campus according to an eight-weeks-on, four-weeks-off schedule. The year-round calendar left Canyon's staff fragmented and their resources stretched. Many teachers changed classrooms every four or eight weeks, carting materials and supplies with them in portable cabinets. Many missed longtime colleagues who were on a different rotation and the sense of unity they used to have.

Distributed across three tracks, Canyon teachers were, in the words of one of them, "slotted into camps," and many had "just given up."

Principal Tara Stickley sought to revive her discouraged faculty by joining one of California's middle school networks and seeking a major state grant for school restructuring. Despite her determination to make the school better, her actions inadvertently triggered the worst effects of the reform mill. Falling into the bad habits of packaged brainwork and a structural view of reform, Stickley and her faculty missed their opportunity to nurture educativity, social justice, caring, and democratic participation in their reform work. We should not be surprised, then, that reform exacerbated, rather than relieved the faculty's malaise.

Stickley was active in statewide middle-grade activities and had a reputation for being a leader. She used her growing repute to help the school secure resources and positive press. At her urging, Vice Principal Ron Dickson and a handful of teachers, including technology teacher Harold Roper, applied for and won a $40,000 state planning grant for restructuring. Stickley's next step was to form a restructuring committee and working subcommittees to develop a change strategy. The committees spent much of their grant money on a retreat, where a consultant spoke about his restructuring efforts in Canada. Some teachers talked enthusiastically about the possibilities of restructuring, but many others were clearly put off, calling the retreat "a waste of money," an "embarrassment," and "just another in-service." On their return, the committees were supposed to report their recommendations. Few fulfilled their charge in earnest, and one teacher reported that "no one knew what was going on." Several teachers we spoke with complained that restructuring was "a decision from the top-down," that "it wasn't grass-roots," but rather simply the principal's "pet project."

The restructuring committee turned next to writing the implementation grant proposal, which, if won, would bring in approximately $1 million over the following five years. But rather than engage teachers in a participatory planning process to examine and negotiate their differences, Dickson took a short leave from school to write the proposal on his own. Teachers were angry. Several complained that Dickson and Roper were too focused on technology. Those in elective subjects worried that the proposal would jeopardize their programs, and perhaps their jobs. Others argued that unless teachers did the writing, curriculum and teaching would not be emphasized. To address the complaints and quiet the conflict, Dickson attempted to incorporate everyone's ideas, softening those that teachers might find objectionable. In response, one disgruntled teacher called the result "mush . . . so much drivel." To no one's surprise and to the satisfaction of some, Canyon's bid did not win the lucrative grant.

In an effort to keep reform alive, Stickley and the restructuring committee held a series of cross-track faculty meetings to use up the remaining few thousand dollars of their planning grant. But, here too, the seductive reform mill undermined Stickley's good intentions. At these meetings, she and committee leaders took up most of the time in the manner of conventional staff development: making presentations, tightly controlling the agenda, and assiduously avoiding dialogues about the faculty's individual or shared norms and values. For example, at one meeting, faculty sat quietly and listened as Stickley displayed overhead transparencies and explained eight components of a learning community; at another, her presentation reviewed the district's restructuring goals and definitions of such reform terms as stakeholders, shared governance, restructuring, and consensus.

After several years of "reform," Canyon Middle School had little to show for its efforts, its trauma, or the many thousands of dollars it had spent.

Betterment: The Chavez Way

Cesar Chavez Middle School's classrooms and corridors offer an oasis, a safe haven in the school's West Coast port-of-entry community of Latino immigrants. Morning and afternoon "graffiti sweeps" and school rules prohibiting any evidence of gang affiliation (dress, hand signs, slang, tattoos, etc.) leave few visible traces of the violence and drugs that plague the inner city. But protecting students from their lives outside is not the Chavez's faculty's main goal. As we've seen in earlier chapters, they expect both to help all their students succeed academically in middle school and to prepare them all for college. Students regularly visit college campuses, teaching teams are named after local universities, and years after they graduate from Chavez some students get help from counselors to fill out college applications. Going above and beyond is the norm; it's what teachers and students alike call "the Chavez Way." As one teacher put it, "I don't think you come to teach here unless you are going to buy into that philosophy."

Their continuous quest to go above and beyond has led Chavez staff to reach out for any program or reform that might help their students. The much admired principal, Ken Lawson, is quick to point out, however, that they are careful to weigh the costs and benefits of each new program, deciding whether the extra effort contributes to the Chavez Way or just burns people out. For instance, like Canyon, Chavez joined one of California's middle-grade partnerships. But the faculty withdrew after a couple of years, partly frustrated by their partner schools' lack of progress, but mostly disillusioned by the emphasis placed on the status of being a reforming school rather than on the substance of reform. Belonging to the state partnership was "not an honor" but, according to one Chavez faculty leader, "a farce."

Chavez, like Canyon, sought California's one-year restructuring planning grant and lucrative five-year implementation grant. But unlike Canyon, whose bid for the planning grant was successful, Chavez's proposal was rejected. If they wanted to write for the major implementation grant, they would have to do it without state encouragement or resources.

The Chavez faculty had failed from the perspective of the reform mill, but they kept on going. Vice Principal Serena Menendez was excited by the energy created in writing the planning grant; she set in motion a schoolwide process in hopes of winning the five-year implementation grant anyway. Even more remarkable was how the Chavez faculty eschewed reform-mill norms and practices and made the planning process itself educative, socially just, caring, and participatory.

Faculty used a routinely scheduled meeting to fill twenty-four pieces of chart paper with reform ideas. For several days afterward, the charts hung in the library for teachers to read and modify. Three teachers distilled the core ideas on the charts and distributed their initial analysis of reform ideas. Menendez posted relevant research articles in the faculty lunchroom; many faculty requested copies so that they could read and think more about the ideas they'd generated.

Like other faculties, the Chavez teachers did not agree about reform. Some veterans worried that their influence would be outweighed by younger teachers who were enthusiastic about the latest reform trends. However, Menendez, Lawson, and others made it possible for those who felt marginalized to join the process without having to give up their reservations. Some of these veterans organized a survey, asking all teachers for their ideas about the changes that had emerged in discussion (for example, teaming, heterogeneous grouping, and community involvement). With results in hand, a team of seven grant writers that included four teachers wrote for five days straight—three of them school holidays—to craft a proposal that drew on local and research knowledge and was framed by rich stories about their school and community. Throughout the five days, the team called in other teachers, parents, and a county office consultant. They submitted the rough draft to the whole staff for review and revision, and a few weeks later, the grant lay in the hands of the state reform mill.

So buoyed were Chavez staff by the betterment process they'd set in motion that they wasted no time in taking the first steps toward restructuring. They set up twelve teams for the fall, with more than half of the staff assigned to them. Teachers decided who they would team with, and each team framed the structure for its relationship. One five-member team (made up of three core teachers, a physical education teacher, and a resource specialist) shared the same set of students all day and worked out a novel plan to teach their own elective courses. Most others opted for teams of two or three members, each with its own particular emphasis. For example, one all-male team decided to make home visits its core strategy. Committed to respecting differences, however, the faculty also agreed that teachers who were wary could take up to three years to prepare for being part of a team. They named this group the "anchors," explaining that every moving ship needed an anchor to ground it but that at some point the anchor had to be pulled on board. Teachers met over the summer to construct for themselves what teaming should mean, and hammer out plans for the fall.

That August, the school learned it was not among the finalists for the restructuring grant. Staff members described themselves and their colleagues as "surprised" and "devastated." Capturing everyone's response to the reform mill, a district administrator commented: "It's a sin they didn't get the money . . . they went about it in a purer way than I've ever seen anybody go about the change process . . . it was done cleanly, and they came off with these ideas really from a draft room, and [they] included everybody."

In most schools, lost funds would have meant canceling or postponing reform plans. But Chavez's "pure" betterment process had created a confidence not easily swayed; as one teacher told us: "We didn't do it simply for the money. We did it because we think this is what our kids' needs are. So why wouldn't we go for it?" Mindful, however, of the human cost of adding yet another program, Lawson knew they had to figure out a way to ensure that the teachers who were launching teams had time to meet and plan throughout the school year. With representatives from every department, Chavez's governance council symbolized, as the principal put it, "real empowerment . . . they make some pretty hard decisions." Digging deep into their site funds, the governance council came up with money to pay for two team-planning periods a week.

Throughout the year, the teams met to discuss their progress. By May, they were all exhausted. Menendez gathered impressions of how the year had gone. Once again, the library filled with chart paper and committees formed to develop a survey. Though, as one teacher commented, they had "a lot of kinks to work out," most of the faculty were convinced that teaming was a good idea. Standing in the lunchroom looking over the survey results, teachers discussed their plans for next year. Many teams planned to stay together; some were breaking up and looking for new members; and some of the anchors were eagerly joining teams. They generated, as one teacher said, "a tremendous amount of dialogue about the next layer of change." True to the Chavez Way, the teachers embraced teaming, driven by the internal goods of betterment.

Chapter Nine

A Passion for the Public Good

No book that presumes to use the words *civic virtue* in its subtitle can be large enough to contain all the caveats and equivocations that its authors crave. No chapter called "A Passion for the Public Good" can fully distinguish *its* passion and *its* good from others' conceptions, let alone establish its intellectual or moral claim to stand alongside them. Yet we so presume—fortified with an appropriation of Cornel West's words:

It is rare in human history, of course, that the notion of individuality and the civic are so coupled that a democratic project is generated. . . . A democratic sensibility cuts against the grain of history. . . .

What then are we to do? There is no overnight solution or panacea, of course. We need to begin with something profoundly un-American, namely, recalling a sense of history, a historical sensibility linked to empathy. Empathy is not simply a matter of trying to imagine what others are going through, but having the will to muster enough courage to do something about it. In a way empathy is predicated upon hope. . . .

To be part of the democratic tradition is to be a prisoner of hope. And you cannot be a prisoner of hope without engaging in a form of struggle that keeps the best of the past alive. To engage in that struggle means that one is always willing to acknowledge that there is no triumph around the corner, but that you persist because you believe it is right and just and moral. . . .

We are not going to save each other, ourselves, America, or the world. But certainly we can leave it a little bit better.[1]

We, like many of the educators we studied, are prisoners of hope. Yet, like them, we see no triumph around the corner. We persist because we believe that schooling grounded by educativity, social justice, caring, and democratic participation is right and good and moral.

Reform, or Counterculture?

Also in our book's title, and on nearly every page, we refer to *education reform*. We have argued—trying to be neither subtle nor overtly rude—that most of what we saw and heard presented as education reforms were terribly flawed enterprises. More deeply, it was not just the reform activities that were flawed, but the very assumptions and the core concepts of reform as embodied in a reform mill. We have tried to use this metaphor to capture the cultural aspect of the social reality of school reform policies and their implementation.[2] In an effort to grasp the culture of school reform and guard against reification, we have inferred the nature and power of the reform mill from the structures, ideologies, and rituals enacted by ordinary people, written policies, actual agencies, and concrete practices. But we do not want to characterize the reform mill simply as the people, policies, agencies, and practices themselves. Instead, we are concerned with how their words and actions symbolize or express the dominant culture. It goes against the very point of this book if the reform-mill argument is turned to focus sharply on the "flaws" of individual people, agencies, and so on, for the purpose of fixing them one by one.

The Reform Mill's "Improvements"

One reason that it's so difficult to sort out the pernicious effects of being encapsulated in a reform-mill culture is that the mill embraces and coopts both progressive and conservative reforms. The reform mill has in fact fostered some significant educational and policy improvements over the past thirty or so years, including such advances as ending de jure school segregation, pressing for constructivist teaching, and exposing the limits of top-down management styles. In each of these cases and many others, the reform mill has been a forceful, rational mover of the school culture, making schools as good as society wants them to be—but no better. Although such reform may result in individual structural or technical alterations of existing school structures, they are rarely anything more than a reconfigured (perhaps improved) status quo. Throughout this book, we write of reformers for whom we have much admiration. In the end, however, we have come to largely reject the idea of reform. In its place, we offer a conception that we call betterment.

Betterment: A Countercultural Alternative

Betterment does not deny that there are important technological changes needed in schools: better ways to organize the school day, better ways to teach mathematics, better ways to increase minority enrollments in college prep classes, and so forth. But betterment also reaches deep into the culture, into history, to keep the best of the past alive as West says, by making schools places of civic virtue. In contrast to reform, betterment asks schools to confront the cultural contradictions that define civic life; it therefore asks them to be countercultural—to be, in West's sense, un-American. It also asks them to be un-American in ways that would address Langston Hughes's poignant claim that "America was never America to me." We contend that for good American schools to be un-American schools in these ways is no more an oxymoron, no more an irony, than for reform—locked in a reform-mill culture—to be a guardian of the status quo.

Collective Action and Betterment in American Schools

We believe that what we saw in sixteen schools and five states demonstrates that, even as the reform mill's work is largely a failure, not all that takes place in schools in the name of reform must be condemned as such. On the contrary, we found reformers engaged in betterment in all of the schools. Their countercultural work is a struggle both against and with history; it is similar to the struggles for betterment of Thomas Jefferson, Abraham Lincoln, Jane Addams, and Martin Luther King, Jr., who, in their own times, were similarly un-American. Embedded in the cultural conflicts of their times, these historical personages were equivocally received by society, sparking intense debate about what it meant to be educative, socially just, caring, and participatory. As we argued in Chapter Two, we Americans use these historic figures, and others like them, to anchor our democratic sense making. If we simply valorize them as cultural icons, however, we risk overlooking the messiness of the social inquiry process that grounds action. Betterment in schools requires that educators engage in the same messy enterprise and muster the same courage.

Educative Practice

Consider Tom Katzir, Doris Davis, and other teachers' highly interactive lessons, which we highlighted in Chapter Three. They envisioned and enacted new theories of learning and classroom practice that approach Dewey's notion of educativity. Memorization and repetition were not options in Katzir's math lessons, which favored using baseball statistics; students had to form answers from their experience and use the language of the discipline to communicate what they knew. Davis consistently guided her students' activity toward a deeper understanding of established disciplinary content, in this case experimental scientific inquiry. As the classrooms of these two teachers and several others illustrate, practice, driven by the internal goods of educativity, did change. Students in these classrooms clearly benefited from these new practices.

Socially Just Practice

Inland principal Ben McCall, in the From Neighbors to Friends project, turned the racial divisiveness problem in his school community into a civil rights obligation. Reaching beyond structural detracking, Inland embarked on a broad moral pursuit of social justice, seeking to change the culture of instruction, curriculum, and relationships among adults and children so as to reflect and respect the racial differences rupturing the community outside of school. As they engaged in this ambitious betterment process, a remarkable thing happened. A school community, once deeply divided, came together—or, we might say, contentiously stumbled together—to grapple collectively with alternatives not only to tracking but also to racism and discrimination.

Caring Practice

Bethany Houston at Carver, among many others, refused to accept less than her students' best efforts. Rather than serving her students to make up for their deficiencies and in the process lowering her expectations, Houston provided them with the best, most rigorous learning opportunities she could. Was she too tough? Did she drive away these needy youngsters? No. She held on to her students with a welcoming hand—a sympathetic touch. Middleton's principal, Wally Vincent, reached out to parents. He did not just get parents involved by placing them on a committee; he responded, making their concerns his own agenda. Houston's teaching was not just the means, an instrumental activity designed to bring students to a particular level of knowledge. Similarly, Vincent's listening was more than the means to solve or avoid a problem. Their teaching and listening were also ends in themselves, because at those moments, for teacher and student, for principal and parent, nothing was more important than working together in a respectful, democratic, relationship.

Participatory Practice

True to Vermont's tradition of public deliberation, many Van Buren teachers approached reform through day-in, day-out discussion and joint activity. Built on trusting, noncompetitive relationships, their working together allowed formerly private concerns such as teaching to become public. In Texas, Tubman's Rebecca Owens worked alongside grassroots organizer Felicia Landers to make the school the center of communitywide empowerment. Enlisting the help of local churches and businesses, VOICES engaged parents in their children's education by helping them recognize their power and leverage in changing schools. In a remarkable countercultural political sentiment, Owens told us: "We are trying to empower [parents] so they will demand change. It is threatening, but it makes the school a better place because parents will demand more of us."

Betterment: A Critical Struggle
That Combines Means and Ends

No school, principal, or reform can replicate Owens's school context, her personality, or her achievements; nor should they try. But many would serve their students and communities well by emulating her—by seizing local, context-specific opportunities; empowering parents; demanding change; and guiding those changes along the dimensions of educativity, care, social justice, and participation. Owens did not ignore the reform mill—nobody can do that—but she resisted its rational, sequential model of change, which views struggle as a sign of weakness, defeat, technical incompetence, or simply a bad attitude because (according to the mill) only achieving the goal is worthwhile. Instead, Owens acted as if empowerment itself, and action itself, made her life, her students' lives, and those of her community dignified and satisfying. In such a place, the work of educating children for democratic participation has begun.

Oliver Bradley at Van Buren explained his sense that struggle is not an enervating instrument to achieve an ephemeral goal, but rather a collective and energizing way to conduct one's personal and professional life: "I think that to say that we're working on reform would not be a correct way to describe it. . . . We're constantly trying to improve, trying to get better, and trying a few things the best way that we can. And that's where we're going. It's a struggle, and whenever you have a large group of people with diverse interests and needs, you're always going to find [that it's] kind of a struggle, but it's a positive one."

Good Is in the Doing

At every turn, breaking from the dichotomy of means versus ends is associated with sustaining the quest for civic virtue. Betty Carlson and Mike Crawford plunged into integrated curricula while other teams were stuck revisiting familiar work and problems such as grading and discipline. Carlson and Crawford did so not because they were driven to raise test scores or handed a package but because they made sense of integration's educative benefits in their everyday work with students. Chavez staff elevated their struggle above the state reform mill that failed to recognize the value of their "pure" reform process; they wanted a grant to further their work but would not change their work to get the grant. Mandeville College broke with tradition when it eschewed the individualistic and competitive norms that universities use; instead it rewarded employees with and for a truly collaborative relationship with Mountain View. Foster Davies sustained an uphill battle for social justice, possibly jeopardizing career advancement and definitely inviting aggravation. None of these people expressed self-sacrifice or martyrdom.

We encountered very few who signed up for reform as an act of compliance, to keep the mill running, or to garner external rewards such as higher test scores, grants, or special designations. Many of the most intensely committed educators intimated that they felt what John Adams may well have meant by "a positive passion for the public good." As one teacher explained, her dedication and long hours are rooted in a "sense of loyalty" and are bolstered by "the sense we get when we know that we've made a difference." Rather than being daunted by the enormousness of their task, such educators seemed to thrive. They stayed late after meetings, spent lunch discussing philosophy, and put themselves on the line to uphold their beliefs. They were practical and they were dreamers. Thinking deeper, reflecting harder, and acting more bravely than most is what sets betterment apart from reform. One teacher put it plainly: "This is my job. This is what I'm here to do. I'm going to do this no matter how difficult it is today."

A Critical Temper

The ideals we hold for schools are the analogs of the ideal characteristics found in the American citizenry: Americans are smart; America is a cultural melting pot; Americans pitch in to help their neighbors; and America requires civic contribution from everyone. Yet even the most generous observers of the culture must concede that many Americans are not well educated; the cultural melting pot has long been exposed as a fanciful metaphor; Americans often neglect some of their neighbors; and far too few of us pay attention to, much less participate in, civic affairs.

It is tempting for citizens to view social and schooling deficits solely in terms of deficiencies of these and other ideals and values.

Many believe, for example, that some Americans (or some groups) do not value education enough; that nonwhite and immigrant Americans do not try hard enough to enter the American cultural mainstream; that urban Americans care too little about their neighbors; and that nearly all are too lazy to participate in civic affairs. At best, these commonplace, deficiency-based, weak-commitment analyses tell only a partial and misleading story of what happens in and out of schools.

The reform mill builds upon deficiency-based analyses by portraying deep cultural contradictions as a neutral and unproblematic landscape. A critical temper, though, reveals these contradictions as if they were rifts and fault lines; it exposes the rubble of shoddy constructions of the past, and it posts warnings to tell those who inquire: do not go there. Nowhere in our data do we find schools that consistently enacted a critical approach to betterment. Yet we did catch glimpses of people probing the reform mill to make public what the mill's rhetoric meant to them and how it affected them in the context of their own experiences. In this way, individual, privately held deficiencies became contextual, collectively held problems.[3]

Reconciling Betterment and Reform Policy

The stories of these schools and state projects reveal a fascinating disjuncture between the worlds of policy making and schools. On the one hand, wherever we looked, people in schools embraced the reform rhetoric, many of the policies, much of the technical assistance, and the small amount of money that came their way. On the other hand, we saw little evidence of the scaling-up rhetoric and policies helping these schools grapple with the local obstacles they faced.

The policy questions raised are already many, but we offer the following:

- How might reform policies acknowledge and assist with the cultural and political challenges that reforming educators face, as well as building their technical capacity?
- How might policy help schools explicitly cultivate civic virtue while averting the reform mill's (and its own) tendency to refashion whatever it touches into a new version of the status quo?

- How might policies and policy-making processes mirror betterment—the educative, socially just, caring, and democratic conditions that educators hope to create for their students?
- How might policy makers and the public engage with schools to become ongoing participants in their betterment?

Certainly, framing reform as a quest for betterment requires policy makers, educators, and the public to pull back from an exclusive focus on such narrow outcome indicators as test scores. Success must be judged in terms of schools' becoming more educative, socially just, caring, or participatory, as well as improving on the conventional indicators. When we view these efforts through a wider lens—one that allows us to see betterment as a battle with cultural contradictions—some (but certainly not all) of what most call reform failures may actually represent significant breaks with the status quo of the schooling culture. Just as important, we find that some of what is now called successful reform may represent only superficial structural changes.

Betterment and the Process of Educational Change

During the past two decades, many school-restructuring initiatives reflected the growing body of research showing that school change will not occur unless local educators and their communities support it and make it their own in a school culture that supports change. Much of the *Turning Points* work followed in this tradition. In fact, the Carnegie staff, staff of the Council of Chief State School Officers who supported the national network of state middle-grade projects, and the state project leaders were quite familiar with the change literature. Most took it as axiomatic that change is nonrational, nonlinear, and unlikely to proceed as planned; that reform is a process, not an event; that change requires mutual adaptation; that reforms differ with the unique culture of each school; and that state leaders help set the conditions for effective change, but local practitioners must develop the specific practices.[4]

Reforms predicated on these principles of change (including *Turning Points*) fell far short of what policy makers had hoped for. As necessary conditions of change, the principles still hold strong.

But they are clearly not sufficient to sustain a passion for the public good. Their neutral tone reads more like an autopsy of reform than an inspiration to rise up and take on the dominant culture. There is no mandate for betterment embedded in these processes.

In response to these highly analytic principles that called for bottom-up reforms, policy makers again missed the point. The next round of reforms, recognizing that significant change was not likely if local school communities were left to invent and implement change pretty much on their own,[5] added top-down mandates to the bottom-up ones. We see this top-down, bottom-up combination when states adopt standards and accountability systems but leave to local schools the decisions about how best to meet the standards. Current federal regulations governing categorical funding also combine the top-down and bottom-up strategies. Local schools select from an approved list of "proven" designs and models of effective practice, and the additional funding affords the resources and technical assistance for educators to replicate them in their local context.

Neither traditional top-down mandates nor local reform initiatives are sufficient to establish and sustain educativity, caring, social justice, and participation. Furthermore, the putative hybrid of top-down, bottom-up does not appear much more promising. In fact, the claim of local adaptation seems to us disingenuous, considering the massive imbalance between national and state initiatives and local capacity to influence them or not be influenced by them. It is a sterling, perhaps unparalleled, example of the reform mill's subtle and invisible operation—this capacity to coopt, at least rhetorically, both those who favor powerful outside control and those who favor laissez faire. Some may argue that the top-down, bottom-up combination is the heart and soul of democratic political compromise, but we find it to be an inadequate paradigm for making schools places of civic virtue.

Advocacy and Political Clout for Betterment

What we saw in schools leads us to favor context-sensitive, locally initiated reforms; however, we also recognize the importance of pressure and support from outside the local community. Few maxims are as well accepted in the change literature as the conclusion that policy makers "cannot mandate what matters."[6] Yet history and our own observations have also shown that leaders with status and power can inspire and educate on behalf of nonneutral, even countercultural, reforms. Policy makers and reformers outside the school must create the political clout and capacity for betterment. That is, they must press educators to go against the dominant grain of schools serving the narrowly instrumental and individualistic ends often demanded by powerful local constituents. They can provide a strong voice, a bully pulpit, that calls for schools to serve the common, public good by becoming educative, socially just, caring, and participatory. This pressure and support can create an environment, a necessary safe space for school-site learning to occur, especially during the early, traumatic stages of reform, when resistance may be great and reformers are most vulnerable. Schools also need technical assistance from the outside, but before they can use technical assistance sensibly they need political space to take on cultural change and to have the conditions created for their own learning and critical inquiry.[7]

Betterment as Inquiry

Moreover, this outside support—in the form of personal relationships, legislation, access to public opinion, or technical assistance (including training, materials, research, and inquiry)—needs to follow the same path the reformers are asking schools to follow. Once educators move beyond a neutral perspective regarding the reform, they find few tools to help them consider what their critique implies for making the change process educative, socially just, caring, and participatory. However, some promising beginnings do exist in scholarship on the moral purposes of schools and teaching, as well as in work from the feminist and critical traditions.[8] These traditions interrupt the typical course of reform conversations, which jump to "practical" future applications of policy; they seek to ground the talk in history, in the present, and in the meanings of the status quo. Although these traditions and our own study may not suggest particular strategies, they do help establish a nonneutral standard or grounding for reform. Advocating a disposition of critical inquiry as a route to realizing moral purposes in schools, they provide principled arguments for seeing betterment as legitimate means and ends for schooling.[9]

Another scholarly approach also captures the best of what we saw in schools. This approach frames betterment as social problem solving and may assuage those worried about overinvesting in *process* at the expense of *content*. Through a broad, open-ended, and diffuse process, social inquiry or problem solving guards against self-indulgence and uncritical acceptance ("Everyone has to do his own thing," "Everyone has her own teaching style," etc.). As Charles Lindblom argues, the reforms needed must reduce the many impairments to thinking clearly: "Societies do not need to urge citizens to probe; they need only to permit them to do so. They need only to reduce the disincentives to probe, the diversions and obfuscations that muddle or dampen probing, the misinformation and indoctrinations that misdirect it, and the intimidations and coercions that block it."[10]

Accordingly, if changes are to be more than refinement of the status quo—in terms of fundamental school goals and norms—then the status quo must be critically examined as an indispensable part of the change process, so that countercultural ideas start to make sense to reform participants. Thus, a disposition toward critical inquiry doesn't simply stress the process of change per se—for example, whether teachers have time to think, talk, and plan together—but rather the substance of what those discussions are about.

We started this chapter by saying that no amount of caveats would satisfy us. Here, we must include the caution of how betterment-as-inquiry, which has the promise of escaping the reform mill, can itself easily get milled.

Betterment That Is Educative

School reformer Deborah Meier reminds us that "you can't replicate a school any more than you can replicate a family, but you can learn from a good school like you can learn from a good family."[11]

Most reform projects start with a small cadre of model programs or schools. A disposition toward educativity does not view these models as products to be emulated, but as sites where more sophisticated peers are engaging in their own learning. The model itself would do well to assume that it too is imperfect and struggling and has much to gain from questions, challenges, and dialogues on its practices.

But a critical, educative process demands many types of knowledge in addition to that gained from various relationships with other practitioners, including results of research about pedagogy, learning, historical precedents, and so on. This knowledge, when brought into the school with a critical perspective, raises such questions as "What are we doing now? How did it come to be that way? What do these practices tell us about how we conceptualize teaching and learning?" Participants in such inquiry constantly remind themselves that the problems they face have current and historical context, and that the routine problems of schooling—using time effectively, staff communication, grouping students for instruction, and the like—must be situated in these contexts to be understood.

Betterment That Is Socially Just

Critical inquiry can allow educators to systematically explore and critique deeply held beliefs and ideologies about intelligence, racial and gender differences, social stratification, and elite privilege as powerful forces to be reckoned with inside and outside of schools.[12] Social theorists doing work that is sometimes identified as "postcolonial" suggest that social constructions such as race and class help constitute our personal, societal, national, and international worlds, and that any fundamental alteration of social institutions must necessarily include reconstructing these ideas.[13] Such inquiry asks us to recognize and contend with embedded values and human interests in school practices by asking, "Whose interests are (and are not) being served by the ways things are?"

As a radical bottom-up strategy, such an approach can be a helpful accompaniment to schools seeking to create practices grounded in principles of equity and fairness. Outsiders who have developed respectful and trusting relationships with schools can sometimes raise questions such as these when those who work in schools would find it difficult to do so. Others outside the school who have positions of influence and power can recognize that such

questions are not a threat to the well-being of the school and community, but a necessary, usually neglected, component of betterment. For schools, it also means recasting resistant old-guard
teachers and other marginalized groups as valuable members of
the adult learning community.

Betterment as Care

Betterment must also be a process in which the needs of local educators and communities are received and responded to. Care, a
necessary condition for civic virtue, is conspicuously absent from
current moves to get to scale. For example, care is diminished if
raising standardized test scores is the sole measure of school
improvement, and low-income schools are written off as incapable
of improvement or subjected to threats and humiliation if they
don't improve. Caring means that low-performing schools should
be seen as potentially rich intellectual environments for students
and teachers that must be helped and expected to improve through
contextually sensitive supports. For example, schools that lack qualified teachers; that need instructional materials such as textbooks,
science labs, or computers; or whose physical plants create health
risks for students should be viewed as targets for capital investment
rather than public abandonment. Schools would be given ade-
quate time to improve; but this does not mean that policy makers
should issue their mandates and resources and return in five years
instead of two years. "Time to improve" means giving teachers
the time they need to learn about and share new practices with
their colleagues—time to collectively critique the implications of
these new practices for their students, themselves, and their local
communities.

Relationships are fundamental to betterment-as-caring. As a
change in the Illinois state administration was sending the middle
school project to another division in the agency, Will Darlington
confessed his shaken faith that reform could be transported and
sustained on the basis of its intrinsic value and a good process
for scaling up: "The goal, of course, is for [the schools] to continue
on their own, eventually, when this all goes away. We have told
the schools from the beginning that it's not the people that make

the difference, it's the process. But since our transition internally, Patrice [Sherwood, his colleague at the ISBE] and I have realized it's not true. We haven't been honest. We really believed that if the process is done well, it wouldn't matter who was there. But, I retract that statement. It is the people. We've learned that here."

Betterment as Participation

At root, critical inquiry means that educators and communities engage in a deliberative process that takes into account both local conditions and the school's role in the common, public good. Since inquiry is not instrumental, is not a means to a predetermined end (unless participation itself, or care, or learning about others' perspectives is seen as an end), no one need feel coerced to compromise or rush to agreements that leave them with reservations. On the other hand, "participants must continually remind themselves that all is not talk; that, notwithstanding the omnipresent ambiguity in educational organizations like schools, actions can and must be taken, reviewed, revised, retaken, reviewed. . . ."[14] Just as inquiry encourages freely made decisions, its imperative for freely made revisions also allows risks. The questions to ask at every opportunity include "Is this the way we want things to be?" and "What are we going to do about it?" Such participatory processes rely less on fidelity to a reform (or faithful implementation of preestablished practices, or even unyielding commitments to recent agreements) than on renegotiating to remain faithful to a principle.

Inquiry is public, open to anyone with a legitimate long-term purpose and obligation to participate. Public critique is necessary not just to correct the cultural press toward seeing the problems of the school as an aggregate of individual problems but also to be sure that the collective (perhaps, but not necessarily, the majority) does not overwhelm minority views and individual voices. The public nature of participation ensures that all views and voices are responded to. Full participation in this process means having the courage to engage in public learning, talking aloud about difficult issues of race and equity, marshaling support through a public appeal to the higher moral ground.

Betterment as Nation Building

The struggles for civic virtue that we observed in reforming schools have their origin in a larger American attempt to reconcile commitment to private interests and individual gain with the passion for the common, public good. This larger struggle embeds schools in cultural contradictions and ambivalence, not only about the meaning of education but also about forging social justice out of deep divisions of race, gender, and social class. It is expressed in schools' inextinguishable penchant for acting with kindness and care while they also assign to very young children and their parents responsibility for their own misfortune. The larger cultural struggle makes schools sites for resolving our democratic sensibilities for political equality with our social hierarchies of wealth, position, and power that distort political participation.

Schools have served as the location for similar cultural struggles since the nation's founding, making the reforms of the 1980s and 1990s part of a long tradition. As such, school reform is more akin to a social movement intent on reinvigorating public life and reactivating citizenship than it is to a technical reengineering of a corporation. Principled collective social action has far more promise as an antidote to both individual, parochial interests and large, centralized government control than do neutral reform technologies. Benjamin Barber, for example, argues for a "strong democracy" in which citizens participate actively and centrally in public debate. Barber argues that our public institutions, including our schools, and civil society generally have been left in shambles by decades of "government gargantuanism and private greed." According to Barber:

> Although in eclipse today, civil society was the key to America's early democratic energy and civic activism. Its great virtue was that it shared government's regard for the commonweal, yet unlike government made no claim to exercise a monopoly on legitimate coercion. Rather, it was a voluntary, "private" realm devoted to "public" goods. . . . Americans want, need, and have a right to civil liberty—the liberty earned by citizens engaging in self-government, willing neither to turn over their destinies to government proxies nor to pretend that commercial markets can produce the social

goods and values that are necessary for democratic community
life. . . . A third way needs to be found between private markets
and coercive government, between anarchic individualism and
dogmatic statism. . . . If we fail to find it, we seem fated to enter
an era in which America's public voice, the nation's civic soul,
will be left forever mute.[15]

Since Barber wrote of this "third way" in 1995, a political cadre
of "third wayers," whose notable proponents include Bill Clinton
and Tony Blair, have coopted the term and developed the ideas to
suit their unique standpoints. One representative group places first
among its "five strategies for renewing democracy" this statement:
"We must restore the American Dream by expanding wealth,
rather than redistributing it. . . ." Some might read this (we do) as
a guarantee that the nation's colossal disparities in wealth and well-
being will continue to increase. A deep tension, then, plagues
attempts to realize this third way. Rooted in the legacies of Reagan
and Thatcher, the power of privatization and deregulation are
offered as opportunities for all citizens to achieve economic success. Finally, the third way rejects redistribution without regard for
how past opportunities were distributed among those who now
have or do not have them; this holds even in the modest arena of
providing the conditions necessary for a common education.

The third wayers rely on market forces and choice as central
strategies for generating a collective commitment to advancing the
common good. In 1999, Robert Reich called this road to implementing such a third way perilous. The third way's success will
depend, Reich argues, on emergence of a political movement: "a
collection of people who, because they are linked by culture and
belief, are willing to pool certain of their resources so that all of
their members have a fair chance of succeeding."[16]

Democratic energy and civic activism mobilized on behalf of
all young Americans is, we believe, at the heart of educational betterment. But on the basis of our study of reforming schools, we
caution school-focused third wayers about the treacherous road
ahead. We remind them of the disappointing effects of the reform
mill on nationwide efforts to improve schools. The mill rejected
the independence of local schools as a way to reform. Likewise, it
rejected top-down central authority to control the course of

change. Recently, it has been exploring another approach, a third way: top-down, bottom-up. From our perspective, direction is irrelevant if what is being passed along is devoid of principled content. We have suggested that this content be looked for, with a critical eye, in the educativity, social justice, caring, and participation at each school and in the attention given these dimensions by public-schooling policy.

The reformers whom we studied undertook their ambitious efforts in an education policy environment marked by twenty years of tilt toward self-interested social policies. Since the oil crisis of the 1970s—and certainly during the Reagan and Bush presidencies—schools, like other social institutions, have looked increasingly to individual action as the key to political and cultural stability, and economic growth. Public policies and public sentiment have leaned toward deregulation, leaner bureaucracies, union busting, and the privatization of social services and schools. Market forces have been relied upon to ensure liberty and prosperity, with particular reliance on accountability. With little critical inquiry and public deliberation, the third way's emphasis on the freedom to follow one's individual volition (like that of the social conservatives that preceded them) has kept individual well-being some distance from—and well ahead of—community interests.

This distance between the emphasis on civic interest and self-interest is sharply apparent in today's schools, and growing more so with the proliferation of third-way policies that favor standards, accountability, deregulation, and choice as tools for systemic education reform. The dominant order of concern about schooling has been that if *my own child* does well, the community will do well (not: my own child will only do well in a strong community). The century's end has brought the ascendance of policy makers and social theorists who argue that only a reemergence of individual morality, accountability, and volunteerism can mitigate the hard edges of self-interest. How far this is from collective work to create educative, socially just, caring, and participatory schools to raise all of the community's children!

We think it will take something else to fan the flames of the nation's civic soul. In the schools we studied, we saw those flames, though often barely rising above a smolder. The flames were, as Cornel West might see them, "a form of struggle that keeps the best of the past alive." The best of the past? Not techniques or programs. Not forgotten morals or buried heroes. The best of the past is the struggle to leave "each other, ourselves, America, [and] the world . . . a little bit better." Schools can do this. They need our help.

Appendix: Studying the Technical, Normative, and Political Dimensions of School Reform

This Appendix describes the methods we used throughout our study and writing of this book. We include it here for two major reasons. First and most conventionally, it summarizes our research methodology: how we designed the study and selected sites; how we collected and analyzed data; how we verified case report findings; how we analyzed our findings across sites. Second, it explains how this book, which differs so dramatically from the final monograph we envisioned at the beginning of this project, came to look and read as it does: how we moved from cross-site analysis to the thematic representations, school vignettes, and cultural analysis contained in *Becoming Good American Schools*.

Becoming a Reflective, Constructivist Multiple-Case Study

How do we capture the spirit as well as the substance of five years of collected data—filling more than twenty-five file cabinet drawers and dozens of computer disks—and tell a story that gives voice to the individuals who opened up their classrooms, welcomed us to their meetings, and shared their successes and frustrations with us? How can we maintain our attention to those voices and, at the same time, address the broader cultural contradictions that underlie their individual and collective struggles? How can we share what we learned about teaching and learning, schooling, and educational policy making in America today, without reducing the lessons to a bulleted list or a recipe of best practices that decontextualize what we could only learn in context?

The structure of this book is our attempt to answer these questions. The stories and analysis contained herein are not meant to summarize the data stored in those twenty-five file drawers. Instead, this book provides a broad analysis of the study's findings. It represents our latest (and, perhaps, last) point in an iterative cycle of theory and data. The cycle began with formulating research questions; continued through conceptualizing and designing the study; came to life through selecting sites and collecting data; and concluded with conducting multiple layers of data analysis, collecting further data, and carrying out still more analysis. Research papers and dissertations, as well as this book, emerged from the process of the study and from the findings themselves.

We do not argue that this is the only story that could be told from this voluminous data. What we offer in this book is a construction of our experience and thinking, guided by our initial conceptual framework, grounded in extensive data, and shaped by our evolving sense of the reform process and the lived experiences of the individuals whom we reluctantly refer to merely as our respondents. Others analyzing these data might well tell a different tale, although not one that, we believe, would be fundamentally inconsistent with what we report here. We've attempted to capture the essence of the data and offer an interpretation that adds new and useful perspectives as school reformers and policy makers go about their work.

This work is informed by a constructivist research paradigm,[1] which acknowledges that the conceptual framework we developed at the outset of the study represented only a temporary construction of school reform processes, one that would likely be modified throughout the course of data collection and analysis.[2] This was, of course, what happened. Although our initial conceptual framework is still conspicuous in our analysis here, the more narrative style we have adopted in *Becoming Good American Schools* caused us to pay closer attention not only to what we knew and what we wanted to say about it but also how we wanted to say it. This latter point contributed to a more reflective methodological stance and prose than existed in previous reports of this work. Several blind reviewers of earlier drafts of the manuscript also contributed significantly to this reflective process.

As we pushed our analysis by probing ("What happens if . . . ?" "Why does it happen this way?"), we began to hear our collected data speaking to a broader audience—one less concerned with the particulars of middle school reform (did teams improve learning? how did schools implement an interdisciplinary curriculum?) and more concerned with understanding the relationships between educational policy and practice. Furthermore, early on we saw that our data could do much to reveal how both policy and practice are nested in broader cultural patterns and that any story told must reflect the meaning and the dignity of our schools' struggles not just within their buildings but within those cultural patterns.

Initial Conceptual Framework

In 1991, we began a three-year study aimed at providing an independent, empirical look at the impact of the Middle Grades Schools State Policy Initiative (MGSSPI) on efforts for middle school reform in a sample of twelve schools in four states—Texas, California, Massachusetts, and Vermont. These states were among the group sponsored by the Carnegie Corporation of New York, with a series of two- and three-year grants. As a part of their participation in the project, these states received technical assistance from the Council of Chief State School Officers (CCSSO) and joined the national network intended to foster cross-state collaboration and assistance.

Our goal in undertaking in-depth case-study research was to describe the strategies that widely contrasting states use to build the capacity and commitment of local schools for restructuring middle-grade education. We wanted to learn whether and how state policy initiatives and state-led implementation efforts can encourage schools to undertake significant reform and assist those schools that make the attempt. We began by reviewing the literature of school change and policy implementation, guided by a set of general questions about Carnegie's strategy: How might state-level actors, working as outside change agents, help local educators make dramatic and comprehensive changes in the structure and culture of schools? What approaches might states use? How might these approaches develop and vary across state and local contexts, and how might the state-school relationships have an impact on school reform? How do educators in schools experience their participation in a state-led reform initiative? How does the local school context facilitate, inhibit, or condition this experience?

We did not propose to evaluate the effectiveness of middle-grade reform in the four states, although that's what many participants expected us to do. Rather, we wanted to learn more general lessons about how states and schools connect on ambitious reforms. We were curious from the very start as to how actors across the entire spectrum of the reform—parents, students, teachers, principals, school district officials, county and state providers of technical services, university and other education partners, policy makers in state departments of education, foundation executives, an occasional governor, and so on—would work with, understand, and receive one another's participation. By investigating MGSSPI, we hoped to understand more about how policy is transformed as it makes its way from a widely heralded foundation report to state policies and structures and then to school practice.

The conceptual framework we developed to guide our work premised the *Turning Points* reform as complex and ambitious, one that was asking schools and others within the broader culture to make changes across technical, normative, and political dimensions.

This framework drew directly from a growing body of theory and research on policy and curriculum implementation, paying special attention to (among others) Seymour Sarason's work on the need for changes in the regularities in the culture of the school; John Goodlad's work on the importance of the sociopolitical context to curriculum change; Michael Fullan's emphasis on the centrality of "meaning making" by those engaged in reform; David Cohen and Deborah Ball's work on the transformation of reform policies as they make their way into practice; and Jon Snyder, Frances Bolin, and Karen Zumwalt's distinction between fidelity, mutual-adaptation, and enactment approaches to implementing new curriculum. We also drew on other work that has noted the importance of normative (or cultural) and political aspects of schooling (for example, Firestone and Corbett; and Louis and Miles).[3] Depicting this framework as a triangle with two-way arrows, we intended to be sensitive to the interconnectedness

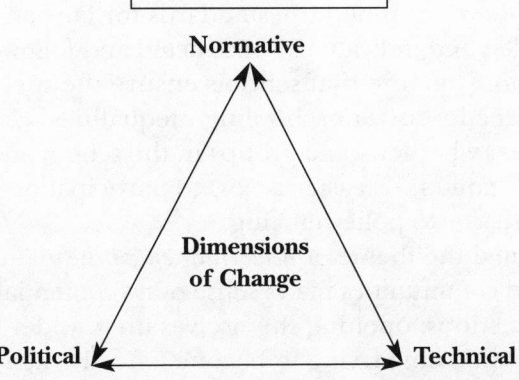

of norms and politics with the technical aspects of reform. Our attention, then, would be directed not just to recommended curriculum, organizational, and classroom changes but also to concomitant alterations in deeply entrenched beliefs, values, relationships, and power dynamics that characterize the cultures of most schools.

Working from this conceptual framework, we identified four themes to guide our inquiry at the school level. These themes represented substantive issues that, given our analysis of the rhetoric and recommendations of *Turning Points,* early MGSSPI documents, and our round of preliminary site visits and interviews with fifteen state project teams, we expected schools to struggle with as they built commitment and capacity for reform.[4]

The first theme, *individualism versus community,* spoke to the tensions that might arise as educators attempted to follow *Turning Points* directives that required subtle shifts toward a communitylike ethos and less focus on individualistic interests and competition.

We expected a variety of responses—resisting change, embracing change, threatening self-interest, openness to collective interests, and so on—as the reform pressed people to create a new kind of school community.

Social justice examined the standards for fairness that schools, communities, and individuals constructed and followed, in light of *Turning Points'* charge that schools ensure the success of all students and rectify current schooling inequalities. Here, we would also consider whether some groups in the school and community had more frequent or easier access to participation and learning opportunities or to policy making.

We coined the theme of *democratic enterprise* to encompass how schools and communities made sense of two potentially conflicting reform directions: opening themselves up to wider participation and at the same time trying to become effective at accomplishing predetermined outcomes, such as improved student learning. Also under this theme, we would try to identify how various school and community members expressed their understanding of democratic participation.

Finally, *inquiry* acknowledged *Turning Points'* emphasis on learning as becoming "intellectually reflective." This theme helped us pay attention to what counted as important knowledge worth informing deliberations about school, and the extent to which meaningful inquiry was encouraged at the schools—within both the broader organizational structures and the classroom. Though the reader may see some continuity between these themes and the four "Becoming" chapters, these themes also weave through the fabric of the book.

Project Scope and Design

What began as a three-year study of four states and twelve schools in 1991 expanded, with additional support in 1994, to add another state and four additional schools; we continued our research until 1996. During the first phase of the study (1991–1994), we set out to understand the interactive nature of reform. We conducted longitudinal, comparative case studies in the twelve schools and four states to examine how schools began to implement *Turning Points* reforms. We wanted to know which particular technical changes schools tackled and why, the change strategies they employed, and the local factors that enabled or impeded adoption and implementation. At the state level, we were interested in understanding the state policy context, specific state policy goals, and how the context and goals related to the state's strategies for building local capacity for reform. Also, we wanted to account for how policy initiatives were transformed as schools adapted them for local practice.

A two- or three-person team visited each school at least twice (many schools were visited three or four times) for three to five days. Often during the same data collection trip, project staff also met with state staff. Individual site visits were never long enough, but they still allowed us to tap into the complexities of reform activities. Even if we necessarily missed most of the significant reform "moments," our multiple visits generally gave us enough snapshots and interview opportunities to reconstruct sequences as they occurred. A typical site visit day consisted of back-to-back classroom observations, interviews, and meetings that lasted well into the evening.

During the second phase, intensive data collection continued at two of the original schools and in three of the original states, while four new schools and Illinois were added to the sample. We maintained some contact with the state and the schools that did not continue into phase two of on-site data collection (using telephone interviews with the schools, and interactions with people in Texas at Carnegie-sponsored conferences). At this point, Carnegie and the MGSSPI asked states to place greater emphasis on schools that face the greatest challenges: low-resource schools with concentrations of disadvantaged students. Carnegie also pressed schools to focus specifically on *Turning Points'* curriculum and health reforms. Our research focus shifted as well during this phase. Thus, three schools that were added to our sample for the second phase—Carver in California, Mitchell in Massachusetts, and Irving in Illinois—brought us many of our richest examples of classroom practice in low-income neighborhoods.

Selecting Good American Schools

We spent a considerable amount of time during the first year participating in a variety of Carnegie and CCSSO MGSSPI activities, including visits to nine states that we considered good candidates for our cases. We selected sites that evinced the wide variability of school contexts and state policy approaches that we witnessed as we reviewed grant proposals and site reviews and attended national MGSSPI meetings. We took seriously the challenge that case study research could yield sophisticated theoretical conclusions if cases were chosen to elaborate or extend emergent theory.

Our theoretical sampling began with the states. We chose states where a lot was happening, but the four cases provide tremendously interesting variation in the state plans, in the nature of state-local interactions and perceptions, and in the states' policy contexts. As you can see from Chapter Seven, we selected states that differed in their historical experience with education reform, the nature of their middle school efforts, their capacity to support changes, and their ideas about and approach to the normative and political aspects of middle school reform. Finally, we wanted states that varied in size and population.

Educational policy in Texas had been historically centralized. The state's penchant for prescriptive policy mandates contributed to contentious relations between state and local officials and some suspicion on the part of local educators. A new state education chief in Texas had recently embarked on efforts to change these patterns by championing reforms that promoted local autonomy (for example, site-based management). California also had a history of centralized reforms, but they had been less prescriptive. California policy subscribed to the principle of "no unfunded mandates" and relied on strong inducements with technical assistance. As we began our project, several state curriculum frameworks had set a standard for local involvement in state policy making.

In Massachusetts, policy making similarly relied on recommendations rather than mandates, but its history of local control and participation made participation seem more voluntary than in Texas or California. State officials did make considerable use of their bully pulpit to set the tone of reform, arguing persuasively that middle-grade reform had a moral as well as an empirical foundation. Vermont sat on the other end of the centralization continuum, with state policy developing consensually and adoption nearly always being voluntary. When we added Illinois to our study for the second phase, we sought a state whose policy environment seemed to fall at a midpoint between centralized and decentralized, and whose size was between large and small. We were also interested in adding a Midwestern state to our sample.

The differences across states contributed to the variety of approaches to middle school reform. As Texas and California officials sought to empower local districts, their counterparts in Massachusetts and Vermont attempted to maintain local control, even as they assumed more centralized influence in the direction of reform. Recent events in Massachusetts reveal how difficult the balancing act can be, and the state is currently embroiled in the kind of contentious state-versus-local relationships we would have believed highly improbable as we started our work.

The schools we selected make up a fascinating array of American middle schools. To identify school cases in each state, we worked with state project staff (as we collected state-level data) and conducted half-day school visits. We sought schools that would let us examine how policies play out in local contexts, selecting one school serving predominantly middle-class, white students; one school serving a racially, ethnically, or socioeconomically mixed student body; and one school serving predominantly disadvantaged or minority students. Across states, this sampling permitted us to compare how schools in similar local contexts responded to contrasting policy-making structures and practices. Importantly, we deliberately avoided model schools—those schools that state officials considered farthest along in reform. Rather, we sought schools that were actively engaged with state project activities and that were working to make reform (and, we hoped, something good) happen. To a person, state staff were enormously cooperative, though sometimes openly concerned that we might not see much. Nevertheless, they directed us to a diverse array of potential sites for the study. They were curious about which ones we chose to include, and although they understood that we could not reveal our choices to them, it was clear that they wished they could steer us toward schools they thought represented their best examples.

Collecting Data

Next we designed and piloted our data-collection protocols. The conceptual framework and the four research themes guided our protocols, which consisted of questions to be answered during interviews and observations at the school sites and in follow-up discussions with state staff. In addition to individual data-gathering instruments, we constructed a case protocol that created initial categories for sorting our collected data. At the school level, it was divided into three main sections—context, goals and strategies, and reform components—and several subsections. The subsections all included a place for descriptive data, and most had sets of questions that fit within each of the research themes. For example, one of the questions in the teacher-teaming subsection of the section on reform components addressed a knowledge-and-inquiry theme: "How does being a part of a team facilitate the construction and use of knowledge and inquiry?" A social justice question related to the section on classroom regularities asked how expectations, opportunities, and status were distributed to students.

We scheduled interviews and observations—in classroom, during teacher and governance team meetings, and in a variety of nonformal settings—prior to arriving at the site. Generally, we made these arrangements with a principal or project director, as we explained to this contact person how we conducted our work. Our contact person sent us relevant documents—grant proposals, vision statements, newspaper articles—that would help us get an idea of the school context and the scope and depth of local reform efforts. We collected additional relevant documents on site.

We began each site visit with classroom and teacher-team observations, which constituted about one-fourth of our time in the field. These observations helped ground our subsequent interviews in teachers' individual and collective practice and helped us get a sense of what it was like to be a student at the school. We generally observed and interviewed every seventh grade teacher, about three-fourths of the remaining academic teachers, at least half of the exploratory teachers, and as many administrators and support staff as possible. We also interviewed groups of students during advisory or homeroom periods, as many parents as we could, district officials, and other professionals attached to the school sites (such as university faculty who were teaching courses on site). We usually interviewed the principal and project director several times, often in small chunks of informal time, throughout our visits.

Even though state officials helped us choose schools, and principals gave us access to their buildings, we assured teachers that meeting with us was completely voluntary and confidential. In approximately fifty site visits of three to five days, each with two or three researchers, we conducted hundreds of observations and more than one thousand interviews; only a few participants across the schools declined to be observed or interviewed. We never surprised teachers or teams; nor did we ever sense that the schools were simply putting on a show for "the team from UCLA" (as we were often called). Our two- or three-person team generally arrived at schools around the time the first teachers would drive up and stayed well past the end of the official school day. We gained a certain reputation among many staff members for working hard and sincerely trying to understand what was going on. Despite our densely packed schedules, we also attempted to set aside informal time for observation and conversation; and we often gained a textured understanding of life on a team or in a school or community by hanging around hallways, scribbling field notes at lunch time, and driving around town in the late afternoon and early evening. School or district administrators and community members often preferred dinner meetings, at which they felt they could be most forthcoming with their views.

The protocols focused our attention broadly on theoretically useful phenomena, but we tailored our data collection to fit individual sites. Occasionally a faculty member would tell us that we *had* to talk to one of her colleagues about a particular matter, and we'd furiously shift our schedules to find a moment with that individual. In one instance, we tracked down a teacher on her way to a convenience store. At one school, we conducted an interview as we accompanied a teacher in the school's jog-a-thon fundraiser.

Keeping all elements from our case-study protocol, we made adjustments to account for a change in school schedules, a highly charged meeting on the hiring of a new principal, an unexpected media event at the school, and, in one sad instance, the death of a student. These events helped us understand the day-to-day issues facing reforming schools and gave us opportunities to explore relations between faculty and administration, parental support, or beliefs about students. Occasionally, we would not uncover an issue until our last day in the field; in these cases, we scheduled phone interviews with key staff members for follow-up.

We often changed how we used observation protocols as well. For example, Mitchell teachers generally shared a large, open classroom, and we sometimes felt like observers of a fast-paced tennis match, as we doggedly completed two classroom observations at the same time. Since we visited each school at least twice and some as many as five times, we could occasionally follow a teacher's development as he or she adopted a new teaching strategy (say, cooperative learning techniques), and we might focus on that particular aspect of his or her teaching practice. We were never satisfied with our protocols for observing teacher-team meetings—meetings that took myriad forms—and generally resorted to extensive note writing in the field instead.

Respondents often had divergent views or disagreed with their colleagues' recollection of events. On occasion, after we finished our last interviews, the researchers would debrief one another and discover that they had heard two completely contradictory accounts of the same event. We sometimes worried that a few respondents were telling us what they thought we wanted to hear, so we relied on data triangulation to increase the trustworthiness of our amassed data—checking several times with a variety of sources, through observations, interviews, and documentary evidence before giving weight to disputed accounts. Our fundamental ground rule was that we didn't stop collecting data until we stopped being surprised by what we saw and heard.

That we acted as a research team amounted to another source of triangulation. Although one researcher was designated the "chief worrier" for each site and returned for all visits (which added continuity between our respondents and us), she or he was joined by a different partner (or partners) for each visit. This helped us maintain a fresh perspective on a site and enlivened our inquiry process, since the junior researcher tended to ask more *how-come* questions of the chief worrier to help make sense of what she or he had seen, heard, or read during the visit.

Analyzing Cases

The data analysis process was far less predictable than data collection. After each site visit, the chief worrier read through field notes, catalogued audiotaped interviews—which were transcribed verbatim—

and began coding and analyzing a sample of the collected data using the case report protocol.[5] Prior to the next site visit, we drafted very preliminary case reports, which included a description of the site context and key respondents, analysis of the gaps in our current data, and questions to be explored during the next visit. Importantly, we did not attempt to make sense of much of this data, seeking instead to lay out for each other what we thought we had learned during earlier site visits.

Following the last site visit, one project member was assigned the task of analyzing all collected data and writing a draft case report. For each school, the large number of documents, the thirty-plus classroom and team observations, and the more than one thousand pages of interviews yielded a pile of files for the case report writer to read, code, and organize. This was a daunting task, since our semistructured or open-ended interviews allowed respondents considerable freedom to make their own connections between issues or events—which did not necessarily fit neatly into our case protocol.[6]

Case report writers began drafting reports after reading and coding a sample of significant data; they worked interactively with further data and the early report to develop the first draft, which gradually became more analytic. This approach was arduous, but it generally yielded reports that were enjoyable to read, as well as to write. To make sure that the writer was crafting a trustworthy account of the case, he or she sent early versions of the case to another research team member who was very familiar with the site. Often several months after data analysis began, case report writers handed over their "first" drafts to a third researcher for an internal review. The primary purpose of the internal review process was to assess the plausibility of conclusions and the authenticity of the case. This process generally yielded substantial conversation about the importance of adding, deleting, clarifying, modifying, or reframing particular passages or sections of the draft case. Typically, it sent researchers back to the data for additional data and analysis. It also facilitated cross-case analyses.

Following this revision process, the school case reports—which ranged from less than forty pages to more than eighty—were sent to a group of external reviewers at the site. Although these reviewers were all very knowledgeable about the reform, they represented a cross-section of perspectives. In a couple of cases, when we worried that the case might do more harm than good at the school, only the principal reviewed this draft. We sent external reviewers questionnaires that requested input related to factual and interpretive accuracy. We also asked reviewers to give us an update on reform activities. We conducted hour-long follow-up interviews with these external reviewers, in which we were able to explore their questionnaire responses and gain much greater understanding of the progress of reform at the school. Once we completed the external review process, we again revised the case report—usually a much less significant amount of revision than occurred during the internal review.

Becoming a Book

One of our goals in writing this Appendix is to explain how this book evolved through nonlinear stages as we reflected on the meaning of what we learned throughout the study. So much writing about social science methodology, even qualitative methodology, presents the writing process as a rather smooth transition from (or as an embedded part of) data analysis. We do not mean to suggest that our writing was separate from our data analysis; however, we do suggest, along with many others, that writing is itself a sense-making process, and that as we wrote successive drafts of sentences, paragraphs, sections, chapters, and the book itself, we came to an ever deeper understanding of what we were writing about, what we wanted to say about it, and what we wanted the reader to hear.

It would be misleading for us to say that we did not begin writing this book until all of the case reports were drafted, reviewed, and revised. In some important ways, we began writing it in 1990 when we proposed our study. However, the conception of the book emerged during the consuming task of drafting case reports, as we weighed the study's major findings. Other cross-case analyses—MGSSPI project meeting presentations, American Educational Research Association symposium papers, two dissertation studies, journal articles, and a book chapter—had focused on particular reform processes or components. We list these below. This book would be our first chance to think broadly about the study's implications for practice, policy, and research.

For the next several months, as we finished our case report writing we began seeing patterns in the evidence that showed the schools attempting to become educative, caring, democratic, just, and better in a broader sense. During our project meetings over these months, we took turns sharing initial concepts for papers we would present at a 1996 AERA symposium entitled "Becoming Good American Schools: The Struggle for Virtue in Middle School Reform." We discussed the organizational structure of the papers, asked for leads to significant data sources that might serve as important examples of the concepts we had in mind, and helped clarify one another's thinking. Following the symposium, we were invited to publish these papers as a special issue for the *Research in Middle Level Education Quarterly*.

For a while, substantially revised versions of some of those early papers remained in place as chapters for this book, and we tried to write the book around them. However, as our analyses deepened, we began framing the book in a way that spoke to broader concepts of goodness in American culture. We began to explore the tension in American culture between individual freedom and the public good, or civic virtue, and looked to the cultural and historical precedents of the specific struggles we found in the schools. We did not romanticize this history; rather, we wanted to focus on how the sociohistorical contexts in which particular cultural icons lived placed them in a situation where their vision for America pushed contemporary society to be "better" than it wanted to be. We also began to see many of the local educators we studied as deeply involved and committed to a civic virtue that had historical roots and modern-day significance. We saw (and see) great hope in the stories of these educators and their schools as we framed our larger story of school reform as a cultural struggle, a struggle for civic virtue, a struggle to become good American schools.

Technical Reports and Publications of the Study

Gong, J. "Renegotiating the Power to Change: The Political Perspective." Annual meeting of the American Educational Research Association, New Orleans, Apr. 1994.

Gong, J. "Realizing Power: Creating Democratic Relations Through Participatory Policymaking Processes." Annual meeting of the American Educational Research Association, San Francisco, Apr. 1995.

Gong, J. "Becoming Just: The Role of Power in Ensuring the Democratic Ends of Participatory Policymaking Processes." *Research in Middle Level Education Quarterly*, 1996, *20*(1), 69–101.

Guiton, G., and Serna, I. "Becoming Egalitarian." Paper presented at the American Educational Research Association annual meeting, New York, Apr. 1996.

Guiton, G., and others. "Teaming: Creating Small Communities of Learners in the Middle Grades." In J. Oakes and K. Hunter Quartz (eds.), *Creating New Educational Communities*. [Ninety-fourth yearbook of the National Society for the Study of Education]. Chicago: University of Chicago Press, 1995.

Oakes, J. "Normative, Technical and Political Dimensions of Creating New Educational Communities." In J. Oakes and K. Hunter Quartz (eds.), *Creating New Educational Communities*. [Ninety-fourth yearbook of the National Society for the Study of Education]. Chicago: University of Chicago Press, 1995.

Oakes, J., Serna, I., and Guiton, G. "Introduction." *Research in Middle Level Education Quarterly*, 1997, *20*(1), 1–10.

Oakes, J., Vasudeva, A., and Jones, M. "Becoming Educative: Reforming Curriculum and Teaching in the Middle Grades." *Research in Middle Level Education Quarterly*, 1997, *20*(1), 11–40.

Oakes, J., and others. "Recreating Middle Schools: Technical, Normative, and Political Considerations." *Elementary School Journal*, 1993, *93*(5), 461–480.

Quartz, K. H. "Becoming Better." *Research in Middle Level Education Quarterly*, 1995a, *20*(1), 102–124.

Quartz, K. H. "The Culture of School Reform." Unpublished Ph.D. dissertation, University of California, Los Angeles (1995b).

Quartz, K. H. "Sustaining New Educational Communities: Toward a New Culture of School Reform." In J. Oakes and K. Hunter Quartz (eds.), *Creating New Educational Communities*. [Ninety-fourth yearbook of the National Society for the Study of Education]. Chicago: University of Chicago Press, 1995c.

Ryan, S. "Establishing Collaborative Cultures in Middle Schools: Are Structural Changes Enough?" Paper presented at the annual meeting of the American Educational Research Association, San Francisco, Apr. 1995.

Ryan, S. "Characterizing Teacher Collaboration in Three Schools: Contrasting Individual and Institutional Definitions." Paper presented at the annual meeting of the American Educational Research Association, Chicago, Mar. 1997a.

Ryan, S. "Defining Teaching: Individual Teachers' Perspectives on Their Work in a Collaborative Setting." Paper presented at the annual meeting of the American Educational Research Association, Chicago, Mar. 1997b.

Ryan, S. "Examining the Impact of Collaborative Structures on Teachers' Work: Contexts, Characteristics, Consequences, and Complications," Unpublished Ph.D. dissertation, University of California, Los Angeles (1998a).

Ryan, S. "Understanding the Consequences of Teacher Collaboration: Workplace Conditions, School Ethos, and Micro-Politics." Paper presented at the annual meeting of the American Educational Research Association, San Diego, Apr. 1998b.

Ryan, S. "Constructing Knowledge Together: Teacher Teams as Learning Communities." Paper presented at the annual meeting of the American Educational Research Association, Montreal, Apr. 1999.

Ryan, S., and Friedlaender, D. "Strengthening Relationships to Create Caring School Communities." *Research in Middle Level Education Quarterly,* 1996, *20*(1), 41–68.

Vasudeva, A., and Ryan, S. "Why Some Teacher Teams Work: The Role of Social Capital in Teacher Efficacy." Paper presented at the annual meeting of the American Educational Research Association, Chicago, Mar. 1997.

Notes

Introduction

1. As cited in Sandel, M. *Democracy's Discontent: America in Search of a Public Philosophy.* Cambridge, Mass.: Harvard University Press, 1996, p. 126.
2. West, C. "The Limits of Neopragmatism." *Southern California Law Review,* 1990, *63*, pp. 1747, 1749.
3. For an elaborated analysis of the intersection of democracy and schooling, see Rogers, J. "Education as Politics, Politics as Education: John Dewey and Critical Intelligence." Unpublished Ph.D. dissertation, Sanford University, 1994.
4. Moreover, just slightly below the lofty values that unite all Americans (one of the highest being Adams's own "positive passion for the public good"), these abstractions diverge to become more concrete and useful in propping up and legitimizing the nation's public policies and schooling practices. Thus, each American lays claim to the verities of American democracy, sharing the Constitution, the founding fathers, and the cultural icons of our history. But only by looking deeply into our public institutions—in our case, schools—can we probe beneath the historical sound bites to find, in practice, what people actually mean and how their lives are affected by others' often contradictory meanings of "positive passion," "public good," and so on.
5. For a comprehensive collection of the school change literature, see Hargreaves, A., Lieberman, A., Fullan, M., and Hopkins, G. (eds.). *International Handbook of Educational Change. Parts 1 and 2.* Dordrecht, The Netherlands, and Norwell, Mass.: Kluwer, 1998.
6. Carnegie Council on Adolescent Development. *Turning Points: Preparing Youth for the 21st Century.* New York: Carnegie Corporation of New York, 1989.
7. Gough, P. B. "Editor's Page: Making the Connection." *Phi Delta Kappan,* 1997, *78*(7), 486.

8. Felner, R. D., and others. "The Impact of School Reform for the Middle Years: Longitudinal Study of a Network Engaged in *Turning Points*-Based Comprehensive School Transformation," *Phi Delta Kappan,* 1997, *78*(7), 528–532, 541–550.

9. Felner and others (1997), p. 530.

10. Felner and others (1997), p. 530.

11. Lipsitz, J., Mizell, M. H., Jackson, A. W., and Austin, L. "Speaking with One Voice: A Manifesto for Middle-Grades Reform." *Phi Delta Kappan,* 1997, *78*(7), 533–540.

12. Lipsitz, Mizell, Jackson, and Austin (1997).

13. We spell out our research methodology and list the other published work that has come from our study in the Appendix.

14. We've given all the schools pseudonyms designed to ease the reader's task of sorting the schools out. Each California school has a name beginning with the letter C, the Illinois school names begin with I, Massachusetts schools have M names, and so forth. In addition, we've given the two affluent schools botanical names (Verbena and Tanglewood), the six diverse schools place names (Middleton, Canyon, and so on), and the eight poverty schools names of famous Americans (Cesar Chavez, Washington Irving, and so on).

15. Dewey, J. *Experience and Education.* New York: Macmillan, 1938.

16. Sarason, S. B. *The Culture of School and the Problems of Change.* Boston: Allyn & Bacon, 1982.

Chapter One

1. Carnegie Council on Adolescent Development. *Turning Points: Preparing Youth for the 21st Century.* New York: Carnegie Corporation of New York, 1989.

2. The most salient version of this approach is the current wave of "systemic reforms" that align curriculum standards, testing, and teachers' training. See Smith, M., and O'Day, J. "Systemic School Reform." In S. H. Furhman and B. Malen (eds.), *The Politics of Curriculum and Testing.* Bristol, Pa.: Falmer Press, 1990. See also McDonnell, L. *Getting the Job Done: Alternative Policy Instruments.* Santa Monica, Calif.: RAND, 1987.

Chapter Two

1. *Turning Points,* p. 42.

2. Benjamin Barber's essay "Jefferson and Education" offers a clear discussion of the centrality of education in Jefferson's conception

of democracy. In Barber, B. *A Passion for Democracy: American Essays.* Princeton, N.J.: Princeton University Press, 1998.

3. In the twentieth century this idea has its modern counterpart in what Jurgen Habermas (1962) termed "the public sphere." Habermas, J. *The Structural Transformation of the Public Sphere: An Inquiry into a Category of Bourgeois Society.* (T. Burger with F. Lawrence, trans.). Cambridge, Mass.: MIT Press, 1989.

4. Jefferson, T. "Notes." In G. Lee (ed.), *Crusade Against Ignorance: Thomas Jefferson on Education.* New York: Teachers College Press, 1961, p. 96; as cited in Spring, J. *The American School.* White Plains, N.Y.: Longman, 1990, p. 45.

5. *Turning Points,* p. 15.

6. Dewey, J. "Democracy and Education in the World of Today." *Essays.* (Pamphlet). New York: Society for Ethical Culture, 1938, p. 296.

7. Jefferson's vision of a virtuous and free society has both classical and liberal roots, making the theoretical terrain thorny at times. On the classical side, it follows from Aristotle's view that the virtuous republic requires the individual to sacrifice self-interest for the common good. But it also has a liberal debt to Locke and others who acknowledged that our human nature is to be free and equal, and that to strive toward self-preservation humans need to be independent. Thus a willing sacrifice was required that could be motivated by the most instrumental self-interest but could not be limited to self-interest. At some point, citizens might be challenged to give up something for which there were no immediate and tangible benefits for them, individually.

8. Jefferson added the phrase "the pursuit of happiness" in place of Locke's original emphasis on property or estate.

9. The reforms, along with the theories on which they stand, proposed that individuals' capacities are mostly similar and mostly shared in common; and when varying capacities are noted, these differences are of little significance when it comes to children learning most of the things that schools think it is important to teach. However, this research on learning, along with appeals to democratic traditions, only slowly penetrated conventional convictions that individual capacities are largely fixed, easily sorted and ranked, and capable of predicting which children would benefit from learning the most important knowledge and which children would not. These two dispositions toward understanding knowledge, learning, and the value of students to society derived from (as well as reinforced) two profoundly different conceptions of civic virtue and images of the public good as enacted in schools.

10. For an excellent treatment of the contradictions in Jefferson and his legacy, see the Epilogue to Ellis, J. *American Sphinx*. New York: Vintage Books, 1998.

11. Again, Barber's 1998 essay is interesting on this point.

12. The Civil War also effectively shattered Jefferson's presumption that free and equal individuals could deliberate reasonably and agree—even temporarily—about how to accommodate the inevitable contradictions between the pursuit of virtue and the pursuit of freedom. Although still occupying a central place in our culture, Jefferson's ideal of an institutional neutral ground in which free white men reason together about the common good was instantly complicated by the diverse citizenry created with the Thirteenth, Fourteenth, and Fifteenth Amendments, and by the Nineteenth Amendment and the civil rights laws passed (and contested) in the twentieth century. Once the descendants of African slaves were nominally admitted into membership in American civil society, the presumption that the power of ideas would prevail over the power of social location lost considerable credibility.

13. Woodward, C. V. *The Strange Career of Jim Crow*. New York: Oxford University Press, 1966, p. 21; see also Carnoy, M. *Faded Dreams*. New York: Cambridge University Press, 1994.

14. On the centennial of the Emancipation Proclamation in 1963, Vice President Lyndon B. Johnson said, "Until justice is blind, until education is unaware of race, until opportunity is unconcerned with the color of men's skins, emancipation will be a proclamation but not a fact." Historian John Hope Franklin notes the difference between the positions of Lincoln in 1863 and Americans in 1993: "The law itself is no longer an obstruction to justice and equality, but it is the people who live under the law who are themselves an obvious obstruction to justice. One can only hope that sooner rather than later we can all find the courage to live under the spirit of the Emancipation Proclamation and under the laws that flowed from its inspiration." Since schools increasingly have become the institution that people of color turn to in the quest for a more racially just society, it's not surprising that today's school reformers struggle mightily with this ambivalent legacy of the color line.

15. For thoughtful analyses of Lincoln's views on race and slavery, see Fredrickson, G. *The Arrogance of Race: Historical Perspectives on Slavery, Racism, and Social Equality*. Hanover, N.H.: Wesleyan University Press, 1988; and Foner, E. *Reconstruction: America's Unfinished Revolution, 1863–1877*. New York: HarperCollins, 1988.

16. Spring (1990); Schultz, S. *The Culture Factory: Boston Public Schools, 1789–1960*. New York: Oxford University Press, 1973.

17. See, for example, Orfield, G., Eaton, S. C., and Jones, E. R. *Dismantling Desegregation: The Quiet Reversal of Brown v. Board of Education*. New York: New Press, 1997.

18. Oakes, J. *Keeping Track: How Schools Structure Inequality*. New Haven, Conn.: Yale University Press, 1985.

19. These gains also included equal employment and housing laws that denied an individual's freedom not to work with or live near another person based on personal preferences for race or other categories such as gender and age.

20. Addams, J. *Twenty Years at Hull House*. New York: Macmillan, 1910, p. 112.

21. Addams, J. "The Subjective Necessity for Social Settlements." (Reprint). Chicago: Jane Addams Hull House Museum, University of Illinois at Chicago, 1892.

22. Addams (1892), n.p.

23. Addams (1892), n.p.

24. Kleibard, H. M. *The Struggle for the American Curriculum: 1893–1958*. (2nd ed.). New York: Routledge, 1995, p. 6.

25. Rogers, J. "Community Schools: Lessons from the Past and Present." (Report to the Charles S. Mott Foundation). Los Angeles: UCLA, 1998.

26. *Turning Points*, p. 16.

27. *Turning Points*, p. 9.

28. *Turning Points*, p. 9.

29. Noddings, N. *The Challenge to Care in Schools: An Alternative Approach to Education*. New York: Teachers College Press, 1992, p. 65.

30. See, for example, Sergiovanni, T. J. *Building Community in Schools*. San Francisco: Jossey-Bass, 1994; Beck, L. G. "Meeting the Challenge of the Future: The Place of a Caring Ethic in Educational Administration." *American Journal of Education*, Aug. 1992, vol. 100, pp. 454–495.

31. Rogers (1998).

32. See also Ayers, W. "Democracy and Urban Schooling for Justice and Care." *Journal for a Just and Caring Education*, 1996, 2(1), 85–92.

33. Ayers (1996).

34. For an inspiring and insightful account of this dimension of the civil rights movement, see Payne, C. *I've Got the Light of Freedom: The Organizing Tradition and the Mississippi Freedom Struggle*. Berkeley: University of California Press, 1995.

35. King, M. L., Jr. *I Have a Dream: Writings and Speeches That Changed the World.* (J. M. Washington, ed.). New York: HarperCollins, 1992, p. 85.

36. Pateman, C. *Participation and Democratic Theory.* Cambridge, England: Cambridge University Press, 1970, p. 25.

37. West, C. "The Limits of Neopragmatism." *Southern California Law Review,* 1990, *63*(1747), 1749.

38. West (1990), p. 1749.

39. See, for example, Alinsky, S. *Reveille for Radicals.* New York: Vintage Books, 1969. For a discussion specifically related to middle-school reform, see also Friedlaender, D. "Building Community: The Struggles of an Urban Middle School." Unpublished Ph.D. dissertation, UCLA (1998).

40. For an elaboration of this line of thinking, see, for example, Barber, B. *Strong Democracy: Participatory Politics for a New Age.* Berkeley: University of California Press, 1984; Barber, B. *An Aristocracy of Everyone: The Politics of Education and the Future of America.* New York and Oxford: Oxford University Press, 1992; Dewey (1938); Gutman (1987); and West (1990).

41. "Local Elections Canceled Due to Lack of Interest." *Los Angeles Times,* Feb. 21, 1999 (Internet edition, n.p.).

42. Boyte, H. C., and Kari, N. N. *Building America: The Democratic Promise of Public Work.* Philadelphia: Temple University Press, 1996. Excerpted at fount.journalism.wisc.edu/cpn/sections/new_citizenship/theory/building_america1.htm.

43. Knight, M. *Unearthing the Muted Voices of Transformative Professionals.* Unpublished Ph.D. dissertation, UCLA (1998).

44. Dewey (1938), p. 296.

45. Rogers (1998).

46. *Turning Points,* p. 54.

47. *Turning Points,* p. 33.

48. Sandel (1996), p. 126.

49. Bellah, R. N., and others. *Habits of the Heart: Individualism and Commitment in American Life.* Berkeley: University of California Press, 1985. Since the days of the founders, much intellectual energy has been devoted to reconciling the liberal and classical roots of American society, and in much contemporary literature these ideas have been subsumed in a lively discussion of *communitarianism* and *individualism.* The moral theory of individualism is based on the concept of self-interest and draws heavily from constitutional guarantees of freedom; the good life is one that satisfies individual interests or preferences. Moreover, each individual, according to this theory,

has the right to determine what he or she considers good. Individualism assumes that people are autonomous, have private interests, and are capable of self-determination, that is, respect for every person's liberty and right to choose a way of life. Communitarianism contrasts with individualism because it values collective conceptions of the good over the self-interested right to choose a way of life. Individual liberty is subordinated to the collective on the grounds that what is good is essentially social; the good is not constituted by individuals but must be constructed through social practice. Communitarians speak of duties and obligations rather than rights; they expect each member of a community to participate in the shared conception of what is good.

Stated in these terms, neither position taken by itself sounds very attractive. Unfettered individualism can approach anarchy or tyranny by a few; strict communitarianism, no matter how altruistic, can approach groupthink, stifling conformity, or tyranny by the many.

Therefore, while some social theorists plant themselves in one camp or the other, most stand somewhere on a bridge connecting civic virtue and individual freedom. Such theorists as John Rawls, Amy Gutmann, and Kenneth Strike lean toward the liberal side, but with communitarian sympathies. Others, such as Jane Mansbridge and Alastair MacIntyre, tilt toward the communitarian side, but with liberal sympathies. Clearly, most Americans who are not theorists also struggle to balance their moral commitment to ideals of both liberty and community.

50. To Americans' credit, they are often tantalized by the promise that somehow, through their conversations and ballot boxes, they might balance or harmonize virtue and freedom by adding more of each— instead of what they sometimes accuse their adversaries of doing: creating greater imbalances by removing a pinch here, a pound there.

Chapter Three

1. Berliner, D. C., and Biddle, B. J. *The Manufactured Crisis*. Reading, Mass.: Addison-Wesley, 1996.
2. Smith and O'Day (1990).
3. Here California's "wars" over standards in reading, math, and science are among many examples nationwide.
4. Over the years, educators have enacted a good many wrongheaded schooling "reforms"—many under the easily caricatured banners

of "John Dewey" or "progressive" or (lately) "constructivist." Here, suffice it to say that when reformers call for fun and interesting lessons, they are not asking for trivial ones; when they ask for pedagogy that is child-centered, they do not demand that children do whatever they want; and a constructivist curriculum does not require that whatever students decide to present as an answer is accepted as having great merit. For an extensive treatment of the theories and practice of reform curricula, see Oakes, J., and Lipton, M. *Teaching to Change the World*. New York: McGraw-Hill, 1999.

5. King, from Martin Luther King Foundation. *Montgomery to Memphis*. (Videorecording). Beverly Hills, Calif.: Pacific Arts Video, 1988.

6. Veteran teachers (most of whom were African American) made up about a third of Carver's faculty. Nevertheless, the dangerous reputation of the neighborhood made hiring qualified teachers difficult, and long-term substitutes filled several positions.

7. For an elaborate discussion of the importance of teacher collaboration in reform, see Ryan, S. P. "Examining the Impact of Collaborative Structures on Teachers' Work: Contexts, Characteristics, Consequences, and Complications." Unpublished Ph.D. dissertation, UCLA (1998).

8. Part of the argument is that even recent calls for students to learn more academic content (for example, Hirsch, E. D. *Cultural Literacy: What Every American Needs to Know*. Boston: Houghton Mifflin, 1987) can easily become the antithesis of teaching for depth. Lists such as those offered by Hirsch and lists of facts ask students, teachers, and the public to think of knowledge not as deep, but as a thin veneer of terms and famous people.

9. For further discussion of these ideas, see, for example, Billett, S. "Situated Learning: Bridging Sociocultural and Cognitive Theorising." *Learning and Instruction*, 1996, *6*(3), 263–280; Grennon Brooks, J., and Brooks, M. G. *In Search of Understanding: The Case for Constructivist Classrooms*. Alexandria, Va.: Association for Supervision and Curriculum Development, 1993; Eisenhart, M., and Borko, H. *Designing Classroom Research: Themes, Issues, and Struggles*. Needham Heights, Mass.: Allyn & Bacon, 1993; and McGilly, K. (ed.). *Classroom Lessons: Integrating Cognitive Theory and Classroom Practice*. Cambridge, Mass.: MIT Press, 1994.

10. *Turning Points*, pp. 49–50.

11. Tharp, R., and others. *Transforming Teaching*. Boulder, Colo.: Westview Press, forthcoming).

12. *Turning Points*, p. 43.

13. Hargreaves, A. *Changing Teachers, Changing Times: Teachers, Culture, and Work in the Postmodern Age*. New York: Teachers College Press, 1994.

14. For a thoughtful analysis of the current reform debates and dilemmas related to challenging academic content in middle schools, see Wheelock, A. *Safe to Be Smart: Building a Culture for Standards-Based Reform in the Middle Grades*. Columbus, Ohio: National Middle School Association, 1998.

15. Anyon, J. "Social Class and the Hidden Curriculum of Work." *Journal of Education*, 1980, *62*(1), 67–92.

16. Newmann, F. M., Secada, W. G., and Wehlage, G. G. *A Guide to Authentic Instruction and Assessment: Vision, Standards and Scoring*. Madison: Wisconsin Center for Education Research, 1995.

Chapter Four

1. Finney, R. *A Sociological Philosophy of Education*. New York: Macmillan, 1929, p. 387.

2. See, for example, Oakes, J. *Keeping Track*. New Haven, Conn.: Yale University Press, 1985; and Oakes, J., Ormseth, T., Bell, R., and Camp, P. *Multiplying Inequalities*. Santa Monica, Calif.: RAND, 1990.

3. *Turning Points*, p. 29.

4. For example, Gardner, H. *Frames of Mind: The Theory of Multiple Intelligences*. New York: Basic Books, 1983; Sternberg, R. J. *Beyond IQ: A Triarchic Theory of Human Intelligence*. New York: Cambridge University Press, 1984; and Sternberg, R. J. *Applied Intelligence*. Orlando: Harcourt Brace, 1986, are examples of work that argues compellingly that intelligence is multifaceted and developmental and that learning is a complex process of constructing meaning.

5. McDonough, P. M. *Choosing Colleges: How Social Class and Schools Structure Opportunity*. Albany: State University of New York Press, 1997.

6. Any catalogue of these reasons might include the following: the actual decline in public support for schools, increasing numbers of uncertified and unqualified teachers, the perception that affirmative action made it harder for qualified whites to get into college, the trumpeting of international comparisons claiming to prove low school standards, and so on.

7. Ehrenreich, B. *Fear of Falling: The Inner Life of the Middle Class*. New York: Perennial Library, 1990.

8. For a compelling elaboration of this argument regarding merit and competition, see Lemann, N. "Rewarding the Best, Forgetting the Rest." *New York Times*, Apr. 26, 1998 (Internet edition, n.p.).

Chapter Five

1. Banks, J. A. "The Historical Reconstruction of Knowledge About Race: Implications for Transformative Teaching." *Education Researcher*, 1995, *24*(2), 15–25.

2. Spargo, J. "The Problem of Hungry School Children." In *The Bitter Cry of the Children.* New York: Macmillan, 1906, pp. 2145–2147.

3. Riley, R. W., Smith, M. S., Peterson, T. K., and Ginsburg, A. L. *Keeping Schools Open as Community Learning Centers: Extending Learning in a Safe, Drug-Free Environment Before and After School.* Washington, D.C.: U.S. Department of Education, 1997, p. 1.

4. Riley, Smith, Peterson, and Ginsburg (1997), p. 3.

5. For a more detailed description of our theory of care, see Ryan, S., and Friedlaender, D. "Strengthening Relationships to Create Caring School Communities." *Research in Middle Level Education Quarterly*, 1996, *20*(1), 41–68.

6. Noddings (1992), p. 1.

7. Ayers, W. "Democracy and Urban Schooling for Justice and Care." *Journal for a Just and Caring Education*, 1996, *2*(1), 85–92.

8. Noddings (1992) looks at the notion of continuity at a number of levels: continuity between students' real lives and the curriculum, that of the school and the community, and that between students and teachers over time. See also Mitchell, B. "Children, Youth, and Restructured Schools: Views from the Field." In B. Mitchell and L. L. Cunningham (eds.), *Educational Leadership and Changing Contexts of Families, Communities, and Schools.* Chicago: National Society for the Study of Education, 1990.

9. W.E.B. Du Bois. "Does the Negro Need Separate Schools?" *Journal of Negro Education*, 1935, *4*(3), 328.

10. In her seminal work, *In a Different Voice: Psychological Theory and Women's Development* (Cambridge, Mass.: Harvard University Press, 1982), Carol Gilligan describes the ethic of care as "an activity of relationship, of seeing and responding to need, taking care of the world by sustaining the web of connection so that no one is left alone" (p. 62). Gilligan offers justice and care as "the ideals of human relationship—the vision that self and other will be treated as of equal worth" (p. 63).

11. By 1993, Harriet Tubman Middle School had made dramatic gains. Although still failing to have all students reach the state's minimum standard, the school moved from the bottom-ranked of the district's twenty schools to fourth.

Chapter Six

1. *Turning Points,* p. 54.
2. For example, see the work of theorists Jurgen Habermas and Nancy Fraser. Also, Robert Putnam and his colleagues write that conditions create "horizontal" dialectal exchanges with opportunities for all voices to be heard, and relationships where participants reach across their differences to solve problems that affect all of them. Habermas (1962); Fraser, N. *Justice Interruptus: Critical Reflections on the "Postsocialist" Condition.* New York: Routledge, 1996; Putnam, R. D., Leonardi, R., and Nanetti, R. Y. *Making Democracy Work: Civic Traditions in Modern Italy.* Princeton, N.J.: Princeton University Press, 1994.
3. Some theorists and activists also emphasize the need for participation to go beyond dialogue to include collective action or "public work" that alerts people to the conditions standing in the way of democracy. See, for example, Boyte and Kari (1996).
4. For an interesting discussion of the Industrial Areas Foundation's work with Texas Schools, see Shirley, D. *Community Organizing for Urban School Reform.* Austin: University of Texas Press, 1997.
5. *Turning Points,* p. 85.
6. For discussions of this principle, see, for example, Boyte and Kari (1996); Follett, M. P. *Dynamic Administration: The Collected Papers of Mary Parker Follett.* New York: HarperCollins, 1942. See also the literature on power as production: Gore, J. "What We Can Do for You! What *Can* 'We' Do for 'You'?" In C. Luke and J. Gore (eds.), *Feminisms and Critical Pedagogy.* New York: Routledge, 1994; Weiler, K. *Women Teaching for Change: Gender, Class, and Power.* New York: Bergin & Garvey, 1988; Foucault, M. *Power/Knowledge: Selected Interviews and Other Writings, 1972–1977.* New York: Pantheon, 1980; Kreisberg, S. *Transforming Power: Domination, Empowerment, and Education.* Albany: State University of New York Press, 1992. Wartenberg describes the feminist theorists of power as having "two faces of power": domination and transformation (Wartenberg, T. E. *The Forms of Power: From Domination to Transformation.* Philadelphia: Temple University Press, 1990, p. 184).

Chapter Seven

1. The self-study project, led by Robert Felner (then a professor at the University of Illinois), administered a survey instrument and

analyzed school data to help develop the capacity of individual state and school projects as well as to collect information to evaluate the reform.

2. Hargreaves (1994) notes that a worthy school reform goal is to move to a "better class of problems."

3. Edwards, T. M. "Revolt of the Gentry." *Time,* June 15, 1998, p. 34.

4. Vermont Department of Education. *The Middle Matters.* Burlington: Vermont Department of Education, 1991, n.p.

5. Elmore, R. F. "Getting to Scale with Good Education Practice." *Harvard Educational Review,* 1996, *66*(1), 1–26.

Chapter Eight

1. A more recent concept of betterment is offered by Lindbloom, C. E. *Inquiry and Change: The Troubled Attempt to Understand and Shape Society.* New Haven and London: Yale University Press, 1990. Building on a long tradition of liberal democratic thought as well as philosophical skepticism regarding the nature of knowledge, Lindbloom argues for a self-guided society that recognizes that inquiry and change are broad, open-ended, social, and political processes. Because these processes involve a "constant re-consideration of both ends and means, there exists no route to be discovered, only those they must create" (p. 302).

2. This distinction between internal and external goods is based on Alasdair MacIntyre's Aristotelian account of the virtues. Typically, however, a practice is defined more narrowly as a shared activity with clear rules and standards of excellence. For this reason, thinking of education as a practice does present some problems, most notably the lack of consensus on the rules or methods and standards. MacIntyre also warns: "Practices must not be confused with institutions. Chess, physics and medicine are practices; chess clubs, laboratories, universities and hospitals are institutions." For this reason, it's important to distinguish between education and betterment as practices and schools as institutions. See MacIntyre, A. *After Virtue.* (2nd ed.). Notre Dame, Ind.: University of Notre Dame Press, 1984, especially chapter fourteen.

3. These structures, ideologies, and rituals are patterns of culture and present objects for studying the values that underlie social institutions such as schools, as well as the collective acceptance of, commitment to, and erosion of these values. See Wuthnow, R. *Meaning and Moral Order: Explorations in Cultural Analysis.* Berkeley: University of California Press, 1987.

4. Taylor, F. *Shop Management.* New York and London: Harper Brothers, 1919, p. 39.

5. Taylor, F. *Principles of Scientific Management.* New York and London: Harper Brothers, 1911, p. 141.

6. Quoted in Braverman, H. *Labor and Monopoly Capital: The Degradation of Work in the Twentieth Century.* New York: Monthly Review Press, 1975, p. 113.

7. Westbrook (1991) notes that although some of Dewey's critics tried to align his view of "scientific intelligence" with Taylor and others, there were few grounds for doing so. Westbrook, R. B. *John Dewey and American Democracy.* Ithaca, N.Y.: Cornell University Press, 1991.

8. Dewey, J. *Ethics: The Middle Works.* Carbondale, Ill.: Southern Illinois University Press, 1976–1983, as cited in Westbrook (1991), p. 185.

9. Berman, P., and McLaughlin, M. W. *Federal Programs Supporting Educational Change.* Vol. 8: *Implementing and Sustaining Innovations.* (No. R-1589/8-HEW). Santa Monica, Calif.: RAND, 1978.

10. Haycock, K. "Creating New Educational Communities: Implications for Policy." In J. Oakes and K. Quartz (eds.), *Creating New Educational Communities.* (Ninety-fourth yearbook of the National Society for the Study of Education). Chicago: University of Chicago Press, 1995.

11. Fullan, M. G. *The New Meaning of Educational Change.* New York: Teachers College Press, 1991, p. 4.

12. Datnow, A., Hubbard, L., and Mehan, H. *Educational Reform Implementation: A Co-Constructed Process.* Santa Cruz: Center for Research on Education, Diversity, and Excellence, University of California, 1999.

13. Examples such as this illuminate the symbolic-expressive dimension of the reform mill. The observable acts, objects, events, and utterances that characterize these training sessions dramatize the nature of social relations and thereby communicate what the reform mill expects. See Wuthnow (1987) on the dramaturgic approach to cultural analysis.

14. For an elaborated analysis, see Ryan (1998).

15. Datnow offers a useful example of reform's collision with gender issues. Datnow, A. *The Gender Politics of Educational Change.* London: Falmer Press, 1998.

16. Hargreaves (1994).

17. Van Buren's exploratory teachers constituted a team as well, one that was quite active in leading schoolwide reform efforts.

18. Dewey, J. *Democracy and Education. Middle Works.* Carbondale: Southern Illinois University, 1976–1983, p. 93. (Originally published 1916.)

19. All of the schools had trouble figuring out how to weave together competing reforms, but some even had problems seeing the connection between ostensibly compatible reforms. At Horace Mann, for example, a district site-based management reform was introduced at the same time as the middle-grade reforms. Because no one thought to frame the district effort as part of the middle-grade reform agenda, the two reforms produced so much confusion that "we ended up doing a half-day in-service on just distinguishing the two." It is a symbol of the mill run amok—spending half a day to learn how two compatible reforms are different—when professional development often dissolves into an empty pursuit.

Chapter Nine

1. West, C. "The Moral Obligations of Living in a Democratic Society." In D. Batstone and E. Mendieta, *The Good Citizen*. New York: Routledge, 1999, p. 12.
2. Wuthnow (1987) argues that cultural analysis is most productively framed as a specialized analytic strategy to understand the symbolic-expressive aspect of social behavior rather than a distinct subject matter. Since culture penetrates all aspects of social life, it must be isolated strictly for analytic purposes.
3. A colleague at UCLA, John Rogers, has been helpful on this point.
4. These findings draw from a wide body of research, including Elmore, R. R., and McLaughlin, M. W. *Steady Work: Policy, Practice, and the Reform of American Education*. Santa Monica, Calif.: RAND, 1988; Firestone, W., and Corbett, D. H. "Planned Organizational Change." In N. Boyan (ed.), *Handbook of Research on Educational Administration*. New York: Macmillan, 1989; Fullan (1991); Louis, K. S., and Miles, M. B. *Improving the Urban High School*. New York: Teachers College Press, 1990; Sarason, S. *The Culture of the School and the Problem of Change*. (2nd ed.). Boston: Allyn & Bacon, 1982; Sarason, S. *The Predictable Failure of Educational Reform*. San Francisco: Jossey-Bass, 1990; Tyack, D., and Cuban, L. *Tinkering Toward Utopia*. Cambridge, Mass.: Harvard University Press, 1995; and Wise, A. "Why Educational Policies Often Fail: The Hyperrationalization Hypothesis." *Curriculum Studies*, 1987, *9*(1), pp. 43–57.
5. Lipsitz, J., Mizell, M. H., Jackson, A. W., and Austin, L. M. "Speaking with One Voice: A Manifesto for Middle-Grades Reform." *Phi Delta Kappan*, 1997, *78*(7), 533–540. See also Cohen, D. K., and Barnes, C. A. "Pedagogy and Policy." In D. K. Cohen, M. W. McLaughlin, and J. E. Talbert (eds.), *Teaching for Understanding:*

Challenges for Policy and Practice. San Francisco: Jossey-Bass, 1993; Elmore (1996); Elmore, R. F., Peterson, P. L., and McCarthey, S. J. *Restructuring in the Classroom: Teaching, Learning, and School Organization.* San Francisco: Jossey Bass, 1996; Muncey, D. E., and McQuillan, P. J. *Reform and Resistance in Schools and Classrooms: An Ethnographic View of the Coalition of Essential Schools.* New Haven, Conn.: Yale University Press, 1996.

6. McLaughlin, M. W. "Learning from Experience: Lessons from Policy Implementation." *Educational Evaluation and Policy Analysis,* 1987, vol. 9, p. 173.

7. For a detailed discussion of this point, see Oakes, J., Welner, K., Yonezawa, S., and Allen, R. L. "Norms and Politics of Equity-Minded Change: Researching the 'Zone of Mediation.'" In A. Hargreaves, A. Lieberman, M. Fullan, and D. Hopkins (eds.), *International Handbook of Educational Change.* Part 2. London: Kluwer, 1998.

8. See, for example, the work of Patricia Hill Collins, Nancy Fraser, Henry Giroux, bell hooks, Peter McLaren, Ira Shor, and many others.

9. For example, John Goodlad and his colleagues have also begun to frame teaching and school change as a moral, rather than technical, enterprise. They point to schools as having the unique moral responsibility of enculturating all of the young into a political democracy—a charge that requires commitment to social justice, caring, and inquiry, as well as knowledge and competence. In this view, then, teaching decisions and organizational planning are essentially seen as moral issues. Moreover, although individual commitments and actions are essential, the moral commitments of schooling must also be institutional imperatives that "go to the very heart of the moral ecology of the organization itself" (Sirotnik, K. "Society, Schooling, Teaching, and Preparing to Teach." In J. I. Goodlad, R. Sodor, and K. Sirotnik (eds.), *The Moral Dimensions of Teaching.* San Francisco: Jossey-Bass, 1990, pp. 298ff.

10. Lindblom, C. *Inquiry and Change.* New Haven, Conn.: Yale University Press, 1990, p. 230.

11. As quoted in Schorr, L. B. *Within Our Reach: Breaking the Cycle of Disadvantage.* New York: Anchor Books, 1989, p. 245. Models of good schools also give reformers a set of principles—the external norms Elmore calls for—that help focus learning (much as learning objectives may help focus student learning in a classroom). These principles act as scaffolds that are present even in the absence of models and that can gradually be removed as local schools internalize reform, such that reform becomes part of the "reformed" school culture. This process, following principles of sociocultural

and cognitive perspectives on learning, enables adults to change how they participate in a community of practice to create a better school.

12. Sirotnik, K., and Oakes J. "Critical Inquiry." In K. Sirotnik and J. Oakes (eds.), *Critical Perspectives on the Organization and Improvement of Schooling.* Boston: Kluwer, 1986; Sirotnik, K. "Making Sense of Educational Research." *Phi Delta Kappan,* 1999, *80*(8), 606–610.

13. hooks, b. *Black Looks: Race and Representation.* Boston: South End Press, 1992; West, C. *Race Matters.* Boston: Beacon Press, 1994.

14. Sirotnik and Oakes (1986), p. 192.

15. Barber, B. "The Search for Civil Society." *The New Democrat,* Mar.–Apr. 1995, *7*(2) (Internet edition, n.p.).

16. Reich, R. B. "We Are All Third Wayers Now." *American Prospect,* Mar.–Apr. 1999, no. 43, p. 51.

Appendix

1. Guba, E. G., and Lincoln, Y. S. "Competing Paradigms in Qualitative Research." In N. K. Denzin and Y. S. Lincoln (eds.), *Handbook of Qualitative Research.* Thousand Oaks, Calif.: Sage, 1994; Schwandt, T. A. "Constructivist, Interpretivist Approaches to Human Inquiry." In N. K. Denzin and Y. S. Lincoln (eds.), *Handbook of Qualitative Research.* Thousand Oaks, Calif.: Sage, 1994; Wells, A. S., Hirshberg, D., Lipton, M., and Oakes, J. "Bounding the Case Within Its Context: A Constructivist Approach to Studying Detracking Reform." *Educational Researcher,* 1995, *24*(5), 18–24.

2. Guba and Lincoln (1994); Kaplan, D., and Manners, R. A. (1986). *Culture Theory.* Prospect Heights, Ill.: Waveland Press; Smith, J. K. "Hermeneutics and Qualitative Inquiry." In D. J. Flinders and G. E. Mills (eds.), *Theory and Concepts in Qualitative Research.* New York: Teachers College Press, 1993.

3. Sarason (1982, 1990); Goodlad, J. I. *A Place Called School.* New York: McGraw-Hill, 1984; Goodlad, J. I. *The Dynamics of Educational Change.* New York: McGraw-Hill, 1979; Fullan (1991); Cohen, D. K., and Ball, D. L. "Policy and Practice: An Overview." *Educational Evaluation and Policy Analysis,* 1990, *12*(3), 347–353; Snyder, J., Bolin, F., and Zumwalt, K. "Curriculum Implementation." In P. A. Jackson (ed.), *Handbook of Research on Curriculum,* New York: Macmillan, 1992; Firestone, W., and Corbett, H. D. "Planned Organizational Change." In N. Boyan (ed.), *Handbook of Research on Educational Administration.* New York: Macmillan, 1992; Louis and Miles (1990).

4. We explicate in greater detail how these themes relate to the specific Turning Points recommendations in Oakes, J., and others. "Recreating Middle Schools: Technical, Normative, and Political Considerations." *Elementary School Journal,* 1993, *93*(5), 461–480.

5. Miles, M. S., and Huberman, A. M. Qualitative Data Analysis. Thousand Oaks, Calif.: Sage, 1994.

6. Yin, R. K. *Case Study Research: Design and Methods.* Thousand Oaks, Calif.: Sage, 1989.

Index